ISLAMIC JURISPRUDENCE

SHĀFIʿĪ'S *RISĀLA*

al-Imām Muḥammad ibn Idrīs al-SHĀFIʿĪ'S

al-RISĀLA

FĪ UṢŪL AL-FIQH

Treatise on the Foundations
of Islamic Jurisprudence

TRANSLATED WITH AN
INTRODUCTION, NOTES, AND
APPENDICES

by Majid Khadduri

SECOND EDITION

THE ISLAMIC TEXTS SOCIETY

DEDICATED TO THE MEMORY OF MY FATHER

First published as
Islamic Jurisprudence: Shāfiʿī's *Risāla*
by Johns Hopkins Press, 1961

This edition published in 1997 by
The Islamic Texts Society
Miller's House
Kings Mill Lane
Great Shelford
Cambridge CB22 5EN, U.K.

Reprint 1997, 2003, 2008, 2011, 2012

British Library Cataloguing-in-Publication Data.
A catalogue record for this book is
available from the British Library.

ISBN 978 0946621 15 6 cloth

Preface

THE PART OF THE world in which Islam grew up is renowned for possessing the oldest legal systems known in recorded history, and Islamic law, more than a millenium old, is relatively new in comparison with other systems. In Islamic legal theory the law preceded society and is considered to be as eternal as God. Tradition has it that God revealed himself through a divine law, communicated to men by His Prophets, either written by God's own finger on tablets made of stone, or sent down to the nearest Heaven to be available for revelation by Angel Gabriel.

Originating from so high a source, law always held a paramount place in the eyes of peoples who lived under divine guidance. It is no wonder that the prestige of the divine law among peoples in that world is without parallel in history. For the law was not only founded on religion and sanctioned by God, but in it the whole spirit of the faith may be said to be epitomized.

Islamic law has preserved its basic character since its formative period. In modern times the greatest challenge has come from the West, and Islamic law is bound to feel the impact. Many a Muslim country has adopted legal concepts from abroad without regard to their suitability for the social milieu. Muslim and Western legal systems have often operated side by side and conflicts between them have been inevitable. But the new law has not been able to command the respect of the public nor has the old law met the necessities of modern life. However, the advocates of the traditional system have had little to offer in the way of a constructive legal reform which might adapt Islamic law to modern conditions of life. In the second and third decades of the twentieth century critics of the two systems keenly felt that the widening gulf between them should be bridged.

Following World War II a revival in the study of Islamic law set in, stemming partly from the rise of several Islamic countries to statehood. Some of the new states stressed the Islamic creed, and the older states declared Islamic law to be a source of legislation. The most constructive approach to modernizing Islamic law is reflected in the new civil codes, notably in the law of contract and property, which Dr. ʿAbd al-Razzāq al-Sanhūrī has drafted for Egypt, Syria, ʿIrāq, and Libya. As a result, a growing interest in the study of Islamic jurisprudence has become noticeable in the Muslim world, in an effort to gain a deeper understanding of the nature of legal reform.

The Muslim world today is facing a problem of legislation not unlike that which faced it in the first two centuries of its existence. During that time Islam expanded rapidly and absorbed new elements of culture and tradition. As a result, the Muslim world abounded in legal doctrines, the advocates of each vying for supremacy over the others. It was Shāfiʿī who provided in the ninth century of the Christian era a systematic legal method by which to synthesize the various legal doctrines into a coherent system. A thorough study of that system will explain how legal problems were resolved in the formative period as well as the approach and the method of reasoning employed in their solution. It is impossible to understand the implications and the trends in modern Islamic legal reforms without an appreciation of the nature and development of classical Islamic jurisprudence.

I have been assisted by important suggestions and comments made on the work as a whole or in part. I should like to thank in particular Shaykh Muḥammad Abū Zahra and Dr. ʿAbd al-Ḥalīm al-Najjār for their valuable assistance, and Dr. ʿAbd al-Razzāq al-Sanhūrī and Dr. Chafīk Cheḥata for helpful suggestions. Comments on one part of the work or another have been gratefully received from Sir Hamilton Gibb, Emil Lang, Nabia Abbott, Leo Strauss, and Marshall G. D. Hodgson. Above all I should like to thank Edwin E. Calverley and Harold Glidden for their invaluable assistance and suggestions. Finally, I wish to acknowledge the aid given by the School of Advanced International Studies of The Johns Hopkins University, and the grant extended by the Rockefeller Foundation, which enabled me in 1958 to work in Cairo and Damascus on manuscripts and other works connected with this study. None of these persons and institutions, however, is responsible for any errors which may be found in the volume or for the views expressed in it.

May, 1961 MAJID KHADDURI

Contents

TRANSLATION OF SHĀFIʿĪ'S *Risāla*

ISLAMIC JURISPRUDENCE

SHĀFIʿĪ'S *RISĀLA*

Translator's Introduction

THE HISTORICAL BACKGROUND OF THE *RISĀLA*

Islamic Jurisprudence before Shāfiʿī

LAW IS A SYSTEM of social control established for the purpose of maintaining an ordered society among men. Different societies develop different legal systems, but every matured system reveals the ways in which the society from which it sprang endeavors to protect what it honors. Islamic law, the product of Islam's centuries of stored experience, is the embodiment of the Islamic ideal life. It is the framework of Islam itself. For although religion describes what the ideal life should be, the law indicates the right road to follow (indeed the term sharīʿa bears this meaning) in order to arrive at the ideal life. Thus the law of Islam, the sharīʿa, has the character of a religious obligation; at the same time it constitutes a political sanction of religion. As a consequence, the sharīʿa has greater practical importance to Muslims than the creed, and its study is ranked higher than a supererogatory prayer by Shāfiʿī, the founder of a school of law and the author of the *Risāla*.

In Islamic legal theory the sharīʿa is derived from a high divine source, embodying God's will and justice. Unlike positive law, it is regarded as the ideal legal order; but, like positive law, it mirrors the character of the society in which it developed.

The idealization of the sharīʿa as the perfect legal system was the product of legal speculation which occupied the minds of jurists for generations; but the one who for the first time laid down a systematic legal reasoning for such an idealization was Muḥammad b. Idrīs al-Shāfiʿī. The impress of his systematic method, which has never been superseded in Islam, has remained permanent.

In what circumstances did Shāfiʿī develop his system?

The Founder of Islam, whose main preoccupation was with religious reform, had, perhaps, little reason to alter the sunna, the customary law prevailing in Arabia.[1] Muḥammad's opponents argued, however—not without good reason—that he had violated the established law of the land. Notwithstanding Muḥammad's reiteration that he merely intended to replace false idols by Allāh, the repudiation of idolatry itself implied the violation of the sunna, since idolatry was part of the customary law of Arabia. Law and religion were so closely intertwined in primitive societies that an attack on religion was a violation of law at the same time. Muḥammad's call to abandon idolatry in favor of the Deity resulted inevitably in the establishment of the supremacy of God's law—as communicated in the Qur'ān—over " idolatrous" law. Thus the Qur'ān became the basic source of legislation. The sunna, though it continued to supply raw material for legislation, took second place in the eyes of the Muslim community.

Muḥammad's death, though coinciding with the sudden expansion of Islam, brought prophetic legislation to an end.[2] The administrative decrees issued by the early caliphs (successors to Muḥammad) supplied answers to many legal problems; but disputes and legal questions relating to purely local matters were bound to be settled on the basis of the custom and precedent

[1] The sunna was the common law of Arabia before Islam, and it comprised legal and moral principles. The sunna grew out of the custom of the forefathers and its enforcement by practice established its legal validity. See I. Goldziher, "The Principles of Law in Islam," *The Historians' History of the World* (New York, 1907), Vol. VIII, pp. 294-304.

[2] Muḥammad is regarded as the last of the prophets (Q. XXXIII, 40); thus divine legislation came to an end by his death.

of each locality. Tribal customary law existed in Arabia before Islam, just as laws and customs in Syria and ʿIrāq were inherited from earlier civilizations. Roman (Byzantine) and Persian (Sasanian), to say nothing of earlier Babylonian and Aramaic, laws must have supplied the Muslim jurist with raw material on the strength of which he issued opinion whenever an authoritative text failed to provide an answer.[3]

Several centers for legal study developed, stemming from local differences in legal traditions and social conditions, but the two principal centers which radiated their influence to other parts of the empire were those of ʿIrāq (Kūfa and Baṣra) and the Ḥijāz (Madīna and Makka). The ʿIrāqī jurists seem to have won the reputation of exercising personal reasoning more than the Ḥijāzī jurists, and Abū Ḥanīfa (d. 150/767), founder of a school of law, as well as his followers were credited with the liberal use of analogy as the basis for their legal reasoning. Abū Ḥanīfa's method of reasoning, reputed to have been applied more extensively than those of other jurists, was in fact the common method used by the ʿIrāqī jurists, while the Ḥijāzī jurists, who claimed to follow the tradition more consistently, actually used personal reasoning no less than their ʿIrāqī contemporaries. The Ḥanafī jurists in fact paid more attention to traditions than their contemporary critics claimed despite their reputation that they were unacquainted with these traditions. Opinions of early ʿIrāqī jurists, such as Ibrāhīm al-Nakhaʿī (d. 95/713) or Ḥammād b. Abī Sulaymān (d. 120/737) were invoked on the strength of traditions traced back to the Prophet Muḥammad through a transmitter like Ibn Masʿūd or Caliph ʿAlī.[4] These

[3] For a discussion on the influence of foreign laws on Islamic law, see J. Schacht, "Foreign Elements in Ancient Islamic Law," *Journal of Comparative Legislation and International Law,* 3rd series, Vol. XXXII (November, 1950), pp. 9-17; and S. V. Fitzgerald, "The Alleged Debt of Islamic to Roman Law," *Law Quarterly Review,* Vol. 67 (1951), pp. 81-102.

[4] See Shāfiʿī's *Risāla,* paragraphs 650-52, below; Muḥammad b. al-Ḥasan al-Shaybānī, *Kitāb al-Aṣl,* ed. Chehata (Cairo, 1954), Vol. I, pp. 1-2. See also J. Schacht, "Pre-Islamic Background and Early Development of Jurisprudence," in M. Khadduri and H. J. Liebesny (eds.), *Law in the Middle East* (Washington, D. C., 1955), Vol. I, pp. 45-46.

traditions may have included the sunna of the Prophet as well as traditions from his Companions. But the attempt to justify the adoption of local custom on the strength of traditions was as much a recognition of the overriding authority of an authoritative text as it was an unconscious effort to Islamize the developing body of law in the newly conquered territory.

The re-assertion of the sunna after Muḥammad's death was probably more visible in the Ḥijāz than elsewhere. For in Arabia it was customary that the sunna, whether laid down by forefathers or by an individual of some weight, should be binding on the community. When Muḥammad first introduced Islam, he was denounced as the violator of the sunna for attacking traditional idolatry. But when Islam was established, the Prophet as the spokesman of the community was cited to provide guidance for legal decisions. After his death Muḥammad's sayings and decisions became precedents on the strength of which jurists made decisions. These precedents constituted the sunna of the Prophet and provided the substance of traditions.[5]

Against such a background the Ḥijāzī jurists could claim that their school represented the school of tradition. They resided in the cradle of Islam, where the sunna was better known, and they set forth the doctrine that the sunna was an overriding authoritative source. Thus the Mālikī school, known as the school of tradition, claimed that its legal opinion represented the Islamic tradition more closely than the Ḥanafī school. It criticized the ʿIrāqī jurists for their use of personal opinion and analogy on the grounds that their knowledge of the Prophet's sunna was palpably lacking. However, a close examination of Mālik's opinions indicates that he made use of personal opinion no less than his Ḥanafī contemporaries.

[5] After the rise of Islam the term sunna came to mean the sayings, acts, and decisions of the Prophet Muḥammad; later on the substance of the sunna, in addition to the authorities who transmitted it, was called ḥadīth or tradition. See Chaps. IX and X, below. See also I. Goldziher, *Étude sur la tradition Islamique*, tr. Léon Bercher (Paris, 1952); and Alfred Guillaume, *The Traditions of Islam* (Oxford, 1924).

One may even discern that Mālik had departed from the Prophet's sunna in favor of personal opinion. A case in point is Mālik's insistence that a contract, once concluded by an offer and acceptance, regardless of the *khiyār al-majlis* (right of option of the parties to a contract as long as they have not separated), was binding on the two parties.[6] Mālik's opinion was based on local practice; but sound though it may seem from a legal viewpoint, it conflicted with the doctrine of the Mālikī school that the authority of tradition was always overriding.[7]

The place occupied by Shāfiʿī in Islamic legal history is determined largely by the character of the age in which he lived. In a later age, once the gate of *ijtihād* (personal reasoning) had closed, he would have been a great jurist with a moderate view as to the development of the law. But in his age a great jurist was necessarily drawn into *ikhtilāf* (disagreement), or the controversy between the schools of tradition and personal opinion. What was to be the position of tradition in relation to the Qur'ān and other sources of the law? What was to be the position of opinion and analogy in relation to the Qur'ān and tradition? At a time when scholars were raising such questions, a man profoundly learned in the tradition, and passionately convinced of its significance, was compelled to take part in the controversy between the advocates of tradition and the advocates of opinion in order to defend the former's claim to supremacy. At first, Shāfiʿī aroused those in favor of tradition, giving them leadership and supplying methods of defense against the advocates of opinion. Later on, after settling in Egypt, Shāfiʿī seems to have felt more strongly the need to strike a balance between the two schools of thought, and he sought to find a common ground of agreement.

[6] See Chap. X, section 7, below; and Mālik, *al-Muwaṭṭa'*, ed. M. Fu'ād ʿAbd al-Bāqī (Cairo, 1951), Vol. II, p. 671.

[7] The tradition concerning *khiyār al-majlis*, however, might have been circulated after Mālik's death. See J. Schacht, *Origins of Muhammadan Jurisprudence* (Oxford, 1950), pp. 159-60.

Shāfiʿī's Life

It was in this milieu that Shāfiʿī played so significant a role in resolving the conflict between the two schools of law. Growing up in the Ḥijāz, the home of tradition, he became a follower of Mālik and then went to ʿIrāq, where he was exposed to the legal reasoning of the ʿIrāqī jurists. In the latter part of his life, in Egypt, where he could reformulate his legal opinions with detachment and rewrite his books, he founded a new school of law by synthesizing the two other schools. Shāfiʿī's career falls, therefore, into three well-marked periods. The first, the period of apprenticeship, begins with his study of the law in Makka and Madīna, where he was given a thorough training in the traditions, and extends to his deportation to ʿIrāq. The second, in which he was exposed to the legal reasoning of the ʿIrāqī jurists, ends with his departure for Egypt; and the third lasts from his settlement in Egypt, where he became the "master," to his death.

A number of biographical accounts of Shāfiʿī have come down to us, although the very earliest are apparently lost. Even in biographical sketches written by Dāwūd al-Zāhirī (d. 270/884) and Zakarīya b. Yaḥya al-Sājī (d. 307/920), reproduced in later accounts, a great deal of legend had already crept into the story of Shāfiʿī's life. The chronology presents great difficulties, as the conflicting narratives about Shāfiʿī's visits to ʿIrāq and his return to Madīna indicate.

The biographical account by Abū Muḥammad ʿAbd al-Raḥmān b. Abī Ḥātim al-Rāzī (d. 327/938) is the earliest that has reached us.[8] Rāzī's work is scarcely more than a collection of oral reports dealing with certain aspects of Shāfiʿī's life and character, some of them reproduced from earlier biographical sketches such as those of al-Zāhirī and al-Sājī. But this source is quite inadequate as a complete account. Later writers, who dealt more fully with the subject, have often drawn heavily

[8] Ibn Abī Ḥātim al-Rāzī, *Kitāb Ādāb al-Shāfiʿī wa Manāqibuh*, ed. Muḥammad Zāhid b. al-Ḥasan al-Kawtharī (Cairo, 1953).

on Rāzī's biography and have reproduced many of the legends that had gathered around Shāfiʿī's life. The great works of Abū Nuʿaym[9] and al-Khaṭīb al-Baghdādī[10] add very little to Rāzī's account. The first full story is given by al-Bayhaqī (d. 458/1065)[11] and reproduced in a well-organized and attractive manner by al-Fakhr al-Rāzī;[12] inevitably, it includes a great deal of legend. Later biographers, notably Ibn ʿAbd al-Barr,[13] Subkī,[14] Ibn Ḥajar,[15] and Nawawī,[16] add but little to earlier accounts. More recent sketches by Ibn Kathīr[17] and Murtaḍa al-Zabīdī,[18] draw heavily on earlier authorities. There are also several unpublished biographical accounts[19] which add practically nothing new. A full critical study of Shāfiʿī's life has not yet been written.[20]

The earliest authorities disagree as to whether Shāfiʿī was born at Gaza, a small provincial town on the Mediterranean Sea, or at ʿAsqalān (Askelon), a larger town not far away, in the year 150/767.[21] Probably Shāfiʿī's mother, shortly after Shāfiʿī's

[9] Abū Nuʿaym al-Iṣfahānī, *Kitāb Ḥilyat al-Awliyā' wa Ṭabaqāt al-Aṣfiyā'* (Cairo, 1938), Vol. IX, pp. 63-163.

[10] al-Khaṭīb al-Baghdādī, *Ta'rīkh Baghdād* (Cairo, 1931), Vol. II, pp. 56-73.

[11] Abū Bakr Aḥmad b. al-Ḥusayn b. ʿAlī al-Bayhaqī, *Kitāb Manāqib al-Imām al-Shāfiʿī* (MS, including a sequel, in 312 folios).

[12] al-Fakhr al-Rāzī, *Kitāb Manāqib al-Shāfiʿī* (Cairo, n. d.).

[13] Ibn ʿAbd al-Barr, *al-Intiqā'* (Cairo, 1350/1932).

[14] Tāj al-Dīn al-Subkī, *Ṭabaqāt al-Shāfiʿīya al-Kubra* (Cairo, 1324/1907). Vol. I, pp. 100-107.

[15] Ibn Ḥajar al-ʿAsqalānī, *Tawālī al-Ta'sīs bi-Maʿālī Ibn Idrīs* (Cairo, 1801/1883).

[16] Abū Zakarīya al-Nawawī, *Kitāb Tahdhīb al-Asmā'* (Biographical Dictionary), ed. Ferdinand Wüstenfeld (Göttingen, 1842-45), pp. 56-86.

[17] Ibn Kathīr, *Kitāb al-Bidāya wa al-Nihāya* (Cairo, 1352/1932), Vol. X, pp. 251-254.

[18] Murtaḍa al-Zabīdī, *Sharḥ Iḥyā' ʿUlūm al-Dīn* (of al-Ghazzālī), Vol. I, pp. 191-201.

[19] In addition to Bayhaqī's *Manāqib,* there is at the Institute of Arabic Manuscripts of the Arab League in Cairo a photographic copy of Quṭb al-Dīn b. Sulaymān al-Khayḍarī, *Zahr al-Riyāḍ fī Radd mā Shannaʿahu al-Qāḍī ʿIyāḍ ʿala al-Imām al-Shāfiʿī* (MS, No. 181). There are three MSS on Shāfiʿī's life at the Zāhirīya Library of Damascus; one of them is by Shahrazūrī, and the other two are extracts from earlier sources which add no new material.

[20] For works on Shāfiʿī's life and jurisprudence, see Select Bibliography, pp. 356-363.

[21] The tomb of the ancestor of the whole clan, Hāshim, can still be visited at

father died, spent some time in Palestine among the Yamanite tribes—to whom her ancestors (the Azd tribe) belonged—before she and her son arrived at Makka, for the authorities state that Shāfiʿī was scarcely two years old when he left Gaza, but that he had reached his tenth year when he arrived at Makka.[22] We know little about Shāfiʿī's early life, except that he was brought up in Makka in poor circumstances and that from his youth he was devoted to learning. Traditional stories, legendary for the most part, give an account of his early devotion to poetry, chivalry, and legal studies. Such traditions have him learning the Qur'ān by heart at the age of seven, committing Mālik's *al-Muwaṭṭa'* to memory at the age of ten, and being declared fit to give legal opinions at the age of fifteen.[23]

Certain facts about his parentage may conceivably have affected the future course of his life.[24] His father belonged to the tribe of Quraysh, the tribe of the Prophet Muḥammad, and his grandfather al-Muṭṭalib was a brother of Muḥammad's grandfather. The descendants of al-Muṭṭalib took an active part, on both sides, in the struggle between Muḥammad and the Makkans, but they all supported Muḥammad after his first victory at Badr in 2/624. This history may have given Shāfiʿī prestige, arising from his belonging to the tribe of the Prophet and from his great grandfather's kinship to the Prophet. It also may have inspired him with the idea that to him was bequeathed the mantle of the Prophet's tradition and that he should stand to defend it. These facts made him, like other descendants of the

Gaza. Apparently it was to southern Palestine that some of the Banū Hāshim went with the conquering Arab armies in the early days of the expansion of Islam.

[22] Ibn Abī Ḥātim al-Rāzī, p. 26; Abū Nuʿaym, Vol. X, pp. 67-68; al-Khaṭīb al-Baghdādī, Vol. II, p. 59; al-Fakhr al-Rāzī, p. 8; Ibn Ḥajar, *Tawālī al-Ta'sīs,* pp. 49, 50.

[23] Ibn Abī Ḥātim al-Rāzī, pp. 39-40; Abū Nuʿaym, p. 70; Bayhaqī, folio 23; Ibn ʿAbd al-Barr, p. 71.

[24] Shāfiʿī's full name and that of his family is: Muḥammad b. Idrīs b. al-ʿAbbās b. ʿUthmān b. Shāfiʿ b. al-Sā'ib b. ʿUbayd b. ʿAbd Yazīd b. Hāshim b. al-Muṭṭalib b. ʿAbd Manāf.

same clan, a beneficiary of the Prophet's share of one-fifth of the spoils of war.[25]

After spending some time among the Beduins, Shāfiʿī returned to Makka to study law under Muslim b. Khālid al-Zanjī (d. 180/796), Muftī of Makka, Sufyān b. ʿUyayna (d. 198/813), and others.[26] Although he was declared qualified to practice law by al-Zanjī, Shāfiʿī desired further legal training and set out to study under the leading jurist of the Ḥijāz, Mālik b. Anas (d. 179/796). He was probably twenty years old when he left Makka for Madīna.

There are several accounts of how Shāfiʿī became the disciple of Mālik. The traditional story is that he went to the Governor of Madīna, armed with a letter of introduction from the Governor of Makka, and requested an audience with Mālik. After some hesitation, the Governor made his way to Mālik's house in the company of Shāfiʿī. Mālik seems to have been impressed by Shāfiʿī's intelligence, and he allowed him to read *al-Muwaṭṭa'* under his guidance. As a follower of Mālik, Shāfiʿī remained in Madīna until Mālik's death, by which time he had already gained distinction as a brilliant jurist.[27]

Shāfiʿī had the good fortune to attract the attention of the Governor of al-Yaman, who was on a visit to the Ḥijāz, and who was impressed by his learning and industry. He helped Shāfiʿī to enter the service of the state at about the age of thirty and to rise rapidly in it. This service was short-lived, however. Shāfiʿī proved to be a just administrator, but he was soon entangled with local interests and factional jealousies, which brought him not merely

[25] al-Fakhr al-Rāzī, p. 7. For the legal position of the Prophet's one-fifth share from the spoil, see Khadduri, *War and Peace in the Law of Islam* (Baltimore, 1955), pp. 121-22.

[26] For the names of jurists under whom Shāfiʿī studied at Makka, see al-Fakhr al-Rāzī, pp. 11-13; Ibn Ḥajar, *Tahdhīb al-Tahdhīb* (Hyderabad, 1326/1909), Vol. IX, p. 25; and *Tawālī al-Ta'sīs*, pp. 79-82.

[27] Traditional accounts differ on whether Shāfiʿī visited ʿIrāq before Mālik's death or whether he went to al-Yaman as a judge. See Abū Nuʿaym, p. 29.

dismissal from his post but also deportation in chains to ʿIrāq, on the alleged charge that he was a secret follower of the Zaydī Imām Yaḥya b. ʿAbd-Allāh, a pretender to the caliphate and an opponent of the ruling dynasty in Baghdād.[28]

Shāfiʿī appeared before Caliph Hārūn al-Rashīd at al-Raqqa (ʿIrāq) with other conspirators in 187/803. The other conspirators were put to death, but he was pardoned when he eloquently defended his loyalty to the caliph on the ground that he was the descendant of a great grandfather who was related to the great grandfather of the caliph himself. Some authorities state that the famous Ḥanafī jurist, Muḥammad b. al-Ḥasan al-Shaybānī (d. 189/805), who was present at the court when Shāfiʿī appeared before the caliph, defended him and said that he was a well-known student of the sacred law.[29] Most authorities agree that the caliph was delighted with Shāfiʿī's conversation and became his patron.[30] This incident brought Shāfiʿī into close contact with Shaybānī, whose books he had copied, and impelled him to devote the rest of his career to legal studies, never again to seek government service.

The contact with Shaybānī's circle had a great impact on Shāfiʿī's legal reasoning. Until that point, as a follower of Mālik, he had been exposed to the teaching of only one school of law. He had, it is true, known of the opinions and arguments of the ʿIrāqī jurists, but he had not heard them at first hand. We are told that he took an active part with Ḥanafī jurists in discourses and arguments, that he strenuously defended Mālik's position, and that he seems to have earned the reputation of being the Upholder of Traditions for his efforts to establish

[28] Another account places the story of the deportation in Makka, where Shāfiʿī had returned from al-Yaman. He may have been there on a short visit from al-Yaman. See Ibn ʿAbd al-Barr, pp. 95-96. For Shāfiʿī's difficulties during his tenure of office in al-Yaman, see Bayhaqī, folio 24; Ibn Ḥajar, *Tawālī al-Ta'sīs*, p. 69.

[29] Bayhaqī states that Shaybānī's intercession on Shāfiʿī's behalf took place after Shāfiʿī was thrown into prison in ʿIrāq. See Bayhaqī, folio 26.

[30] al-Fakhr al-Rāzī, pp. 22-27; Ibn ʿAbd al-Barr, pp. 94-98.

the supremacy of traditions.[31] But those discussions must have made him aware of the weaknesses of the Mālikī school, which Shāfiʿī began to appreciate after settling in Egypt, as well as the points of strength in the legal reasoning of the ʿIrāqī jurists. Some authorities stress the difficulties encountered by him in his arguments with the Ḥanafī jurists, and one declares that Shāfiʿī was driven out of ʿIrāq by them.[32] Most authorities, however, believe that Ḥanafī followers complained to Shaybānī of Shāfiʿī's criticism, but that Shāfiʿī, though avoiding a stand against Shaybānī directly, determined to stand on his own in his legal reasoning. Some authorities state that Shaybānī, upon hearing the complaints of his followers, invited Shāfiʿī to a debate on the points of difference between them;[33] they also state that Shāfiʿī emerged triumphant over Shaybānī, although Ḥanafī sources insist that Shāfiʿī was defeated.[34] These circumstances must have been difficult for Shāfiʿī, who, as protégé of Shaybānī, may have tried honestly to avoid an open conflict with him, as some authorities indicate.[35] Nor was Shāfiʿī's position strong enough to take an open position against Shaybānī, an influential man at the court, and his followers.

This uncomfortable situation must have influenced Shāfiʿī in the decision to leave ʿIrāq in 188/804 and to settle elsewhere. He went via Ḥarrān and Syria to Makka, where he had begun his early legal studies. As a disciple of Mālik, he was well received and began to lecture at the Sacred Mosque. His teachings, however, revealed unexpected differences with Mālik, for his thorough grasp of the Mālikī and Ḥanafī legal opinions made him aware of the shortcomings of both. He made a deep impression on many students of law, including Aḥmad b. Ḥanbal (d. 241/855), who was studying in Makka at that

[31] Ibn Abī Ḥātim al-Rāzī, pp. 170-82; Bayhaqī, folios 24-26; Abū Nuʿaym, p. 107; and al-Khaṭīb al-Baghdādī, Vol. II, p. 68.

[32] See Ibn al-Bazzāz al-Kirdarī, *Manāqib al-Imām al-ʿAzam* (Hyderabad 1321/1904), Vol. II, p. 153.

[33] Ibn Abī Ḥātim al-Rāzī, p. 160; Abū Nuʿaym, Vol. IX, pp. 71-72; al-Fakhr al-Rāzī, pp. 32, 31.

[34] al-Kirdarī, Vol. II, p. 153.

[35] Bayhaqī, folio 25.

time, but his influence in the Ḥijāz must have been limited. His departure from Mālik's opinions disappointed many a Mālikī admirer at a time when Shāfiʿī had not yet won the reputation of the "master."[36]

Shāfiʿī returned to Baghdād in 194/810. His legal reasoning had matured, and his stature as a jurist had grown sufficiently to permit him to follow an independent line of legal speculation. It was during this period that he accumulated the material for the legal system that was destined to leave so deep a mark upon Muslim law. After a span of three or four years, Shāfiʿī decided to leave Baghdād for Egypt. It is not quite clear why he made this decision. The authorities state that while in Baghdād he attached himself to ʿAbd-Allāh b. Mūsa, who invited him to settle in Egypt. We are told that the Caliph al-Ma'mūn (d. 218/833) offered him the position of a judge, but he declined it.[37]

Shāfiʿī's departure from ʿIrāq took place in 198/814. It was the same year that the Caliph al-Ma'mūn established himself in Baghdād, having defeated his brother al-Amīn a year earlier and inaugurated a regime in which the rationalist philosophy of al-Muʿtazila assumed a predominant position. In 213/827 the Caliph officially proclaimed the doctrine of "the creation of the Qur'ān" in opposition to the Orthodox view of its eternal nature as co-existing with God. In 218/833 he decreed that no qāḍī who did not subscribe to this doctrine could hold an office in the state, and an inquisition for the trial of those who rejected the doctrine was instituted.[38] This anticipated atmosphere of intolerance to orthodox views, it has been suggested by a recent writer,[39] drove Shāfiʿī to settle in Egypt. At the age of fifty Shāfiʿī seems to have made his final choice between his love

[36] Ibn Abī Ḥātim al-Rāzī, pp. 165, 168.

[37] Some of the sources state that such a position was offered to him toward the end of his life after he settled in Egypt. See Bayhaqī, folio 38; Ibn Ḥajar, *Tawālī al-Ta'sīs*, p. 84.

[38] For an account of the history and ideas of the Muʿtazila and their influence on Caliph al-Ma'mūn, see De Lacy O'Leary, *Arabic Thought and Its Place in History* (London, 1922), Chap. 5; A. J. Wensinck, *The Muslim Creed* (Cambridge, 1932), passim; Zuhdī H. Jār-Allāh, *al-Muʿtazila* (Cairo, 1947).

[39] Abū Zahra, *al-Shāfiʿī* (Cairo, 1948), p. 28.

for power and his love for the law, and he decided to settle in a place where he could concentrate on legal speculation in relative quiet.

Remote from the center of court intrigues, and on good terms with the Governor of Egypt, Shāfiʿī found himself in a congenial position. During the five years he lived in Egypt, he devoted all his time to teaching and to dictating his works to his students. We are told that his leading disciples—al-Rabīʿ b. Sulaymān al-Murādī (d. 270/880), Abū Yaʿqūb al-Buwayṭī (d. 231/845), and Abū Ibrāhīm Ismāʿīl b. Yaḥya al-Muzanī (d. 274/877), to mention but three—were in the habit of writing down Shāfiʿī spoken words, and that Shāfiʿī would correct the text when it was read aloud before him.[40] Thus, Shāfiʿī's disciples in Egypt were responsible for all of the books that are known to us now, whether copied or dictated from his original writings. Doubts have been raised as to whether some of Shāfiʿī's writings—such as the *Kitāb al-Umm*—were not actually composed by a disciple.[41] If some of his words have been changed or rephrased, however, the contents of the books must comprise Shāfiʿī own legal reasoning and ideas, for Shāfiʿī biographers agree that his books were handed down to us as recorded by his students and one of the students, who wrote a *Summary* (Mukhtaṣar), agrees with Shāfiʿī's fundamental opinions as recorded in his collected works.[42]

Shāfiʿī had difficulty persuading his opponents to accept his opinions. He followed an independent line of legal reasoning, often disagreeing with leading jurists, among them his great master Mālik. The disagreement aroused Mālikī opponents, who presented themselves to his circle to take issue with him, but his great abilities as an attractive teacher and skillful debater silenced them. One authority asserts that in an argument with Fityān, a Mālikī follower in Egypt, Shāfiʿī triumphed, but the intemperate loser, failing in persuasion, resorted to abuse. The Governor, a patron of Shāfiʿī, ordered that Fityān be

[40] Ibn Abī Ḥātim al-Rāzī, p. 71; Ibn Ḥajar, *Tawālī al-Ta'sīs*, p. 77; Bayhaqī, folio 49.

[41] Zakī Mubārak, *Kitāb al-Umm* (Cairo, 1934).

[42] Cf. Muzanī's *Mukhtaṣar* with the relevant parts in *Kitāb al-Umm*.

punished by being paraded through the streets of the city bearing a plank and stating that this was the penalty for abusing a descendant of the Prophet's near of kin. Enraged by this degrading punishment, Fityān's followers turned upon Shāfiʿī after one of his lectures and resorted to violence. Shāfiʿī badly injured, was taken to his house, where he died a few days later.[43] The incident gives us a picture of the consequences which heated controversies between rival schools of thought could generate.

It is possible that Shāfiʿī's death was not caused entirely by his opponent's attack. Shāfiʿī was known to suffer from a serious intestinal illness which kept him frail and ailing during the latter years of his life. He died on the last day of Rajab, 204 (20 January 820), in Fusṭāṭ (Old Cairo), and was buried in the vault of the Banū ʿAbd al-Ḥakam, near Mount al-Muqaṭṭam. The *qubba* (dome), still in existence, was built by al-Mālik al-Kāmil, the Ayyūbid Sulṭān, in 608/1212. It has always been a prominent place of pilgrimage, and it was still impressive and revered by many a Shāfiʿī admirer when visited by the present writer in 1958.

Shāfiʿī's Personality and Character

Tradition paints Shāfiʿī as a handsome man who paid attention to his appearance. When his hair turned grey in later years, he was in the habit of dyeing it dark red. He was tall and slender with an attractive face and a pleasing voice.[44] He was a man of impressive personality, respected for his straightforwardness and revered for his piety. Although a man of meager resources, gaining little remuneration from his study of the law, he was generous with his friends as well as with the poor. That generosity became the favorite theme of many later biographers,

[43] Yāqūt, *Muʿjam al-Udabāʾ*, ed. D. S. Margoliouth (London, 1981), Vol. VI, pp. 394-95; Ibn Ḥajar, *Tawālī al-Taʾsīs*. p. 86; cf. Muḥammad Zāhid al-Kawtharī, *Maqālāt al-Kawtharī* (Cairo 1373/1953), pp. 463-66.

[44] Nawawī, p. 83; Ibn Ḥajar, *Tawālī al-Taʾsīs*, pp. 60-61.

who described him as giving away to the poor everything that his hands had acquired.[45] His will shows his concern for the emancipation of his slave, as well as for the welfare of all his relatives and associates.[46]

From early childhood Shāfiʿī seems to have displayed a sharp intelligence and a good memory. We are told that at an early age he had memorized a great deal of ancient Arab poetry, in addition to the Qur'ān and Mālik's *al-Muwaṭṭa'*. Eloquent in speech and an expert in the Arabic language, his interest in poetry and language preceded his interest in law. Only when he was reminded, as one authority puts it, that it was more dignified to become a jurist than a poet, did he turn to the study of the law.[47] Whether or not this story was invented afterwards to account for Shāfiʿī's legal pursuit, he did grow up in a center where the legal profession tempted many a Muslim scholar. He certainly chose a field in which he distinguished himself not only as a great thinker and a skillful jurist, but as an expositor of the sharīʿa without equal.

Although the study of law was Shāfiʿī's main concern, his early biographers state that he was acquainted with other branches of Islamic learning. Later biographers tend to depict him as a scholar whose knowledge was encyclopedic. One of these stories, related by al-Balawī, paints him as discussing with Caliph Hārūn al-Rashīd, in his first audience with that caliph, almost every conceivable branch of knowledge, including Greek medicine and philosophy in their original language.[48] The early sources of his life give the impression that he was opposed to theology and prohibited discourse on it in his presence.[49]

Traditional accounts seem to give contradictory impressions of Shāfiʿī's loyalties. He is depicted as a man who gave secret

[45] Ibn Abī Ḥātim al-Rāzī, pp. 126-28; Abū Nuʿaym, p. 77; Ibn ʿAbd al-Barr, pp. 93-94; Ibn Ḥajar, *Tawālī al-Ta'sīs,* p. 55.

[46] For full text of his will (dated February 203/819), see Shāfiʿī, *Kitāb al-Umm* (Cairo, 1322/1905), Vol. IV, pp. 48-49.

[47] It is also stated that al-Zanjī, Muftī of Makka, persuaded him to study law. Ibn Ḥajar, *Tawālī al-Ta'sīs,* p. 51; Nawawī, p. 59.

[48] al-Fakhr al-Rāzī, p. 26; Ibn Ḥajar, *Tawālī al-Ta'sīs,* pp. 51, 62, 66.

[49] Ibn Abī Ḥātim al-Rāzī, p. 188.

support to an ʿAlīd pretender to the caliphate, but who, upon appearing before Caliph Hārūn al-Rashīd, demonstrated that his loyalty was to the ʿAbbāsid rather than to the ʿAlīd house.[50] When reproached afterward for betraying a certain sympathy for the ʿAlīds, Shāfiʿī did not deny it, on the ground that he was a distant kinsman of theirs. Proof that he took an active part in a conspiracy against the central authority appears insufficient. At any rate, Shāfiʿī seems to have removed himself completely from politics and palace intrigues and never again accepted a position in the service of the state. His single-mindedness and straightforwardness prompted him to stay above factional differences and personal jealousies.

Nor was he ready to compromise with the fellow members of his profession. He did not shrink from showing disagreement with the Ḥanafī jurists in ʿIrāq, despite Shaybānī's intercession with the caliph to secure his pardon, because Shāfiʿī's differences with Ḥanafī doctrines were genuine legal differences. When he lectured afterward in Madīna, he showed just as much legal disagreement with Mālikī followers, although he never ceased to pay high tribute to his great master Mālik. He betrayed, perhaps, a certain inflexibility in his relations with rival schools because he maintained so high a standard of legal reasoning that his disagreement with others appeared sharp and uncompromising. He was too much of a scholarly perfectionist for his contemporaries.

Tradition also depicts him as a great debater who emerged triumphant from every argument with his rivals. Ibn ʿAbd al-Ḥakam, one of his disciples in Egypt, pays high tribute to the ability of his master in the art of defeating his critics.[51] The Mālikī jurist Fityān, it will be recalled, resorted to violence because his tongue failed him when he sought to challenge Shāfiʿī's persuasive argument. Although Ḥanafī jurists reject Shāfiʿī's ability to withstand a discussion with Shaybānī, early accounts state that Shāfiʿī conducted debates with Ḥanafī jurists

[50] Ibn ʿAbd al-Barr, pp. 91, 95-98.
[51] *Ibid.*, pp. 73, 78.

with great skill.[52] Both the *Risāla* and the *Kitāb al-Umm* bear witness to Shāfiʿī's scholastic ability in pursuing an argument to its logical conclusion. A great portion of the *Risāla* is, in fact, written in the form of a debate between Shāfiʿī and an interlocutor, who, in most cases, is a disguised critic of Shāfiʿī's doctrines.

THE COMPOSITION AND STRUCTURE OF THE *RISĀLA*

Composition of the Risāla

MOST AUTHORITIES are agreed that the *Risāla* was written after Shāfiʿī resided in ʿIrāq.[53] It was perhaps one of his earliest works, although we are told that before he left ʿIrāq he had composed another book, entitled *Kitāb al-Ḥujja*, and perhaps others, which have failed to reach us.[54]

Traditional accounts state that the *Risāla* was originally written at the request of ʿAbd al-Raḥmān b. Mahdī[55] in order to explain the legal significance of the Qur'ān and the sunna. While an invitation from a leading ʿIrāqī traditionist to Shāfiʿī, who had made a reputation as the Upholder of Traditions, seems quite conceivable, the earliest extant sources on Shāfiʿī's life are silent on the point. Neither Ibn Abī Ḥātim al-Rāzī (d. 327/938) nor Abū Nuʿaym al-Iṣfahānī (d.

[52] Ibn Abī Ḥātim al-Rāzī, p. 42.

[53] Few of them hold that the *Risāla* was written when Shāfiʿī was still in Makka. See al-Khaṭīb al-Baghdādī, Vol. II, pp. 64-65; and Yāqūt, *Muʿjam al-Udabā'*, Vol. VI, pp. 388-89.

[54] Nawawī, p. 61; Ibn Ḥajar, *Tawālī al-Ta'sīs*, p. 76. Cf. Ibn al-Nadīm, *Kitāb al-Fihrisṭ*, ed. G. L. Flügel (Leipzig, 1871), pp. 295-96.

[55] A leading traditionist in Baṣra (d. 198/813). See Ibn Abī Ḥātim al-Rāzī, *Taqdimat al-Maʿrifa li-Kitāb al-Jarḥ wa al-Taʿdīl* (Hyderabad, 1952), pp. 250-62; and Abū Nuʿaym, Vol. IX, pp. 3-63.

430/1038) gives the slightest suggestion that the *Risāla* was written at Ibn Mahdī's request. Abū Nuʿaym merely states that Ibn Mahdī once remarked that al-Shāfiʿī was "an intelligent young man"[56]—a statement which may mean that Ibn Mahdī had read either the *Risāla* or any one of Shāfiʿī's other books and concluded that he was an intelligent man; it does not necessarily suggest that the *Risāla* was written at Ibn Mahdī's request.

Nor do the sources mention that Ibn Mahdī and Shāfiʿī ever met. A tradition related by Shāfiʿī on the authority of Ibn Mahdī, recorded in one of his books,[57] was sharply contradicted by al-Sarrāj al-Bulqīnī, on the ground that the two men had not met; but al-Bulqīni accepted the traditional story that the *Risāla* was sent by Shāfiʿī to Ibn Mahdī. That the two men may never have met does not weaken the possibility that Ibn Mahdī had requested Shāfiʿī to write the *Risāla;* but it does raise doubts as to the reliability of later reports that such a request had been made.

The first authority to state that Shāfiʿī composed the *Risāla* in response to Ibn Mahdī's request was Bayhaqī. One of his narratives, based on information transmitted by Mūsa, son of ʿAbd al-Raḥmān Ibn Mahdī, states that Mūsa's father had complained to Shāfiʿī that Mālik's legal opinions had been distorted in Baṣra, and that Shāfiʿī responded by writing the *Risāla* to Ibn Mahdī. Mūsa, moreover, claims that he had seen the text of the *Risāla* written in Shāfiʿī's own hand.[58] Bayhaqī also reports a narrative, on the authority of al-Ḥārith b. Surayj al-Naqqāl, to the effect that al-Ḥārith, who earned the name of al-Naqqāl (the carrier) because he carried the *Risāla,* had himself delivered the work to Ibn Mahdī.[59] Later authorities repeat virtually the same version of the story that Ibn Mahdī had invited Shāfiʿī to write the *Risāla.*[60]

[56] Abū Nuʿaym, p. 93.
[57] Shāfiʿī, *Kitāb al-Um,* Vol. I, p. 117.
[58] Bayhaqī, folio 46.
[59] *Ibid.;* Ibn ʿAbd al-Barr, p. 72; Shāfiʿī, *Kitāb al-Umm,* Vol. I, p. 118.
[60] al-Khaṭīb al-Baghdādī, Vol. II, pp. 64-65; al-Fakhr al-Rāzī, p. 18; Ibn Ḥajar, *Tawālī al-Ta'sīs,* p. 55.

Perhaps Ibn Mahdī made known to Shāfiʿī his desire for a book in support of the authoritative sources of the law and against the prevailing tendency to use personal opinion. It was unlikely that Shāfiʿī could produce a work as original as the *Risāla* virtually on the spur of the moment, the impression given us by the sources. The theme of such a work must have been in Shāfiʿī's mind for a long time, and the book was either ready when Ibn Mahdī asked for it, or it was simply a matter of putting into writing what had already crystallized in Shāfiʿī's mind. A methodical legal reasoning, inferior in quality though it may have been in the first version of the *Risāla,* must have been in preparation for a long while. It is even conceivable that the narrative concerning Ibn Mahdī's request may have been circulated after he had seen or received the *Risāla* from Shāfiʿī. How Shāfiʿī conceived the idea of writing a book dealing with the subject of *uṣūl* (sources of the law) in a completely novel manner is exceedingly difficult to determine. But the age in which he lived and his involvement in the controversy between two opposing schools of thought must have given him the external stimulus to reflect on the subject. His keen intellect and extensive knowledge of the law made him eminently qualified to search fruitfully for the interrelationship of the sources which separated rival schools of law. But the structure and arguments of his reasoning must have evolved in his mind after long study and reflection.

The Old and the New Risāla

Shāfiʿī's treatise on jurisprudence has become universally known as *Kitāb al-Risāla Fī Uṣūl al-Fiqh,* often abridged as *Kitāb al-Risāla* or simply *al-Risāla.* The word risāla, which means an epistle, or a communication in writing made to an absent person, came to be used as a result of the traditional story that this book had been sent in the form of an epistle to ʿAbd al-Raḥmān Ibn Mahdī, who had asked Shāfiʿī to write a treatise on the authoritative sources of the sharīʿa. Thus the book at first acquired the unofficial title of al-Risāla, and this later became the formal title in all the manuscripts that have been preserved or published. Most of the writers who refer to this treatise, whether in the original or the revised form, call it *Kitāb al-Risāla* or *al-Risāla.* Thus the *Risāla* has become for all students of Islamic law the recognized title of Shāfiʿī's book on jurisprudence.

Internal evidence shows that Shāfiʿī himself never called his treatise by this name. More than half a dozen times, Shāfiʿī refers to it either as " Our Book," " My Book," " this Book," or simply the " Book."[61] These references demonstrate that the title of *al-Risāla* became current after Shāfiʿī's death and that Shāfiʿī himself, if the name was current in his time, did not recognize it as the proper title of his book.

The authorities are agreed that Shāfiʿī composed two treatises on jurisprudence, both referred to as *al-Risāla;* the old one was composed in ʿIrāq and the new in Egypt.[62] The old *Risāla* is described as a book in which Shāfiʿī set forth a systematic study of the Qur'ān, including its general and particular rules and its abrogating and abrogated communications, and of the sunna as the authoritative sources of the law. Some authorities state that it also dealt with *ijmāʿ* (consensus) and *qiyās* (analogy).[63] Since the text of the old *Risāla* has failed to reach us, except perhaps for a few passages reproduced in some later authorities,[64] it is difficult to define precisely its scope and arguments. We are told, however, by some authorities who were acquainted with both versions that the new *Risāla* was superior in quality to the old.[65]

[61] See paragraphs 22, 109, 131, 149, 173, 182, below.

[62] Bayhaqī cites the two works as two separate books (folio 50). Ibn Ḥajar states that Aḥmad b. Ḥanbal possessed a copy of both the old and the new *Risāla,* which were regarded as two different works (Ibn Ḥajar's *Tawālī al-Ta'sīs,* p. 77).

[63] al-Fakhr al-Rāzī, p. 55.

[64] See Bayhaqī, folio 98.

[65] For a statement to this effect by Aḥmad b. Ḥanbal (d. 239/855), a student of Shāfiʿī and founder of a school of law, see Ibn Abī Ḥātim al-Rāzī, p. 60; Abū Nuʿaym, p. 97.

It is likely that the old *Risāla,* dealing as it did with the authoritative sources, must have been in the nature of an apologia for the school of tradition, owing to Shāfiʿī's preoccupation during his first residence in ʿIrāq with arguments against Ḥanafī jurists. Although the old *Risāla* may have dealt with Shāfiʿī's opposition to personal opinion and the free use of analogy, it is inconceivable that it dealt with Shāfiʿī's differences with Mālik, as expounded in the new *Risāla,* since in ʿIrāq Shāfiʿī had taken the position of a supporter of Mālikī doctrine against the criticism of Ḥanafī jurists. In the brief quotation which Bayhaqī cites from the old *Risāla,* there is evidence that Shāfiʿī clearly supported the position of the Ḥijāzī traditionists, who held that the narratives of the Prophet's companions were authoritative, since they had been in close association with the Prophet and understood the meanings of his sunna. He also accepted the opinions of the Successors, if there was agreement among them.[66]

The new *Risāla,* however, reflects the mature thinking of Shāfiʿī after he settled in Egypt, and as its substance and arguments indicate, it deals with the whole subject of the sources as they were reconstructed in his mind in his later years. Internal evidence not only bears witness that the new *Risāla* was composed in Egypt, since it contains cross references to books which were written or dictated by Shāfiʿī after he settled there,[67] but it also demonstrates that in its present form the new Risāla was written or revised toward the end of its author's life.[68] Thus it reflects his mature legal speculations at the height of his career as a leading jurist.

The new *Risāla* is a compact treatise composed in a style which demonstrates that its author was an expert in the Arabic language. However, his use of a new terminology and new legal concepts often compelled him to repeat or redefine his terms and arguments. This is specially noticeable in his discourse with an interlocutor who demands explanation or repetition of ideas which Shāfiʿī may already have discussed in other

[66] Bayhaqī, folio 98.
[67] See paragraph 1184, below.
[68] See paragraph 1173, below. Cf. Shāfiʿī, *Kitāb al-Umm,* Vol. VI, p. 77.

sections of the book. Moreover, the problem of proper cross-referencing, which confronted other scholars, was not always satisfactorily solved,[69] and compelled Shāfiʿī at times to repeat his ideas. Often he refers the reader to other sections of the *Risāla* without a precise indication as to which section he means.[70]

However, the *Risāla*'s structure seems fairly sound and logical, and Shāfiʿī's arguments are set forth in a systematic manner and carried to their logical conclusions. The author begins his subject with a discussion of general topics in jurisprudence, supported by detailed examples, and then takes up the authoritative sources of the law. He pays particular attention to the sunna and traditions, not only because of the complexity of the subject, but also because he sought to establish their overriding authority. Finally, he discusses rather briefly the two other sources of the law, consensus and analogy, and concludes with a critical evaluation of certain other methods of reasoning such as *istiḥsān* (juristic preference) and *ikhtilāf* (disagreement). From this logical order the author makes some three or four digressions in which he discusses certain topics which belong more appropriately to other sections of the book.[71]

Shāfiʿī's knowledge of ancient Arabic literature assisted his literary style. In those days no one could be a great scholar unless he was a master of the Arabic tongue. He must also have had the gift of lucid and eloquent expression and the ability to quote freely from the Qur'ān and from ancient Arabic poetry. It is precisely these qualities of exactness and eloquence which are characteristic of his style. He could, moreover, arrest attention by a turn of expression, or a fine classical phrase, and he could sum up a point of law tersely in a maxim. Though he had all these gifts, Shāfiʿī's style is at times discursive and, in the *Risāla* in particular, too compact for clarity and, not infrequently,

[69] Cf. F. Roseuthal, *The Technique and Approach of Muslim Scholarship* (Rome, 1947), pp. 37-39.

[70] E.g., paragraphs 16, 22, 28, 135, 166, 168, etc.

[71] E.g., Chaps. III and VIII, below.

obscure. In comparison with other jurists, however, his style rises to eloquence.

The Order and Sources of the Risāla

Since the structure and substance of the old *Risāla* are not known to us, it is extremely difficult to state precisely to what degree the text of the new *Risāla* was based on the old. Both internal evidence and the narratives of the authorities seem to indicate that Shāfiʿī had, perhaps, composed the second *Risāla* anew. Once asked about Shāfiʿī's books, Ibn Ḥanbal replied: "The books Shāfiʿī wrote in ʿIrāq were far from perfect; after settling in Egypt, they were rewritten and perfected."[72] Bayhaqī, as well as other authorities, endorse the idea that the *Risāla* was rewritten in Egypt, and they give the impression that the old and the new editions were two different books.[73] Internal evidence suggests that not all of Shāfiʿī's earlier works were at his disposal after he settled in Egypt. In Chapter X of the new *Risāla,* Shāfiʿī states that the transmitters of some of the traditions that he cited were omitted because not all his earlier books were with him.[74] In his *Kitāb Ikhtilāf al-Ḥadīth* Shāfiʿī again apologizes for the fact that he did not have the first version of the book.[75] These statements indicate that some of the works Shāfiʿī composed in ʿIrāq, perhaps including the old *Risāla,* were no longer available to him after he settled in Egypt.

Finally, we may raise the question of the sources from which Shāfiʿī drew inspiration and information. This is not an easy question to answer specifically, since Shāfiʿī makes no reference in the *Risāla* to books which he may have consulted. In his other works, the *Kitāb al-Umm* in particular, he devotes whole

[72] Ibn Abī Ḥātim al-Rāzī, p. 60.

[73] Bayhaqī, folio 47; al-Fakhr al-Rāzī, p. 57.

[74] See paragraph 429, below.

[75] Shāfiʿī, *Kitāb Ikhtilāf al-Ḥadīth,* on the margin of *Kitāb al-Umm,* Vol. VII, p. 252. See also Ibn Ḥajar, *Tawālī al-Ta'sīs.* p. 78.

sections to discussions with other jurists—such as Awzāᶜī, Mālik, Abū Ḥanīfa, Abū Yūsuf and Shaybānī—which clearly indicate that he had studied the works of these eminent jurists with care.[76] His biographers give the impression that Shāfiᶜī was acquainted with almost all scholarly works.[77]

Traditional accounts portray Shāfiᶜī as taking an early interest in learning. He committed the Qur'ān to heart at seven and Mālik's *Muwaṭṭa'* at ten. These two books undoubtedly left a great impression on his mind and supplied indispensable sources for his legal training and speculation. The Qur'ān served the double purpose of supplying raw material for legislation, as the basic source of law, and an inspiring ideal for the scholar who aimed at shaping his system of law in harmony with that model. There are 220 Quranic citations in the *Risāla,* given either as specific rules of law or as examples for formulating principles or maxims of law.

Next to the Qur'ān, Shāfiᶜī stressed the Prophet's sunna. We are told that the old *Risāla* was written mainly to defend the viewpoint of traditionists concerning the overriding authority of the sunna. In the new *Risāla,* not only does Shāfiᶜī study the sunna as a source of law, but he also draws heavily on it in formulating his rules and maxims of law. Over a hundred traditions are cited in the *Risāla,* several of them repeated as examples at various points. Most of these traditions, it seems, Shāfiᶜī related on the authority of the masters under whom he studied in Makka and Madīna. His two greatest authorities are, of course, Mālik, from whom he quotes thirty-eight traditions,[78] and Sufyān b. ᶜUyayna, from whom he quotes thirty-five traditions.[79] From his other masters, he cites six traditions from ᶜAbd al-ᶜAzīz al-Darāwardī (Madīna),[80] four from Ibn

[76] Shāfiᶜī, *Kitāb al-Um,* Vol. VII, pp. 87 ff., 177 ff., 277 ff., 303 ff.

[77] See Ibn Abū Ḥātim al-Rāzī, pp. 136 ff.; and al-Fakhr al-Rāzī, pp. 19-21.

[78] See paragraphs 86, 112, 113, 119, 120, 142, 145, 148, 149, 161, 223, 231, 233, 255, 266, 271, 306, 318, 319, 322, 328, 332, 336, 337, 338, 346, 417, 419, 428, 435, 438, below.

[79] See paragraphs 6, 64, 94, 121, 129, 139, 144, 154, 161, 199, 223, 281, 310, 311, 321, 332, 338, 344, 346, 348, 413, 417, 420, 428, 440, 443, 483, 533, 647, 740, below.

[80] See paragraphs 92, 97, 413, 420, 551, below.

Abī Fudayk (Madīna),[81] four from Muslim b. Khālid al-Zanjī (Madīna),[82] three from Saʿīd b. Sālim al-Qaddāḥ (Makka),[83] two from Ibrāhīm b. Abī Yaḥya (Madīna),[84] and one from ʿAbd al-Majīd b. ʿAbd al-ʿAzīz (Makka).[85] From al-Yaman he quotes five traditions on the authority of Yaḥya b. Ḥassān, to whom he refers as the "trustworthy authority" without mentioning his name,[86] and from ʿIrāq he relates three traditions on the authority of ʿAbd al-Wahhāb b. ʿAbd al-Majīd al-Thaqafī.[87] A few other traditions either are related without authority or are cited with an incomplete list of authorities.

From the viewpoint of legal speculation we are inclined to believe that Shāfiʿī's main inspiration was derived from the intense debate with Ḥanafī jurists in ʿIrāq to which he had been subjected. He not only had to study their works, Shaybānī's in particular, which he copied, but also to reflect on the underlying principles separating him from those jurists. His arguments with the Ḥanafī jurists must have had greater influence on his legal speculation than his biographers indicate. After settling in Egypt, Shāfiʿī acknowledged his indebtedness to the Ḥanafī jurists and paid high tribute to the contributions of Abū Ḥanīfa and Shaybānī to the sharīʿa.[88]

Much of his legal material and many of his ideas Shāfiʿī owed to the teachings of his masters, which he stored in his memory. His debates with his rival scholars and his discussions of legal questions with colleagues and disciples must have contributed greatly to his knowledge and to the final formulation of his opinions. To be specific on these matters is difficult, however, for even if a disciple did contribute his share in a discussion, it was customary for the disciple to record the account in his notes on the authority of his master.

[81] See paragraphs 120, 148, 226, below.
[82] See paragraphs 148, 344, 438, 440, below.
[83] See paragraphs 348, 450, below.
[84] See paragraph 447, below.
[85] See paragraph 338, below.
[86] See paragraphs 122, 258, 319, 348, 474, below.
[87] See paragraphs 122, 129, 230, below.
[88] Ibn Abī Ḥātim al-Rāzī, pp. 204-207, 210-11.

SUBSTANCE AND ARGUMENT OF THE *RISĀLA*

The vocabulary of the Risāla

THE VOCABULARY of the *Risāla* raises questions not only of legal nomenclature, but also of literary and philosophical terminology. Shāfiʿī rarely defines his terms, assuming that his followers and readers will be familiar with the general and technical words from the context of his writings or from the common usage of the time. Thus before we proceed to the fundamental ideas embodied in the *Risāla,* it may be useful to discuss briefly the meaning of some of its cardinal terms and expressions. Four sets of terms deserve particular examination.

In the first set, there are general terms which need elucidation, such as *ʿilm* (knowledge), *al-bayān* (declaration), and *ʿadl* (justice). By *ʿilm*, Shāfiʿī always means legal knowledge derived from the authoritative sources of the law; some rules are obligatory for men individually (*farḍ ʿayn*), such as prayer and fasting, and some are obligatory for them collectively, such as the *jihād*. He equates knowledge with certainty and states that it is the duty of the jurist to seek the truth in his legal reasoning.[89] By *al-bayān*, which Shāfiʿī applies to Quranic communications, he means a clear declaration embodying a rule or a principle of law. The term is frequently used in the *Risāla* either in the sense of mere declaration, embodying a rule of law, or in clarifying the meaning of a certain rule of law.

The term *ʿadl* is used either in the general sense of justice, which implies conformity with the law, or as the necessary qualification for a witness. Although no precise

[89] See Chap. III, below; cf. Sharīf ʿAlī al-Jurjānī, *Kitāb al-Taʿrīfāt,* ed. G. L. Flügel (Leipzig, 1845), pp. 160-62.

definition is given by Shāfiʿī, the term *ʿadāla*, the quality of *ʿadl*, is described by al-Māwardī, a Shāfiʿī jurist, as a state of moral and religious perfection.[90] Thus the term *ʿadl* signifies probity or justness of character. This is the sense in which it is frequently used in the *Risāla*. The witness must be *ʿadl* (just in character), and the minimum requirement is that he must display justness at the time when his testimony is given. It is possible, Shāfiʿī argues, that the witness may not be *ʿadl* at another time. The testimony of one witness of just character must be supported by another witness of just character, and the justness of character of each witness must be confirmed by another person of just character.[91]

The second set of terms is made up of those which Shāfiʿī uses in his discussions of the Qur'ān. The terms "general" and "particular" as applied to rules, which are familiar to modern students of the law, were introduced to Islamic jurisprudence for the first time by Shāfiʿī.[92] The precise meaning of these terms will be explained in the following section. He also introduced the terms "explicit" and "implicit," the first being equivalent to the literal meaning of the communication and the second to the meaning implied either in the text or in the context of the communication. Shāfiʿī also uses the term al-naskh or the abrogation of divine legislation, which is well known to contemporary jurists as the repeal of legislation. The term as well as the principle of abrogation are to be found in the Qur'ān (Q. XVI, 103), but Shāfiʿī argues that a Quranic communication can be abrogated only by another Quranic communication and that neither does the Qur'ān abrogate the sunna, nor the sunna the Qur'ān. It is true, he goes on to argue, that a sunna can be superseded by a Quranic communication, but not until the

[90] al-Māwardī, *Kitāb al-Aḥkām al-Sulṭānīya,* ed. M. Enger (Bonn, 1853), p. 108; and paragraph 16, below.

[91] See paragraphs 364-367, below.

[92] Ibn Abī Ḥātim al-Rāzī, p. 57. Ibn Ḥanbal is reported to have said that he had not understood the rules of the Qur'ān until he heard Shāfiʿī's classification of these rules into general and particular, etc. See Abū Nuʿaym, p. 97.

sunna is first abrogated by another sunna laid down by the Prophet.[93]

In the third set of terms, there are certain words used in connection with Shāfiʿī's discussion of the sunna and ḥadīth (tradition). Although sunna and ḥadīth mean the same thing in practice, in pre-Islamic Arabia *sunna* meant usage or custom and it formed the common law observed by the Arabs. After the rise of Islam, the term sunna was applied to the sayings and decisions of the Prophet Muḥammad, and ḥadīth meant the communication of the sunna, or the Prophet's custom. In the words of Wensinck, "ḥadīth is the external, sunna the internal side of tradition; ḥadīth is the form, sunna the matter."[94] The sunna is reported in the form of a general statement—usually short—preceded by a chain of authorities or transmitters (*isnād*), cited to prove the authenticity of the report. The *isnād* begins with the latest authority and goes back to a Companion who relates the Prophet's custom (i. e., his saying or decision). This transmission must be uninterrupted and must be made on the authority of an eye or ear witness, and all the transmitters must be thoroughly reliable. Thus, the criticism of Muslim scholars was restricted to a thorough examination of the *isnād* (transmission), and the scholars were satisfied if the tradition passed such an external test.

The traditions were collected in the third century (ninth century of the Christian era) in a number of digests, and six digests became recognized as authoritative. These are the two *Ṣaḥīḥs* of al-Bukhārī (d. 256/869) and Muslim (d. 261/874), and the four *sunans* of Abū Dāwūd (d. 275/888), Tirmidhī (d. 279/892), Ibn Māja (d. 283/886), and al-Nasā'ī (d. 303/915). Other digests of traditions, well known to students of the sharīʿa, are by Ibn Ḥanbal (d. 241/856), al-Dārimī (d. 255/869),

[93] See Chap. V, below. For a full discussion of the rules of abrogation, see Abū Jaʿfar (surnamed al-Naḥḥas) Muḥammad b. Aḥmad b. Ismāʿīl al-Ṣaffār, *Kitāb al-Nāsikh wa al-Mansūkh* (Cairo, 1323/1905); and al-Ḥāzimī, *al-Iʿtibār Fī al-Nāsikh wa al-Mansūkh Min al-Āthār* (Cairo, 1346/1927).

[94] A. J. Wensinck, "The Importance of Tradition for the Study of Islam," *Moslem World*, Vol. XI (1921), p. 239.

al-Dāraquṭnī (d. 385/996), al-Bayhaqī (d. 458/ 1065), and others. Although Shāfiʿī is critical of narratives transmitted by unreliable authorities, and is unwilling to accept traditions from authorities unknown to him, he himself cites in the *Risāla* several traditions without *isnād*.[95] Such traditions are known to traditionists as *mursal*, or traditions lacking some or all the names of the transmitters. Shāfiʿī also accepts some traditions that were transmitted by a single authority. Such traditions are called *al-khabar al-wāḥid*, or the single-individual tradition.[96]

In the fourth set of terms, words such as *ijtihād*, *qiyās*, *ijmāʿ*, and *istiḥsān* are used in the exercise of legal reasoning. Literally, *ijtihād* means the exercise of effort. Originally it was used as the exercise of discretion and personal opinion, but in Shāfiʿī's time the term was narrowed down to mean the discretion of the scholar. Shāfiʿī limited *ijtihād* to the use of *qiyās* (analogy), prohibiting the exercise of personal opinion unless it were based on a precedent. *Ijtihād*, Shāfiʿī says, is the method of reasoning, based on certain indications, leading to the correct decision.[97] *Qiyās* is equated with *ijtihād* of which Shāfiʿī approves, provided there is a relevant text in the Qur'ān or tradition on the strength of which analogy could be applied. It is generally defined as the method of legal reasoning by which a decision is made on the strength of a precedent in which a common reason, or an effective cause, is applicable.[98] Shāfiʿī's conception of analogy perhaps may be best seen in the following statement:

> Analogy is of various kinds... They differ from one another in the antecedence of the analogy of either one of the two, or its sources,

[95] See paragraphs 7, 19, 82, 112, 124, 133, 196, 239, 333, 713, 869, below.
[96] See Chap. X, below.
[97] See Chap. XIII, below.
[98] Sarakhsī, *Uṣūl,* Vol. II, p. 121. For the possibility of deriving this concept from Hebrew or Aramaic sources, see J. Schacht, *Origins of Muhammadan Jurisprudence,* p. 99; and S. G. Vesey-Fitzgerald, " Nature and Sources of the Sharīʿa," in M. Khadduri and H. J. Liebesny (eds.), *Law in the Middle East* (Washington, 1955), Vol. I, pp. 96-97.

> or the source of both, or the circumstance that one is more clear than the other. The strongest kind [is the deduction] from an order of prohibition by God or the Apostle of the small quantity that the equally strong or stronger order of prohibition of the great quantity shall be applicable owing to the [compelling] reason in the greater quantity. Similarly the commendation of a small act of piety implies the presumably stronger commendation of a greater act of piety; and similarly the order of permission of a great quantity would render permissible that of a smaller quantity.[99]

By *ijmāᶜ* (consensus) Shāfiᶜī does not mean merely the agreement of a few scholars of a certain town or locality, as the Ḥijāzī and ᶜIrāqī jurists seem to have held, but the majority of leading jurists in Muslim lands. He also universalized *ijmāᶜ* on matters of fundamentals to include agreement of the Muslim community.[100] On matters of fundamentals arrived at by consensus, Shāfiᶜī argues, there should be no disagreement (*ikhtilāf*), but on matters of detail for which there may be two answers, one answer might be chosen by *istiḥsān* (discretion or preference). The earlier jurists seem to have permitted a greater degree of discretion than Shāfiᶜī was inclined to accept.[101]

Fundamental Ideas of the Risāla

A brief summary of the content of the *Risāla* hardly does justice to it, for only a complete translation of the text, such as is provided in the following pages, can present a full expression of the ideas and the method of reasoning of its author. However, a description of the *Risāla,* its fundamental ideas and problems, may serve the reader as a guide.

The *Risāla* opens with an introductory chapter on the religious basis of Islamic jurisprudence. After the usual homage

[99] See paragraph 387, below.

[100] See Chap. XI, below; and al-Ghazzālī, *al-Mustaṣfa Min ᶜIlm al-Uṣūl* (Cairo, 1356/1937), Vol. I, pp. 115-21.

[101] See Chap. XV, below.

and expressions of gratitude to God, Shāfiʿī points out that at the time Muḥammad was charged with his prophetic mission, mankind was divided into two classes. There were those who did not believe in God and who worshipped idols and stones and other natural objects, and there were the "People of the Book,"[102] who believed in God and in the teachings of His earlier prophets, but who had changed God's commands and forged falsehood by their tongues, mixing it with the truth that God had revealed to them. Because of this state of misbelief, God decided to send forth the last of his prophets, Muḥammad, to repair and reconstruct the world into a God-fearing community. Thus Muḥammad's mission, embodied in the term "Islam," was to provide mankind with the final and definitive religion.

Shāfiʿī discusses briefly the place of the Qur'ān in the Islamic religion and the duty of the Muslims to obey the orders of Muḥammad, and concludes that it is the duty of all those who seek legal knowledge to gain it by constant appeal to God's Book as communicated to the Prophet. For "no misfortune will ever descend upon any of the followers of God's religion for which there is no guidance in the Book of God to indicate the right way."[103]

The Qur'ān, Shāfiʿī points out, is the basis of legal knowledge. Its provisions constitute a "perspicuous declaration" (Q. III, 132) on all matters, spiritual and temporal, which men are under obligation to observe. The second chapter of the *Risāla* is therefore devoted to a discussion of the nature of the legal provisions of the Qur'ān under the title "*al-bayān*" (perspicuous declaration). "*Al-bayān,*" Shāfiʿī says, "is a collective term" which includes general principles of law as well as detailed rules. The term *al-bayān* has been discussed by several leading jurists. Some say that it merely

[102] Ahl al-Kitāb, the people who possess a scripture, include Christians, Jews, Magians (Zoroastrians), Samaritans, and Sabians. For a discussion of their status in Islam, see my *War and Peace in the Law of Islam*, Chap. 17.

[103] See paragraph 11, below.

means a declaration, embodying certain legal provisions; others argue that it not only declares them, but also makes them clear.[104] Shāfiʿī, however, seems to emphasize the legal content of the provisions on the grounds that all Quranic communications are clear, "although some are more sharply clarified than others," and only to those who are ignorant of the Arab tongue do some communications seem less clear than others. He then divides *al-bayān* into five categories. The first consists of a specific legal provision in the text of the Qur'ān, such as the basic duties that are owed to God (credal witness, prayer, payment of alms, fasting, and pilgrimage). The second includes certain provisions, whose modes of observance are specified by an order of the Prophet Muḥammad (such as the number of prayers each day and the amount of alms to be paid). The third consists of broad legal provisions which Muḥammad particularized. The fourth includes all the legal provisions laid down by Muḥammad in the absence of a specific Quranic text. The fifth and final category is comprised of rules which are sought by the exercise of *ijtihād* (personal reasoning) by means of *qiyās* (analogy).

Although in his chapter on *al-bayān* Shāfiʿī discusses certain characteristics of the Qur'ān, that chapter is, apparently, intended to be only an introduction to a fuller treatment of the Qur'ān, from a juridical viewpoint, in subsequent chapters. At the end of chapter II, on *al-bayān*, he discusses the Arabic eloquence of the Qur'ān—one of its distinguishing features—which, to the Muslims, is the chief evidence of the miracle (*iʿjāz*) of this Book.[105]

[104] For a discussion on the meaning of *al-bayān* see al-Ghazzālī, *al-Mustaṣfa*, Vol. I, pp. 304-66; Abū Isḥāq al-Shāṭibī, *al-Muwāfaqāt*, ed. ʿAbd-Allāh Durāz (Cairo, n. d.), Vol. III, pp. 308-14; Sayf al-Dīn al-Āmidī, *al-Iḥkām Fī Uṣūl al-Aḥkām* (Cairo, 1347/1928), Vol. II, pp. 121-34.

[105] The doctrine of the miracle of the Qur'ān has been discussed by several Muslim scholars. For a full exposition of the doctrine, see al-Bāqillānī, *Kitāb Iʿjāz al-Qur'ān*, ed. Aḥmad Ṣaqr (Cairo, 1954); ʿAbd al-Qāhīr al-Jurjānī, *Dalāʿil al-Iʿjāz*, ed. M. Tawit (Tetuan, n. d.), 2 vols. For a survey of works dealing

Shāfiʿī's critical study of the Qur'ān from a juridical viewpoint led him to the keen observation that the Quranic rules and principles fall into various categories. To begin with, he divides them into general and particular rules. Some of the general rules, he observes, are intended to be general, in which the particular rules are included. There are general rules in which both the general and particular rules are included, and there are general rules which are intended to be particular rules.

Then Shāfiʿī divides the Quranic legislation into a different set of categories. There are, he observes, general rules the meaning of which may be clarified by the context, and there are those only the wording of which indicates the implicit meaning. There are general rules, he adds, which only the sunna can specify as general or particular.

Shāfiʿī's classification of the Quranic legislation into the foregoing categories was not only novel but was hailed as a great contribution to the understanding of the Qur'ān as a source of law. His distinction between the general, which embodies general rules and principles of law, and the particular, which means specific rules, clarified for his contemporaries the way toward a deeper understanding of the sources and principles of Islamic law. Shāfiʿī's contribution elicited high praise. To cite but one example, al-Karābīsī told Aḥmad b. Ḥanbal—founder, of another school of law—that he had understood the precise meaning of the Qur'ān only after he had read the *Risāla*.[106]

Shāfiʿī's specific reference to the sunna, the Prophet's sayings and decisions, to clarify the meaning of a particular piece of Quranic legislation or an ambiguous text, brings the sunna into the field of Islamic legislation and indicates its specific role as a source of law. It is in his discussions of the sunna and traditions that we find one of Shāfiʿī's greatest contributions to Islamic jurisprudence. For although the school of tradition laid sufficient emphasis on the sunna, in opposition to the school of opinion, in which Shāfiʿī himself took an active part in

with the question of *iʿjāz*, see Naʿīm al-Ḥimṣī, *Ta'rīkh Fikrat Iʿjāz al-Qur'ān* (Damascus, 1955).

[106] Ibn Abī Ḥātim al-Rāzī, p. 57; al-Fakhr al-Rāzī, p. 20.

his early career, it was Shāfiʿī who made it clear that only an authentic tradition from the Prophet is binding and constitutes an authoritative source of legislation. Both the Ḥijāzī and the Irāqī jurists often accepted traditions that were based on local custom or embodied a personal opinion as valid for legislation. Shāfiʿī made a distinction between an authentic tradition from the Prophet and a narrative which embodies the opinion of a Companion or a leading jurist; the latter may be useful in clarifying the meaning of a text, but it should not be as binding as a tradition from the Prophet.

Shāfiʿī goes on, in the following chapters, to discuss the principle of abrogation, by virtue of which a Quranic communication was repealed by a later one. Here he indicates again the role of the sunna in its relation to the Qur'ān, pointing out that the sunna merely states which of the Quranic communications are the abrogating ones and which are the abrogated, but he rejects the Ḥanafī doctrine which states that the sunna can abrogate the Qur'ān. The Qur'ān does not abrogate the sunna directly nor does the sunna abrogate the Qur'ān; the Prophet, says Shāfiʿī, always provided a new sunna, in conformity with Quranic legislation, when the Quranic legislation contradicted an earlier sunna. Thus although he stresses the significance of the sunna, he gives it a precise definition as a second authoritative source of law in its relation to the Qur'ān.

The sunna includes Muḥammad's sayings and decisions. It is, therefore, not on the same level as the infallible Quranic communications. However, Shāfiʿī argues, God had imposed on men the duty of obedience to His Prophet as well as to Him, and he goes on to give evidence that God regards disobedience to the Prophet as disobedience to Him. Accordingly, in practice the sunna of the Prophet is a source of legislation as valid as the Qur'ān.

But since Shāfiʿī emphasizes the rule that only an authentic sunna, transmitted by reliable authorities, constitutes a valid source of law, he devotes a large portion of the *Risāla* to a study of what constitutes an authentic tradition, who are the reliable transmitters, and why certain authentic traditions are contradictory to one another. This latter category, to which he pays attention, is as novel as his distinction in the Quranic legislation between the general and particular.

To Shāfiʿī there are no contradictory traditions. They appear contradictory only to those who do not know the circumstances in which they were laid down and who do not realize that certain traditions merely qualify others. Shāfiʿī's contribution to this field of legal reasoning, although it may raise certain doubts as to the historical evidence of his interpretation, resolved a serious problem for the jurists who were faced with a great mass of contradictory traditions. Shāfiʿī's method of reconciliation, called *al-ta'wīl* (interpretation),[107] encouraged the acceptance of many a tradition which otherwise would have been in danger of being rejected. Thus his solution supplied further material for legal development, but for the critical historian it rendered more difficult the problem of separating the historical elements from the mass of traditions which Muslim publicists accepted without question.

The latter part of the *Risāla* deals briefly with *ijmāʿ* (consensus), *qiyās* (analogy), *ijtihād* (personal reasoning), *istiḥsān* (juristic preference), and *ikhtilāf* (disagreement). Although these are important jurisprudential subjects, Shāfiʿī devotes much less space to them than to the Qur'ān and sunna.

Shāfiʿī's doctrine of consensus, as Schacht rightly points out, develops continuously in his writings.[108] It begins as the consensus of a few scholars in a certain locality, following Mālik's method,[109] and becomes a concept that includes the entire Muslim community. If the view that the new *Risāla* was written or revised as the last of Shāfiʿī's writings is correct, his doctrine of consensus as defined in this work should represent his final formulation. In various parts of the *Risāla*,

[107] *Ta'wīl* became the subject of further study by many Muslim scholars. See Ibn Qutayba al-Dīnawarī, *Kitāb Ta'wīl Mukhtalaf al-Ḥadīth* (Cairo, 1326/1909).

[108] J. Schacht, *Origins of Muhammadan Jurisprudence*, p. 88.

[109] Mālik, however, recognized the *ijmāʿ* of the scholars of his own locality—Madīna.

Shāfiʿī refers to the consensus of the scholars as a method of expounding the law acceptable to contemporary jurists, but in his references to the consensus of the community at large, specially in the chapter on consensus,[110] he undoubtedly tends to invest it with higher authority. Shāfiʿī ends his chapter on consensus by asserting: " He who holds what the Muslim community holds shall be regarded as following the community, and he who holds differently shall be regarded as opposing the community he was ordered to follow. So the error comes from separation... "

The concept *vox populi, vox Dei,* embodied in a tradition which states " My people will never agree on an error," is not cited by Shāfiʿī in this form, a fact which perhaps indicates that it was circulated after his time. But the concept does appear in the *Risāla,* which may well be the source of the final formulation of the principle embodied in the tradition ascribed to the Prophet Muḥammad.[111] Shāfiʿī's doctrine of the community at large was opposed by other scholars, including his own followers, although Ghazzālī (d. 1111) tried to confine the agreement to fundamental principles, leaving matters of detail to the consensus of the scholars.[112] The fundamental weakness in the doctrine of the consensus of the community was procedural—the lack of an adequate method which would provide means for the community to arrive at an agreement.[113]

Shāfiʿī discusses *ijtihād* (personal reasoning) and *qiyās* (analogy) at greater length than consensus, because he tried to limit the use of personal reasoning, in the wide and unrestricted sense, to the use of analogy. He often uses the terms *qiyās* and *ijtihād* interchangeably, but obviously he permits personal

[110] See Chap. XI, below.

[111] Goldziher has suggested a possible Roman influence on the Islamic doctrine of consensus, but a primitive form of consensus was not new to the Arabs. See J. Schacht, *Origins of Muhammadan Jurisprudence,* pp. 83, 91.

[112] Ghazzālī, *al-Mustaṣfa,* Vol. I, p. 115.

[113] The lack of a method by which to arrive at an agreement remained the perennial weakness of the doctrine of consensus, and no adequate solution was provided by jurists who came after Shāfiʿī. See remarks on this point in my *War and Peace in the Law of Islam,* pp. 38-34.

reasoning only through analogy. "Analogy is of two kinds," says Shāfiʿī, "the first, if the case in question is similar to the original meaning [of the precedent]... The second, if the case in question is similar to several precedents, analogy must be applied to the precedent nearest in resemblance and most appropriate."[114] He tried, however, to limit the use of analogy to matters of detail; it cannot supersede an authoritative text. Neither should it be based on a special or an exceptional precedent; analogy must conform to the spirit and the general rules and principles of the law. In taking such a position Shāfiʿī established a balance between those who used analogy extensively as a source of law and those who rejected it altogether. As to *istiḥsān*, which the ʿIrāqī jurists used as a method for rejecting one precedent in favor of another, it is declared unacceptable by Shāfiʿī because it permits virtually unlimited use of discretion and personal reasoning. Only one form of personal reasoning is acceptable to Shāfiʿī—analogy. Even this method is regarded as a weak instrument. In summing up the sources of the law at the end of the *Risāla*, Shāfiʿī says: "Although I have made decisions [on the basis of consensus and analogy] just as I have made decisions on the basis of the Book and the sunna, [in the case of consensus and analogy] the principle on which I made my decision varies."[115]

Finally, the *Risāla* ends with a discussion of *ikhtilāf* (disagreement). Although the jurists before Shāfiʿī seem to have tolerated a greater freedom in the use of disagreement, the trend toward the systematic use of the sources as defined by Shāfiʿī set in motion the movement to limit disagreement. Shāfiʿī states that there are two kinds of disagreement. The one is prohibited and the other permitted. He goes on to say:

> On all matters concerning which God provided clear textual evidence in His Book or [a sunna] uttered by the Prophet's tongue, disagreement among those to whom these [texts] are known is

[114] See paragraph 497, below.
[115] See paragraph 821, below.

> unlawful. As to matters that are liable to different interpretations or derived from analogy, so that he who interprets or applies analogy arrives at a decision different from that arrived at by another, I do not hold that [disagreement] of this kind constitutes such strictness as that arising from textual [evidence].[116]

Thus Shāfiʿī restricts disagreement only on matters on which the scholars may exercise personal reasoning (*ijtihād*) and on which each may take a decision which is right in his own way. A case in point is the search for the *qibla*, the direction of the Sacred Mosque. Everyone will have to determine his own *qibla*, by *ijtihād*, and although each may take a slightly different position from another, everyone is right in his own way.

SIGNIFICANCE OF THE *RISĀLA*

Shāfiʿī as the Founder of the Science of Islamic Jurisprudence

THE *RISĀLA*, a novel work in the literature of Islamic law, gave Shāfiʿī a name as the founder of the science of *uṣūl al-fiqh* (roots or sources of the law). The *uṣūl* had been the subject of study by other jurists as attested by the fact that Abū Yūsuf (d. 182/798) discusses certain aspects of it in his *Kitāb al-Kharāj*,[117] and Shaybānī, one of Shāfiʿī's early friends in ʿIrāq, is reputed to have written a book on *uṣūl*. But this term had not yet acquired the technical meaning of a science dealing specifically with the sources of the law which Shāfiʿī had attached to it. No other jurist seems to have discussed the subject in so coherent and systematic a manner, and the *Risāla*

[116] See paragraph 721, below.

[117] Abū Yūsuf, *Kitāb al-Kharāj* (Cairo,1852/1934). Abū al-Mu'ayyad b. Aḥmad al-Makkī regards him as the first who wrote on the subject of *uṣūl* from a Ḥanafī point of view. See Makkī's *Manāqib al-Imām al-Aʿẓam* (Hyderabad, 1321/1904), Vol. II, p. 245.

appears to be the first complete and well-organized survey of the *uṣūl*, their interrelationship, and how the detailed rules and decisions were derived from the authoritative sources. It proved to be so excellent a guide of the sharīʿa that it was always referred to as the leading work on the subject.[118] Some of the subjects of this book, such as *istiḥsān* (juristic preference) and *ʿilm* (legal knowledge), are dealt with more fully in the *Kitāb al-Umm,*[119] and a separate work is devoted to the study of the Qur'ān;[120] but the *Risāla* is the only comprehensive treatise dealing with the subject of *uṣūl* which Shāfiʿī had written.

The *Risāla,* however, is not a complete work on jurisprudence dealing with the nature and principles of law, although the reader may well form an idea about Shāfiʿī's conception of the nature of law since several sections are devoted to an exposition of the broad principles and rules of the sharīʿa. The *Risāla* is in the main a treatise on the nature and use of the sources of the sharīʿa. It was written originally as an apologia for the supremacy of traditions, but after its fundamental ideas and arguments had been reformulated in Egypt, it represented a systematic and critical study of all the sources of the law.

The significance of the *Risāla,* therefore, lies not so much in the detailed matters it discusses, although these have had their influences on Muslim jurists, as in the comprehensive view of the whole subject of *uṣūl* and in the logical and systematic method Shāfiʿī provided for legal reasoning. The originality of the book lies in its new departure in the study of jurisprudence.

From Shāfiʿī's time onward, the *Risāla* became a textbook for students of Muslim jurisprudence. It has been carefully

[118] ʿAbd al-Raḥmān Ibn Khaldūn, *al-Muqaddima,* ed. E. M. Quatremère (Paris, 1858), Vol. III, p. 22; trans. F. Rosenthal (London, 1958) , Vol. III, pp. 27-28; and M. Z. al-Kawtharī, *Bulūgh al-Amānī Fī Sīrat al-Imām Muḥammad b. al-Ḥasan al-Shaybānī* (Cairo, 1355/1937), p. 67.

[119] Shāfiʿī, *Kitāb al-Umm,* Vol. VII, pp. 250-65, 267-303.

[120] Shāfiʿī, *Kitāb Aḥkām al-Qur'ān,* ed. M. Z. al-Kawtharī (Cairo, 1371/ 1951), 2 vols.

studied by Shāfiʿī's followers as well as by the followers of other schools of law. Al-Muzanī, one of Shāfiʿī's disciples, said that he had read the *Risāla* five hundred times; from each reading he had derived a fresh thought.[121] Ibn Ḥanbal often suggested the *Risāla* to his followers and ranked it in his mind among the best of Shāfiʿī's writings. It became a model for both jurists and theologians who wrote on the subject. Al-Ghazzālī, perhaps the greatest Muslim theologian, wrote a work on jurisprudence in which he elaborated the theme of the *Risāla* and set forth a study of the sources of law in a highly logical and systematic manner in accordance with the Shāfiʿī school of law.[122]

The *Risāla* became a favorite subject for commentaries written by later jurists. Although none of the commentaries has been found, we are told by some authorities that at least five were composed. One of them was by Abū Bakr al-Ṣayrafī (d. 330/932), who was hailed by al-Subkī, a Shāfiʿī follower, as the greatest writer on jurisprudence since Shāfiʿī himself. Other commentators were al-Naysābūrī (d. 349/960), al-Shāshī (d. 365/976), al-Jawzaqī (d. 378/989), and al-Juwaynī (d. 438/1046). These commentators were all learned in the law and theology, and their books were highly regarded in Islamic lands.[123]

The Islamization and Idealization of Law

By providing a precise method of legal reasoning, Shāfiʿī achieved two important results. First, he rationalized on an Islamic basis all the law that earlier generations had handed down. Not only did he reject the use of sources that were

[121] Bayhaqī, folios 47-48; Ibn Ḥajar, *Tawālī al-Ta'sīs*, p. 77.

[122] al-Ghazzālī, *al-Mustaṣfa*. He also devoted two other volumes to an exposition of the law according to the Shāfiʿī school, entitled *Kitāb al-Wajīz* (Cairo, 1317/1900) , 2 vols.

[123] Subkī, Vol. II, pp. 169-70. See also Ibn al-Nadīm, p. 300; and Ḥajjī Khalīfa, *Kashf al-Ẓunūn*, ed. G. L. Flügel (Leipzig and London, 1835-58), Vol. II, p. 873.

not Islamic, such as custom and personal opinion, but he also defined the method by which legal reasoning was restricted within the framework of the authoritative sources. Although historically the law was derived from both Islamic and non-Islamic sources, the process of Islamizing the law was perhaps an unconscious movement set in motion from the very beginning of Islam. It was Shāfiʿī, however, who consciously laid down a method of jurisprudence that was intended to confine legal reasoning within the framework of Islamic sources. To achieve the purpose he inevitably narrowed the free use of legal reasoning, and the tendency toward *taqlīd* (literally, imitation, i. e., to follow the doctrine of a recognized authority) may be said to have begun at that time. In the following century, *taqlīd* became the dominating rule.

Furthermore, Shāfiʿī's logical method led him to assume that the decisions and actions of the Prophet had always been consistent and rational. In making use of the Prophet's sunna as a source of law, he always assumed that there was no contradictory sunna; if one was ever found, either it must be lacking in authenticity or, Shāfiʿī argued, the circumstances in which the contradictory sunna had been provided were not the same. In following this line of reasoning, Shāfiʿī subordinated positive rules to the sunna and rejected old legal doctrines, even though based on sound legal reasoning, whenever they contradicted the authority of the sunna.

Shāfiʿī's method of jurisprudence was concerned less with developing the law that existed in his age than with systematizing a body of law that had already reached a high degree of growth. Thus in the *Risāla* Shāfiʿī paid less attention to the problem of developing new principles of law than to the problem of how to demonstrate that all the principles and rules that existed in his time were derived from recognized Islamic sources.

Closely associated with the Islamization of law, perhaps the inevitable result of it, was the tendency to idealize the sharīʿa as the perfect legal order. It is true that Quranic legislation was regarded as divine from the very beginning, but pre-

Islamic law, customary or otherwise, that was not repealed by divine legislation was incorporated into Islam after a long process of synthesis. All the early Muslim jurists unconsciously contributed to the harmonizing of the law with the spirit of divine legislation by making decisions in the form of answers to practical questions. Thus the idea of regarding as divine not only Quranic legislation, but all Islamic law, may be said to have begun in early Islamic history. The philosophical elaboration of this idea, however, had not yet been fully achieved until Shāfiʿī's time. One of Shāfiʿī's main preoccupations, it will be recalled, was his constant disputations with fellow jurists against the use of sources which might infuse into the law elements of human legislation. The development of the sharīʿa after Shāfiʿī's time tended to become gradually divorced from the practical needs of the individual and oriented toward the common interests of Islam, embodying its ethical and religious ideals.

Not unlike the idea of natural law in medieval Christendom, Islamic law was regarded as transcendental and perfect. In contrast with positive law, Islamic law was revealed in a supernatural way and for a supermundane purpose. The *jus divinum* was regarded as the ideal, eternal and just, designed for all time and characterized by its universal application to all men.[124] The ideal life was the life led in strictest conformity with this law.

In theory the divine law preceded the state and was independent of man's own existence. The state was created to enforce the law, but if it fails to do so—and in such a case the state forfeits its *raison d'être*—the individual still remains under an obligation to observe the law even in the absence of anyone to enforce it. The sanction of the law, which is distinct from the validity of that law, need not exist. For the object of the law is to provide for the individual the right path (*sharīʿa*), or the ideal life, regardless of the existence of the proper authority to enforce it.[125]

[124] See Q. XVIII, 27; XXXIII, 6.
[125] al-Shāṭibī, Vol. II, pp. 8 ff.

The need for a rational justification of such a system is so great that man often seeks to justify it by mere self-conviction.[126] Shāfiʿī's legal reasoning supplied a rationale for the Islamic legal order. Deriving his system from the Qur'ān, the very word of God, and from the model conduct set forth by God's Prophet, Shāfiʿī demonstrated how every rule of law can conform in letter or in spirit to the norms provided by the authoritative sources. In the final formulation of the classical system of Islamic law Shāfiʿī's impress remained permanent.

Shāfiʿī's Influence

It is not difficult to understand the reason for Shāfiʿī's pre-eminence. His vast capacity for work, his extraordinary knowledge of the law as well as his broad knowledge of Islamic studies, his powerful intellect and his eloquent and lucid exposition were devoted exclusively to the study of law. No less favorable for his great success were the circumstances in which he played his role as the founder of a new school of law. He appeared at a time when two rival schools of law were competing for supremacy. There is a saying related by a Muslim scholar that the reason Shāfiʿī's life was relatively short was that there was still need for some differences of opinion, and had he lived longer, no differences would have survived.[127] Shāfiʿī probably never intended to found a school of law after his name. His biographers often quote him as saying that he merely wished to teach the truth and had no desire to have his name cited as an authority.[128] Shāfiʿī's precise legal methodology, however, inevitably limited the number of schools

[126] Submission and self-conviction are urged in many a Quranic communication: Q. II, 2; IV, 136; VI, 155; VII, 204; VIII, 8; XXXIX, 41, etc.

[127] See Muṣṭafa ʿAbd al-Rāziq, *Tamhīd li Ta'rīkh al-Falsafa al-Islāmīya* (Cairo, 1944), p. 237.

[128] Ibn Abī Ḥātim al-Rāzī, pp. 91, 93; Ibn ʿAbd al-Barr, p. 84; Muzanī's *Mukhtaṣar* (on the margin of *Kitāb al-Umm*, Vol. I, p. 2); Ibn Ḥajar, *Tawālī al-Ta'sīs*, p. 62.

of law that were developing and led to the establishment of a separate school of law.

After Shāfiʿī's death, many legends surrounded the story of his life and his influence. A tradition from the Prophet has it that at the end of every century a great reformer from his house would appear. It has been held that ʿUmar b. ʿAbd al-ʿAzīz (d. 101/720), the eighth Umayyad caliph, was the religious reformer who appeared at the end of the first century of the Islamic era; at the end of the second, it was Shāfiʿī. Other traditions have been related to prove that Shāfiʿī's legal doctrine was anticipated and approved by the Prophet.[129] Later accounts of his life abound with similar stories which raised him to the highest saintly position. Although these stories lack historical foundation, they should not be dismissed as without value, because for centuries they influenced the minds of generations that followed.

Yet Shāfiʿī's role as the founder of a new school of law was not the product of a hero cult arising after his death, as in the case of Ibn Ḥanbal; nor was he, like Abū Ḥanīfa, the titular head of a group of distinguished jurists who all contributed to Ḥanafī law. His was the active career of a jurist who provided the foundation of a new school of law. Shāfiʿī's influence as the founder of a school of law began after he settled in Egypt, and it rose steadily. Among the leading disciples who were already active in spreading his earlier doctrines in ʿIrāq were men such as Abū ʿUbayd al-Qāsim b. Sallām (d. 224/838),[130] al-Zaʿfarānī (d. 260/873),[131] Abū Thawr (d. 240/854),[132] Aḥmad b. Ḥanbal

[129] al-Khaṭīb al-Baghdādī, Vol. II, p. 69.

[130] Ibn ʿAbd al-Barr, p. 107; Subkī, Vol. I, pp. 272-74; Ibn Khallikān, *Wafayāt al-Aʿyān*, ed. Muḥammad al-Ḥamīd (Cairo, 1948), Vol. III, pp. 225-27.

[131] Ibn ʿAbd al-Barr, pp. 105-106; Ibn Khallikān, *Wafayāt al-Aʿyān*, Vol. I, pp. 356-57; Subkī, Vol. I, pp. 250-51.

[132] Ibn ʿAbd al-Barr, p. 107; Subkī, Vol. I, pp. 227-31.

(d. 241/856),[133] and al-Karābīsī (d. 245/860).[134] In Makka, he had been followed by Abū Bakr al-Ḥamīdī (d. 219/835),[135] Abū Isḥāq al-Shāfiᶜī (d. 237/852),[136] and others.[137] In Egypt his leading disciples were al-Buwayṭī (d. 231/845),[138] al-Muzanī (d. 264/877),[139] al-Rabīᶜ b. Sulaymān al-Jīzī (d. 256/869),[140] al-Rabīᶜ b. Sulaymān al-Murādī (d. 270/833),[141] and others.[142] These jurists not only recorded Shāfiᶜī's words and expounded his legal doctrines, but they also spread his teachings to other countries and bequeathed his collected writings to succeeding generations.

Cairo and Baghdād, and to a lesser degree Makka, were the chief centers from which Shāfiᶜī's doctrines first radiated. Within a century after his death, the Shāfiᶜī school gradually spread into Madīna, Syria, and Central Asia. Shrinking in Egypt under Fāṭimid rule (909/1171), it again became predominant under Ṣalāḥ al-Dīn (d. 564/1169). In the last centuries before the occupation of the central lands of Islam by the Ottoman sultans, the Shāfiᶜī school had become the most widespread. Adopting the Ḥanafī school as official, the Ottoman government helped to establish this school in Constantinople and in many other Islamic centers. With the rise of the Ṣafawī dynasty at the opening of the sixteenth century, Persia gradually adopted the

[133] Ibn al-Jawzī, *Manāqib al-Imām Aḥmad b. Ḥanbal* (Cairo, 1349/1931); W. M. Patton, *Aḥmad Ibn Ḥanbal and the Miḥna* (Leyden, 1897); Abū Zahra, *Aḥmad Ibn Ḥanbal* (Cairo, 1947).

[134] Ibn ᶜAbd al-Barr, p. 106; Ibn Khallikān, *Wafayāt al-Aᶜyān,* Vol. I, p. 399; al-Khaṭīb al-Baghdādī, Vol. II, p. 57; Subkī, Vol. I, pp. 251-56.

[135] Ibn ᶜAbd al-Barr, p. 104; Subkī, Vol. I, pp. 263-64.

[136] Subkī, Vol. I, pp. 225-27. Ibn ᶜAbd al-Barr, p. 105; and Subkī, Vol. I, pp. 186 ff.

[137] Ibn ᶜAbd al-Barr, p. 105; and Subkī, Vol. I, pp. 186 ff.

[138] Ibn ᶜAbd al-Barr, pp. 109-10; Subkī, Vol. I, pp. 275-79.

[139] Ibn ᶜAbd al-Barr, pp. 110-11; Ibn Khallikān, *Wafayāt al-Aᶜyān,* Vol. I, pp. 196-97; Subkī, Vol. I, pp. 242-44.

[140] Ibn Khallikān, *Wafayāt al-Aᶜyān,* Vol. II, pp. 53-54; Nawawī, pp. 242-43.

[141] Ibn ᶜAbd al-Barr, p. 112; Ibn Khallikān, *Wafayāt al-Aᶜyān,* Vol. II, pp. 52-53; Nawawī, pp. 243-44; Subkī, Vol. I, pp. 259-63.

[142] Some members of the ᶜAbd al-Ḥakam family, especially ᶜAbd-Allāh b. ᶜAbd al-Ḥakam (d. 214/830) and his sons. See Ibn ᶜAbd al-Barr, pp. 113-14; Subkī, Vol. I, pp. 223-25.

Shīʿī system. However, the Shāfiʿī school remained predominant in Egypt, Syria, the Ḥijāz, South Arabia, parts of the Persian Gulf, East Africa, the Malay Archipelago, Daghistan, and parts of Central Asia.

THE TEXT OF THE *RISĀLA*

Manuscripts

THERE ARE two manuscripts of the *Risāla* at the Dār al-Kutub, the National Library in Cairo. No others have been discovered. The first, known as the manuscript of Ibn Jamāʿa, consists of 124 folios. The other, known as the manuscript of al-Rabīʿ, is the older and by far the more interesting. In its present form, it consists of 78 folios; 62 constitute the text, and the rest, of more recent vintage, presumably, consist of the certificates of readers—persons who had read or heard the reading of the original text. The size of the manuscript is 5½ x 10¼ inches. On the whole the writing is clear, although not as legible as the manuscript of Ibn Jamāʿa. Rarely, however, is it obscure or impossible to read.

The manuscript of al-Rabīʿ is divided into three parts, each forming a *juz'* (tome). This artificial division should not be taken to mean that the *Risāla* was originally divided into three volumes, since a *juz'* is more likely to end abruptly in the middle of a paragraph rather than at the end of a chapter. Such a division was necessitated by the use of three sets of notebooks, each set called a *juz'* and consisting of some twenty folios. The copying of books in separate sets of notebooks seems to have been a practice common among Muslim writers. The artificiality of this division seems to make it advisable not to follow it in the present translation.

The so-called al-Rabīʿ manuscript, alleged to have been the text written by al-Rabīʿ himself rather than one copied from an older text of al-Rabīᶜ, has become a subject of controversy among several scholars. Moritz held that it was written in the middle of the fourth century (the latter part of the tenth century A.D.).[143] He gave no explanation as to how he arrived at this date of the manuscript, but Shaykh Aḥmad Shākir (d. 1958), an editor of the *Risāla,* with whom the present writer had the opportunity of discussing this problem shortly before his death in Cairo, pointed out that probably Moritz arrived at this conclusion on the basis of a statement in the margin of the Ibn Jamāᶜa manuscript in which it was stated that the latter was compared with an older one—the Rabīᶜ manuscript—copied in the year 358 of the Hijra.[144] Shākir is of the opinion that the Rabīᶜ manuscript must have been about a century earlier, at least shortly before the death of al-Rabīᶜ in 270/883.

Although the difference between Moritz and Shākir in the dating of the Rabīᶜ manuscript is less than a century, Shākir's opinion raises a number of problems. If the date were shortly before 270/883, the manuscript would probably have been written on papyrus rather than on paper, which had just been introduced into Egypt. Moreover, the style of writing, except the titles of each *juz'*, which are in Kufic, is a cursive book hand. To these objections Shākir replied that paper had already been introduced into Egypt in the late second century of the Islamic era and the shift of style from Kufic to cursive had already begun. He quoted a statement from al-Qalqashandī maintaining that although it is commonly accepted that Ibn Muqla (d. 328/939) was the first to introduce the new style of writing, it had already been in vogue since the second century of the Islamic era.[145] Furthermore, he pointed out that

[143] See B. Moritz, *Arabic Palaeography* (Cairo, 1905), Vol. II, plate 117.

[144] See the introduction to Shākir's edition (Cairo, 1940), pp. 22-23.

[145] Abū al-ᶜAbbās Aḥmad al-Qalqashandī, *Kitāb Ṣubḥ al-ᶜAsha* (Cairo, 1922), Vol. III, p. 15; Shākir's introduction, pp. 18-19. For a critical evaluation of the commonly accepted fact that Ibn Muqla was the first to introduce the new Arabic style, see Nabia Abbott, "The Contribution of Ibn Muqlah to the North Arabic Script," *American Journal of Semitic Languages and Literatures,* Vol. LVI (1939), pp. 70-83; and *The Rise of the North Arabic Script* (Chicago, 1939), pp. 33 ff.

there is at the Dār al-Kutub in Cairo a papyrus dated 195/810, which resembles the Rabīʿ manuscript in style. However, this apparent resemblance, which Shākir advanced in support of his argument, can be very misleading to non-experts in paleography. Finally, he asserted that the certificates of readers often refer to this manuscript as belonging to al-Rabīʿ, which, in Shākir's view, was evidence of its being al-Rabīʿ's own copy.

There seems to be no conclusive argument in favor of the viewpoints of either Shākir or Moritz on the strength of internal evidence alone. The manuscript would probably have been on papyrus were it written in al-Rabīʿ's time, although this argument cannot be regarded as conclusive evidence against its having been one of the first books written on paper in Egypt.[146] The style of the manuscript, which became the common style only a century after the time of al-Rabīʿ, tends to support the viewpoint of Moritz. Professor Nabia Abbott, an expert in Arabic paleography (with whom the writer discussed the problem of style on the basis of photographic copies of samples of the manuscript), is inclined to accept a fourth-century dating.

As internal evidence fails to support either viewpoint, we must call upon external evidence for a more conclusive argument. The present writer has examined the manuscript and the condition of its paper in particular. The paper, though undoubtedly ancient, can give us no final answer on the basis of its present condition. A revealing external examination may be conducted on the strength of a chemical analysis of the paper and ink, an examination which the authorities of the Dār al-Kutub seem unprepared to undertake at the present moment. Until that is done, an expert opinion on whether the manuscript

[146] There are books written on paper in the third century of the Islamic era, but not from Egypt. Professor Abbott states that "while one might expect a few paper documents to come out of the third-century Egypt, no one would ever expect the Egypt of the early third century to produce a paper book on any subject whatsoever" (Nabia Abbott, "A Ninth-Century Fragment of the 'Thousand Nights'," *Journal of Near Eastern Studies,* Vol. VIII (1949) , p. 144.

was written in the third or the fourth century of the Islamic era cannot be formed.

Editions

Of the four known editions of the *Risāla*, only two deserve serious consideration, the Būlāq and the Shākir editions. The other two are inferior in quality and at any rate are based on no other known manuscript.

The Būlāq edition is based on the Ibn Jamāʿa manuscript and constitutes some eighty-two pages of the first volume of the *Kitāb al-Umm,* published by the Būlāq Government Press in Cairo in 1321/1904. The editor did an extremely competent piece of work in examining the manuscript, but he confined himself, unfortunately, to one manuscript only. With all its merits, this remains an uncritical edition of the *Risāla*, lacking, among other things, any comparison with the Rabīʿ manuscript.

The Shākir edition, published in Cairo by the Ḥalabī Press in 1358/1940, is a more elaborate work running to some 670 pages and including an introduction, notes, and eight appendices. The erudition and competence of the late learned Shaykh, universally recognized by scholars, have rendered possible not only the publication of the *Risāla* in a separate volume, but also the editing and the publication of several other works.

Shākir's edition is based on the so-called al-Rabīʿ manuscript. Shākir confines himself to that text rather than seeking to reproduce a reconstruction of the two manuscripts. He indicates in the footnotes, however, the verbal differences between the Būlāq edition and the al-Rabīʿ manuscript. His edition is enriched by a number of linguistic and historical comments with virtually full references to the Quranic communications. His references to ḥadīth digests are less full and often incomplete. He seldom explains Shāfiʿī's terms and legal concepts. Nor is the bibliography (pp. 609-610) satisfactory; indeed some of the references in the footnotes are more helpful than the bibliography. In comparing the original manuscript with the Shākir edition, it is evident that Shākir has usually avoided the incorporation of corrections and comments on the original text, and that when he did incorporate them in certain instances in the belief that they would improve the text, he has indicated them by parentheses. But Shākir's edition is far from being critical; and the need for a more complete and scholarly edition continues to exist.

The Translation

To the present writer's best knowledge, a complete translation of the *Risāla* has not been made into any foreign language. A brief summary of it is available in Dutch,[147] but this lays no claim to completeness of translation.

Written in broad and often abstract terms, the *Risāla* presents a number of difficulties to the translator. A translation of the meaning only serves to deprive the reader of the spirit and significance of the original text; a closely literal translation may render the broad abstract concept in the English language more specific than the author intended. Shāfiʿī is often fond of expressing his ideas in terse or incomplete sentences which would probably become meaningless in another language. The present writer has, therefore, provided the equivalent in English in as close and literal a translation as possible, with occasional words or sentences added in parentheses to complete the meaning of a sentence or to clarify an abstract concept. No attempt was made to recast the original in a completely modern style. The definitions of basic terms and concepts and the supplementary material in the notes may help to explain the meaning of the text in translation. The notes are also intended to indicate the principal sources available for the material dealt with in the *Risāla*.

[147] L. I. Graf, *al-Shāfiʿī's Verhandeling over de Wortelen van den Fikh* (Leiden, 1934).

Although the original text of the *Risāla* has undergone several revisions and the rewriting of certain portions, some of Shāfiʿī's ideas have been repeated over and over again, though in different forms, and no attempt has been made in this translation to omit repetitions. Two chapters of the *Risāla* do not appear to fit into the logical order of the book. These are the chapters " On the Nature of God's Orders of Prohibition and the Prophet's Orders of Prohibition" and " On Legal Knowledge." In the original text they follow the chapter " On Traditions," which may have been inserted to answer certain points raised by an interlocutor. As the chapter on legal knowledge consists of a discussion of a general jurisprudential nature, it was deemed necessary to transfer it so that it follows the chapter " On *al-Bayān*"; and the chapter on the nature of God's orders of prohibition and the Prophet's orders of prohibition was transposed to the position preceding the discussion on traditions. The latter portion of the chapter on *al-Bayān*, dealing with the Arabic character of the Qur'ān, has been shifted to form the first section of the chapter " On the Book of God." In order to preserve the character and the general scheme of the book which the author laid down, no other attempts have been made to change or completely recast the structure of the work.

Neither the original Arabic texts nor the Būlāq edition were divided into subdivisions in addition to the basic divisions into chapters. The Shākir edition, however, is subdivided into numbered paragraphs. Shākir's system, artificially divides the book into so many paragraphs that it has been abandoned here. The present writer, accordingly, has followed a different method in subdividing the chapters into paragraphs.

POSTSCRIPT

COMPARED with the Ibn Jamāʿa manuscript, the al-Rabīʿ manuscript is relatively free from the frequent citations of blessings which may be found in abundance in later classical writings. Although most of the blessings in the text of al-Rabīʿ have been rendered into the nearest English equivalents, it did not seem essential to retain all of them.

References to such works as the *Encyclopaedia of Islam*, Brockelmann's *Geschichte der Arabischen Literatur,* and leading dictionaries, which are well-known to students of Islam, have been considered unnecessary.

The abbreviations most frequently used are the following:

The letter b., if inserted between two names, stands for ibn or bin, which means "the son of."

Q is the abbreviation for Qur'ān.

1/632 cites the date according to the Hijra and the Gregorian calendars.

B and S stand for the Būlāq and Shākir editions. They appear in the margin of the translation to indicate the end of the corresponding pages of the Būlāq and Shākir editions.

Translation of Shāfiʿī's *Risāla*

Chapter I

[INTRODUCTION]

IN THE NAME OF GOD, the Merciful, the Compassionate.

Abū ʿAlī al-Ḥasan b. Ḥabīb b. ʿAbd al-Malik, on the authority of al-Rabīʿ b. Sulaymān al-Murādī, from al-Imām Muḥammad b. Idrīs. . . al-Shāfiʿī, said:[1]

1. Praise be to God (Allāh) who created the heavens and the earth, and made the darkness and the light; yet the unbelievers attribute equals to their Lord.[2] Praise be to God to whom gratitude for one of His favors cannot be paid save through S7
another favor from Him, which necessitates for the giver of thanks for His past favors to repay it by a new favor which [in turn] makes obligatory upon him gratitude for it. Those who describe Him cannot attain to the utmost of His greatness, which is as He has described Himself [in the Qur'ān] and above what His creatures can attribute to Him. I praise Him with such praise as is obligatory on account of His kindness and the might of His majesty. I ask help of Him: The help of one save in whom there is no power or might at all. I ask Him for His guidance: The guidance whereby no one who takes refuge in it will ever be led astray. I ask Him for His forgiveness for whatever [offence] I

[1] Būlāq ed., p. 2. The first few lines of the Rabīʿ MS are not legible. The Būlāq edition is filled with blessings, especially after such names as those of God and the Prophet.

[2] Cf. Q. VI, 1.

have already committed and for what I have deferred—with the pleading of one who confesses himself in a state of servitude[3] and who knows that none but He can forgive his offence and save him from it. I bear witness that there is no god but God alone, who has no associate whatever, and that Muḥammad is His servant and Apostle.[4]

2. He [God] sent him [to mankind] at a time when men were divided into two groups.

One of them being the People of the Book,[5] who had changed some of its rules, and misbelieved in God, since they forged falsehood fashioned by their tongues and mixed it with the
S8 Truth that God had revealed to them. For God, Blessed and
B2 Most High, mentioned to His Prophet[6] some of their misbelief, saying:

> Among them there is a party that twist their tongues with the Book, in order that you may reckon it to be a part of the Book, and they say: ' It is from God,' although it is not from God; and they speak falsehood against God knowingly [Q. III, 78].

[3] I. e., in the service of the Lord.

[4] The recital of this formula, called the profession of faith, constitutes the first of the Five Pillars of Islam (*al-arkān al-khamsa*), and it is the duty of every Muslim to recite it whenever it is deemed necessary or commendable. Any individual who desires to become a Muslim must first recite it. The other four pillars are: prayer, payment of alms, fasting of the month of Ramaḍān, and pilgrimage. See Shāfiʿī's *Risāla,* Chap. VI. For a detailed discussion of this subject, see Shāfiʿī, *Kitāb al-Umm,* Vols. 1-2.

[5] Ahl al-Kitāb—People of the Book—are those who possess a Scripture. They include Christians, Jews, Samaritans, Sabians, and Magians (Zoroastrians). For a discussion on their status in Islamic law, see Majid Khadduri, *War and Peace in the Law of Islam,* Chap. 17.

[6] Although Shāfiʿī uses the terms " Apostle" (*rasūl*) and " Prophet" (*nabī*), no distinction is made between the two, and they seem to him to be synonymous. Muslim publicists, however, have distinguished between the two terms: A Prophet is a man who receives divine revelations; an Apostle is a man who not only receives divine revelations but also communicates them to men. Thus every Apostle is a Prophet, but not every Prophet is an Apostle. See Nasafī's *Creed* (with a commentary by al-Taftazānī), ed. E. E. Elder (New York, 1950), p. 21; Ṣadr al-Dīn b. ʿAlī b. Abī al-ʿIzz, *Sharḥ al-Ṭaḥāwīya,* ed. Aḥmad Muḥammad Shākir (Cairo, 1373/1954), pp. 95-96; A. J. Wensinck, *The Muslim Creed* (Cambridge, 1932), pp. 203-204. For a broad philosophical treatment, see F. Rahman, *Prophecy in Islam* (London, 1958).

And He said:

> So woe to those who write the Book with their hands and then say: ' This is from God,' that they may sell it for a little price. Woe to them for what their hands have written, and woe to them for their earnings [Q. II, 79].

And He, Blessed and Most High, said:

> The Jews say: ' ʿUzayr[7] is the son of God,' and the Christians say: ' The Messiah is the son of God'; that is the utterance of their mouths, conforming to what was formerly said by those who had previously disbelieved—God oppose them! How they are perverted! They have taken their rabbis and their monks as lords rather than God, although the Messiah is the son of Mary, and they were commanded to worship only one God. There is no God at all but Him. Exalted is He above what they associate [with him] [Q. IX, 30-31].

And He, Blessed and Most High, said:

> Didst thou not see those who have received a portion of the Book believing in the idol and the vain thing and saying to those who misbelieved: ' These are better guided than those who have believed S9
> [in the revelation of the Qur'ān]'? Those are they whom God cursed, whomsoever God curses shall never find for himself any defender [Q. IV, 51-52].

The other [group] was that of those who misbelieved in God and created [something] that God did not permit. They set up with their hands stones and wood and images that they found pleasing and gave them names that they forged and called them gods and worshipped them. When they were pleased with [something] other than what they worshiped, they cast [the latter] away and set up with their hands that other [thing] and worshiped it—those were the Arabs.[8]

[7] Although the Jews can hardly think of Ezra as the son of God, ʿUzayr has been generally identified with Ezra. See Ṭabarī, *Tafsīr* (Cairo, 1958), Vol. XIV, pp. 201-205; J. Walker, " Who is ʿUzayr," *Moslem World,* Vol. XIX (1929), pp. 303-306; and ʿUzayr in *Shorter Encyclopedia of Islam,* p. 617.

[8] Shāfiʿī refers to the religious practices of the Arabs before the rise of Islam.

3. A group of the Persians followed their path in this respect and in the worship of whatever they pleased, whether fish or beast or star or fire or something else.

Wherefore God mentioned to His Prophet one of the answers of some of this sort [of men] who worshiped other than Him, quoting from them:

> We, indeed, found our fathers forming a community, so we follow in their footsteps [Q. XLIII, 22].

And He, Blessed and Most High, quoted their saying:

> Do not abandon your gods; do not abandon Wadd or Suwāʿ, or
> S10 Yaghūth and Yaʿūq, or Nasr.[9] Thus they led many astray [Q. LXXI, 23-24].

And the Most High said:

> And mention Abraham in the Book; surely he was a trusty man, a prophet, when he said to his father: ' Father, why worshipest thou that which neither hears nor sees, nor avails thee anything?' [Q. XIX, 41-42].

And He said:

> And recite to them the story of Abraham. When he said to his father and his people: ' What do you serve?' They said: ' We serve idols, and to them we continue cleaving.' He said: ' Do they hear you when you pray, or profit you or harm?' [Q. XXVI, 70-73].

Concerning this group, reminding them of his favors, and warning them all of their erring, and His favor to those of them who believed, He said:

> Remember the favor of God to you when you were enemies; for He brought your hearts together and by His favor you became brothers. You were on the brink of a pit of fire and He delivered you from it. Thus God makes His signs clear for you, perchance you will let yourselves be guided [Q. III, 103].

[9] Wadd, Suwāʿ, Yaghūth, Yaʿūq, and Nasr were idols worshipped by the Arabs before Islam. See Hishām b. al-Kalbī, *Kitāb al-Aṣnām;* English translation by Nabih Faris, *Book of Idols* (Princeton, 1952), pp. 8, 9, 10. These idols, according to Bayḍāwī, were originally the names of saintly persons whom the Arabs raised to the level of divinity. See Bayḍāwī's *Tafsīr* (Cairo, 1305/1887), p. 762.

4. [Shāfiʿī] said: Before His deliverance of them by Muḥammad, God's blessing and peace be upon him, they were misbelievers, individually and collectively, having in common
the gravest of things: The disbelief in God and committing what S11
He does not permit. God is High above what they profess. There is no God other than He, exalted be He with praise of him, Lord and Creator of all things. Whoever of them is alive is as [He] described his state: living, working, speaking under the anger of his Lord, increasing his disobedience. Whoever has died is as [He] described his word and his work: He has gone to his punishment.[10]

5. When [the revelation embodied in] the decree of the heavenly Book reached its appointed time and the Providential order became a reality through the manifestation of His religion, which He chose, after the predominance of disobedience to Him, which He disapproved—He opened the gates of His heavens by His mercy, just as His Providential order did not cease to be executed in His foreknowledge at the time of the revelation of His law in the past centuries. For He, Blessed and Most High, said:

> The people were one nation; then God set forth the prophets as bringers of good tidings and warners [Q. II, 213].

The One whom He chose for His revelation, the Elect One for His message, the One favored above all His creatures through the gift of His mercy and the sealing of His prophecy and the most universal of whatever He sent any messenger with previously, was Muḥammad, His servant and His Apostle. Mention of him is upraised together with mention of Him in
this life. He is the intercessor whose intercession is looked for S12
in the next life. He is the purest of His creatures in soul; the One who combines most fully every character that is pleasing to Him in spiritual and temporal life. He is the best [in mankind] in ancestry and family.

[10] Cf. Q. III, 185; and XI, 19.

And He acquainted us and all mankind with his [Muḥammad's] special graces and their universal benefit for religion and the life of this world.[11] For of him He said:

> There has come to you an apostle from among yourselves; grievous unto him is the difficulty you have experienced,[12] who is watchful over you, and who is gentle and compassionate with the believers [Q. IX, 128].

And He said:

> ... That you might warn the Mother of Cities and those around it [Q. XLII, 7].

The Mother of Cities is Makka, the city of his [Muḥammad's] people.

And He said:

> And warn thy clan, thy nearest kin [Q. XXVI, 214].

And He said:

> Surely it is a reminder to thee and to thy people, and assuredly you will be questioned [Q. XLIII, 44].

6. Shāfiʿī said: Concerning [God's] saying, "Surely it is a
S13 reminder to thee and to thy people," [Q. XLIII, 44] [Sufyān] b. ʿUyayna, on the authority of Ibn Abī Najīḥ from Mujāhid, told us: It has been asked: "To whom did the man [Muḥammad] belong?" "To the Arabs," was the reply; and it was asked: "To what [tribe] of the Arabs?" "To Quraysh," was the reply.

7. Shāfiʿī said: Mujāhid's comment on [God's saying] is so clear in the text [of the Qur'ān] that it needs no explanation.

God, praise be to Him, specified [Muḥammad's] people and his nearest of kin in [the message of] warning—and included all mankind in it after them—and raised the Apostle's renown
S14 through the Qur'an;[13] furthermore, He distinguished his people
B3 in the message when He commissioned him to warn, in
S15 accordance with His saying [in the Qur'ān]: "Warn thy clan,

[11] Cf. Būlāq ed., p. 3.
[12] See Lane's *Lexicon*, p. 2168.
[13] Cf. Q. XCIV, 4.

thy nearest of kin" [Q. XXVI, 214].

A few of those who are learned in the Qur'ān have asserted that the Apostle said:

> Men of ʿAbd-Manāf![14] God has sent me to warn my nearest of kin, and you are those nearest of kin.

8. Shāfiʿī said: [Sufyān] b. ʿUyayna told us from Ibn Abī Najīḥ from Mujāhid who [in giving the meaning of God's saying]: "And we have raised for thee thy reputation" [Q. XCIV, 4], said: "Whenever I [God] am mentioned, you [Muḥammad] are mentioned too" [e. g., in the word of witness]: "I profess that there is no god at all but God and that Muḥammad is the Apostle of God."[15]

9. [Shāfiʿī said]: This means (but God knows best) the inclusion of [Muḥammad's] name in [pronouncing] the profession of the faith and in the calling of the believers to prayer. It may also mean mentioning his name in reading the Qur'ān, in acts of obedience and avoiding disobedience.

May God bless and give peace to our Prophet whenever his name is mentioned by those who may remember, or omitted by those who disregard him. May God bless him among the first and the last generation, with the most favorable, most abundant and most gracious blessing that He has bestowed upon any of His creatures. May He grant you and us virtue by His blessing upon Him more than he granted to any of his nation by His blessing and peace. May His peace and mercy and blessing be upon [Muḥammad]. May God reward him on our behalf with the most abundant reward bestowed on any messenger sent on behalf of those to whom he was sent. For God has delivered us from falsehood[16] through him and made us members of the best community established for men by

[14] Descendants of ʿAbd-Manāf b. Quṣayy of the tribe of Quraysh. See Ibn Hishām, *Kitāb Sīrat Sayyidinna Muḥammad,* ed. Ferdinand Wüstenfeld (Göttingen, 1858-60), pp. 68-75; Musʿab b. ʿAbd-Allāh al-Zubayrī, *Kitāb Nasab Quraysh,* ed. Levy Provençal (Cairo, 1953), pp. 14-17.

[15] See Q. XXXVII, 34; XLVIII, 29.

[16] Which in turn leads to death (*tahlika*).

following His religion with which he was well-pleased, He chose for us and by virtue of which [religion] He made pure His angels
S16 and those of His creatures He favored with it. No blessing—hidden or visible—has ever descended upon us, through which we obtained spiritual or temporal gain or by which spiritual or temporal hurt was dispelled, but Muḥammad was the cause of its dispatch, the leader to its benefit and guide to its right way; he is the defender against falsehood and [dissipator of] the sources of evil, which oppose righteousness, and warner against whatever causes falsehood, and he is ever ready with advice for guidance and warning [against evil]. May God's blessings be upon him and his family as His blessings were upon Abraham and his family. Thou [God] art praiseworthy and glorious!

10. God revealed to him His Book, of which He said:

> And verily it is a Book sublime, falsehood comes not to it from before or from behind; a revelation from One who is All-Wise and Praiseworthy [Q. XLI, 41-42].

[By virtue of this Book] He brought forth [Muḥammad's people] from misbelief and ignorance[17] into the light and guidance. He made clear to them [in the Book] what He permitted—showing favor by permitting His creatures—and what He prohibited, as He knows best what pertains to their felicity by avoidance of it in this world and in the hereafter. He tested their obedience by placing them under obligation in word and deed, and by enjoining abstinence from forbidden things from which He has warded them off, and He rewarded
S17 them for their obedience by granting eternal life in Paradise and deliverance from His vengeance, whereby His bounty was made abundant. Praiseworthy is He. And He taught them what He made due [as punishment] for those who disobey Him, in contrast to what He made due [as reward] for those who obey Him.

And He admonished them by calling their attention [to the experiences] of former people who had more property and

[17] Literally: " blindness."

children and who lived longer and left [behind them] more memorable deeds. They enjoyed their fortune during their earthly life. When He made His judgement, death took them suddenly for their lapses and they received [God's] punishment at the end of their terms of life so that they take prior warning of future happening and understand [God's commands] as stated clearly [in the Qur'ān] in order to be awake before being taken by surprise, and perform [their deeds] before the end of the period when an offender is not reproved and a ransom is not taken " on the day when each soul will find brought before it the good and the evil that it has done, it will wish that there were a far distance between it and that day" [Q. III, S18
30].

All that [God]—glorified be His praise—has revealed in His Book is a mercy [from Him] and an evidence [for His existence]. Whoever knows [the Book], knows it; and whoever is ignorant of it, is ignorant of it. He who is ignorant of it, does not know it, and he who knows it, is not ignorant of it. For the public is divided into classes with regard to knowledge. Their status in learning is according to their rank in knowledge of it.

It is obligatory upon him who seeks knowledge to exert his utmost energy in increasing his knowledge, to be patient with every obstacle that may stand in his way, and to be sincere to God in understanding His knowledge—whether [to be found] in the text [of the Book] or [obtained] by deductive reasoning—and to appeal to God for help, for nothing good is obtainable save by God's help.

For he who has obtained knowledge of God's commands from His Book, whether as [provided] in the text or through *istidlāl* (inductive reasoning), and—had God's help in word and deed in whatever he learned of it—attains virtue in his spiritual and temporal [life], doubt leaves him, wisdom en- lightens his heart and is entitled to the position of Imāma: leadership in religious matters.

We pray to God—who offers His blessings ere we deserve them and who continues to do so in spite of our negligence to our obligatory gratefulness to Him, and who made us the best nation on earth—to provide us with an understanding of His S19

Book, of the sunna of His Prophet, and word and deed which would fulfil for us our obligation to Him, and makes obligatory upon us supererogatory [service].

11. Shāfiʿī said: No misfortune will ever descend upon any of the followers of God's religion for which there is no guidance in the Book of God to indicate the right way. For God, Blessed and Most High, said:

> A Book we have sent down to thee that thou mayest bring forth mankind from darkness to light, by the permission of their Lord, to the path of the almighty, the Praiseworthy [Q. XIV, 1].

And He said:

> And we sent down to them the reminder, that thou mayest make clear to mankind what was sent down to them; and so haply they may reflect [Q. XVI, 44].

And He said:

> And we have sent down to thee the Book as a clarification for everything and as a guidance and a mercy and good tidings to the Muslims [Q. XVI, 89].

And He said:

> And we have revealed to thee a spirit of our bidding. Thou didst not
> B4 know what the Book was, nor the faith; but We made it a light by
> S20 which We guide whomsoever We will of our servants. And, verily,
> thou shalt be a guide unto a right[18] path. [Q. XLII, 52].

[18] Literally: "straight."

Chapter II

[ON *AL-BAYĀN* (PERSPICUOUS DECLARATION)][1]

What is al-Bayān?

12. Shāfiʿī said: *Al-Bayān* is a collective term for a variety of meanings[2] which have common roots but differing ramifications. The least [common denominator] of these linked but diverging meanings is that they are [all] a perspicuous declaration for those to whom they are addressed, and in whose tongue the Qur'ān was revealed;[3] they are of almost equal value for these persons, although some declarations were made emphatically clearer than others, though they differed [in clarity] to persons ignorant of the Arab tongue.

13. Shāfiʿī said: The sum-total of what God has declared to His creatures in His Book, by which He invited them to worship Him in accordance with His prior decision, includes various categories.

[1] *Al-bayān* may mean either the substance of a certain Quranic communication or making clear the meaning of that substance. The nearest equivalent for the first is speech or declaration; for the second, making lucid or perspicuous. Since both meanings are often implied in Shāfiʿī's usage, the combined terminology " perspicuous declaration" has been chosen. For the meaning of *al-bayān*, see al-Ghazzālī, al-Mustaṣfa, Vol. I, pp. 153-54; al-Bāqillānī, *Iʿjāz al-Qur'ān*, ed. Aḥmad Ṣaqr (Cairo, 1954), pp. 69-70, 319-320; and the Translator's Introduction pp. 33-84, above.

[2] *Maʿānī* (singular: *maʿnā*) may signify either an intention or an expression of meaning or reason. The English equivalent of meanings, in the sense of ideas, is used here.

[3] I. e., the Arabs.

One of these is what He has declared to His creatures by texts [in the Qur'ān], such as the aggregate of duties owing to Him: That they shall perform the prayer, pay the *zakāt* (alms tax), perform the pilgrimage, and observe the fast. And that He has forbidden disgraceful acts[4]—both visible and hidden—and in the textual [prohibition of] adultery, [the drinking of] wine, eating [the flesh of] dead things and of blood and pork; and He has made clear to them how to perform the duty of [the major] ablution as well as other matters stated precisely in the text [of
S21 the Qur'ān].

A second category consists of [those duties] the obligation of which He established in His Book, but the modes of which He made clear by the tongue of His Prophet. The number of prayers [each day] and the [amount of] *zakāt* and their time [of fulfilment] are cases in point; but there are other [similar] duties which He has revealed in His Book.

A third category consists of that which the Apostle of God established by example or exhortation, but in regard to which there is no precisely defined rule from God [in the Qur'ān]. For God has laid down in His Book the obligation of obedience to His Apostle and recourse to his decision. So he who accepts [a duty] on the authority of the Apostle of God accepts it by the obligation imposed by God.

A fourth category consists of what God commanded His creatures to seek through *ijtihād* (personal reasoning)[5] and by it put their obedience to the test exactly as He tried their obedience by other duties which He had ordered them [to fulfil], for the Blessed and Most High said:

> And We shall put you to the trial in order to know those of you who
> S22 strive and endure, and We will test your accounts [Q. XLVII, 31].

[4] *Al-fawāḥish.*

[5] *Ijtihād* literally means personal effort to understand the meaning implied in a certain rule of law in order to form an opinion. It implies personal legal reasoning which should be exercised by applying analogy (*qiyās*) to an authoritative text such as the Qur'ān or tradition. For a discussion on the use of *ijtihād*, see Chap. XIII, below; and J. Schacht, *Origins of Muhammadan Jurisprudence*, pp. 105 f., 127 f., 132.

And He said:

> And that God might try what was in your breasts and sift out what was in your hearts [Q. III, 154].

And He said:

> Perchance your Lord will destroy your enemy, and will make you successors in the land, that He may see how you will act [Q. VII, 129].

14. Shāfi'ī said: [God ordered the performance of prayer] in the direction[6] of the Sacred Mosque[7] and said to His Prophet:

> Sometimes We see thee turning thy face about toward the heaven. So We will turn thee to a direction that will satisfy thee. Turn thy face in the direction of the Sacred Mosque, and wherever you are, turn your faces in its direction [Q. II, 144].

And He said:

> And from whatever place thou hast gone forth, turn thy face in the direction of the Sacred Mosque; and wherever you may be, turn your faces in its direction [Q. II, 150].

Thus [God], glorified be His praise, guided [men]—should they be at a distance from the Sacred Mosque—by using the reasoning powers which he has implanted in men and which discriminate between things and their opposites and the S23
landmarks which [He] set up for them when the Sacred Mosque, towards which He commanded them to turn their faces, is out of sight. For God said:

> For it is He who has made for you the stars, that you might be guided by them in the darkness of land and sea [Q. VI, 97].

And He said:

> And by landmarks and by the stars they are guided [Q. XVI, 16].

[6] The *qibla*, i. e., the facing of Makka while performing the prayer ritual.

[7] The Sacred Mosque is at Makka. In the center of the Mosque is al-Ka'ba, the sacred shrine of Islam.

15. Shāfiʿī said:[8] Such landmarks may be the mountains, the nights and the days, which have winds of known names though they blow from different directions, and the sun and the moon and the stars whose risings and settings and whose places in the sky are known.

Thus [God] prescribed to men the use of personal reasoning in turning in the direction of the Sacred Mosque by means of guidance to them, which I have described, and so long as men use their personal reasoning they will not deviate from His command, glorious be His praise; but He did not permit them to pray in any direction they wished if the Sacred Mosque were out of sight. And He also instructed them
S24 about His will and providence and said: "Does man think that he will be left roaming at will?" [Q. LXXV, 36]. "Left roaming at will" means one who is neither commanded nor prohibited.

16. [Shāfiʿī said]: This [communication] indicates that no one—other than the Prophet—is allowed to make a decision except by *istidlāl* in the way that I have described concerning these matters and concerning justice and penalties in hunting; nor should any man make use of *istiḥsān*[9] (juristic preference), for to decide by *istiḥsān* means initiating something himself without basing his decision upon a parallel example.

God commanded men that they should call as witnesses two men of just character.[10] Just character means acting in obedience to God. Thus was the path showing the knowledge of justice or

[8] Būlāq ed., p. 5.

[9] *Istiḥsān* is the method of legal reasoning through which the jurist seeks an opinion for which there is either no authority in the tradition or for which there are two authorities, one of them being preferred. For Shāfiʿī's arguments against *istiḥsān*, see Chap. XIV, below; and *Kitāb al-Umm,* Vol. VII, pp. 267 ff.

[10] Two men of just character (*ʿadl*) constitute the minimum number of witnesses required in testimony (*shahāda*). The witness must be *ʿadl*—equitable, just, well-known for telling the truth—therefore it means the possession of a character which renders his testimony valid. The nearest equivalent therefore is the combination "just character." See Ibn Farḥūn, *Tabṣirat al-Ḥukkām* (Cairo, 1302/1884), Vol. I, pp. 173, 204; and E. Tyan, *Histoire de l'organisation judiciaire en pays d'Islam* (Paris, 1938), Vol. I, pp. 349-72.

injustice. This [subject] has been dealt with in its proper place,[11] and I have cited examples which I hope have indicated [the meaning] of others not dealt with in parallel situations. S25

al-Bayān I

17. Shāfiʿī said:[12] With respect to visitation [of the Kaʿba],[13] God, Blessed and Most High, said:

> Whoever makes use of the minor pilgrimage in order to perform the [great] Pilgrimage, shall bring as an offering what he can easily afford; but if he finds none, then a fast of three days in the course of Pilgrimage, and seven upon your return, that is ten altogether; that applies to those whose families are not present at the Sacred Mosque [Q. II, 196]. B5

Thus it was clearly understood by those to whom this communication was addressed that the three-day fasting during Pilgrimage and the seven-day [fasting] after the return [from Pilgrimage] make ten days altogether. For God said: "These are ten altogether" [Q. II, 196]. This communication was either intended to state precisely [the meaning] or to instruct men that S26
if three are added to seven the total is ten. And He said:

> We had an appointment with Moses for thirty nights, and We completed them with ten [more] so that the full period of his Lord's appointment was forty nights [Q. VII, 142].

[11] See Chap. XIII, below.

[12] Būlāq ed., p. 5.

[13] There are two kinds of pilgrimages: the major and the minor; the first (*al-ḥajj*) is the fifth of the five pillars (*arkān*) of Islam (see Chap. 1, note 4; and paragraph 155, below), which must be performed at the tenth of the month of Dhū-al-Hijja, during the ʿĪd al-aḍḥa; the second (*ʿumra*) is the minor or lesser pilgrimage which might be performed at any other time. The major pilgrimage is a duty to be performed by those who are able, at least once in a lifetime; the other is supererogatory. See paragraph 156, below.

So it was clearly understood by those to whom this communication was addressed that thirty and ten nights make forty.

Shāfiʿī said:[14] God's saying: "Forty nights" may either mean the same as the foregoing communication, namely, that if thirty are added to ten the total is forty, or it may have been intended to specify more clearly the meaning.

18. Shāfiʿī said:[15] God said:

> Fasting is prescribed for you as it was for those before you; perhaps you will show piety. A certain number of days [of fasting], but if any of you be sick or on a journey, then a number of other days [Q. II, 183-184].

And He said:

> The month of Ramaḍān in which the Qur'ān was sent down as guidance for the people and as clear signs of the guidance and the salvation[16] (*furqān*)—so let those of you who witness [the arrival of] the month fast it; but if anyone is sick or on a journey [let him fast] a number of other days [Q. II, 185].

Thus [God] laid down the duty [for men] to fast, specifying
S27 that it shall be for a month; and the month, according to [the Arabs] is the period between two [successive] crescents, which may be either thirty or twenty-nine [days]. The guidance implied in this legislation, as well as in the two foregoing ones, is to state more clearly the total number.

The most likely interpretation [of this communication] is that it specifies the total number of seven and three, and thirty and ten, that is, to state more precisely the meaning, since men surely must have known these two numbers and their totals just as they have known the month of Ramaḍān.

[14] Būlāq ed., p. 6.

[15] *Ibid.*

[16] The meaning of this word in the various communications of the Qur'ān cannot always be precisely determined. It may mean salvation, separation, proof, or simply a communication. See Jurjānī, p. 111; Nöldeke and Schwally, *Geschichte des Qorans* (Leipzig, 1919), Vol. I, p. 84; and Richard Bell, *Introduction to the Qur'ān* (Edinburgh, 1953), pp. 136-38.

al-Bayān II

19. Shāfiʿī said:[17] God, Blessed and Most High, said:

> When you stand, up for the Prayer, wash your faces and your hands up to the elbows, and wipe your heads, and your feet up to the ankles; and if you are polluted, purify yourselves [Q. V, 6].

And He said:

> Nor [when you are] polluted, then purify yourselves, unless you be S28
> travellers on the road.[18]

Thus God's Book has provided a precise definition of [the duty of] ablution, which must be distinguished from cleansing with stones (*istinjā'*), and purifying from pollution.[19]

It has been laid down that [the duty of] washing the face and the limbs must be performed by a minimum of one [washing] for each, and it may mean more than once. The Prophet has specified that [the duty of] ablution shall be performed once, but he himself performed it three times. It follows that the minimum requirement in performing [ablution] is to wash the limb once. The minimum requirement for [complete] washing is likewise once. Since only once is [the legal] requirement, the three [washings] are optional.

The sunna laid down that three stones are required to perform cleansing (*istinjā'*), and the Prophet indicated what constitutes ablution and complete washing. He also indicated that the ankles and the elbows should be included in the washing, for the text [in the Qur'an] may mean washing [the body], either excluding the two limits (the ankles and elbows) or including

[17] Būlāq ed., p. 6.

[18] Q. IV, 43. The latter part of this communication is not given by Shāfiʿī.

[19] For the meaning of ablution, see Chap. VII, section 2, below. Cleansing with stones after defecation is *istinjā'*, and cleaning from *janāba* (pollution) is prerequisite for purification. See Shāfiʿī's *Kitāb al-Umm*, Vol. I, pp. 18, 38.

them. Since the Apostle of God said: "Woe to the [unwashed] heels from the fire of hell," he obviously specified washing rather than wiping.

20. Shāfiʿī said:[20] God said:

> His parents receive, each of them, a sixth of what he has left, if he has
> S29 children; but if he has no children and his heirs are his parents, then
> his mother receives a third; if, however, he has brothers, his mother
> receives a sixth [Q. IV, 11].

And He said:

> A half of what your wives leave belongs to you if they have no children; but if they have children, a fourth of what they leave belongs to you, after any bequests they may have made or debts [have been paid]...If a man—or a woman—whose property is inherited has no direct heirs, but has a brother or a sister, each of the two receives a sixth; if they be more than that, they share in a third, after any bequests he may have made or debts [have been paid], without prejudice one to the other—a charge from God; verily God is All-Knowing, All-Gracious [Q. IV, 12].

These textual legislations [in the Qur'ān] have rendered other narrative unnecessary. God, however, made a condition that [an estate should not be distributed] until bequests are executed
S30 and debts are paid. Thus the narrative indicates that a bequest
should not exceed one third [of the estate].[21]

al-Bayān III

21. Shāfiʿī said:[22] God, Blessed and Most High, said:

> Verily the Prayer has become for the believers a thing prescribed for stated times [Q. IV, 103].

[20] Būlāq ed., p. 6.
[21] See Ṭabarī, *Tafsīr.* Vol. VIII, pp. 30 ff.
[22] Būlāq ed., p. 6.

And He said:

> Observe the Prayer and pay the alms tax (*al-zakāt*) [Q. II, 43; and other similar communications].

And He said:

> And perform the major (*ḥajj*) and minor (ʿ*umra*) pilgrimages to God [Q. II, 196].

Then He specified clearly by the tongue of His Apostle the required number of prayers, their times and the modes of their performance; the amount of *zakāt* and the times of its payment; the performance of the major (*ḥajj*) and minor (ʿ*umra*) pilgrimages and when these duties are required or not required and when [the Prophet's] sunnas are in agreement or contradictory with each other. Other parallels may be found in S31
the Qur'ān and the sunna. B6

al-Bayān IV

22. Shāfiʿī said: [*al-Bayān*] includes all that the Apostle has provided in the sunna concerning which there is no [legislation in the] Book. There is in this book,[23]—concerning God's favoring mankind [with the ability] to understand the Book and Wisdom—a proof that Wisdom is the sunna of the Apostle of God.[24]

Included in what I have stated concerning God's command to His creatures ordering obedience to the Apostle and specifying

[23] See paragraph 87, below.

[24] In a broad sense *al-ḥikma* is synonymous with the Truth and it includes, legally speaking, all the orders of prohibition and permission. See Jurjānī, pp. 96-97; and al-Muṭarrazī, *Kitāb al-Mughrib* (Hyderabad, 1328/1911), Vol. I, p. 133. Shāfiʿī, however, uses the term specifically for legal orders derived from the sunna, distinguishing it from legal orders based on divine communication. His opinion is based on the following Quranic communications; Q. II, 123, 231, 146; IV, 113; XXXIII, 34; and LXII, 2, in which wisdom follows the Qur'ān and is interpreted to mean the sunna. See paragraphs 160-62, 192-95; and Ṭabarī, *Tafsīr,* Vol. III, pp. 86-88.

the place it has in religion,[25] is a proof of the precise definition of the duties stated in the Qur'ān, which consists of the following categories:

The first category is what the Book has laid down with such clarity that nothing further—in addition to revelation (*tanzīl*)—was needed.

The second category consists in what is clearly stated in the obligation imposed [by God] ordering obedience to the Prophet. The Apostle in his turn precisely stated on the authority of God what the duties are,[26] upon whom they are binding, and in what
S32 circumstances[27] some of them are required or not required, and when they are binding.

The third category consists in what [God] has specified only in the sunna of His Prophet, in the absence of a textual [legislation in the] Book.

23. Shāfiʿī said:[28] Everything [in the sunna of the Prophet] is a clear explanation for the [divine communication in the] Book of God.

So he who accepts the duties to God [laid down] in His Book should accept the sunna of the Apostle by God's command ordering His creatures to obey the Apostle and to have recourse to his decision. For he who accepts [a duty] on the authority of the Apostle accepts it from God, since God has imposed the obligation to obey [the Prophet].[29]

The acceptance of [all the duties] laid down in both the Book of God and the sunna of the Apostle means the acceptance of each one as imposed by God, despite the differing reasons for the acceptance of what He permitted or prohibited, commanded, or punished in various ways as He pleased, glorified be His praise. For He said " He will not be questioned
S33 about what He does, but they will be questioned" [Q. XXI, 23].

[25] See paragraph 88, below.
[26] Singular in the Arabic text.
[27] Literally: " at what time."
[28] Būlāq ed., p. 7.
[29] See Chap. VII, below.

al-Bayān V

24. Shāfiʿī said:[30] God, Blessed and Most High, said:

> And from whatever place thou hast gone forth, turn thy face in the direction of the Sacred Mosque; and wherever you may be, turn your faces in its direction [Q. II, 150].

Thus [God] laid down the duty that wherever men may be they must turn their faces in the direction [of the Sacred Mosque].[31]

The [use of the] term "direction" means that if the object [the Sacred Mosque] is seen, then [the prayer] in that direction is determined [by sight]; but if [the Mosque] is out of sight, the direction is determined by *ijtihād* (personal reasoning)—that is all that one is required to do. S34

God said:

> It is He who has appointed for you the stars, that by them you may be guided through the darkness of land and sea [Q. VI, 97].

And He said:

> And by landmarks and by the stars they might be guided [Q. XVI, 16].

Thus [God] has set landmarks [for men to be guided by] and erected the Sacred Mosque in whose direction they were ordered to turn their faces [in prayer]. Their turning in that direction [is determined either] by the landmarks set up by Him or by the reasoning powers which He implanted in them to recognize the landmarks. All this is a clear declaration and a favor from Him, glorious be His praise.

25. And He said:

> And call in as witnesses two persons of just character from among yourselves [Q. LXV, 2].

[30] Būlāq ed., p. 7.

[31] Part of paragraph 105 to the end of paragraph 110 [Shākir's ed.] are omitted because they merely explain the literal meaning of the words *shaṭr*, and *jiha*, equivalent to "toward" or "direction" (i. e., of the Sacred Mosque in Makka).

And He said:

> Such witnesses as you approve of [Q. II, 282].

[God] specified that [the person] of just character is he who acts in accordance with [the command to obey God]. Thus any one who seemed to be acting in accordance with [the command to obey God] was regarded as of just character, and any one who acted contrary [to the command to obey God] was regarded as lacking in just character.

26. [God], glorified be His praise, said:

> Do not kill game when you are in pilgrim sanctity; whoever of you
> S38 kill it intentionally, there shall be compensation equal to what he has killed from [his] flocks, as two persons of just character among you shall decide—an offering to be delivered at the Kaʿba [Q. V, 95].

Equal compensation in kind literally means the nearest in size to the body [of the game killed]. The viewpoints of the Companions of the Apostle who expressed an opinion on game are at one that compensation should be the nearest in size to the body of the game. We should therefore examine the game killed, and whatever of the livestock is found to resemble it in size should be paid in compensation.

Equal compensation in kind for the livestock does not mean compensation in price save in a far-fetched interpretation. Of the two meanings, the literal is the more appropriate. This
B7 [literal meaning] is sought by *ijtihād*, which any man who makes a decision should apply in [determining] equal compensation.

27. This kind of [legal] knowledge is an example of what I have already discussed, [namely], that no one at all should [give an opinion] on a specific matter by merely saying: It is permitted or prohibited, unless he is certain of [legal] knowledge, and this knowledge must be based on the Qur'ān and the sunna, or [derived] from *ijmāʿ* (consensus) and *qiyās* (analogy). The subject dealt with in this chapter belongs to analogy, on the strength of which the right direction in prayer, just character,
S39 and equal compensation are to be determined.

Analogy is [the method of reasoning] through which indications are sought from parallel precedents in the Qur'ān or the sunna—since these are the authoritative sources of the truth—in determining what I have already stated such as the direction in prayer, just character, and equal compensation. [Analogy's] conformity [to precedent] should be based on two conditions:

The first is that God or His Apostle have either prohibited a certain act[32] by an [explicit] text [in the Qur'ān and the sunna] or permitted it by an [implied] reason. If such a reason is found in the absence of a specific text in the Book or the sunna, the act should be prohibited or permitted in conformity with the [implied] reason of permission or prohibition.

[The second] is that we may find a certain act analogous to only one aspect of a certain precedent and analogous to another aspect of another precedent, but neither the latter nor the former provides a close analogy. In such a case, analogy should be applied to the closest one as I have stated [in] the example of the killing of game.

28. Shāfiʿī said: There are two [categories of] viewpoints concerning [legal] knowledge: one of them is *ijmāʿ* (agreement) and the other is *ikhtilāf* (disagreement). These will be dealt with elsewhere [in this book].[33] A case in point of our knowledge of the Book of God is that the entire Book of God has been revealed in the Arab tongue. And [our] knowledge of the S40
abrogating and abrogated [communications] of the Book of God,[34] the duties imposed [by God] through His revelations, the ethics [of the Book], guidance and permissibility [as provided in the Book]. And knowledge of the position in which God has placed His Prophet as it is precisely defined in the commands of His Book and in the utterances of His Prophet; and of what He meant by the sum total of the duties imposed by Him and upon whom [they are binding], whether upon all His creatures or only upon some of them, rather than others; and [the obligation] laid down by God ordering obedience to His Prophet and recourse to his decision; and knowledge of the parables demonstrating

[32] Shāfiʿī uses the broad term *shay'* which means, literally, a thing.

[33] See Chaps. XI and XV, below; and *Kitāb al-Umm*, Vol. VII, pp. 250-65.

[34] For *al-nāsikh wa al-mansūkh*, see Chap. V, below.

obedience to God and indicating how to avoid disobedience to Him as well as how to avoid missing one's own fortune and how to increase supererogatory favor [are all provided in the Book of God].

It is the duty of those who have [legal] knowledge never to express an opinion unless it is based on certainty. There are cases where men have discussed matters relating to [legal] knowledge when, if only they had abstained from so doing, abstention
S41 would have been more appropriate and safer, I trust.

Chapter III

[ON LEGAL KNOWLEDGE][1]

29. Someone asked me:[2] What is [legal] knowledge and how much should men know of it?

30. Shāfiʿī replied: Legal knowledge is of two kinds: one is for the general public, and no sober and mature person should be ignorant of it.

31. He asked: For example?

32. [Shāfiʿī] replied: For example, that the daily prayers are five,[3] that men owe it to God to fast the month of Ramaḍān, to make the pilgrimage to the [Sacred] House whenever they are able, and to [pay] the legal alms in their estate; that He [God] has prohibited usury,[4] adultery, homicide, theft, [the drinking of] wine, and [everything] of that sort which He has obligated S357
men to comprehend, to perform, to pay in their property, and to abstain from [because] He has forbidden it to them.

This kind of knowledge may be found textually in the Book of God, or may be found generally among the people of Islam.

[1] The heading is not in Shākir's edition, but may be found in the Būlāq edition, p. 50. This section, moved from its place following the chapter on traditions, deals with a broad jurisprudential subject, not on traditions as a source of the sharīʿa. The subject matter of this chapter has been dealt with more fully in Shāfiʿī's *Kitāb al-Umm,* Vol. VII, pp. 250-65; edited and published in a separate booklet by Aḥmad Muḥammad Shākir under the title Jumāʿ al-ʿIlm (Cairo, 1940).

[2] The opening statement, " Shāfiʿī said," is omitted.

[3] Būlāq ed., p. 50.

[4] Būlāq ed., p. 50.

The public relates it from the preceding public and ascribes it to the Apostle of God, nobody ever questioning its ascription or its binding force upon them. It is the kind of knowledge which
S358 admits of error neither in its narrative nor in its interpretation; it is not permissible to question it.

33. He asked: What is the second kind?

34. Shāfiʿī replied: It consists of the detailed duties and rules obligatory on men, concerning which there exists neither a text in the Book of God, nor regarding most of them, a sunna. Whenever a sunna exists [in this case], it is of the kind related by few authorities, not by the public, and is subject to different interpretations arrived at by analogy.

35. He asked: Is [legal knowledge of] this kind as obligatory as the other, or is it not obligatory so that he who acquires such knowledge performs a supererogatory act, and he who neglects
S359 it falls not into error? Or, is there a third kind, derived from a narrative (*khabar*) or analogy?

36. [Shāfiʿī] replied: There is a third kind [of knowledge].

37. He asked: Will you explain it, give its source, and state what [portion] of it is obligatory, and on whom it is binding and on whom it is not binding?

38. [Shāfiʿī] replied: The public is incapable of knowing this kind of knowledge, nor can all specialists obtain it. But those who do obtain it should not all neglect it. If some can obtain it, the others are relieved of the duty [of obtaining it]; but those who do obtain it will be rewarded.

39. He asked: Will you cite a narrative or any other relevant
S360 information as a basis for [using] analogy?

40. [Shāfiʿī] replied: God has imposed the [duty of] *jihād* as laid down in His Book and uttered by His Prophet's tongue. He stressed the calling [of men to fulfil] the *jihād* [duty][5] as follows:

> God has bought from the believers their selves and their possessions against [the gift of] Paradise. They fight in the way of God; they

[5] For the legal meaning of *jihād*, see M. Khadduri, *War and Peace in the Law of Islam,* Chap. 5.

> kill, and are killed; that is a promise binding upon God in the Torah and Gospel and the Qur'ān; and who fulfils his covenant better than God? So rejoice in the bargain you have made with Him. That is the mighty triumph [Q. IX, 111].

And He said:

> Fight the polytheists totally as they fight you totally;[6] and know that God is with the godfearing [Q. IX, 36].

And He said:

> Slay the polytheists wherever you find them, and take them, and confine them, and lie in ambush for them everywhere. But if they repent and perform the prayer and pay the *zakāt*, then set them free. God is All-Forgiving, All-Compassionate [Q. IX, 5].

And He said:

> Fight those who do not believe in God nor in the Last Day, who do not forbid what God and His Apostle have made forbidden, and who do not practice the religion of truth, of those who have been S361
> given the Book, until they pay the *jizya* out of hand and have been humbled [Q. IX, 29].

41. ʿAbd al-ʿAzīz b. Muḥammad al-Darāwardī[7] told us from Muḥammad b. ʿAmr b. ʿAlqama from Abū Salāma [b. ʿAbd al-Raḥmān] from Abū Hurayra, who said that the Apostle of God said:

> I shall continue to fight the unbelievers until they say: ' There is no god but God,' if they make this pronouncement they shall be secured their blood and property, unless taken for its price, and their reward shall be given by God.[8]

And God, glorified be His praise, said:

[6] Bell's substitution of the word " continuously" is fitting in this communication, but it alters the literal meaning of the text. See Richard Bell, *The Qur'ān*, Vol. I, p. 178.

[7] Būlāq ed., p. 50.

[8] See Abū Dāwūd, *Sunan* (Cairo, 1935), Vol. III, p. 44.

> O believers, what is the matter with you, that when it is said to you: 'Go forth in the way of God,' you sink down to the ground? Are you so content with this present life as to neglect the Hereafter? The enjoyment of this life is little in comparison with the Hereafter. If you do not go forth, He will inflict upon you a painful punishment, and instead of you He will substitute another people; and you will not hurt Him at all, for God is powerful over everything [Q. IX, 38-39].

And He said:

> Go forth, light and heavy! Struggle in God's way with your
> S362 possessions and yourselves! That is better for you, did you but know [Q. IX, 41].

42. [Shāfiʿī] said: These communications mean that the *jihād*, and rising up in arms in particular, is obligatory for all able-bodied [believers], exempting no one, just as prayer, pilgrimage and [payment of] alms are performed, and no person is permitted to perform the duty for another, since performance by one will not fulfil the duty for another.

They may also mean that the duty of [*jihād*] is a collective (*kifāya*) duty different from that of prayer: Those who perform it in the war against the polytheists will fulfil the duty and
B50 receive the supererogatory merit, thereby preventing those who have stayed behind from falling into error.

But God has not put the two [categories of men] on an equal footing, for He said:

> Such believers who sit at home—unless they have an injury—are not the equals of those who fight in the path of God with their
> S363 possessions and their selves. God has given precedence to those who fight with their possessions and their selves over those who sit at home. God has promised the best of things to both, and He has preferred those who fight over those who sit at home by [granting them] a mighty reward [Q. IV, 95].

The literal meaning of this communication is that the duty is obligatory on all men.[9]

[9] Cf. Būlāq ed., p. 51, which incorporates this statement with the question of the interlocutor. See Shākir's comment in the *Risāla*, p. 364, n. 2.

43. He asked: Where is the proof for your opinion that if some people perform the duty, the others would be relieved of punishment?

44. [Shāfiʿī] said: It is in the communication [that I have just cited].

45. He asked: In what part of it? S364

46. [Shāfiʿī] replied: God said: "Yet to each God has promised the best of things."

Thus God has promised "the best of things" for those who stayed behind and could not go to the *jihād*, although he clearly specified his preference for those who went to the *jihād* over those who stayed at home. If those who stayed at home were in error, while others were fighting, they would be committing a sin, unless God forgives them, rather than receiving "the best of things."

47. He asked: Is there any other [proof]?

48. [Shāfiʿī] replied: Yes, God said:

> It is not for the believers to go forth all together, but why should not a party of every section of them go forth, to become learned in religion, and to warn their people when they return to them, perhaps they will beware [Q. IX, 122].

[When] the Apostle went to battle he was accompanied by some of his companions while others stayed at home; for ʿAlī b. Abī Ṭālib stayed at home during the battle of Tabūk. Nor did God ordain that all Muslims were under obligation to go to battle, for He said: "Why should not a party of every section of them go forth?" So He made it known that going into battle was obligatory on some, not on all, [just] as knowledge of the law is not obligatory on all but on some, save the fundamental duties which should be known to all men. But God knows best.

49. Shāfiʿī said:[10] In like manner are other duties,[11] the fulfilment of which is intended to be collective; whenever they

[10] Būlāq ed., p. 51.

[11] Singular in the Arabic text.

are performed by some Muslims collectively, those who do not perform them will not fall in error.

If all men failed to perform the duty so that no able-bodied man went forth to battle, all, I am afraid, would fall into error (although I am certain that this would never happen) in accordance with [God's] saying:

> If you do not go forth, He will inflict upon you a painful punishment [Q. IX, 39].

S366 50. He asked: What is the meaning [of this communication]?

51. [Shāfiʿī] replied: It means[12] that it is not permissible that all men should fail to "go forth"; but that if some go forth, so that a sufficient number fulfils [the collective duty], the others do not fall into error, because the going forth by some would fulfil the [duty of] 'going forth.'

52. He asked: Are there examples other than the *jihād*?

53. [Shāfiʿī] replied: [Yes, such as] the funeral and burial prayers, the performance of which should not be neglected; but men are not all under the obligation to attend to their
S367 performance, for those who perform them will relieve those who do not from falling into error.

In the same [category falls the duty to] reply to a salutation. For God said:

> When you are greeted with a greeting, respond with a better one, or return it. Verily God keeps account of everything [Q. IV, 87].

The Apostle of God said:

> He who is standing shall greet him who is sitting. If [only] one replies to a greeting, he would fulfil [the duty] on behalf of the others.[13]

These are merely intended to mean that a reply must be made. So the response of the few fulfils the duty for all who are obligated to reply, for the [collective] response is sufficient.

[12] Literally: "The indication in it."

[13] Mālik, *al-Muwaṭṭa'*, ed. M. F. ʿAbd al-Bāqī (Cairo, 1951), Vol. II, p. 959; Abū Dāwūd, Vol. IV, p. 351.

So far as I have been informed, the Muslims have continued to act as I have stated, from the time of the Prophet to the present. Only a few men must know the law, attend the funeral service, perform the *jihād* and respond to greeting, while others are
exempt. So those who know the law, perform the *jihād*, attend S368
the funeral service, and respond to a greeting will be rewarded,
while others do not fall into error since a sufficient number fulfil S369
the [collective] duty. B51

Chapter IV

[ON THE BOOK OF GOD]

[*Arabic Character of the Qur'ān*][1]

S41 54. One of them said: There are in the Qur'ān Arabic and foreign [words].

55. Shāfiʿī replied:[2] The Qur'ān indicates that there is no portion in the Book of God that is not in the Arab tongue. He who expressed such an opinion [concerning foreign words in the Qur'ān] may have found some [men] who accepted it by [sheer] submission (*taqlīd*)[3] to his authority, leaving the matter of proof up to him and to those who have disagreed with him. However, by mere submission they have neglected [their duty]; God forgiveth them and us.[4] But, perhaps, he who expressed the opinion that there are in the Qur'ān [words] which are not of the Arab tongue—and his opinion was accepted by others—meant that there are certain particular [words] which are not understood by some Arabs.

Of all tongues, that of the Arabs is the richest and the most extensive in vocabulary. Do we know any man except

[1] This section constitutes the latter part of the chapter on *al-bayān*. Cf. Shākir's ed., paragraph 133.

[2] Būlāq ed., p. 8.

[3] Literally: "imitation." This word is used as the opposite of *ijtihād* or the exercise of personal reasoning.

[4] For Shāfiʿī's warning against *taqlīd*, see Muzanī's *Mukhtaṣar* (margin of the *Kitāb al-Umm*, Vol. I, p. 2).

a prophet who apprehended all of it? However, no portion of it escapes everyone, so that there is always someone who knows it. Knowledge [of this tongue] to the Arabs is like the knowledge of the sunna to the jurists (*fuqahā'*): We know of no one who possesses a knowledge of all the sunna without missing a portion of it. So if the knowledge of all the scholars is gathered together, the entire sunna would be known. [However], if the S42
knowledge of each scholar is taken separately, each might be found lacking in some portion of it, yet what each may lack can be found among the others.

They [the scholars] may be divided into various classes: Those who possess the greater portion [of the sunna], although they may have lacked some of it, and others who know less than the others. The little of the sunna which may not be known to [the scholar] who possesses the greater part of it is not evidence that knowledge of it should be sought from [scholars of] another class, but that what is lacking should rather be sought from among his colleagues [of the same class] until the entire sunna of the beloved Prophet[5] is gathered by each scholar separately. They [the scholars] vary as to the degree of their comprehension [of the sunna]. S43

In like manner is the [knowledge concerning the] tongue of the Arabs by the scholars[6] and the public: No part of it will be missed by them all, nor should it be sought from other [people]; for no one can learn [this tongue] save he who has learned it from [the Arabs], nor can anyone be as fluent [in this tongue] as they unless he has followed them in the way they learned it. He who has learned it from them should be regarded as one of the people of that tongue.

Those who have adopted [tongues] other [than the Arabic], have done so because they have neglected [this tongue]; if they return to it, they will belong to its people.

Knowledge of the [Arabic] tongue is more widely spread among the majority of Arabs than knowledge of the sunna among the scholars.[7]

[5] Literally: " Whom I love more than my father and mother."
[6] *Al-Khāṣṣa* literally means the few, i. e. the scholars.
[7] Būlāq ed., " Among the majority of the scholars," p. 8.

56. If someone says: May we not find some foreigners who [are capable of] uttering some [words] in the Arab tongue?

This may be explained, as I have said, by the possibility of learning them from [the Arabs]; otherwise[8] none could [possibly] utter more than a few [words]. And he who has uttered a few [words] will be [regarded as] belonging to the Arabs.

But we do not deny that [there may exist] in foreign tongues certain words, whether acquired or transmitted, which may be
S44 similar to those of the Arab tongue, just as some words in one foreign tongue may be similar to those in others, although these [tongues are spoken in] separate countries and are different and unrelated to one another despite the similarity in some of the words.

57. Someone may ask: What is the proof that the Book of God was [communicated] in a pure Arab tongue, unmixed with others?

58. [Shāfiʿī replied]: The proof is [to be found] in the Book of God [itself], for God said:

B8 We never sent any messenger save with the tongue of his people [Q. XIV, 4].

59. But if someone says: [Each of] the messengers before Muḥammad was sent to his own people, while Muḥammad was sent to all mankind. This may either mean that [Muḥammad] was sent with the tongue of his people and that all others must learn his tongue—or whatever they can learn of it—or that Muḥammad was sent with the tongues of all [mankind]. Is there any evidence that he was sent with the tongue of his own people
S45 rather than with foreign tongues?

60. Shāfiʿī replied:[9] Since tongues vary so much that different [people] cannot understand one another, some must adopt the language of the others. And preference must be given to the tongue which others adopt.

[8] Literally: "For if he were not of those who learned it from them."

[9] Būlāq ed., p. 9; Shāfiʿī's reply begins with the statement: "The evidence for it is to be found in the Book of God."

The people who are fit to receive such a preference are those whose tongue is their Prophet's tongue. It is not permissible—but God knows best—for the people of [the Prophet's] tongue to become the followers of peoples whose tongues are other than that [of the Prophet] even in a single letter; but rather all other tongues should follow his tongue, and all the peoples of earlier religions should follow his religion. For God has declared this in more than one communication of His Book. He said:

> Verily it is the revelation of the Lord of the worlds, brought down by the Faithful Spirit, upon thy heart, that thou mayest be of those who warn, in a clear Arabic tongue [Q. XXVI, 192-195].

And He said:

> Thus have We sent it down as an Arabic Law [Q. XIII, 37].

And He said:

> And so We have revealed to thee an Arabic Qur'ān in order that thou mayest warn the Mother of the Towns and the people of its vicinity [Q. XLII, 7]. S46

And He said:

> *Ḥā' Mīm*[10]
> By the clear Book
> Behold, We have made it an Arabic Qur'ān, perchance ye will understand [Q. XLIII, 1-3].

And He said:

> An Arabic Qur'ān with no crookedness in it, perchance they will be God fearing [Q. XXXIX, 28].

61. Shāfiʿī said: Thus [God] has given evidence in each of the [foregoing] communications that His Book is Arabic, and He confirmed this by His disavowal—glorified be His praise—of any other tongue than the Arab tongue in two [further] communications of His Book.

[God], the Blessed and Most High, said:

[10] These are some of the obscure letters that are found at the beginning of certain Quranic chapters.

> We know well that they say: 'It is only a human being who teaches him'; the tongue of him they hint at is foreign, but this is a clear Arabic tongue [Q. XVI, 103].

And He said:

> If We had made it a foreign Qur'ān, they would have said: Why are not its communications made distinct? What, foreign and Arabic [Q. XLI, 44]?

62. Shāfiʿī said: He [God] has made us cognizant of the significance of His favors[11] by virtue of the [Prophet's] place with which He has favored us. For He said:

> There has come to you a messenger from among yourselves, grievous
> S47 to him is your suffering, watchful he is over you, and with the
> believers, he is gentle and compassionate [Q. IX, 128].

And He said:

> It is He who has raised up among the untutored people a messenger from among them to recite to them His signs, and to purify them, and to teach them the Book and the Wisdom, though they were hitherto in manifest error [Q. LXII, 2].

Among those favors which [God] made His Prophet cognizant of, is what He said [to him]:

> It is assuredly a reminder to thee and thy people [Q. XLIII, 43].

Thus [God] has favored the [Prophet's] people by associating their name with his name in His Book.

And He said:

> And warn thy clan, thy nearest kin [Q. XXVI, 214].

And He said:

> In order that thou mayest warn the Mother of the Towns and those around it [Q. XLII, 7].

[11] Būlāq ed., p. 9.

The Mother of the Towns is Makka,[12] the city [of the Prophet] and of His people. Thus [God] mentioned them in His Book as a special [people] and included them among those who were warned as a whole, and decreed that they were to be warned in their Arabic tongue—the tongue of the [Prophet's] people in particular.

It is obligatory upon every Muslim to learn the Arab tongue to the utmost of his power in order [to be able] to profess through it that " there is no God at all but God and Muḥammad is His servant and Apostle," and to recite in it [i. e., the Arabic tongue] the Book of God, and to utter in mentioning what is incumbent upon him, the *takbīr*,[13] and what is commanded, the *tasbīḥ*,[14] the *tashahhud*[15] and others. S48

Whatever is additional of the language which God made to be the language of him [Muḥammad] by whom He sealed His prophethood and by whom He revealed the last of His Books—is for his [man's] welfare, just as it is his [duty] to learn [how] to pray and recite the *dhikr*[16] in it, to visit the [Sacred] House[17] and perform its duties, to turn [in prayer] in the direction to which he should turn,[18] and to be a follower [in the performance] of the duties imposed upon him or recommended to him, [rather] than to be followed. S49

63. Shāfiʿī said:[19] [The reason] I began to explain why the Qur'ān was communicated in the Arab tongue rather than in another, is that no one who understands clearly the total meanings of the [legal] knowledge of the Book of God would be ignorant of the extensiveness of that tongue and of the various meanings

[12] All Muslim commentators are agreed that the Mother of Towns is Makka. Richard Bell, however, suggests that it is probably Madīna. See Richard Bell, *The Qur'ān,* Vol. II, p. 484, n. 3.

[13] Calling " God is greatest."

[14] " God be praised."

[15] The recital of the salutation and the formula of the profession of the faith: " There is no god at all but God and Muḥammad is the Apostle of God."

[16] The *dhikr* is the recital of the praise and glorification of God and of his remoteness from every impurity or imperfection. See Lane, *Lexicon,* p. 969.

[17] Al-Kaʿba. See paragraph 14, above.

[18] I. e., facing the Sacred Mosque in prayer (*al-qibla*).

[19] Būlāq ed., p. 9.

[of its words] to be found [just as] there are various words for a certain meaning. Doubts which occur to one who is ignorant of [the Arab tongue] will disappear from him who knows it.

Calling the attention of the public to the fact that the Qur'ān was communicated in the Arab tongue in particular is [a sincere piece of] advice to [all] Muslims. This advice is a duty imposed upon them which must not be put aside and is the attainment of a supererogatory act of goodness which no one will neglect except him who makes himself foolish and who abandons the field of good fortune. Included in faithfulness is that the truth[20] shall be explained to them. Both the fulfilment of what is right and faithfulness to the Muslims are [embodied in our obligation of] obedience to God. And obedience to God embraces all good.

64. Shāfiʿī said:[21] Sufyān b. ʿUyayna told us from Ziyād b. ʿIlāqa, who said: I have heard Jarīr b. ʿAbd-Allāh saying:
S50 "I have paid homage to the Prophet that [I will be] faithful to every Muslim."[22]

Ibn ʿUyayna [also] told us from Suhayl b. Abī Ṣāliḥ from ʿAṭā' b. Yazīd [al-Laythī] from Tamīm al-Dārī, that the Prophet said: "Religion is faithfulness," repeated three times. "To whom?" the Prophet was asked.[23] "To God, to His Book, to His Prophet and to all the Muslims, their leaders and their public," he replied.[24]

S51 65. Shāfiʿī said: God has addressed His Book to the Arabs in their tongue in accordance with the meanings known to them. Included [in the words] "in accordance with the meanings they know" was the extensiveness of their tongue.

It is [God's] divine disposition to express something, part of which is literally general which is intended to be obviously

[20] *Al-Ḥaqq* is what is right or the truth in terms of law and religion. See Jurjānī, p. 61; al-Muṭṭarrazī, Vol. I, p. 132; and "Ḥaḳḳ," in *Shorter Encyclopaedia of Islam,* pp. 126-27.

[21] Būlāq ed., p. 9.

[22] Muslim, *Ṣaḥīḥ* (Cairo, 1347-49/1929-30), Vol. II, pp. 36-39; Abū Dāwūd, Vol. IV, p. 286.

[23] Būlāq ed., p. 9.

[24] Bukhārī, Vol. I, p. 23; Muslim, Vol. II, pp. 36-39; Abū Dāwūd, Vol. IV, p. 286; Ibn Ḥanbal, *al-Musnad,* ed. Aḥmad Muḥammad Shākir (Cairo, 1956), Vol. 15, pp. 99-100.

general with the first part [of the phrase] not needing the second. [Something] "literally general" means that [the concept of] the particular is included in the general; that is indicated by some [of the words] expressed. Also "literally general" means [only] what is particular, with the word literally recognized in its context to mean what is not literally so. Knowledge of all of this is to be found either in the beginning of what is said or in the middle or at the end. B9

[The Arabs] may begin the subject of a speech whose first word makes the last clear; and they may begin a speech whose last word makes the first clear. And they may speak about [a certain] subject, in which they indicate the meaning—just as gestures indicate—without clarifying it with words. To them this [kind of speech] is of the highest order which only their learned understand, not those who are unlearned. They [also] call [a certain] object by several names, and one word may have several meanings.

All these [categories of] meanings which I have discussed are known to the scholars, although the things they know may vary: [some] having knowledge of some quite well, while others are ignorant of that part of the [Arab] tongue—in which the Book of God was communicated and the sunna uttered—are unfamiliar with them. Whoever undertakes, therefore, to speak in the language they [the Arabs] know, undertakes something part of which he does not know. And whoever was in error without excuse whenever he spoke about something of which his knowledge did not embrace the difference between what was wrong and right.[25] S52

[25] Since the Qur'ān contains quite a few foreign words, the question has often been raised whether these do not qualify the Arabic character which the Qur'ān stresses. There are two schools of thought concerning this question. The early school, whose best exponents were Ibn ʿAbbās (d. 68/687), leading authority in Makka, and Shāfiʿī, argued that although the Arabic language was rich in its vocabulary, it was bound to have certain words in common with other languages. A later school of thought maintained that foreign words had been adopted by the Arabs in an early age, before the Qur'ān was communicated, and had become an integral part of the Arabic language. Thus when the Qur'ān was revealed in "the Arabic language," those words had already been Arabicized. Al-Shāṭibī (d. 790/1388) argues that there is no question that the

General Declaration of the Book Intended to be General in Which the Particular Is Included

66. Shāfiʿī said:[26] God, Blessed and Most High, said:

> God is the creator of everything, and He of everything is a guardian [Q. XXXIX, 62].

S53 And [God], Blessed and Most High, said:

> It is God who hath created the heavens and the earth [Q. XIV, 32].

And He said:

> There is not a living creature[27] in the earth but God is responsible for its sustenance [Q. XI, 6].

These are examples of general declarations in which no particular is included.

67. Shāfiʿī said: Everything, including the heaven and the earth, things having living spirit, trees and the like—God has created them all. And God is responsible for the sustenance of every living creature and He knows its lodging place and its repository.[28]

And God said:

> It is not for the people of Madīna or for the Beduin round about them to tarry behind the Apostle of God or to prefer their own lives to his [Q. IX, 120].

Qur'ān contains foreign words but that, generally speaking, the Book was communicated in the Arabic language and that it cannot be understood save in the way the Arabic language is understood. See al-Shāṭibī, Vol. I, pp. 64-66; al-Ghazzālī, Vol. I, p. 68; al-Suyūṭī, *al-Itqān Fī Ulūm al-Qur'ān* (Cairo, 1370/1951), Vol. I, pp. 135-40; and Arthur Jeffery, *Foreign Vocabulary of the Qur'ān* (Baroda, 1938).

[26] Būlāq ed., p. 10.

[27] Dābba, incorrectly rendered as beast, is any living creature including man (Cf. Richard Bell, The *Qur'ān,* Vol. I, p. 205).

[28] A citation from Q. XI, 8.

The meaning implied in this communication is like the previous one; it specifies those men who [take part] in the *jihād*, whether they are able to fulfil the *jihād* [duty] or not, and that none should put himself before the Prophet. There is in this communication a general as well as a particular [declaration].

And [God] said:

> And the oppressed—men, women and children—who say: Our Lord, take us out of this city of wrong-doing people [Q. IV, 75]. S54

In the same [category] falls God's saying:

> So... until when the two of them came to the people of a city, they asked the people for food, but they refused to receive them hospitably [Q. XVIII, 77].

There is an indication in this communication that not all the people of the town were asked for food. So this communication has the same meaning [as the preceding one].

Moreover, there is in it as well as in [the communication concerning] the "city of wrong-doing people," a particular [declaration], since not all the people of the town were wrongdoing; there lived among them Muslims [too], but they were a few among many others.

There are [several] other examples in the Qur'ān, but these are sufficient, I trust; and there are examples in the sunna cited in their proper places [of this book]. S55

The Explicit General Declaration of the Book in Which the General and the Particular Are Included

68. Shāfiʿī said:[29] God, Blessed and Most High, said:

> O ye people, We have created you male and female and made you peoples and tribes, that you may know one another. Verily, the

[29] Būlāq ed., p. 10.

> noblest among you in the sight of God is the most godfearing of you [Q. XLIX, 13].

And [God], Blessed and Most High, said:

> O ye who have believed, fasting is prescribed for you as it was for those before you; perhaps you will be godfearing. A certain number of days; but if any of you be sick or on a journey, then a number of other days [Q. II, 183-84].

And He said:

> Verily the Prayer has become for the believers a thing prescribed for stated times [Q. IV, 103].

69. [Shāfiʿī] said: It is evident from the Book of God that general and particular [declarations] are included in the two [foregoing] communications.

S56 As to the general, it is in God's saying:

> We have created you male and female and made you peoples and tribes, that you may know one another [Q. XLIX, 13].

For all souls addressed by this communication, whether in the time of the Prophet or before or after him, were created male or female, and [made] peoples and tribes.

The particular may be found in God's saying:

> The noblest among you in the sight of God is the most God-fearing [Q. XLIX, 13].

For fear of God is obligatory on [the person] who can comprehend it and who belongs to those who are mature of the descendants of Adam, excluding the beasts, the lunatics and children who have not yet come of age, including those who can comprehend what fear of God means.

B10 No one should be regarded as god-fearing—or not god-fearing—unless he is capable of comprehending [its meaning] and belongs to [the class of] God-fearing people; if he acts contrary to it, he belongs to another class. The Book as well as
S57 the sunna bear witness to what I have discussed. For the Prophet said:

> No obligation is imposed on three: the one asleep, until he awakes; the child, until he comes of age; and the lunatic, until he recovers.[30]

Divine legislation concerning fasting and prayer belongs to the same [category]: They are obligatory upon the mature and the sane—excluding those who are not mature or who are mature but insane—and menstruant women during the period of menstruation.

The Explicit General Declaration of the Book Intended To Be All Particular

70. Shāfiʿī said:[31] God, Blessed and Most High, said:

> Those to whom the people said: ' The people [i. e., the enemy] have gathered against you, so be afraid of them.' But it increased them in faith, and they said: ' It is on God that we count, and a good guardian is He' [Q. III, 173]. S58

71. Shāfiʿī said: Since there were with the Apostle people other than those who gathered against them [i. e., his people], and those who informed [his people] were people other than those who gathered or were with him—these [also] were certain people—the evidence of the Qur'ān[32] is, therefore, clear from what I have stated that [the Prophet] has gathered for them certain people, excluding others.

[Legal] knowledge conveys certainty that the whole people did not gather against them, nor inform them, nor were they [i. e., the informed] the whole of the people.

Since the term " people" may either be applied to [a minimum of] three persons or to all the people or to any number between S59
three and all, it is correct in the Arab tongue to say that " those

[30] This tradition was transmitted on the authority of ʿĀ'isha and ʿAlī. For the transmission from ʿĀ'isha, see Abū Dāwūd, Vol. IV, pp. 140-41; and for the transmission from ʿAlī, see Ibn Ḥanbal, Vol. II, pp. 188, 197, 279, 335, 348-49.

[31] Būlāq ed., p. 11.

[32] Būlāq ed., p. 11.

to whom the people said" may constitute [only] four persons, and that " the people who have gathered against you," are those who have departed, from [the battle of] Uḥud.[33] Yet these are not too many people [despite the fact that] those who gathered are different from those who gathered against, and those who informed are different from both. But the greater number of the people are those [who remained] in their towns who are other than those people who gathered, those who gathered against and those who informed.

72. [Shāfiʿī] said: And He [God] said:

> O ye people, a parable is coined, so listen to it: Verily those to whom you pray, apart from. God, will not create a fly, even if they were to join together to do it; and if a fly were to snatch anything from them, they would never rescue it from him. Feeble indeed are the beseecher and the besought [Q. XXII, 73].

The[34] meaning commonly implied by this word [i. e., people] is general, applying to all people. But it is clear to those learned in the Arab tongue that the meaning implied [here] is some of the people, excluding others. For no other [people] were addressed by this communication except those who worship other gods than God—exalted be He over what they say—since there are among them believers who are lunatics and minors
S60 who do not worship [other] gods than Him.

73. [Shāfiʿī] said: The meaning implied in this text falls in the same category as the foregoing one, according to those who are learned in the Arab tongue; but the former seems to be clearer to persons who are not among the learned, owing to several [clear] indications in it.

74. Shāfiʿī said: God, Blessed and Most High, said:

> Then pour forth from where the people have poured forth [Q. II, 195].

[33] The people who gathered against the Prophet were the Makkans, who fought Muḥammad at the battle of Uḥud in 3/625. See Ṭabarī's *Tafsīr*, Vol. VII, pp. 404-405. For the battle of Uḥud see Ibn Hishām, Vol. II, pp. 555-56; trans. Guillaume, pp. 370 ff.; W. Montgomery Ward, *Muḥammad at Medina* (Oxford, 1956), pp. 21-29.

[34] " Shāfiʿī said" is omitted.

It is certain that not all the people had been present at ʿArafa[35] in the time of the Apostle, and that it was [only] the Apostle and those who had been with him to whom this communication was addressed. But it is correct in the Arab tongue to say: "Pour forth from where the people have poured forth," meaning [only] some of the people.

75. Shāfiʿī said:[36] The meaning of this communication falls in the same category as the two foregoing ones, and is so regarded by the Arabs. The first communication is clearer than the second to those who are ignorant of the Arab tongue, and the second is clearer to them than the third; but to the Arabs there is no difference in clarity among the three, since the one possessing the least clarity is as adequate [for comprehension] as the one that is clearest to them. For the one who listens wants only to comprehend the [meaning of the] saying of one who speaks: the least [meaning] that makes him comprehend would be suffi- S61
cient.

76. [Shāfiʿī said]: God, glorious be His praise, said:

> People and stones[37] are its fuel [Q. II, 24].

The Book of God indicates that [only] some of the people would be the fuel, in accordance with God's saying:

> Verily those to whom the best [reward] has already [been decreed] by us—they from it will be far removed [Q. XXI, 101].

[35] After performing the circumambulation of the Kaʿba and the *saʿī* (course) from Ṣafa to Marwa, the pilgrims halt at the outlying sanctuaries at places called ʿArafa, Muzdalifa and Minā.

[36] Būlāq ed., p. 11.

[37] Probably brimstone (see Richard Bell, *The Qur'ān,* Vol. I, p. 5, n. 3).

Category [of Declaration] the Meaning of Which Is Clarified by the Context

77. Shāfiʿī said:[38] God, Blessed and Most High, said:

> And ask them about the town which was bordering the sea, when its inhabitants transgressed the sabbath. Their fish came to them on the day of their sabbath, right to the shore, but on the day when they did not keep sabbath, they did not come to them. Thus were we trying them for their ungodliness [Q. VII, 163].

[God], glorious be His praise, has at first mentioned the subject concerning the town that was bordering the sea; but
S62 when He stated "they transgressed the sabbath," He obviously meant the people of the town, since the town [itself] can neither
B11 transgress nor deviate from the sabbath or other [matters]. Thus by transgression [God] meant the people of the town whom He tried for their violation [of the Sabbath].

And He said:

> How many a town which was doing wrong have We broken up, and set up after it another people. When they sensed Our power, there they were from it running [Q. XXI, 11-12].

The meaning implied in this communication falls in the same category as the previous one. [God] mentioned the town which was broken up, but when He said it was doing wrong, it is evident that those who were doing wrong were only the people [of the town], not the houses, which [obviously] have nothing to do with wrongdoing. And when [God] mentioned the people who were established after its destruction and their sense of power of Our [i. e., God's] attack, it is [quite] certain that he
S63 who can sense [Our] power can only be a human being who knows what power is.

[38] Būlāq ed., p. 11.

Category [of Declaration] the Wording of Which Indicates the Implicit, not the Explicit [Meaning]

78. God, Blessed and Most High, citing the saying of Joseph's brothers to their father, said:

> We testify only to what we know, and against the unseen we could not guard. Ask the town in which we have been, and the caravan with which we have come; verily we speak the truth [Q. XII, 81-82].

[The meaning of] this communication [falls in the same category] as the previous one, on which those learned in the [Arab] tongue do not disagree, that [Joseph's brothers] spoke to their father about a matter which touches the people of the town and those of the caravan, since the town and the caravan [by themselves] cannot tell what the truth was.

General [Declaration] Which the Sunna Specifically Indicates Is Meant To Be Particular

79. God, glorious be His praise, said:

> And his parents each receive a sixth of what he has left, if he has children; but if he has no children and his heirs are his parents, then his mother receives a third; if, however, he has brothers, his mother receives a sixth [Q. IV, 11].

And He said: S64

> And half of what your wives leave belongs to you if they have no children; but if they have children, a fourth of what they have belongs to you, after any bequests may have been made or debts [have been paid]... To them belongs a fourth of what you leave, if you have no children; if you have children, an eighth of what you leave belongs to them, after any bequests you may have made or debts [have been paid]. If a man—or a woman—whose property is

> inherited has no direct heirs, but has a brother or a sister, each of the two receives a sixth; if they be more than that, they share in a third, after any bequests you may have made or debts [have been paid], without prejudice one to the other; a charge from God; verily God is knowing, gracious [Q. IV, 12].

Thus, [God] made it plain that fathers and wives are among those He named in various circumstances, the terms being general; but the sunna of the Prophet indicated that this is intended to mean only some fathers and wives, excluding others, provided that the religion of the fathers, children and wives is the same [i. e. Islam] and that each heir is neither a killer nor a slave.[39]

80. And He said:

> After any bequests he may have made or debts [have been paid] [Q. IV, 12].

The Prophet made it clear that bequests must not exceed one third [of the deceased's estate], and the heirs receive the two-
S65 thirds; and he [also] made it clear that debts take precedence over bequests and inheritance and that neither the bequest nor the inheritance [should be distributed] until the creditors are [first] paid.[40]

Thus if it were not for the evidence of the sunna and the consensus of the people, there would be no inheritance until after the bequest [was paid] and the bequest would not fail to take precedence over the debt, or be on equal footing with the debt.

81. And God said:

> When you stand up for Prayer, wash your faces and your hands up to the elbows, and wipe your heads, and your feet up to the ankles [Q. V, 6].

[God], glorious be His praise, meant that the feet are intended to be washed [in the same manner] as the face and the hands.

[39] See Ṭabarī, *Tafsīr,* Vol. VIII, pp. 51-68.
[40] *Ibid.,* pp. 64-68.

The literal meaning of this communication is that the [duty of the washing of the] feet cannot be fulfilled save by what fulfils [the duty of washing] the face or wiping the head. However, what was meant by the washing or the wiping of the feet, was not all—but [only] some—of those who perform the [duty of] ablution.[41]

Since the Apostle [himself] wiped his shoes and ordered those who wore their shoes in a state of purification to do so, the sunna of the Apostle indicated that [the duty of] the washing or the wiping of the feet meant that [it was obligatory on] some of those who [perform] the duty of ablution, not others.

82. God, Blessed and Most High, said:

> As for the thief, male and female, cut off their hands as a retribution **S66**
> for that with which they have charged themselves—a chastisement from God [Q. V, 38].

The Apostle decreed that "Hands should [neither be] cut off [for the stealing] of fruits nor the spadix of a palm tree, and that the hand [of the thief] should not be cut off unless the price of the [thing] stolen is a quarter of a dīnār[42] or more."[43]

83. And God said:

> The fornicatress and the fornicator—scourge each of them with a hundred stripes [Q. XXIV, 2].

And He [God], concerning slave-women, said:

> If they, having been taken under *iḥṣān*,[44] commit an indecency, they shall be subject to half the punishment to which those under *iḥṣān* are subject [Q. IV, 25].

[41] *Ibid.*, Vol. X, pp. 7-81.

[42] From the Greek *denarion*, the gold unit of currency. A dīnār was the equivalent of ten, later more, silver dirhams.

[43] See Mālik, Vol. II, p. 839; Abū Dāwūd, Vol. IV, pp. 136-37; Cf. Shāfiʿī, *Kitāb al-Umm*, Vol. VI, p. 118.

[44] *Iḥṣān* is a term applied to a woman who abstains from what is not lawful or from what induces suspicion. A married woman, having a husband, possesses both of these significations. See Lane, *Lexicon*, p. 586.

Thus the Qur'ān indicated that scourging with a hundred stripes is intended [only] for the free, not the slave-women. And when the Apostle stoned rather than scourged the *thayyib*[45] adulterer, the sunna of the Prophet specified that the hundred stripes are [the penalty] for the free fornicatress and fornicator; and that the cutting off of the hand of the thief was intended to be [the penalty] for one who steals [a thing] from a secure place[46] and that the price [of the theft] should be [at least] a quarter of a dīnār, excluding other things covered under the terms " theft" and " adultery.".

84. God said:

S67 And know that if you have taken anything as a spoil, one-fifth belongs to God and to the Apostle, and to the near of kin, and to orphans, and to the poor and to the wayfarer [Q. VIII, 41].

B12 Since the Apostle [is reported to] have given the Banū Hāshim and the Banū al-Muṭṭalib the portion of the share belonging to " the near of kin,"[47] the sunna of the Apostle gave evidence that the " near of kin"—whom God made partakers of the one-fifth share—were the Banū Hāshim and the Banū al-Muṭṭalib, not others.

Indeed the whole [tribe] of Quraysh is related [to the Prophet]. The [clan of the] Banū ʿAbd Shams is related [to the Prophet] equally with the [clan of the] Banū al-Muṭṭalib, for they were all the descendants of the same father and mother, although some members of the Banū al-Muṭṭalib were distinguished by having been descendants from the Banū Hāshim [too], in distinction from others.[48]

[45] The *thayyib* is a woman who is not a virgin, or a woman whom a man has gone into, or a woman who has become separated from her husband in any manner (by death or divorce).

[46] I. e., the thing which is well protected, not liable to be picked up by people. See a tradition to this effect in Abū Dāwūd, Vol. IV, p. 138.

[47] The term *qurba*, literally meaning " way of approach to God," refers in this Quranic verse, as Shāfiʿī points out, to the Banū Hāshim and the Banū al-Muṭṭalib. See Bayḍāwī, pp. 240-41.

[48] For a study of the Prophet's family relationship with other clans, see Ibn Muṣʿab al-Zubayrī, *Kitāb Nasab Quraysh,* ed. E. Lévy-Provençal (Cairo, 1953).

Since the portion of the share [belonging to the near of kin] was not given to all who belonged to the Banū al-Muṭṭalib, excluding those whose descent from the Banū Hāshim did not give them a portion of the share, this indicated that they [the Banū Hāshim] obtained a special portion which others did not, only because of their relationship to the stock of [the Prophet], although they supported the Prophet—as they always did—when they entered into his pass (*shiʿb*).[49] Yet, God, glorious be
His praise, did not specify [anything] special for them. S68

Most certainly [the clan of] the Banū Hāshim belonged to the [tribe of] Quraysh, but none of them was given a share from the one-fifth on account of their descent. The Banū Nawfal [enjoyed] the same [blood] relationship, although they were distinguished on the grounds of their descent from a different
mother. S69

85. [Shāfiʿī said]: God said:

> And know that if you take anything as spoil, one-fifth belongs to God and to the Apostle [Q. VIII, 41].

Since the Apostle decreed that the booty belongs to the S70
slayer in an attack, the sunna of the Prophet indicated that the spoil, which is subject to the [deduction of the] one-fifth share provided in the Qur'ān, is different from booty, provided that the booty was taken in a battle of attack, in distinction from booty taken otherwise. But the booty taken in [fighting] other than an attack is subject to the one-fifth share in accordance
with the sunna, in the same manner as other spoils.[50] S71

Had it not been for the evidence of the sunna and our decision on the [basis of the] literal [meaning of the Qur'ān], we should
have been in favor of punishing everyone to whom the term S72
stealing applies by the cutting off [of the hand]; and of scourging

[49] This is a reference to the counter-alliance of the clans of the Banū Hāshim and the Banū ʿAbd al-Muṭṭalib against the boycott of the tribe of Quraysh and its attempt to force the Prophet and his followers to abandon Islam. See Ibn Hishām, Vol. I, pp. 230-34. Guillaume, in his translation of Ibn Hishām's *Life of Muḥammad,* uses "alley" for *shiʿb*, p. 159.

[50] Mālik, Vol. II, pp. 454-55; Bukhārī, *Saḥīḥ*, ed. L. Krehl (Leiden, 1862-1908), Vol. II, p. 286; Shāfiʿī, *Kitāb al-Umm,* Vol. IV, pp. 66-67.

every free *thayyib* adulterer with a hundred stripes; and of giving the share of the near of kin to everyone related to the Prophet—which might have been extended to many sections of the Arabs, owing to the [Prophet's] blood relationship with them—and of regarding the booty subject to the one-fifth [rule] in the same manner as a spoil, by treating it like other spoils.

Chapter V

[ON THE OBLIGATION OF MAN TO ACCEPT THE AUTHORITY OF THE PROPHET]

A Declaration Concerning the Duty Imposed by God, as Laid Down in His Book, [Ordering Men] to Follow the Prophet's Sunna

86. Shāfiʿī said: God has placed His Apostle—[in relation to] His religion, His commands and His Book—in the position made clear by Him as a distinguishing standard of His religion by imposing the duty of obedience to Him as well as prohibiting disobedience to Him. He has made His merits evident by associating belief in His Apostle with the belief in Him. For God, Blessed and Most High, said:

> So believe in God and His Apostles, and do not say: "Three." Refrain; [it will be] better for you. God is only one God. Glory be to Him. His having a son is something alien to him [Q. IV, 171]. S73

And He said:

> The believers are only those who have believed in God and His Apostle, and who when they are with him on some common affair do not go away until they ask his permission [Q. XXIV, 62].

Thus [God] prescribed that the perfect beginning of the faith, to which all other things are subordinate, shall be the belief in Him and then in His Apostle. For if a person believes only in Him, not in His Apostle, the name of the perfect faith[1] will never apply to him until he believes in His Apostle together with Him.[2]

So the Apostle laid down the sunna [of reciting the Prophet's name together with that of God] for testing the faith of every man [as the following tradition indicates]:

Mālik b. Anas told us from Hilāl b. Usāma from ʿAṭa' b. Yasār from ʿUmar b. al-Ḥakam, who said:

> I went to the Apostle of God with a slave-girl and I asked him: 'I have taken an oath [to free a slave]; may I free her?' 'Where is God?' the Apostle asked her. 'In heaven,' she answered. 'And who am I?'
> S75 asked he. 'You are the Apostle of God,' she answered. 'You may free her,' [the Prophet] said.[3]

[The transmitter's name, ʿUmar b. al-Ḥakam]—Shāfiʿī says should read Muʿāwiya b. al-Ḥakam, for Mālik, I believe, has not correctly reported the name, as others did.

87. Shāfiʿī said: God has imposed the duty on men to obey His divine communications as well as the sunna of His Apostle. For He said in His Book:

> O our Lord, raise up amongst them an Apostle, one of themselves, to recite to them Thy signs and to teach them the Book and Wisdom
> S76 and to purify them. Verily Thou art All-Mighty, All-Wise [Q. II, 129].

And He, glorious be His praise, said:

> And also we have sent among you an Apostle, one of yourselves, to recite to you our signs, and purify you, to teach you the Book and the Wisdom, and to teach you what you did not know [Q. II, 151].

And He said:

[1] I. e., Islam.
[2] Cf. Ṭabarī, *Tafsīr,* Vol. IX, pp. 422-23; Bayḍāwī, pp. 137-38, 474-75.
[3] Mālik, Vol. II, pp. 776-77.

> God bestowed a favor upon the believers when He raised up amongst them an Apostle, one of themselves, to recite His signs to them, to purify them and to teach them the Book, although they had formerly been in manifest error [Q. III, 164].

And He, glorious be His praise, said:

> It is He who has raised up an Apostle among the untutored people, one of their number to recite to them His signs, to purify them, and to teach them the Book and the Wisdom, though formerly they had been in manifest error [Q. LXII, 2].

And He said:

> But remember the goodness which God has shown you and how much of the Book and the Wisdom He has sent down to you to admonish you thereby [Q. II, 231].

And He said:

> God has sent down to thee the Book and the Wisdom, and has taught thee what thou did not know before; the bounty of God towards thee is ever great [Q. IV, 113].

And He said:

> And call to mind the signs of God and the Wisdom which are recited in your houses; verily God is gentle, well-informed [Q. XXXIII, 34]. **S77**

So God mentioned His Book—which is the Qur'ān—and Wisdom, and I have heard that those who are learned in the Qur'ān—whom I approve—hold that Wisdom is the sunna of **B13**
the Apostle of God. This is like what [God Himself] said; but God knows best! For the Qur'ān is mentioned [first], followed by Wisdom; [then] God mentioned His favor to mankind by teaching them the Qur'ān and Wisdom. So it is not permissible for Wisdom to be called here [anything] save the sunna of the Apostle of God. For [Wisdom] is closely linked to the Book of God, and God has imposed the duty of obedience to His Apostle, and imposed on men the obligation to obey his orders.[4]

[4] See paragraph 22, above.

So it is not permissible to regard anything as a duty save that set forth in the Qur'ān and the sunna of His Apostle. For [God], as we have [just] stated, prescribed that the belief in His Apostle
S78 shall be associated with the belief in Him.

The sunna of the Apostle makes evident what God meant [in the text of His Book], indicating His general and particular [commands]. He associated the Wisdom [embodied] in the sunna with his Book, but made it subordinate [to the Book]. Never has God done this for any of His creatures save His Apostle.

God's Command Ordering Obedience to the Apostle Is Both Associated with Obedience to Him and Ordered Independently

88. [Shāfiʿī said]: God said:

> When God and His Apostle have decreed a matter, it is not for a believing man or a woman to exercise a choice in a matter affecting him; whoever opposes God and His Apostle has deviated into manifest error [Q. XXXIII, 36].

And He said:

> O you who believe, obey God and obey the Apostle and those in authority among you. If you should quarrel about anything, refer it to God and the Apostle, if you believe in God and the Last Day. That is better and fairer in the issue [Q. IV, 59].

Some scholars have held that "those in authority" [means] the commanders of the Apostle's army. That is what more than
S79 one commentator has told us. But God knows best.[5]

This is in accord with what [God] said, for the Arabs who had been around Makka knew nothing about command, and

[5] Ṭabarī adds that it may mean the leaders in matters of religion and law. See Ṭabarī, *Tafsīr*, Vol. VIII, pp. 495-504; Bayḍāwī, p. 115.

[the idea of] some submitting to the command of others was repugnant to them.

When, however, they submitted to [the authority of] the Apostle, they did not think that [such an authority] was fit to reside in any hands other than the Apostle's.

So they were commanded to obey "those in authority"—the ones whom the Apostle appointed, with conditional but not absolute obedience, concerning their rights and duties. However, [God] said: "If you should quarrel about anything, refer it to God," that is, in the event of disagreement.

89. Shāfiʿī said:[6] This [i. e., the meaning implied in the latter command] is, if God will, as He said about "those in authority," namely, that "If you should quarrel" (but God knows best), they [the people] and the commander whom they were ordered to obey—should "refer it to God and the Apostle" for a settlement on the basis of what God and His Apostle said, if they know it. If you do not know what God's commands are, you S80
should ask the Apostle, if you are able to reach him,[7] or any one of you who is able to do so. For this is an obligation concerning which there should be no disagreement, in accordance with God's saying:

> When God and His Apostle have decreed a certain matter, it is not for a believing man or a woman to have a choice in a matter affecting him [Q. XXXIII, 36].[8]

As to the disputes that happened after the Apostle's [death], the matter was decided in accordance with God's judgment [as laid down in the Qur'ān] and then that of His Apostle [as laid down in the sunna]. But if a text were not applicable, the matter was decided by analogy on the strength of a precedent sought [either in the Qur'ān or the sunna] in the same manner as I have [already] explained concerning the *qibla*, [witnesses

[6] Būlāq ed., p. 14.
[7] Ṭabarī, *Tafsīr,* Vol. VIII, pp. 504-505.
[8] See Bayḍāwī, p. 558.

of] just character, equal compensation, and whatever God has prescribed in parallel cases. For He said:

> S81 Those who obey God and the Apostle are with the prophets and the veracious and the martyrs and the upright upon whom God has bestowed favor. Good company are these [Q. IV, 69].

And He said:

> O you who have believed, obey God and His Apostle [Q. VIII, 20].

God's Command Ordering Obedience to His Apostle

90. [Shāfiʿī said]: God, glorious be His praise, said:

> Verily, those who swear allegiance to thee swear allegiance really to God; the hand of God is above their hands. So whoever breaks his oath, breaks it only to his own hurt, and to him who fulfils what he has pledged to God, He will grant a great reward [Q. XLVIII, 10].

And He said:

> Whoever obeys the Apostle has obeyed God [Q. IV, 80].

So God instructed [men] that their homage to the Apostle is homage to Him, and their obedience [to him] is obedience to Him.

And He said:

> But no! by thy Lord, they will not become believers until they make
> thee judge in their disputes and do not afterwards find difficulty in
> S82 thy decisions, but surrender in full submission [Q. IV, 65].

This verse, we have been told, was revealed in connection with a land dispute between al-Zubayr and another man in which the Prophet gave a decision in favor of al-Zubayr. This decision is a sunna laid down by the Apostle, not a command in the text of the Qur'ān.[9]

The Qur'ān indicates what I have just stated; for if this decision were a Quranic decision, it should have been prescribed in the text of the Book of God.

But if men fail to accept a decision based on a clear text of the Book of God, they undoubtedly cease to be believers, for they are rejecting a decision based on divine legislation. For God, Blessed and Most High, said:

> Do not put the Apostle's calling on you for aid on the same footing amongst you as your calling on each other. God knows those of you who slip away secretly, so let those who go against His command beware lest a trial befall them, or a painful punishment [Q. XXIV, 63]. B14 S83

And He said:

> When they are called to God and to His Apostle that he may judge between them, lo, a party of them avert themselves. But if they are in the right, they will come to him in submission.
>
> Is there sickness in their hearts, or are they in doubt, or do they fear that God and His Apostle may act unjustly towards them. Nay, but they are the evildoers.
>
> All that the believers said when they were called to God and His Apostle that he might judge between them was: ' We hear and obey.' These are the ones who prosper.
>
> Whoever obeys God and His Apostle, and fears God and shows piety—these are the ones who attain felicity [Q. XXIV, 48-52].

[9] Yaḥya b. Ādam, in *Kitāb al-Kharāj,* reports the case as follows: " One of the Helpers from among the Banū Umayya had a dispute with al-Zubayr concerning a creek (*sharj*) in the *ḥarra*, and the Prophet said: Irrigate, O Zubayr, and then leave the water alone. Said the man of the Banū Umayya: Justice, O Prophet, even though he is the son of your aunt! And the face of the Prophet changed so that the man knew that what he had said had hurt the prophet. Then the Prophet said: O Zubayr Shut off the water till it reaches the height of two ankles—or he said:—[till it] reaches the fence—and then let the water flow. It was revealed [then]—or he said: recited—: " No, by thy Lord, they do not believe until they make thee judge in the tangles. . . " [Q. IV, 68]. Yaḥya b. Ādam, *Kitāb al-Kharāj,* ed. A. M. Shākir (Cairo, 1347/1929), pp. 106-107; English translation by A. Ben Shemesh, entitled *Taxation In Islam* (Leiden, 1958), p. 74. See also Ṭabarī, *Tafsīr,* Vol. VIII, pp. 519-23.

Through this communication, God instructed men that their recourse to the Apostle to judge among them is a recourse to God's judgment, for the Apostle is the judge among them, and when they accept his judgment they do so only because of an obligation imposed by God.

And He instructed them that the [Prophet's] judgment is His judgment, for his judgment is imposed by Him and by His established knowledge—rendering him a man of destiny and assisting him by preserving him from error and [worldly]
S84 success—and by testifying that He guides him and causes him to obey His order.

So God imposed the obligation upon His creatures to obey His Apostle, and He instructed them that [obedience] to him is obedience to Him.

The sum-total of what He instructed them is the duty to obey Him and His Apostle, and that obedience to the Apostle is obedience to Him. He [also] instructed them that He imposed the duty on His Apostle to obey His order, Glorious be His praise.

The Obligation Made Clear by God to His Creatures That He Imposed upon His Apostle to Follow What He Revealed to Him, and What He Testified to of His Obeying His Commands, His Guidance, and That He Is the Guide of Any Who Follow Him

91. Shāfiʿī said: God, Glorious be His praise, said to His Prophet:

> O Prophet, fear God, and obey not the unbelievers and the hypocrites. Verily God is All-Knowing, All-Wise. But follow what is revealed to thee from thy Lord. Verily God is aware of the things you do [Q. XXXIII, 1-2].

And He said:

> Follow what has been revealed unto thee from thy Lord—there is no
> god but Him—and turn thou away from the polytheists[Q. VI, 106]. S85

And He said:

> Then we set thee upon an open way of the Law; therefore follow it, and follow not the whims of those who do not know [Q. XLV, 18].

So God instructed His Apostle that He has favored him with His established knowledge and that he will preserve him from mankind, for He said:

> O thou Apostle, proclaim what is sent down to thee from thy Lord—if thou do it not thou hast not delivered His message—and God will defend thee from the people [Q. V, 67].[10]

92. Shāfiʿī said:[11] And [He], glorious be His praise, certified [the Prophet's] firm belief in what He commanded him, and in Guidance to himself and to whoever follows him. For He said:

> Thus We have revealed to thee a spirit belonging to Our affair. Thou didst not know what either the Book or the Faith were. But We have made it a light by which We guide whoever We please of Our servants, and verily thou shalt guide unto a straight path [Q. XLII, 52].

And He said:

> Had it not been for the bounty and mercy of God toward thee, a party of them would have proposed to lead thee astray; but they lead only themselves astray; they do not hurt thee at all. God has
> sent down to thee the Book and the Wisdom, and He has taught thee S86
> what thou didst not know; God's bounty to thee is ever great [Q. IV, 113].

[10] See Ṭabarī, *Tafsīr*, Vol. X, pp. 467-72. Previously the Prophet was safeguarded by a few of his followers.

[11] Būlāq ed., p. 15.

Thus God declared that He commanded His Prophet to obey His order, and certified what he proclaimed on His behalf as well as what he certified for himself.[12] We [also] certify for him in order to draw near to God by our belief in Him, and we make entreaties to Him by belief in His words. [For] ʿAbd al-ʿAzīz [b. Muḥammad al-Darāwardī] told us from ʿAmr b. Abī ʿAmr—the freed slave of al-Muṭṭalib—from al-Muṭṭalib b. Ḥanṭab that the Apostle of God said:

> I have left nothing concerning which God has given you an order without giving you that order; nor have I neglected anything concerning which He has given you a prohibition without giving you that prohibition.[13]

93. Shāfiʿī said: What God has informed us of in His established knowledge and in His final and irrevocable judgment—a S87 favor and a blessing from Him—is that He prevented those who attempted to lead [the Prophet] astray, and informed him that they could not hurt him at all.

In certifying that [the Prophet] guides mankind along a straight-forward path—the path of God—and that he delivers His message and obeys His commands—as we have stated before—and in ordering obedience to him and in emphasizing all [of this] in the [divine] communications just cited—God has given evidence to mankind that they should accept the judgment of the Apostle and obey his orders.

[12] Ṭabarī, *Tafsīr,* Vol. IX, pp. 199-201; Bayḍāwī, pp. 126-27.

[13] This is the first part of a tradition, the second part of which Shāfiʿī cites in paragraph 97. In his *Kitāb al-Umm* (Vol. VI, p. 209, margin) the two parts are cited as one tradition. Transmitters have related the tradition in a variety of wordings, but all agree on the substance. See al-Suyūṭī, *al-Jāmiʿ al-Ṣaghīr* (Cairo, 1352/1933), Vol. I, p. 305. For a discussion on the transmission of this tradition and on al-Muṭṭalib b. Ḥanṭab, Companion of the Prophet, see Shākir's edition of the *Risāla,* pp. 93-102, note 8. This Companion should be distinguished from a Successor by the same name who transmitted traditions on the authority of ʿĀ'isha, Abū Hurayra, and Anas b. Mālik (See Ibn Ḥajar, *al-Iṣāba* [Cairo, 1358/1939], Vol. III, p. 404). See also J. Schacht, *The Origins of Muhammadan Jurisprudence,* pp. 53-54.

94. Shāfiʿī said: Whatever the Apostle has decreed that is not based on any [textual] command from God, he has done so by God's command. So God instructed us in His saying:

> And verily thou wilt guide [mankind] to a straight path, the path of God [Q. XLII, 52-53].

For the Apostle has laid down a sunna [on matters] for which there is a text in the Book of God as well as for others concerning which there is no [specific] text. But whatever he laid down in the sunna God has ordered us to obey, and He regards [our] obedience to him as obedience to Him, and [our] refusal to obey him as disobedience to Him for which no man will be
forgiven; nor is an excuse for failure to obey the Apostle's sunna S88
possible owing to what I have already stated and to what the Apostle [himself] has said:

Sufyān [b. ʿUyayna] told us from Sālim Abū al-Naḍr—a freed slave of ʿUmar b. ʿUbayd-Allāh—who heard ʿUbayd-Allāh b. Abī Rāfiʿ relate from his father that the Apostle had said:

> Let me find no one of you reclining on his couch,[14] and when confronted with an order of permission or prohibition from me, say:
> ' I do not know [whether this is obligatory or not]; we will follow S89
> only what we find in the Book of God.'[15] S90

95. Shāfiʿī said:[16] The sunnas of the Apostle together with B15
the [communications of the] Book of God fall in two categories:

[14] In both the Būlāq and Shākir editions there is a statement following this tradition to the effect that Shāfiʿī explained the word *arīka* (a couch) to mean *a bedstead* (*sarīr*); but this statement is perhaps spurious, as Shākir himself suspected, since it is written on the margin of the MS, possibly by one of the readers.

[15] Abū Dāwūd, Vol. IV, p. 200. This tradition is followed by a statement, paragraph 296 (Shākir's edition), which reads: " Sufyān [b. ʿUyayna] said: '[This ḥadīth] was related to me by Muḥammad b. al-Munkadir, who transmitted it from the Prophet without citing the names of [other] authorities'." Such a tradition, lacking the names of other transmitters, is called ḥadīth *mursal*. Shāfiʿī, however, seems to have depended on the authority of ʿUbayd-Allāh b. Rāfiʿ, the son of Abū Rāfiʿ, a freed slave of the Prophet, who transmitted the tradition from his father (See Ibn Ḥajar, *al-Iṣāba,* Vol. I, p. 488).

[16] Būlāq ed., p. 16.

First, for every textual [communication] in the Book the Apostle laid down [a similar sunna] in conformity with divine communication. Second, for any [ambiguous] command the Apostle laid down on God's behalf [a sunna] clarifying the meaning implied by God and specifying what [kind of] duty God imposed, whether general or particular, and how man should carry it out. In both categories [the Prophet] followed the Book of God.

96. [Shāfiʿī] said: I know of no scholar who does not agree that the sunna of the Prophet falls in three categories, two of which were agreed upon unanimously. These two categories agree [on certain matters] and differ [on others].

S91 First, for whatever acts there is textual [legislation] provided by God in the Book, the Apostle [merely] specified clearly what is in the text of the Book. Second, as to any [ambiguous] communication in the Book laid down by God, [the Prophet] specified the meaning implied by Him. These are the two categories on which scholars do not disagree.

The third category consists of what the Apostle has laid down in the sunna and concerning which there is no text in the Book.

97. Some [scholars] have said: God empowered [the Prophet], by virtue of the duty He imposed [on mankind] to obey Him and his success in obtaining [God's] approval in accordance with His established knowledge, to provide sunnas [for matters] on which there is no text in the Book. Others said: No sunna was ever laid down [by the Prophet] unless there was a basis[17] for it in the Book, such as the sunna which specified the number of prayers [each day] and [the modes of] their performance, based on the general duty of prayer. In like manner, [the Prophet] laid down sunnas dealing with sale [of property], as well as others. For God said:

> Do not consume your property among you uselessly [Q. IV, 29].

And He said:

> God has permitted sale and forbidden usury [Q. II, 275].

[17] Literally: " Foundation," i. e., a fundamental principle or a precedent.

Whatever God has provided by [way of] permission or prohibition, he has specified on God's behalf as he did in [the case of the duty of] prayer.

Others said: [The Prophet] received a message from God S92
confirming the sunna by a command from Him.

Still others said: [The Prophet] was inspired with all that he had laid down. The sunna is [divine] Wisdom inspired by God, and so whatever He inspired him with [constitutes] sunna. [For] ʿAbd al-ʿAzīz [b. Muḥammad al-Darāwardī] told us from ʿAmr b. Abī ʿAmr from al-Muṭṭalib, who related that the Prophet said:

> The trustworthy spirit [Gabriel] has inspired me [with the thought]
> that no soul will ever die until it will receive its full provision. Be, S93
> therefore, moderate in your request.[18]

98. Shāfiʿī said:[19] Among the things with which [the Prophet] was inspired is his sunna. This [sunna] is the Wisdom which God mentioned [in His Book], and whatever He sent down to him is a Book—the Book of God—all of these have been given to him as favors from God and by His will. These favors are either embodied in one Favor[20] or take different forms. S94-103
We pray God for protection from error and success.

In whatever form it may take, God made it clear that He imposed the duty of obedience to His Apostle, and has given none of mankind an excuse to reject any order he knows to be the order of the Apostle of God. God has rather made men have need for him in [all matters of] religion and He has given the proof for it by providing that the sunna of the Apostle make clear the meanings of the duties laid down in His Book, so that it might be known that the sunna—whether in the form specifying the meaning of God's commands as provided in the text of the Book which they can read or in the form of legislation in the absence of such a text—in either form represents God's command and is in [full] agreement with that of His Apostle; S104

[18] See note 13, above.
[19] Būlāq ed., p. 16.
[20] I. e., the Message.

both are [equally] binding in all circumstances. This has been confirmed by the Apostle in the tradition of Abū Rāfiʿ which has already been cited.[21]

99. Shāfiʿī said:[22] I shall explain what I have already said about the sunna, [whether] it specifies the Book of God or provides [additional legislation] for matters on which there is no text in the Book, such examples as may clarify the meaning of the subject that was discussed.

The first one I take up will be [a discussion] on the sunna based on the Book of God. I shall discuss by means of *istidlāl* (deductive reasoning) the sunna relating to the subject of the *nāsikh* (abrogating) and the *mansūkh* (abrogated) passages in the Book of God. Next, [I shall] state the duties provided in the text [of the Book] and the sunna which the Apostle has laid down on the basis of the Book; the general duties which the Apostle specified for its modes and its times of fulfillment; next, the general [commands] which were intended to be general and the general [commands] which were intended to be particular;
S105 and [finally] the sunna [of the Prophet] for which there is no text in the Book.

[21] See note 15, above.
[22] Būlāq ed., p. 16.

Chapter VI

[ON THE ABROGATION OF DIVINE LEGISLATION]

The Abrogating and Abrogated [*Communications*]

100. Shāfiʿī said: God indeed created mankind for whatever His established knowledge desired in creating it and for whatever [its destiny] should be. There is no reversal at all of His judgment, He being swift of reckoning.[1] And he revealed to them the Book that explains everything, as a guide and a mercy.[2] In it He laid down some duties which B16 He confirmed, and others which He abrogated, as a mercy to His people so as to lighten their burden and to comfort them in addition to the favors which He had begun to bestow upon them. For the fulfilment [of the duties] He confirmed, He rewarded them with Paradise and with salvation from His punishment. His mercy has included all of them in what He confirmed and what He abrogated. Praise be to Him for His favors.

101. Shāfiʿī said:[3] God has declared that He abrogated [communications] of the Book only by means of other communications in it; that the sunna cannot abrogate [a text in] the Book

[1] This is a citation from Q. XIV, 51.
[2] Cf. Q. XVI, 89.
[3] Būlāq ed., p. 17.

but that it should only follow what is laid down in the Book, and that the sunna is intended to explain the meaning of communications of general [nature] set forth [in the Book]. For God said:

S106 When Our signs are recited to them as Evidences, those who do not look forward to meeting us, say: Bring a Scripture other than this or change it. [You O Muḥammad] say: It is not for me to change it of my own accord; I only follow what is revealed to me; verily I fear, if I go against my Lord, the punishment of a mighty day [Q. X, 15].

Thus God informed [men] that He had commanded His Prophet to obey what was communicated to him, but that He did not empower him to alter [the Book] of his own accord. For there is in His saying: "It is not for me to alter it of my own accord" [Q. X, 15], an evidence for what I stated, that nothing can abrogate the Book of God save His Book. Since [God] is the originator of His [own] commands, He [alone] can repeal or confirm whatever of it He wills—glorious be His praise—but no one of His creatures may do so. For He also said: "God repeals what He wills, or confirms; with Him is the Mother of the Book" [Q. XIII, 39].[4]

Some scholars have maintained (but God knows best) that there is in this communication an evidence that God has empowered His Apostle to set forth rules by [God-given] aid [for matters] on which He provided no communications in the Book. But God knows best.[5]

It is held that [God's] saying: "God will repeal what He wills," means that He repeals and confirms the duties which He

[4] The Mother of the Book is the original copy of the Qur'an which exists or co-exists with God in Heaven (See Bayḍāwī, p. 334). "The original of the Qur'an," says Bell, "is thought of as a book preserved in (the seventh) heaven in the presence of God. This is assumed to be what is meant by the preserved tablet, lawḥ maḥfūẓ, spoken of in Q. LXXXV, 22. Sometimes it is thought of as having been sent down to the nearest heaven on the night of power, lailat al-qadr, described in Q. XCVII, so as to be available for revelation to the Prophet by the angel Gabriel" (Richard Bell, *Introduction to the Qur'ān* [Edinburgh, 1953], p. 37). See also ʿAbd al-Qāhir al-Baghdādī, *Kitāb Uṣūl al-Dīn* (Istanbul, 1928), Vol. I, pp. 106, 108; and Abū al-Ḥasan al-Ashʿarī, *al-Ibāna ʿAn Uṣūl al-Diyāna* (Hyderabad, 2nd ed., 1367/1947), pp. 19-35.

[5] Cf. Bayḍāwī, p. 334.

wills. This resembles [the meaning in] the foregoing [statement]; but God knows best. However, the evidence against it is in the Book of God, in which He said: S107

> For whatever We abrogate or cast into oblivion to forget, We bring a better or the like of it. Knowest thou not that God is powerful over everything? [Q. II. 106].

Thus God has informed men that the abrogation or the deferment of any communication cannot be made valid save by another [Quranic] communication. For He said:

> When we substitute one communication for another—God knoweth best what He sendeth down—they say: 'Thou [Muḥammad] art only a forger' [Q. XVI, 101].[6]

In like manner the sunna of the Apostle of God states: Nothing can abrogate it except [another] sunna of the Apostle. If God were to address to His Apostle [a communication] on a matter on which he [Muḥammad] had provided a sunna different from what God had addressed to him, he [Muḥammad] would provide a sunna in conformity with whatever God had communicated to him, so that he would make clear to men that he had provided a sunna that abrogated one earlier or contrary to it. This is [well] stated in the sunna [of the Prophet], God's blessing and peace be upon him.[7]

102. Someone may ask: The evidence that a Quranic [communication] can abrogate another [of equal status], may be found in the Qur'ān itself, because there is nothing at all to match the Qur'ān; however, can you find such [an evidence] in the sunna [concerning its abrogation by another sunna]?

103. Shāfiʿī replied: The evidence lies in my [earlier] statement concerning God's commands ordering men to obey the S108

[6] For the significance of this communication as an evidence that God permitted the repeal of His commands by others, see Abū Jaʿfar al-Naḥḥās, *Kitāb al-Nāsikh wa al-Mansūkh* (Cairo, 1323/1906), pp. 2-3; Ibn Ḥazm, *Kitāb al-Iḥkām fī Uṣūl al-Aḥkām* (Cairo, 1345/1927), Vol. IV, p. 65.

[7] For a discussion on the doctrine that the Prophet's sunna can only be abrogated by another sunna, see al-Ḥāzimī, *al-Iʿtibār fī al-Nāsikh wa al-Mansūkh Min al-Āthār* (Cairo, 1346/1927), p. 16.

order of the Apostle that the sunna was accepted [as emanating] from God and that he who obeys it does so by [an order in] the Book of God.[8] For there is no other textual order which God has made obligatory upon mankind save that which is in His Book and in the sunna of His Prophet. If the sunna is taken as such, that nothing else by a human being is equal to it, nothing can [therefore] abrogate it save another of equal status. Nothing is equal [to the sunna] save the sunna of the Apostle, since God has never given to any other human being [the power] He gave [to the Prophet]. He commanded men to obey him and made his orders binding upon them. Thus all men are his followers: He who follows shall never disobey what he was ordered to obey, and he who is under obligation to obey the sunna of the Apostle shall not refuse to obey it, for he is not empowered to abrogate any part of it.

104. Someone may ask: Is it possible to assume that there was a transmitted sunna which was abrogated while the abrogating sunna was not transmitted?

105. [Shāfiʿī replied]: That is impossible. For how could the transmitted sunna be possibly abrogated while the one which is binding was abandoned? Were this permissible the whole sunna might be abandoned by men, for they would [then] say: "Perhaps it was abrogated." No duty has ever been abrogated unless it was replaced by another. The abrogation of the *qibla* [i. e., prayer in the direction] of Jerusalem by another [in the
S109 direction] of the Kaʿba is a case in point. For whatever has been abrogated in the Book or in the sunna must have been [replaced by] something else.

106. Someone may ask: Can the sunna be abrogated by the Qur'ān?

107. [Shāfiʿī] replied: If a sunna were abrogated by the Qur'ān, another sunna must have been laid down by the Prophet making clear that his earlier sunna was abrogated so as to demonstrate to men that an act can be abrogated only by something of equal status.

[8] See Chap. V, above.

108. He may ask: Where does the evidence lie for your opinion?

109. [Shāfiʿī replied]: [The evidence lies] in what I have discussed in this book in its [proper] place, where it was made clear that the duties imposed by God—[both] the general and the particular—implied that [the Prophet] makes no pronouncement unless it is based on God's command. If God abrogates any of His commands, the Apostle would also have to abrogate his sunna by another [in conformity with God's new command].

Were it permissible to hold that what the Apostle has laid down in the sunna was abrogated by the Qur'ān and that he has transmitted no abrogating sunna, it would be permissible B17
to hold a similar view concerning [the tradition relating to] the prohibition of all kinds of sale [of property], by holding that [the Prophet] had prohibited them before [God] had laid down [the rule] that "God has permitted sale and forbidden usury" [Q. II, 276]. The same might be held about [the tradition concerning] the stoning of adulterers, namely, that stoning may be regarded as abrogated in accordance with God's saying: "The fornicatress and the fornicator—scourge each one of them with a hundred stripes," [Q. XXIV, 2] and that [the tradition S111
concerning] the wiping of the shoes may also be regarded as abrogated by the communication of ablution. It would also be possible to hold that the cutting off of the hand of the thief should not be dropped even if the stolen article were kept securely or if its value was less than a quarter of a dīnār in view of God's saying: "The thief, male and female, cut off their hand" [Q. V, 42], for the term "thief" is binding upon whomever steals, regardless of the value of the stolen article or of its security. It would be possible to reject all the traditions of the Apostle by saying: "He did not say this [or that]," if they were found to be not in accordance with divine legislation. Thus it would be permissible to reject the sunna on one of two grounds: either if it were in conformity with the general principles of the Book, but its wording were different in certain respects from the wording [of the Book],

or if its wording were phrased at greater length than that in the divine communication, although they might be different in some respects. The Book of God and the sunna of His Apostle, however, provide [ample] evidence in contradiction of this opinion and in support of the one I have stated earlier.

S112 The Book of God [contains] perspicuous declarations by virtue of which blindness[9] will be healed. In it also will be found evidence concerning the position of the Apostle in relation to the Book of God and His religion, [the Apostle's] submission to God, and his clarification [of God's word] on behalf of Him.

The Abrogating and the Abrogated, of Which the Book [of God] Indicates Some and the Sunna Others

110. Shāfiʿī said: I have heard some scholars who related that God had imposed a certain duty for prayer before He laid down that for the five prayers. For He said:

S113 O thou enwrapped in thy robes,
Stay up the night, except a little,
Half of it, or a little less
Or a little more,
And chant the Qur'ān distinctly [Q. LXXIII, 1-4].

God abrogated this [duty] by another, which may be found in the same chapter [of the Book], and it reads as follows:

> Thy Lord knows that thou remainest up nearly two-thirds of the night, or half of it, or a third of it, and a party of those with thee likewise, and God determines the night and the day. He knoweth that ye will never count it up, so He has turned towards you with mercy. So recite what may be convenient [for you] of the Qur'ān; He knoweth that some of you will be sick and others journeying about

[9] I. e., ignorance.

> in the land, seeking the bounty of God, and others fighting in the cause of God. So recite what is convenient of it, and observe the Prayer, and pay the alms [Q. LXXIII, 20].

For after God laid down His order " Stay up the night...half of it...or a little more," He added: " Nearly two-thirds of the night, or half of it, or a third of it, and a party of those with thee," He [merely] shortened it and said: " He knows that some of you will be sick...so recite what is convenient of it... "

111. Shāfiʿī said: So it is evident from the Book of God that: " Thou remainest up nearly two-thirds of the night, etc... " has been abrogated by: " So recite what is convenient S114
of it." God's saying: " So recite what is convenient of it" may mean: First, it is a confirmed duty which superseded another. Second, it is an abrogated duty superseded by another, just as it itself had superseded a previous one in accordance with God's saying:

> And as for the night, keep vigil a part of it, as a work of supererogation for thee; it may be that thy Lord will raise thee up to a laudable position [Q. XVII, 79].

For His saying: " And as for the night, keep vigil a part of it, as a work of supererogation for thee" may mean that " to keep vigil" is a duty in addition to that " to recite what is convenient of it."

112. [Shāfiʿī] said: [In such a case] it is obligatory to seek the evidence of the sunna for [determining] which of the two meanings [is valid]. The sunna of the Apostle of God, however, has indicated that no duty other than that of the five prayers is obligatory. We therefore hold that only the [duty of] five [prayers] is obligatory and that any earlier prayers have been abrogated by that sunna in accordance S115
with God's saying: " ...keep vigil a part of it, as a work of supererogation for thee," and that this has abrogated the one [stipulated in] the " rising up at night, half of it, or a third of it or recite what is convenient of the Book... " This does not mean at all that we recommend abandoning the recital

of what is convenient of the Book in the performance of prayer, for the more the recital is prolonged the more we like it. [For] Mālik [b. Anas] told us from his uncle Abū Suhayl b. Mālik from his father who heard Ṭalḥa b. ʿUbayd-Allāh say:

> A tribesman from Najd, excited and crying, whose voice was hardly intelligible until he came near [the Prophet's company], was really inquiring about Islam. ' Islam [imposes the obligation of] five prayers [every] day and night,' the Prophet said. ' Am I under any other [obligation]?' he asked. ' No, not unless you volunteer,' replied [the Prophet] and he mentioned the fasting during the month of Ramaḍān. ' Am I under any other [obligation]?' asked the tribesman. ' No, not unless you volunteer,' replied the Prophet. The tribesman departed, while murmuring: ' By God I shall neither add to nor drop any of these [obligations].' So the Apostle said: ' If [this man] will
> S116 fulfil his promise, he will be successful [as a Muslim in his life].'[10]

B18 This [tradition] has also been related by ʿUbāda b. al-Ṣāmit from the Prophet as follows:

> Five prayers have been made obligatory on mankind by God. He who fulfils them without neglecting or treating lightly any one of them, has a covenant with God that He will let him enter into Paradise.[11]

[10] Mālik, Vol. I, p. 175; Bukhārī, Vol. I, pp. 19-20; Muslim, Vol. I, pp. 166-68.
[11] Mālik, Vol. I, p. 123; Abū Dāwūd, Vol. II, p. 62.

The Duty of Prayer [the Performance of Which] the Book of God and the Sunna Indicate to Whom it Might Not Apply Owing to [a Valid] Excuse, and Against Him Whose Prayer Is Not Accredited Because of [Some Act of] Disobedience

113. God, Blessed and Most High, said:

> They will ask thee about menstruation; say: It is harmful; so withdraw from women in menstruation, and come not near them until they are clean; but when they have purified themselves, come to them as God has commanded you. Verily, God loves those who turn continually in penitence, and loves those who keep themselves pure [Q. II, 222].

Shāfiʿī said: By means of ablution and washing away pollution, God imposed [the duty of] purity on him who prays, so no prayer will be lawful save for him who is purified. When God mentioned menstruation, He commanded withdrawal from women until they are purified; when they are purified, they become lawful [to men]. We conclude that purification by water shall be performed after the end of menstruation, and that purity cannot be attained by a menstruating woman [merely] by the use of water, since water is always available in towns. But God mentioned purification [by water] only after [women] have become purified, which can be attained only at the ending of menstruation, as stated in the Book of God and the sunna of His Apostle.

Mālik [b. Anas] told us from ʿAbd al-Raḥmān b. al-Qāsim from his father from ʿĀ'isha, who related that she was menstruant during her visitation [of the Sacred Mosque] with the Prophet. So [the Prophet] ordered her to perform the duty in the same manner as a pilgrim " but do not circumambulate S118
[the Kaʿba] until you are purified."[12]

[12] Mālik, Vol. I, pp. 410-11; Bukhārī, Vol. I, pp. 393-94; Muslim, Vol. XIII, pp. 141-44. Cf. Shāfiʿī, *Kitāb al-Umm,* Vol. I, p. 51.

So we concluded that God meant that the performance of the duty of prayer is obligatory on those who have achieved purity by ablution and [complete] washing. Since menstruant women[13] cannot become purified by either [ablution or washing]—as menstruation is a natural occurrence beyond their free will to constitute disobedience—they are excused from prayer during menstruation and they need not make up for what they neglected after the end of their menstruation.

114. Shāfiʿī said:[14] By analogy with the menstruant women, we hold that he who is [either] unconscious or insane, whose mind has become sick by an order of God and not by his own fault, is excused from [the duty of] prayer; for he cannot comprehend it as long as his state makes him incapable of comprehension.

It is generally agreed among the scholars that the Prophet did not order menstruant [women] to perform the [duty of] prayer; but they are agreed that they should fast. We have therefore made a distinction between the two duties on the strength of
S119 the evidence I have just stated on the authority of the scholars and their agreement [on this matter].

Fasting must be distinguished from prayer in the case of the traveller, since he can postpone it until after the month of Ramaḍān, but to neglect the travel-prayer is not permitted for a single day. Fasting is obligatory but one month in twelve, and is not obligatory in the other eleven months, but no man who is capable of prayer is excused from it.

115. [Shāfiʿī said]: God said:

> Draw not near to prayer when you are drunken until you know what you are saying, nor [when you are] polluted, unless you be travelling on the road, until you have washed yourselves [Q. IV, 46].

Some scholars have said: This communication was revealed before the one which prohibited the [drinking of] wine.[15]

[13] Singular in the Arabic text.
[14] Būlāq ed., p. 19.
[15] See Ṭabarī, *Tafsīr,* Vol. VIII, pp. 375-79.

The Qur'ān gives evidence (but God knows best) that the duty of prayer should not be performed until the drunkard can comprehend the things he recites, because the prohibition of prayer [to the drunkard] is stated first and then the person who is in a state of impurity (*junub*). So the scholars are agreed that he who is in a state of impurity shall not pray at all until he is S120 purified.[16]

Since the [performance of] prayer by the drunkard was prohibited before [the drinking of] wine was prohibited, [the performance of prayer by] the drunkard would be more appropriately prohibited after wine was prohibited, for [the drunkard] would be doubly disobedient: First, because he prays in a state [of drunkenness] which was prohibited, and secondly because he drinks wine.[17]

Prayer [must be performed] by word and deed and by abstention [from forbidden acts]. If [he who prays] cannot comprehend the words, the deed, and the abstention, and cannot perform the prayer as ordered, [the duty] is not fulfilled and he must make up for it after he recovers.

He who is insane by God's order and who is in a state beyond the control of his free will must be distinguished from him who is a drunkard, since the latter has himself caused the drunkenness and must make up for it, while he who is insane did not inflict upon himself the disability which caused him to be disobedient.

116. [Shāfiʿī] said:[18] God has commanded the Apostle to turn in the direction of Jerusalem in prayer. Before this direction was abrogated it was not permitted to turn in any other direction. But it was abrogated and [the Apostle] was ordered to turn in the direction of the [Sacred] House: It became unlawful S121 in accordance with a textual command to turn either in the direction of Jerusalem or to any other direction than that of the Sacred House.

[16] Only by a major ablution (*ghusl*) can the state of impurity (*junub*) be transformed into a state of purity. See Shāfiʿī, *Kitāb al-Umm*, Vol. I, p. 33.

[17] See Abū Jaʿfar al-Naḥḥās, pp. 39 ff.

[18] Būlāq ed., p. 19.

117. [Shāfiʿī said: Each [direction] was valid in its time: The turning toward Jerusalem—when God ordered His Prophet to
B19 turn to it—was obligatory; but after it was abrogated it became obligatory to turn only toward the Sacred House, and no other direction is permitted by law, except in the event of fear [of danger] or in a supererogatory prayer in travel as indicated in the Book and the sunna.

The same applies to whatever God has abrogated, for the [word] abrogate means to repeal His command, [the obedience
S122 to] which was right in its time, but its repeal rendered its abandonment right, [too]. He who was aware that [God's] command was abrogated must obey the [new] command and abandon the abrogated one, but he who is not aware of it should continue to obey the abrogated duty. For God said to His Prophet:

> We may see thee turning thy face about toward the heaven. So We shall put thee in possession of a *qibla* that will satisfy thee. Turn thy face in the direction of the Sacred Mosque, and wherever you may be, turn your faces in its direction [Q. II, 144].

118. Someone may ask: Where does the evidence lie [in this communication] that [men] have been ordered to change [the direction] from one *qibla* to another.

119. [Shāfiʿī replied]: It is in God's saying:

> The fools among the people will say: ' What has turned them from the *qibla* which they have been observing?' Say: To God belongs the East and the West; He guideth whom He willeth to a straight path [Q. II, 142].

S123 Mālik [b. Anas] told us from ʿAbd-Allāh b. Dīnār from ʿAbd-Allāh b. ʿUmar, who said:

> When men were [performing] the dawn prayer in [the Mosque of] Qubā',[19] a messenger arrived and said: Quranic communication was

[19] Qubā', situated on the outskirts of Madīna, was the residence of the tribe of the Banū ʿAmr b. ʿAwf, among whom the Prophet passed a few days after he migrated to Madīna (1/622) before he moved into the town. A mosque known by the name of this place was erected later where the Prophet and his followers prayed. See Ibn Hishām, Vol. I, pp. 317, 333; Guillaume's translation, pp. 215, 226-27.

revealed to the Prophet last night by virtue of which he was ordered to turn toward the *qibla* [the direction of the Kaʿba]. So while they were [praying] in the direction of al-Shā'm, they [immediately] turned their faces toward the Kaʿba.[20]

Mālik [b. Anas] told us from Yaḥya b. Saʿīd from Saʿīd b. al-Musayyib, who said: [After he migrated to Madīna], the
Prophet prayed for sixteen months in the direction of Jerusalem S124
ere the *qibla* was changed two months before [the battle of] Badr.[21]

120. [Shāfiʿī] said: The evidence of the Book concerning prayer in a state of fear may be found in God's saying:

> If you fear [danger], pray either on foot or mounted [Q. II, 239].

So it is not permissible in accordance with the text [of the
Book] to pray when mounted unless one is in fear [of danger]; S125
but [in such a case] God did not mention the *qibla*.

Concerning prayer in [a state of] fear, [ʿAbd-Allāh] Ibn ʿUmar related from the Prophet a tradition in which he said:

> In the event there is a serious fear [of danger] you may pray on foot or mounted, regardless of the direction of the *qibla*.[22]

The Apostle prayed supererogatory prayers while riding his camel, facing the direction in which she was travelling.

[20] Mālik, Vol. I, p. 195; Bukhārī, Vol. I, p. 113; Muslim, Vol. V, p. 10; Shawkānī, *Nayl al-Awṭār* (Cairo, 1952), Vol. II, p. 172. The change of the *qibla* from Jerusalem to Makka, as the traditions indicate, was the result of the Prophet's quarrel with Jews. At first, it seems, he prayed toward Jerusalem because of the veneration in which he saw it was held by the Jews. It was also his desire to convert the Jews or reach an agreement with them. Failing to achieve either conversion or a lasting alliance, he decided to break with them. The change of the *qibla*, the first manifestation of this decision, meant that Muḥammad wanted to substitute Makka for Jerusalem as the center of his world. For the events leading up to the change of the *qibla*, see Ibn Saʿd, *Ṭabaqāt*, eds. Eugen Mittwoch and Edward Sachau (Leiden, 1905-40), Vol. I, pp. 241-44; Ṭabarī, *Taʾrīkh*, Series I, pp. 1279-81; al-Maqrīzī, *Kitāb Imtāʿ al-Asmāʿ*, ed. A. M. Shākir (Cairo, 1941), Vol. I, pp. 59-60.

[21] Mālik, Vol. I, p. 196; Bukhārī, Vol. I, p. 112; Muslim, Vol. V, p. 10.

[22] Mālik, Vol. I, p. 184; Bukhārī, Vol. III, p. 209; Shawkānī, *Nayl al-Awṭār*, Vol. II, pp. 176-77. Cf. Shāfiʿī, *Kitāb al-Umm*, Vol. I, 197.

This [tradition] was transmitted by Jābir b. ʿAbd-Allāh, Anas b. Mālik and others.[23] [The Prophet, however], never performed the required prayer while travelling except on the ground and in the direction of the *qibla*.

Ibn Abī Fudayk told us from Ibn Abī Dhi'b from ʿUthmān b. ʿAbd-Allāh b. Surāqa from Jābir b. ʿAbd-Allāh, who said:

> S126 During the campaign of the Banū Anmār[24] the Prophet, mounted on his camel, prayed in the direction of the east.[25]

121. Shāfiʿī said:[26] God said:

> O thou prophet, stir up the believers to fight: If there be twenty of you who endure, they will overcome two hundred, and if there be a hundred of you, they will overcome a thousand of those who have disbelieved, because they are a people who do not understand [Q. VIII, 65].

He [God] then declared in His Book that He relieved them of the obligation calling for one believer to fight ten [unbelievers] and confirmed the one which imposed the obligation that one believer should fight two unbelievers in accordance with His saying:

> Now God has made it lighter for you and knows that there is weakness in you. So if there be a hundred of you who endure, they will overcome two hundred, and if there be a thousand of you, they will overcome two thousand, by the permission of God. God is with those who endure [Q. VIII, 66].

Sufyān [b. ʿUyayna] told us from ʿAmr b. Dīnār from Ibn ʿAbbās, who said:

[23] Bukhārī, Vol. I, p. 279; Ibn Ḥajar, *Bulūgh al-Marām,* ed. R. M. Riḍwān (Cairo, 1954), p. 25; cf. Shawkānī, *Nayl al-Awṭār,* Vol. II, pp. 177-78.

[24] This was an abortive campaign (A. H. 4/A. C. 626), for when the news reached the Prophet that the Banū Anmār b. Baghīḍ and the Banū Saʿd b. Thaʿlaba b. Dhubyān b. Baghīḍ were preparing for war in Najd, an expedition, headed by the Prophet, proceeded to the east but found that the enemy had already left. It was during this campaign that the Prophet prayed, mounted on his camel, in the direction of the east. For an account of this campaign, see al-Maqrīzī, Vol. I, pp. 188-89.

[25] Cf. Shāfiʿī, *Kitāb al-Umm,* Vol. I, p. 84.

[26] Būlāq ed., p. 20.

> When the divine communication: ' If there be twenty of you who endure, they will overcome two hundred' was revealed, it became obligatory upon the twenty [believers] never to retreat [in battle] before two hundred [unbelievers]; and when God revealed: ' Now God has made it lighter for you and knows that there is weakness in you—If there were twenty of you, etc.'—it became obligatory on a hundred [believers] never to retreat before two hundred [unbelievers].[27] S127

[Shāfiʿī] said: This is in conformity with the opinion of Ibn ʿAbbās. But God made this so clear in [His] communications that it needs no explanation.[28]

122. [Shāfiʿī said]: God said:

> Those of your women who commit indecency—seek four witnesses against them, and if they testify, confine them to their houses until death takes them or God appoints for them a way out. And when two of you commit [indecency] punish them both; but if they repent and reform, then desist from them. Verily God always has been relenting, compassionate [Q. IV, 15-16]. S128

God, however, abrogated [the penalty of] confinement and the inflicting of harm [by another communication] in which He said:

> The fornicatress and the fornicator—scourge each of them with a hundred stripes [Q. XXIV, 2].

Thus the sunna specified that the scourging of a hundred stripes should be [inflicted] on the unmarried fornicators.

ʿAbd al-Wahhāb [b. ʿAbd al-Majīd al-Thaqafī] told us from Yūnus b. ʿUbayd from al-Ḥasan from ʿUbāda b. al-Ṣāmit that the Apostle said:

> Take it from me [repeated twice], God has decided on a way [for their punishment]: For [the fornication of] the unmarried couple [the penalty] shall be scourging with a hundred stripes and banishment

[27] Cf. Shāfiʿī, *Kitāb al-Umm,* Vol. IV, p. 92; and Ṭabarī, *Tafsīr,* Vol. XIV, pp. 50-58.

[28] Shāfiʿī, *Kitāb al-Umm,* Vol. IV, p. 92.

for a year; for [the adultery of] the married couple, scourging with a hundred stripes and stoning [to death].[29]

S129 We are told by the trusted authority[30] from Yūnus b. ʿUbayd
S130 from al-Ḥasan from Ḥiṭṭān al-Raqāshī from ʿUbāda b. al-Ṣāmit
from the Prophet a similar [tradition].

123. [Shāfiʿī] said: The sunna of the Apostle specified that the penalty of scourging with a hundred stripes for [fornication on the part of the] free unmarried couple was confirmed, but that it was abrogated concerning the married; and that the penalty of stoning for [adultery on the part of the] free married couple was confirmed.[31] For when the Apostle's ruling: ["Take
S131 it from me, etc."] was laid down, it abrogated the [penalty of]
B20 banishment and scourging for the adulterers.

Since the Prophet ordered the stoning of Māʿiz [b. Mālik al-Aslamī] rather than scourging him, and he ordered Unays [b. al-Ḍaḥḥāk al-Aslamī] to inquire from the wife of Aslamī and to stone her if she confessed adultery—this [precedent] indicated that the scourging of the free married adulterers was abrogated and that [the penalty of] stoning was confirmed, since this was
S132 a later decision [which superseded an earlier one].[32]

But the Book of God and the sunna of the Prophet indicate that slave-adulterers are excluded from this [punishment].

Concerning slave-women, God, Blessed and Most High, said:

[29] Abū Dāwūd, Vol. IV, p. 144; Abū Jaʿfar al-Naḥḥās, p. 97; Ibn Ḥajar, *Bulūgh al-Marām,* p. 153; Shāfiʿī, *Kitāb al-Umm,* Vol. VI, p. 119, and Vol. VII, p. 252 (margin).

[30] It is held, on the authority of al-Rabīʿ al-Murādī, that Shāfiʿī applied the term "trusted authority" to Yaḥya b. Ḥassān (see Bayhaqī, *Manāqib,* folio 278); but it is obvious that in this instance the trusted authority must be someone else, since Yūnus was born in 144/761 after Ḥassān had died in 139/756.

[31] There is in the Būlāq edition part of a tradition cited by Shāfiʿī in the following paragraph which adds nothing but verbal changes. This addition, as Shākir has pointed out, is spurious. See *al-Risāla,* Shākir's ed., p. 131, n. 3.

[32] Cf. Shāfiʿī, *Kitāb Ikhtilāf al-Ḥadīth* (*Umm*, Vol. VII, p. 251). Shāfiʿī's citation of the name of the wife of "Aslamī" is perhaps an error, as other ḥadīth digests do not cite the name of the woman. Traditions indicate that Māʿiz confessed in the presence of the Prophet four times to his having intercourse with the woman and the Prophet ordered him to be stoned to death. See Abū Dāwūd, Vol. IV, pp. 145-51; and Shawkānī, *Nayl al-Awṭār,* Vol. VII, pp. 100-106. Cf. Mālik, Vol. II, pp. 820-21.

> If, then, having been taken under *iḥṣān*,[33] they commit an indecency, they shall be subject to half the punishment to which those under *iḥṣān* are subject [Q. IV, 25],

It is evident that half [the punishment] cannot be executed except in scourging—which it is possible to divide—while stoning, which leads to death, cannot be halved, for he [who S133
is subject] to stoning might die either by the first stone cast on him or by a thousand or more. So it is impossible [to determine] what half [of the punishment] is. The [limit of such] penalties is specified by the destruction of life, and the destruction of life is dependent on the number of strokes and the size of the stones. Obviously no half of such a limit can be determined.[34] S134

124. Shāfiʿī said:[35] The Apostle of God said:

> If it is proved that the slave-women of any one of you has committed adultery, she should be scourged.[36]

But [The Prophet] did not say that she should be stoned. Nor did the Muslims differ on [the dictum that] slaves who commit adultery are not subject to stoning.

The taking of a slave-woman under *iḥṣān* is performed by accepting Islam. We hold this [opinion] on the strength of the evidence of the sunna and the agreement of the majority of the scholars.

Since the Apostle decreed: "If the slave-woman of any one of you, etc." without stipulating: "Whether she was taken under *iḥṣān* or not," we concluded that God's saying concerning slave-women [which runs as follows]: "If then, having been taken under *iḥṣān*, they commit an indecency, they shall be subject to half the punishment to which those under *iḥṣān* are subject," [Q. IV, 25], must mean: If they [the slave-women] S135
have become Muslims, not that if they were taken as wives

[33] For the meaning of this term, see paragraph 83, n. 44, above.

[34] Cf. Shāfiʿī, *Kitāb al-Umm,* Vol. VI, pp. 75, 122, for slight verbal changes. These changes may have been made by copiers. See Shākir's edition of the *Risāla,* pp. 134-35, notes 2-3.

[35] Būlāq ed., p. 21.

[36] Cf. Mālik, Vol. II, pp. 826-27, for a different wording.

and the intercourse were performed in marriage, nor if they were freed although the intercourse was not performed [in marriage].[37]

125. Someone may ask: Does it not appear that you give *iḥṣān* a variety of meanings?

126. [Shāfiʿī] replied: Yes, for the aggregate meaning of *iḥṣān* is that there should be a bar against forbidden acts. Islam may be one of them;[38] freedom [from slavery] is another; the taking [of the woman] as a wife and the performance of intercourse [through marriage] are still others; and finally detainment in the house. [As a rule] anything that may prevent [indecency] constitutes *iḥṣān*. For God said:

> We taught him the making of garments for you to protect you from each other's violence [Q. XXI, 80].

And He said:

> They will not fight against you all together, except in fortified towns [Q. LIX, 14].

[The term fortified] means protected [towns].

127. [Shāfiʿī] said: The first and the last part [of the
S136 communication] indicate that the meaning of *iḥṣān*—which is stated in general [terms] in [this] place, not in others—is Islam, not intercourse or freedom or confinement or chastity. These are the various [possible] meanings of *iḥṣān*.

[37] For the meaning of *iḥṣān* in this communication, see Ṭabarī, *Tafsīr*, Vol. VIII, pp. 195-202.

[38] I. e., a bar against one of the forbidden acts.

The Abrogating and Abrogated [*Communications*] *Which Are Indicated by the Sunna and Consensus*

128. [Shāfiʿī said]: God, Blessed and Most High, said:

> Prescribed for you, when death draws nigh to one of you, and he leaves behind some property, is the making of a testament in favor of his parents and relatives who are reputable—an obligation on the God-fearing [Q. II, 180].

And He said:

> And those of you who die, leaving wives, let them make testament for their wives, provision for a year without expulsion; but if they
> go forth, there is no fault in you what they may do with themselves S137
> honorably. God is All-Mighty; All-Wise [Q. II, 240].

Thus God provided [legislation] for the inheritance of parents as well as for near relatives whether together with them or as successors, and for the inheritance of the husband from his wife and the wife from her husband.

The two [foregoing] communications may be interpreted either to confirm bequests for the parents and the near relatives, bequest for the wife, and inheritance together with bequests, so that inheritance and bequests are lawful; or that [the legislation concerning] inheritance abrogates [that concerning] bequests.[39]

Since both interpretations are possible, as we pointed out, it is obligatory upon the learned to find an evidence in the Book
of God [as to which of the two is valid]; if nothing is found S138
in the text of the Book of God they should try the sunna of the Apostle. If such an evidence is found, it should be accepted from the Apostle, as [if] accepted from God by virtue of God's command to obey His [Apostle].

We have found that those learned in legal interpretation and the authorities in the campaigns [of the Prophet]—whether from

[39] Cf. Ṭabarī, *Tafsīr*, Vol. III, pp. 384-96; V, pp. 250-62.

[the tribe of] Quraysh or other [tribes]—are agreed that in the year of the capture [of Makka (8/630)] the Prophet said:

> No bequest to a successor [is valid], nor shall a believer be slain for [the blood of] an unbeliever.[40]

B21 This tradition has been transmitted from those who have heard it from the authorities on the [Prophet's] campaigns. So this is a transmission by the public from the public and is therefore of greater authority than the transmission of one [individual] from another. Further, we have found that the scholars are agreed [on the acceptance of this tradition].

129. [Shāfiʿī] said: Some of the Syrian [transmitters] have related [this] tradition [with an *isnād* or authorities] which those who are learned in traditions do not confirm, because
S139 some of the transmitters are unknown.[41] So we have related this tradition [directly] from the Prophet as an interrupted [tradition].[42]

We have accepted this tradition, as I pointed out, on the authority of those learned in the [Prophet's] campaigns and the agreement of the public, just as we have already related it on the authority of all those who are learned in the campaigns and the agreement of the public. [For] Sufyān [b. ʿUyayna] told us from Sulaymān al-Aḥwal from Mujāhid that the Apostle said: "No
S140 bequest to a successor [is valid]."[43]

We have concluded that the Prophet's ruling: "No bequest for a successor [is valid]," as I have stated, [means] that [the legislation on] inheritance has abrogated that on bequests for the parents and the wife, on the strength of the information related by those learned in matters concerning the [Prophet's]

[40] Abū Dāwūd, Vol. III, p. 113; Shawkānī, *Nayl al-Awṭār,* Vol. VI, p. 43; Shāfiʿī, *Kitāb al-Umm,* Vol. IV, pp. 27, 36, 40.

[41] I. e., this tradition, well-known to those learned in traditions in the Ḥijāz, was related without the names of the transmitters; but it was related by Syrian authorities with the names of the transmitters.

[42] An interrupted tradition is a tradition reported without the full chain of transmitters.

[43] See Shāfiʿī, *Musnad,* Vol. II, p. 189; and note 40, above.

campaigns, interrupted traditions from the Prophet, and the agreement of the public.

A great number of the public also have held that the [legislation concerning] bequests for relatives was abrogated and is no longer obligatory; for whenever they are entitled to inherit, they are so by virtue of the [law of] inheritance; but S141-142
when they are not entitled to inherit, it is not obligatory that they should inherit by a bequest.

Ṭāwūs [b. Kaysān] and a few other [authorities], however, held that the [legislation concerning] bequests for parents has been abrogated, though it was confirmed for relatives not entitled to inherit. So it is not permissible for him who bequeaths to do so [to persons] other than relatives.

Since it is possible to maintain with Ṭāwūs that [the legislation] affecting relatives is [still] valid—in as much as the tradition transmitted by the authorities on [the Prophet's] campaigns merely states that the Prophet said: " No bequest for a successor [is valid]," it is deemed obligatory upon scholars to seek an evidence either in support or against Ṭāwūs's opinion.

We have found that the Apostle made a decision [concerning] six slaves owned by a man who possessed no other property and who had set them free at the time of his death. The Prophet divided them into three groups, freeing two [slaves] and leaving four in slavery. This [tradition] had been related to us by ʿAbd S143
al-Wahhāb [al-Thaqafī] from Ayyūb al-Sakhtiyānī from Abī Qilāba from Abī al-Muhallab from ʿImrān b. Ḥusayn from the Prophet.[44]

130. [Shāfiʿī] said: Thus the indication of the sunna, as provided in the tradition of ʿImrān b. Ḥusayn, is that the Prophet's decree to free [the slaves] at the time of death constitutes a bequest. Since the person who freed the slaves was S144
an Arab—and the Arabs own foreign [slaves] with whom they had no blood relationship—the Prophet allowed a bequest to them to be valid. This [precedent] indicates that if a bequest

[44] Abū Dāwūd, Vol. IV, p. 28; Shāfiʿī, *Kitāb al-Umm,* Vol. IV, pp. 24, 27; Vol. VII, pp. 370-71 (margin).

in favor of persons other than relatives were void, it would be void concerning the freed slaves [too], as they were not blood relatives of [the man] who set them free.

It also indicates that the bequest of the deceased cannot exceed one third of his estate; that what exceeds one third is illegal; that bequests in favor of freeing slaves [already] earning money for their freedom (*istisʿā'*)[45] are void; and that [the choosing of two freed slaves out of six] by dividing them [into three groups] is confirmed [on the basis of] the casting of lots.[46]

Bequests to parents are no longer valid, since their [right to] inheritance as successors is confirmed. A bequest made by a deceased [person] to anyone—if he is not a successor—is valid. It is commendable—in my opinion—if [the deceased] leaves a bequest to his relatives.

131. Shāfiʿī said:[47] There are in the Qur'ān other [examples] concerning abrogating and abrogated [legislation], which may be found in their [proper] places, in the *Kitāb Aḥkām al-Qur'ān*.[48] I have discussed only some of the general principles on the strength of which the meaning of other examples may be sought. I am satisfied that these examples suffice for others hitherto not dealt with. May I ask God [for His] protection [from error] and for success [in following the right]. I have dealt
S145 with the duties imposed by God, the general and the specified, together with the sunna of the Apostle, so that those who have

[45] This term is applied to the slave who is partially freed provided he pays out of his labor the price of the remaining portion in slavery.

[46] On the strength of a tradition related by ʿImrān b. Ḥusayn the Ḥanafī school permitted *istisʿā'*, on the ground that the freeing of one third of the six slaves means that one third of each one of them can be freed and the remaining two thirds might be freed by *istisʿā'*. Thus the Ḥanafī school does not permit dividing the slaves into three categories or the casting of lots in determining such division. The Shāfiʿī school, however, rejects this interpretation and holds that the meaning of the tradition is clear, that the Prophet permitted the freedom of only two slaves out of six (constituting one third of the bequest), and that his division of the six into three groups meant that he permitted such a division and, finally, that his choice constitutes the casting of lots. For this reason *istisʿā'* is rejected, and the division into categories and the casting of lots were accepted.

[47] Būlāq ed., p. 22.

[48] Shāfiʿī, *Kitāb Aḥkām al-Qur'ān,* Vol. I, pp. 149 ff.

knowledge of the Book will know the place in which God has placed His Prophet in relation to His Book, His religion, and the followers of His religion. They will also know that to obey his orders means to obey God, and that his sunna is in conformity with what God revealed in His Book and that it is not contradictory to it at all. And he who comprehends this book knows that [God's] declaration is of various forms—not just one—, the common feature of which is that to the learned it is either clear or vague; but to those lacking in [legal] knowledge, the declaration varies in vagueness [in accordance S146
with their degree of comprehension].

Chapter VII

[ON DUTIES]

The Duties Laid Down in the Text [of the Qur'ān]

132. God, Glorious be His Praise, said:

> Those who accuse women under *iḥṣān* [of unchastity] and do not then bring forward four witnesses, scourge them with eighty stripes, and do not ever accept any testimony of theirs again; they are the
> B22 ungodly [Q. XXIV, 4].

Shāfiʿī said: The women under *iḥṣān* in question are those who are freewomen and have come of age. This indicates that *iḥṣān* is a collective term covering a variety of meanings.[1] [God] said:

> Those who accuse their wives and have no witnesses except themselves—let one of them testify by God four times, that he is of those who speak the truth. And a fifth time, that the curse of God shall be upon him, if he should be of the liars. It shall avert the punishment from her if she testify by God four times that he is of the
> S147 liars. And a fifth time, that the wrath of God shall be upon her, if he should be of the truthful [Q. XXIV, 6-9].

Since God has distinguished between the ruling [relating to the accusation] of the husband and [the ruling relating to] any

[1] According to Ibn Qutayba, the woman under *iḥṣān* is a free and mature woman, in possession of her faculties and who has had sexual intercourse in a legal marriage. See Ibn Qutayba, *Kitāb Ta'wīl Mushkil al-Qur'ān*, ed. Aḥmad Ṣaqr (Cairo, 1373/1954), p. 391. See also paragraph 83, n. 44.

one who may accuse other [than the husband]—punishing the one other than the husband, unless he produces four witnesses in support of his accusation, and excluding the husband from punishment by virtue of the *liʿān*[2]—this indicates that those who accuse women under *iḥṣān*, who are subject to scourging [as a punishment], are those who accuse free and mature women, not wives.

This is [another] example of what I have already explained that the Qur'ān [was revealed] in Arabic and that some of its communications are explicitly general, intended to have particular [meaning], not that one of the two communications meant to abrogate the other but that each is valid in the manner indicated by God. So a distinction should be made between the two [communications] in the manner God made the distinction and the two be joined together in the manner He united them.

So, if *liʿān* were invoked, the husband would not be punished, just as a party [in a dispute] is acquitted by witnesses; if he refuses to invoke the *liʿān*, he shall be punished if his wife is a free woman and mature of age.

133. [Shāfiʿī] said: The communication concerning *liʿān* was revealed in connection with [the case of ʿUwaymir] al-ʿAjlānī and his wife and the Prophet executed the procedure of the *liʿān* between them. This [precedent of] *liʿān* was related by Sahl b. Saʿd al Sāʿidī and Ibn ʿAbbās; but neither Ibn ʿUmar, **S148**
who witnessed its execution, nor the others related the [actual] words pronounced by the Prophet on the *liʿān*.

These [authorities] related [other] decisions taken by the Apostle, not to be found in the Qur'ān, such as the cancellation [of the marriage contract] between the two parties in the *liʿān*, voiding [the blood relationship of] the child [to the accusing father], and his pronouncement: "If [the mother] gives birth to the child and it possesses [the physiognomy] indicated [by the accusing father], it belongs to the accused person." So if

[2] *Liʿān* is an oath by virtue of which a husband may accuse his wife—without evidence—of adultery without becoming liable to punishment under *qadhf* by stoning. The marriage is dissolved and the husband can deny the paternity of the child borne by the wife.

the child proves to possess after birth similar resemblances [to the accused person], he [the Prophet] said: "the child's status is clear [that it belongs to him who is accused], for has not God laid down the rule [in the Qur'ān]," [that such a case must be decided by *liʿān*, i. e., the cancellation of the marriage contract and the voiding of the blood-relationship of the child].[3] Ibn ʿAbbās [also] related that the Prophet, [on hearing the oath of accusation repeated for the fifth time], said: "Stop him [the husband], for this means punishment [for the wife]."[4]

134. Shāfiʿī said:[5] We conclude that [the authorities] do not relate certain needed portions of the tradition and relate others, for had they known the portion concerning how the Prophet executed the *liʿān* [between husband and wife] they
S149 would have related it. They only knew that whoever was versed in the Book of God knew that the Prophet executed the *liʿān* in accordance with God's communication. They [the authorities] were merely satisfied with what God provided for *liʿān*, such as the number of oaths and that both could bear witness [as stated in Q. XXIV, 6-9] without citing the Apostle's decision on how he executed the *liʿān* [between husband and wife].

135. Shāfiʿī said: There are in the Book of God fully adequate [communications] concerning *liʿān* and the number of oaths; but some [of the authorities] have related [traditions] from the Prophet concerning the cancellation [of the marriage contract between the two parties in the *liʿān*] as I have already
S150 said. Such traditions from the Apostle, which are in agreement with the Book of God, have already been discussed.[6]

[3] See Shāfiʿī, *Kitāb al-Umm,* Vol. V, p. 114; and *Kitāb Ikhtilāf al-Ḥadīth* (margin of the *Kitāb al-Umm,* Vol. VII, pp. 305-306).

[4] Should the husband pronounce a fifth oath, beyond the number necessary for *liʿān*, his accusation of adultery, if not counter-acted by the wife, would entail punishment of the wife by stoning to death. If the husband's fifth oath were false, he would be punished by fire after death for a false oath. See Shāfiʿī, *Kitāb al-Umm,* Vol. V, p. 111.

[5] Būlāq ed., p. 23.

[6] See Shāfiʿī, *Kitāb al-Umm,* Vol. V, pp. 110-22.

136. God said:

> Fasting is prescribed for you as it was for those before you; perhaps you will show piety. A certain number of days [Q. II, 183-184].

And He specified the month by saying:

> The month of Ramaḍān, in which the Qur'ān was sent down as guidance for the people and as evidences of the guidance and Furqān; so whoever of you is present during the month let him fast in it; but if anyone is sick or on a journey [let him fast] a number of other days. God desires ease for you, and desires not hardship for you; and [it is] in order that you may complete the [full] number of [days], and that you may magnify God for the guidance He hath given you; perhaps you will be thankful [Q. II, 185].

Shāfiʿī said: I have known of no authority who related a
tradition from the Prophet specifying that the month for fasting **S151-157**
was the month of Ramaḍān—which falls between Shaʿban and Shawwāl—owing to certainty as to the place of Ramaḍān among the other months; for men have been satisfied that God imposed the duty.

They [men] have obligated themselves to observe fasting during travel, and when they may break it, and they knew how to make up for this duty as well as others on which there is no explicit text in the Book [of God]. Nor have I known anyone besides the scholars who needed [to know] which month was Ramaḍān or whether [fasting in this month] was obligatory. The same may be said about other prescribed duties: That [men] must perform the prayer, [pay] the alms and—for those who can manage it—perform the Pilgrimage; that adultery, homicide, and similar acts are forbidden.

137. [Shāfiʿī] said: Certain traditions have come from the Apostle on these matters for which there are no specific texts in the Qur'ān, but the Apostle has specified on God's behalf
the meaning intended by Him, while the Muslims provided a **S158**
number of derivative rules on which the Apostle laid down no specific sunna.

For instance, concerning the man who divorces his wife by pronouncing the third declaration [of divorce],[7] God said:

> If he divorces her, she shall not be lawful to him after that, until she marries another husband. If he divorces her, then it is no fault for them to return to each other [Q. II, 230].

God's saying: "Until she marries another husband" may mean either until she [formally] marries another husband—this was the meaning accepted by those to whom the communication was addressed and she was regarded as married once the marriage contract was concluded—or until she [actually] had intercourse with another husband, for the term *nikāḥ* may include both intercourse and the marriage contract.[8] So when the Apostle once said to a divorced woman, whose divorce was pronounced three times by her husband and who was then married to another man: "You will not be lawful [to your first husband] until you have tasted the sweetness [of the second husband] and he has tasted yours,"[9] he meant that she
S159 must have intercourse with another husband, and that *nikāḥ* [includes] intercourse.

138. Someone may ask: Will you cite a tradition from the Apostle in support of your statement?

139. [Shāfiʿī] replied: Sufyān [b. ʿUyayna] told us from Ibn
B23 Shihāb [al-Zuhrī] from ʿUrwa [b. al-Zubayr] from ʿĀ'isha, who said:

> S160 The wife of Rifāʿa [al-Quraẓī] once came to the Prophet and said: 'Rifāʿa has divorced me [complete divorce] and ʿAbd al-Raḥmān b. al-Zabīr married me, but [the latter's organ] is as limp as cloth's nap.' 'Do you want to go back to Rifāʿa?' asked the Apostle, [and

[7] Būlāq ed., p. 23.

[8] Literally *nikāḥ* means intercourse, but the legal meaning is marriage contract, which may or may not include intercourse. See Jurjānī, p. 167; and al-Muṭarrazī, Vol. II, p. 229. For the meaning of *nikāḥ* in the Quranic communication, see Ṭabarī, *Tafsīr,* Vol. IV, pp. 385-590; Bukhārī, Vol. III, p. 463.

[9] The figurative meaning of the word *ʿusayla* is used in the Arabic text. See Lane, *Lexicon,* p. 2046.

he stipulated]: ' No, not until you taste his sweetness and he tastes yours.'[10]

140. Shāfiʿī said: So the Apostle made it clear that God made her lawful to the husband who pronounced her divorced thrice [only] after another marriage [was consummated] with *nikāḥ*, that is, if the *nikāḥ* was followed by intercourse with the other husband.

[*Quranic*] *Duties for Which the Apostle Provided Sunna*

141. God, Blessed and Most High, said:

> When you stand up to pray, wash your faces, and your hands up to the elbows, and wipe your heads, and your feet up to the ankles. If you are polluted, purify yourselves [Q. V, 6]. S161

And He said:

> Do not perform the prayer... when you are polluted—unless you are travellers on the road—until you wash yourselves [Q. IV, 43].

So [God] made it clear that cleanliness from *junub* (pollution) must be performed by complete washing (*ghusl*), not by ablution.[11]

142. Shāfiʿī said:[12] The Apostle laid down sunna for ablution in conformity with God's communication: So he [the Prophet] washed his face, and his hands to the elbows; wiped his head; and washed his feet up to the ankles. [For] ʿAbd al-ʿAzīz b. Muḥammad [al-Darāwardī] told us from Zayd b. Aslam from ʿAṭā' b. Yasār from Ibn ʿAbbās from the Prophet that the latter performed the ablution [by washing] each limb once.[13]

[10] Bukhārī, Vol. III, p. 4-77; Abū Dāwūd, *Sunan*, Vol. II, p. 294. See also Shāfiʿī, *Kitāb al-Umm*, Vol. V, p. 229; Vol. VII, p. 314 (margin); and Ṭabarī, *Tafsīr*, Vol. IV, pp. 590-96.

[11] See Ṭabarī, *Tafsīr*, Vol. VIII, pp. 379-84; Vol. X, p. 82.

[12] Būlāq ed., p. 24.

[13] Bukhārī, Vol. I, p. 47; Abū Dāwūd, Vol. I, p. 34; Tirmidhī, *Sunan*, ed. A. M. Shākir (Cairo, 1356/1937), Vol. I, p. 60; Shāfiʿī, *Kitāb al-Umm*, Vol. I, p. 27.

Mālik [b. Anas] told us from ʿAmr b. Yaḥya [al-Māzinī] from
his father who asked ʿAbd-Allāh b. Zayd, the grandfather of
ʿAmr b. Yaḥya, "Are you able to show me how the Apostle
performed ablution?" "Yes," replied ʿAbd-Allāh b. Zayd, and
he asked for water. He poured it over his hands and washed
twice; he rinsed [his mouth] and sniffed [water into his nose]
S162 thrice; he washed his face thrice, and washed his hands up to
the elbows twice [each time], and wiped his head with his hands
moving them from the front and brought them back—he began
with his forehead until he carried them to his neck, then he
brought them back to the place from which he had started—
S163 and [finally] he washed his feet.[14]

The literal [meaning] of God's saying: "Wash your faces" is that the minimum requirement for washing is once [each time], but it may [also] mean more [than once]. So the Apostle decreed that ablution must be performed by washing once [each time], in conformity with the literal [meaning] of the Qur'ān. This is the minimum requirement for washing,[15] but it may mean more than once since [the Prophet] performed it twice and three times.

Since [the Prophet] washed once [also], we have concluded
that if once does not fulfil [the duty], he would not have
S164 performed it once before prayer. More than one ablution is
[therefore] optional—not obligatory—and that less than that,
[i. e., once] does not fulfil [the duty].

This is in conformity with what I have already said concerning other duties, namely that if the traditions were lacking, the Book would be satisfactory without them; but if traditions were found about them, they indicate that they should be in conformity with the Book of God.

143. [Shāfiʿī said]: It may be that the authorities have related traditions to indicate that although the Apostle ordinarily performed the ablution three times, they were intended to be optional, not obligatory, so that the performance of less than

[14] Mālik, Vol. I, p. 18; Bukhārī, Vol. I, pp. 59-60; Shāfiʿī, *Kitāb al-Umm.* Vol. I, pp. 23, 27.

[15] Būlāq ed., p. 24.

that number would not be regarded as failure to fulfil the duty. However, since certain traditions specify that "he who performs the ablution thrice before prayer—and performing a two-cycle prayer twice—without any distracting thought [mixed with the prayer], his [sins] would be forgiven," [men] desired to increase the [number of] ablutions, but such increase is supererogatory.

In the performance of ablution, the Apostle washed his [hands] including the elbows, and [the feet] including the ankles. The [Quranic] communication [concerning washing] may either mean washing including [the elbows and ankles] or washing without them. It was perhaps for clarifying the meanings of this [communication] that the [two] traditions were related. The
one closest to the literal meaning of the divine communication S165
specifies that [the elbows and ankles] should be [included] in the washing. For this [washing] is made clear in the sunna as well as in the Qur'ān. But though this as well as the other [declarations] in the Qur'ān are clear enough to the scholars, to others the clarity in both is not the same.

The Apostle laid down a sunna that washing to free one's self from pollution includes the washing of the genital organs, the ablution—like the ablution before prayer—and the complete washing (*ghusl*). We recommend that [his example] be followed.

I know of no scholar from whom I have learned who has disagreed that any washing should be satisfactory, provided that it is complete, although men prefer otherwise [i. e., ablution and complete washing]. For [the Qur'ān] prescribes washing [only] without any specifications as in the case of ablution.

The Apostle laid down sunnas regulating [the circumstances that call for] ablution, and the [kinds of] pollution which must be washed away, for such matters have not been dealt with in
the Book [of God]. S166

[Quranic] Duties Which the Sunna Specified are Intended to Be Particular

144. God, Blessed and Most High, said:

> They will ask thee for a pronouncement. Say: God pronounces to you concerning the indirect heirs. If a man perishes and has no children, but he has a sister, she shall receive a half of what he leaves and he is her heir if she has no children [Q. IV, 176].

And He said:

> To the men belongs a share of what parents and near relatives leave,
> B24 and to the women belongs a share of what parents and near relatives
> leave, whether it be little or much, a share prescribed [Q. IV, 7].

And He said:

> And to his parents, to each one of the two belongs a sixth of what he
> leaves, if he has children; but if he has no children and his heirs are
> his parents, a third to his mother, or, if he has brothers, to his mother
> a sixth, after any bequests he may bequeath or any debts [have been
> S167 paid]. As to your fathers or your sons you do not know which of
> them is the most advantageous to you. So God apportions; verily,
> God is All-Knowing, All-Wise.
>
> A half of what your wives leave belongs to you, if they have no children; but if they have children, a fourth of what they leave belongs to you after any bequests they may bequeath or debts [have been paid] [Q. IV, 11-12].

And He said:

> To them belongs a fourth of what you leave, if you have no children; but if you have children, an eighth of what you have belongs to them, after any bequest you may bequeath or debts [have been paid] [Q. IV, 12].

The sunna [merely] specified what God has provided for those who are eligible to inherit: Brothers, sisters, children, and the near relatives, parents, spouses, and all those who are eligible

to inherit in accordance with [the text of] the Book, provided that the legator and the legatee [either] profess the same religion [i. e., Islam] and belong to the people of the lands of Muslims[16] or are [non-Muslims] in treaty relations with Muslims [by virtue of which] their lives and property are secured.[17] If they are polytheists, they are eligible to inherit in accordance with their [own law of] polytheism. For Sufyān [b. ʿUyayna] told us from S168
al-Zuhrī from ʿAlī b. Ḥusayn from ʿAmr b. ʿUthmān from Usāma b. Zayd who related that the Apostle said: "The Muslim cannot inherit from a non-Muslim, nor the non-Muslim from the Muslim."[18] S169

Furthermore, the legator and the legatee must be freemen and Muslims. [For] Ibn ʿUyayna told us from Ibn Shihāb [al- Zuhrī] from Sālim [b. ʿAbd-Allāh] from his father that the Apostle said: "He who sells a slave possessing property, the property belongs to the seller unless the buyer stipulated otherwise."[19]

145. [Shāfiʿī] said: It is evident in the sunna of the Apostle that the slave cannot own property, that what he owns belongs to his master, and that ascribing to him title to property—which may be [found] in his hands—merely means that it is added to him [as an additional property], and not that he possesses it, for [the slave] cannot be an owner [so long as] he is incapable of possession, rather he himself is possessed; he may be sold, given in gift, or bequeathed [as a chattel]. For God [made lawful] the transfer of the property of the dead to the living who can own what the dead had owned. So if the slave S170
were to inherit property whether as a father or in any other capacity his share of the inheritance would be owned by his

[16] Dār al-Muslimīn or Dār al-Islām is the territory of Islam. It may be defined, broadly speaking, as the territory whose inhabitants observe Islamic law, or, strictly speaking, the territory under Islamic rule. See M. Khadduri, *War and Peace in the Law of Islam,* pp. 155-57.

[17] Non-Muslims who accepted Muslim rule by virtue of a treaty or a charter are called *ahl al-dhimma* or scriptuaries. See *ibid.,* Chap. 17.

[18] Mālik, Vol. II, p. 519; Muslim, Vol. XI, pp. 51-52; Abū Dāwūd, Vol. III, p. 125; Shāfiʿī, *Kitāb al-Umm,* Vol. IV, pp. 2-3; and Shāfiʿī, *Musnad,* Vol. II, p. 190.

[19] Abū Dāwūd, Vol. III, p. 268; Ibn Ḥanbal, Vol. I, pp. 305-306; Shāfiʿī, *Kitāb al-Umm,* Vol. IV, p. 3.

master on his behalf, [even though] the master is neither the father of the deceased nor an heir entitled to a share in the inheritance. So if the slave were given the right of inheritance as a father, it means the master will have the right of inheritance and we would have given such a right [to a person] to whom God has not given it. For that reason, as I have pointed out, we do not favor giving [the right of] inheritance to the slave, nor to any one who is not in possession of freedom and [the faith of] Islam and who is not devoid of homicidal intent so that he is not regarded as a criminal. For Mālik [b. Anas] related from Yaḥya b. Saʿīd from ʿAmr b. Shuʿayb that the Apostle said: "He who kills [another] cannot inherit [from him]."[20]

146. Shāfiʿī said:[21] So we hold that he who kills [another]
S171 will not inherit from him. For the minimum [penalty] for a killer with a criminal intent is to deprive him of [the right of] inheritance, since he is disobedient to God and incurs His displeasure. There is no disagreement among the learned whom I have known, whether in this country or in another, that the Muslim cannot inherit from another unless he is a freeman and clear of criminal intent. Their agreement—on what I have just stated—is a binding evidence on them that they should never disagree on any of the sunna of the Apostle. For if the sunna on matters for which there are textual communications has the same place as these communications, and is as binding [on men] as the Qur'ān, it indicates that for whatever else the sunna
S172 provided—for which there are no divine communications—it should be as binding [as the Qur'ān]. The scholars should be the last to have doubts as to its binding force, and should know that God's commands and those of His Apostle are not contradictory, but follow the same pattern. [For] God, Blessed and Most High, said:

> Do not consume your property among you in vanity, although there be trading by mutual consent on your part [Q. IV, 29].

[20] Mālik, Vol. II, p. 867; Ibn Ḥanbal, Vol. I, pp. 305-306.
[21] Būlāq ed., p. 25.

147. [Shāfiʿī said]:[22] And He said:

> That is for their having said: Sale is just the same as usury, though God hath permitted sale and forbidden usury [Q. II, 275],

Moreover, the Apostle prohibited certain [kinds of] sale, mutually agreed upon among partners—which become unlawful—such as [the exchange of] gold for gold except in equal quantities, and gold for silver, whether in cash or credit,[23] or whatever S173
is implied in their meaning provided the exchange involves [neither] risk nor the concealment of anything [concerning the sale] from the buyer by the vendor.

So the sunna indicated that God made lawful sales [of every kind] which are not forbidden, except those which He has forbidden through His Prophet's tongue.

Moreover, the Apostle provided sunna for other [kinds of] sale, such as the following: S174

1. [If] a slave is sold with a defect concealed by the vendor [in order] to deceive the purchaser, the latter has the right to return [the slave] and keep any profits [arising from the slave's employment].[24]
2. If a person sells a slave who possesses property, the property belongs to the vendor unless stipulated otherwise [in the contract of sale].[25]
3. If a person sells a pollinated palm tree, the fruits belong to the vendor unless stipulated otherwise [in the contract of sale].[26]

These [traditions] are binding on men for God imposed the S175
obligation that they should obey [the Prophet's] order. B25

[22] *Ibid.*

[23] *Nasī'a* literally means deferred payment.

[24] Abū Dāwūd, Vol. III, p. 284.

[25] Mālik, Vol. II, p. 611; Bukhārī, Vol. II, p. 81; Shāfiʿī, *al-Musnad,* Vol. II, p. 148; and *Kitāb Ikhtilāf al-Ḥadīth* (margin of *Kitāb al-Umm,* Vol. VII, p. 332); Ibn Qutayba, *Kitāb Ta'wīl Mukhtalaf al-Ḥadīth,* p. 286.

[26] Mālik, Vol. II, p. 617; Bukhārī, Vol. II, p. 35; Muslim, Vol. X, pp. 190-92.

General Duties: *[Prayer]*

148. God, Blessed and Most High, said:

Verily prayer has become for the believers a thing prescribed [to take place at] stipulated times [Q. IV, 103].

And He said:

Observe the prayer and pay the *zakāt* (legal alms) [Q. II, 43, 77, 104 etc.].

And He said to His Prophet:

Take of their wealth a *ṣadaqa* (free-will alms)[27] to cleanse and purify them thereby and pray for them [Q. IX, 103].

And He said:

Pilgrimage to the House is a duty to God from the people, whoever is able to make his way there [Q. III, 98].

God has laid down in the Qur'ān the duties of prayer, *zakāt* and pilgrimage and specified the modes [of their performances]
S176 through His Prophet's tongue.

So the Apostle specified that prayers [each day] shall number five; that the number of cycles[28] in the noon, *ʿaṣr*[29] and the evening prayers shall number four repeated twice in the towns; and that cycles at the sunset prayer shall number three, and at the dawn prayer two.

[27] Shāfiʿī seems to use *zakāt* and *ṣadaqa* interchangeably, although the two are not strictly speaking synonymous terms. *Ṣadaqa*, a free-will alms, may be called a poor-rate. Thus *ṣadaqa* is included in the *zakāt*, but the latter is imposed for broader purposes of state, including expenditure for military operations. See G. H. Bousquet and J. Schacht, *Selected Works of C. Snouck Hurgronje* (Leiden, 1957), Chap. 3 on *zakāt*.

[28] The *rakʿa* (cycle) include standing, bowing, prostration and sitting. See Edwin E. Calverley, *Worship in Islam* (London, 1958), p. 72, n. 1.

[29] *ʿAṣr* is the mid-afternoon.

He decreed that in all [the prayers] there should be recitals from [the Qur'ān], audible in the sunset, evening, and dawn prayers, and silent recitals in the noon and ʿ*aṣr* prayers.

He specified that at the beginning of every prayer there shall be the *takbīr* [declaration that God is great] and at the ending the *taslīm* [salutations on the Prophet and his house] and that each [prayer] consists of the *takbīr*, the recital, the bowing, and two prostrations after each inclination, but beyond these nothing is obligatory.

He decreed that prayer while one is on a journey can be shorter—if the traveller so desires—in the three performances that have four cycles, but he made no change in the sunset and dawn prayers when the prayer is performed in town. However, all prayers must be [performed] in the direction of the *qibla* [facing Makka], whether one is in town or on a journey, except
in the case of prayer of fear.[30] S177

He decreed that supererogatory [prayers] must be performed in the same manner; They are unlawful without the purification or the recital or any other requirements for obligatory [prayers] such as the bowings, prostrations and the *qibla* whether performed in the towns or in the country or on the ground during travel. In a supererogatory prayer, however, the rider may pray in any direction that his animal may be moving. [For] Ibn Abī Fudayk told us from Ibn Abī Dhi'b from ʿUthmān b. ʿAbd-Allāh b. Surāqa from Jābir b. ʿAbd-Allāh that in the campaign against the Banū Anmār the Apostle was [seen] praying while riding his camel toward the east.[31] A similar tradition was transmitted by Muslim [b. Khālid al-Zanjī] from Ibn Jurayj from Abū Zubayr from Jābir; but I do not know whether the name of the Banū Anmār was mentioned or
whether the tradition [merely] stated that [the Prophet] prayed S178
during travel.[32]

The Apostle also decreed that in the feast- and rain-prayers the number of bowings and prostrations must be the same;

[30] Prayer of fear may be performed in case of a threat or an attack in war. See Shāfiʿī, *Kitāb al-Umm,* Vol. I, pp. 83-84.

[31] See paragraph 120, above.

[32] Cf. Shāfiʿī, *Kitāb al-Umm,* Vol. I, p. 84.

but he added a cycle to the eclipse-prayer, raising the number [of bowings and prostrations] in each cycle to two. So we are told by Mālik [b. Anas] from Yaḥya b. Saʿīd from ʿAmra [daughter of ʿAbd al-Raḥmān] from ʿĀ'isha from the Prophet. The same [tradition] was related by Mālik [b. Anas] from Hishām from his father from ʿĀ'isha from the Prophet; and from Mālik b. Anas from Zayd b. Aslam from ʿAṭā' b. Yasār from Ibn ʿAbbās from the Prophet. The wording of the Prophet's prayer, related by ʿĀ'isha and Ibn ʿAbbās, may be somewhat different, but all are agreed that [he
S179 performed] the eclipse-prayer in two cycles, each one [repeated] twice.[33]

Concerning prayer, God said:

> Verily the prayer has become for the believers a thing prescribed for stated times [Q. IV, 103].

The Apostle specified on God's behalf the time [of each prayer]. He performed [each] prayer at its specified time, except that when he was besieged in the battle of al-Aḥzāb[34] he could not [perform each] prayer on time for that reason; so he delayed [the prayers] until [he was able to perform] the noon, the ʿ*aṣr*, the sunset, and the evening prayers at the same time.

Muḥammad b. Ismāʿīl b. Fudayk told us from Ibn Abī Dhi'b from al-Maqburī from ʿAbd al-Raḥmān b. Abī Saʿīd from his father who said:

> We were withheld from performing prayer during [the battle of] the Trench for a long while, till [late at] night, but when we were relieved
> S180 from fighting—as God said: ' God relieved the believers of fighting, for God is strong, and mighty' [Q. XXXIII, 25]—the Apostle ordered

[33] Mālik, Vol. I, pp. 186-88; Bukhārī, Vol. I, pp. 264-65; Shāfiʿī, *Kitāb al-Umm,* Vol. I, pp. 214-15.

[34] The battle of al-Aḥzāb or al-Khandaq (The Trench) was waged by the Makkans (the Confederates) against the Prophet in 5/627 to revenge their defeat at Uḥud the year before. This battle figures in the Qur'ān, XXXIII, 9-27, under the name of al-Aḥzāb and in the Arab annals as al-Khandaq. See Ibn Hishām, Vol. II, pp. 669 ff.; Guillaume's translation, pp. 450 ff.

Bilāl[35] [to call believers to prayer], and they performed the noon-prayer as fully as if it were at its time, and then performed the *ʿaṣr*, the sunset and the evening prayers in like manner. This [incident] took place before the communication concerning the fear-prayer was revealed, which runs as follows: ' If you fear [danger] pray either on foot or mounted!' [Q. II, 239].[36]

149. [Shāfiʿī] said: So Abū Saʿīd made it clear that [the practice of deferred prayers] preceded the communication to the Prophet concerning fear-prayer. The communication in which the fear-prayer is stated runs as follows:

> When thou art journeying in the land, there is no fault in you if you shorten the prayer, if you fear the unbelievers may molest you. Verily S181
> the unbelievers are for you a manifest enemy.
>
> When thou art amongst them and hast set up the prayer for them, let a party of them stand with thee, and let them take their weapons, and B26
> when they prostrate themselves, let them be behind you; and then let another party who have not prayed come and pray with thee, taking their precautions and their weapons [Q. IV, 101-102].

Mālik [b. Anas] told us from Yazīd b. Rūmān, from Ṣāliḥ b. Khawwāt from those who prayed with the Apostle the fear-prayer during the campaign of Dhāt al-Riqāʿ said:

> A company [of believers] stood in rank [for prayer] with [the Prophet] while another watched the enemy. He performed one cycle with those who stood with him and remained standing until the company completed [the prayer]. Having thus taken the position of those facing the enemy, another company stood [with the Prophet], who performed the other cycle and remained sitting while the S182
> company completed their prayer until he [uttered] the salutation with them.[37]

[35] Bilāl was the son of an Abyssinian slave-woman, whom the Prophet called "the first fruit of Abyssinia," and to this day he is known as the Prophet's *mu'azzin*, or the one who calls to prayer. See Ibn Hishām, Vol. I, p. 205; Vol. II, pp. 822, 917; Guillaume's translation, pp. 144, 554, 616.

[36] Ṭabarī, *Tafsīr,* Vol. XV, pp. 237-50; Shāfiʿī, *Kitāb al-Umm,* Vol. I, p. 75.

[37] Mālik, Vol. I, pp. 183-84; Bukhārī, Vol. III, pp. 100-102; Ṭabarī, *Tafsīr,* Vol. IX, pp. 141-62; Shāfiʿī, *Kitāb al-Umm,* Vol. I, p. 186.

The same tradition has been related by ʿAbd-Allāh b. ʿUmar b. Ḥafṣ from his brother ʿUbayd-Allāh b. ʿUmar from al-Qāsim b. Muḥammad from Ṣāliḥ b. Khawwāt from his father Khawwāt b. Jubayr from the Prophet.[38]

It is evident from these [traditions]—as I have already stated
S183 in this book—that whenever the Apostle laid down a sunna inspired by God in order to abandon or abrogate another, he laid it down as an evidence given to men that they should obey this sunna, not the earlier one.

So God abrogated [the communication concerning] the deferment of prayer in the event of fear and [replaced it] by another—as both God and His Prophet have laid it down—directing that it should be [performed] at its [specified] time. The Apostle abrogated his sunna concerning the deferment of this prayer in accordance with God's command by another sunna, and the Apostle [himself] performed this prayer at its specified
S184 time, as I already have pointed out. [For] Mālik [b. Anas] told us from Nāfiʿ from Ibn ʿUmar, who stated concerning fear-prayer that the Prophet said:

> If there is a serious fear [of danger], you may pray on foot or mounted regardless of the direction of the *qibla*.[39]

A similar tradition was related by a certain man on the
S185 authority of Ibn Abī Dhi'b, from al-Zuhrī from Sālim from his father from the Prophet.

150. [Shāfiʿī] said: So the sunna of the Apostle indicated, as I have already said, that [facing] the *qibla* is at all times obligatory except when it is impossible to perform the prayer in the specified direction, such as at the time of sword-play, flight [from battle], or equivalent situations in which it is impossible to pray in the direction [of the *qibla*].

Thus the sunna was confirmed that the prayer must not be deferred beyond its specified time, but that [it should be performed] in whatever direction the person is able to do it.

[38] Cf. Shāfiʿī, *Kitāb al-Umm*, Vol. I, pp. 186-87.

[39] Mālik, Vol. I, p. 184; Bukhārī, Vol. III, pp. 101, 209; Shāfiʿī, *Kitāb al-Umm*, Vol. I, p. 179.

The Zakāt (*Legal Alms*)

151. God said:

> Observe the prayer and pay the *zakāt* [Q. II, 43, 83, 110]. S186

And He said:

> And the observers of the prayer and the payers of the *zakāt* [Q. IV, 162].

And He said:

> So woe to those who pray, who of their prayer are careless, who make a show, but withhold charity [Q. CVII, 4-7].

Some of the scholars said: [These communications refer to] the duty of *zakāt*. God said:

> Take of their goods a freewill offering to cleanse and purify them thereby, and pray for them; thy prayers are comfort for them. God is All-Hearing, All-Knowing [Q. IX, 103].

The reference of this communication is to goods in general, but it may [also refer] to certain goods to the exclusion of others. So the sunna specified that the *zakāt* should be paid on some goods, not on all.

Since goods are of various categories—such as the cattle—the Apostle ordered the payment [of alms] on camels and sheep, S187
and indicated—as we are told—that it should be paid on cows in particular from among the cattle, and a certain percentage has been specified by God through His Prophet's tongue.[40] Since men possessed cattle consisting of horses, donkeys and mules and others which the Apostle exempted from payment—for he laid down the sunna that horses were exempt from alms—it

[40] The Prophet ordered Muʿādh b. Jabal, governor of al-Yaman, that the *zakāt* should be paid on cows: a calf for every thirty cows and one cow for every forty. See Shāfiʿī, *Kitāb al-Umm,* Vol. II, pp. 7-8; Shawkānī, *Nayl al-Awṭār,* Vol. IV, pp. 141-42; Abū Dāwūd, Vol. II, pp. 101-102; Ibn Ḥanbal, Vol. VI, p. 4.

is evident that alms must be paid only on what [the Prophet] specified, not on all.

As to men who possess sown and planted products such as
S188 palm-dates and grapes, the Apostle ordered payment of alms on both on [the basis of] a rough estimate [of the value of each tree]. The rate of payment was one-tenth [of the total value] if [the land] were watered by rain or from a spring and half of the one-tenth if it were watered by wells.[41]

Some of the scholars held by analogy to palm-trees and grapes that [alms] on olive trees [should be one-tenth as well].

Since men possess crops of varied produce other than palm-dates, grapes and olives, such as walnuts, almonds, figs, and others, which the Apostle has exempted from payment, we concluded that God imposed the payment of alms on some crops, but not on all.

152. Shāfiʿī said:[42] Men have produced wheat, barley, millet
B27 and similar products, on which, we are told, the Apostle ordered the payment [of alms]. By analogy of wheat and barley, alms have been paid on grain, suit [kind of barley],[43] *ʿalas* [kind of
S189 wheat],[44] rice, and all other products which men have produced and eaten, such as bread, *ʿaṣīda*, *sawīq*, *udm*,[45] chick-peas and *qaṭṭānī* [general term for lentils, etc.] which may be made into flour or bread, etc., in the same way as the Prophet ordered the
S190 payment of the alms on similar products which men produced for food.[46]

Men have produced other products on which neither the Apostle, nor those who succeeded him, ordered payment [of alms], for they do not fall in the category of products on
S191 which [the Prophet] imposed alms, such as *thufā'*, *asbiyūsh*,

[41] Abū Dāwūd, Vol. II, p. 108; Shawkānī, *Nayl al-Awṭār,* Vol. IV, pp. 149-50.

[42] Būlāq ed., p. 27.

[43] Suit is a species of barley, having no husk, which means either beardless or smooth. Lane, *Lexicon,* Part IV, p. 1401.

[44] *ʿAlas* is a certain kind of wheat, having two grains in one husk, and sometimes one grain or three. Lane, *Lexicon,* Part V, p. 2130.

[45] *ʿAṣīda*, *sawīq*, and *udm* are species of flour made into various kinds of moisted food. Lane, *Lexicon,* S. V.

[46] Shāfiʿī, *Kitāb al-Umm,* Vol. II, pp. 30-31.

kusbara [coriander], *ʿuṣfur*[47] and others. So these are [all] exempt from alms. This indicates that alms are [obligatory] on some products, but not on all.

153. Shāfiʿī said:[48] The Apostle ordered the payment of alms on silver, and the Muslims followed his precedent on gold, either [on the strength of] a narrative which was not transmitted to S192
us[49] or on [the strength of] analogy that gold and silver are measures of price which men used to hoard or pay in exchange for goods in various countries before the rise of Islam and after S193
it.

Men possess other [kinds of] metal such as brass, iron, and lead on which neither the Apostle nor those who succeeded him imposed alms. They are exempt on [the strength of] precedent and they should not, by analogy with gold and silver, be subject to alms, for gold and silver are used as standards for prices in all countries, and all other metals may be purchased by them on the basis of a specific weight at a certain time.

Although ruby and chrysolite are more precious than gold and silver, neither the Apostle nor those who succeeded him have imposed alms on them as far as we know. Since they are possessed by a special [class] and are not used as a medium of exchange—because they are not measures of price—they are S194
exempt [from alms].[50]

154. Shāfiʿī said:[51] According to what the public have related from the Apostle concerning the alms on the cattle and measures of price [i. e., gold and silver], he ordered its payment once a year. For God said:

> Give the due portion of it on the day of its harvesting [Q. VI, 141].

So the Prophet decreed the payment of alms on the produce of sowing and planting, in conformity with God's communication, at the time of the harvest, not at other times. And he specified

[47] Species of spices. See Lane, *Lexicon,* S. V.

[48] Būlāq ed., p. 28.

[49] See Mālik, Vol. I, pp. 246-47; Abū Dāwūd, Vol. II, pp. 100-101; Shāfiʿī, *Kitāb al-Umm,* Vol. II, p. 34.

[50] Mālik, Vol. I, pp. 250-51; Shāfiʿī, *Kitāb al-Umm,* Vol. II, 34-36.

[51] Būlāq ed., p. 28.

that [the alms] on *rikāz* [natural and hidden treasures] shall be
S195 one-fifth, to be paid on the day they are produced, not at other
times.[52] For Sufyān [b. ʿUyayna] told us from al-Zuhrī from
[Saʿīd] b. al-Musayyib and Abū Salāma from Abū Hurayra that
the Apostle said: "One-fifth [shall be paid] on *rikāz*."[53]

If it were not for the evidence of the sunna, all goods would
have been treated on an equal footing on [the basis of] the literal
S196 meaning of the Qur'ān, and the alms would have been imposed
on all, not on some only.

[*Pilgrimage*]

155. [Shāfiʿī said]: God imposed the duty of *al-ḥajj* (Pilgrimage) on all who can perform it.[54] It has been related from the Prophet that the means (*al-sabīl*) consists of the necessary provisions and transport (i. e., donkey or camel).[55] And he [the Prophet] specified the time of Pilgrimage, how to pronounce the formula of fulfilling [the duty],[56] and what is decreed [as recommended acts], and what should be avoided in the wearing of garments and the use of perfumes as well as other procedural matters [such as the halts] at the [sanctuary] of ʿArafa and the [passing of the night at] Muzdalifa, and the throwing [of the

[52] Shāfiʿī, *Kitāb al-Umm,* Vol. II, pp. 31-32.

[53] Mālik, Vol. I, pp. 249-50; Bukhārī, Vol. I, pp. 381-82; Ibn Ḥanbal, Vol. IV, pp. 312-13; Shawkānī, *Nayl al-Awṭār,* Vol. IV, pp. 156-58; Shāfiʿī, *Kitāb al-Umm,* Vol. II, pp. 37-38.

[54] Literally: "On all those who have the means" (*al-sabīl*). Cf. Q. III, 91: "It is the duty of all men toward God to come to the House of Pilgrims, if they are able to make their way there."

[55] In the *Kitāb al-Umm,* Vol. II, pp. 96-98, Shāfiʿī defines the capacity to fulfil the duty of *ḥajj* in broader terms, including physical fitness in addition to the availability of the means of transportation. See also Ṭabarī, *Tafsīr,* Vol. VII, pp. 37-46.

[56] The formula "*labbayk Allahumma*" is uttered by all pilgrims while performing the duty. See Ṭabarī, *al-Qira Li-Qāṣid Umm al-Qura* (Cairo, 1367/1948), pp. 141-48.

stones at Minā], the shaving [of the head], the circumambulation [of the Kaᶜba] and other matters.[57]

If someone was unaware that there was a sunna for matters on which there was a text in the Book of God except what I have already stated concerning the sunna laid down by the Apostle [specifying] the meaning implied in God's general communication, and that [the Prophet] merely explained God's S197
prescribed acts, prohibited or permitted that I have mentioned, and all other matters connected with them, including their time of fulfilment as well as other matters not dealt with [in God's communications], it became obligatory on men that if the sunna of the Apostle confirms [and explains] God's communication in one or more instances it shall do so always.

It is evident that the [Prophet's] sunna never contradicts the Book of God, and that his sunna—even in the absence of legislation in the Book—is binding, as I have already stated here and elsewhere, in accordance with God's command to obey His Apostle. [For] it is obligatory on men to know that God has not given any other [person] such power save His Apostle, and that the word and deed of every person should be in conformity with the Book of God and the sunna of His Apostle. And the words and deeds of every one should conform to the Book of God and the sunna of His Apostle, and that should the opinion of a certain scholar be contradictory to the sunna of the Apostle, S198
one should abandon that opinion when he becomes aware of the contradiction and should obey the sunna of the Prophet; for if one does not do so he is not excused. For what is more obligatory on men than that they should obey the Prophet, an obligation indicating the place in which [God] placed him in B28
relation to His revelations, His religion and the followers of His religion?

[57] For a general discussion on the performance of the *ḥajj* duty in Shāfiᶜī's law, see Shāfiᶜī, *Kitāb al-Umm,* Vol. II, pp. 93-112; and Muzanī, *al-Mukhtaṣar* (on margin of *Kitāb al-Umm),* Vol. II, pp. 39-46. For a detailed account of the *ḥajj*, see the work of a leading eleventh-century Shāfiᶜī jurist, Aḥmad Ibn ᶜAbd-Allāh Muḥibb al-Dīn al-Ṭabarī, *al-Qira Li-Qāṣid Umm al-Qura;* Bousquet and Schacht, *Selected Works of G. Snouck Hurgronje,* Chap. 4.

[*The* ʿIdda *or Waiting Period*]

156. God said:

> Those of you who die, leaving wives, let them keep to themselves for four months and ten days [Q. II, 234].

And He said:

> Divorced women shall keep to themselves for three periods [Q. II, 228].

And He said:

> For those of your women who have despaired of [further] menstru-
> S199 ation, if you are in doubt, their period of waiting shall be three months, as it is for those who have not menstruated as yet. For those who are pregnant, their term is when they are delivered of what they bear [Q. LXV, 4].

Some of the scholars said: Since God has obligated the woman whose husband dies to wait four months and ten [days], and has specified the period of waiting for the pregnant [woman] to last until she has been delivered, [it follows that] if the husband dies and the woman is pregnant she is bound by the two periods concurrently just as she would be bound to fulfil any other two duties combined together.[58]

157. [Shāfiʿī] said: But since the Apostle said to Subayʿa, daughter of al-Ḥārith, who gave birth to a child a few days after her husband's death: " You are lawful [for marriage] and you may get married," this indicates that the ʿ*idda*—whether in the case of death or divorce to be fulfilled by [the expiration of] the required months—was intended to [bind] women who are
S200 not pregnant; but if they are pregnant the ʿ*idda* is dropped.[59]

[58] This is the opinion of Ibn ʿAbbās and, perhaps, ʿAlī. See Shawkānī, *Nayl al-Awṭār,* Vol. VI, pp. 306-307.

[59] See Mālik, Vol. II, pp. 589-90, Abū Dāwūd, Vol. II, p. 293; Shāfiʿī, *Kitāb al-Umm,* Vol. II, pp. 205-206; Shawkānī, *Nayl al-Awṭār,* Vol. VI, p. 305.

[*Forbidden Women*]

158. God said:

> Forbidden to you are your mothers and daughters, your sisters, your aunts, paternal and maternal, your brother's daughters, your sister's daughters, your mothers who have given suck to you, your suckling sisters, your wives' mothers, your stepdaughters who are in your care being born of your wives you have been in to—but if you have not yet been in to them, it is no fault in you—and the spouses of your sons who are of your loins. And it is forbidden for you to take two sisters together, unless it be a thing of the past; God is All-Forgiving, All-Compassionate; and wedded women except what your right hand has possessed. So God prescribes for you. And it is lawful for you to seek what is beyond that by means of your wealth in wedlock and not in debauchery; those of them whom you enjoy thereby pay their hire as stipulated, and it is no fault in you in regard to anything you may give them by mutual agreement beyond the stipulated amount. Verily God is All-Knowing, All-Wise [Q. IV, 23-24].

This communication may have two meanings: [it may mean] that the women whom God has [specifically] forbidden shall be [regarded as] forbidden, and that those whom He has not S201
specifically forbidden, shall be lawful on the ground that He is [both] silent about them and by His saying: " And [it is] lawful for you to seek what is beyond that" [Q. IV, 24]. This may be regarded as the literal meaning of the communication.[60]

But it is evident in this communication that the prohibition concerning the taking of [the two sisters] together as wives must be distinguished from the prohibition of taking mothers [as wives]. So what God specified as lawful shall be lawful; what He specified as forbidden shall be forbidden; and what He prohibited concerning the taking of the two sisters together [as wives] shall be prohibited.

God's prohibition of the taking [of two sisters] as wives is an evidence that He has [merely] forbidden taking them together, but that taking each one separately is lawful in principle while S202

[60] See Ṭabarī, *Tafsīr,* Vol. VIII, pp. 141-79.

the taking of mothers, daughters, and paternal and maternal aunts is unlawful in principle.

The meaning implied in the communication: "And [it is] lawful for you to seek what is beyond that" is to specify those
S203 women who are in principle forbidden as well as others of equal status related by suckling—these can only be married in accordance with [the prerequisites of] lawful marriage.

159. Some one may ask: What is the evidence for that?

160. The answer is:[61] Since [the maximum number of] women who may lawfully be taken as wives is four, the taking of a fifth [would be unlawful] and the marriage contract would have to be dissolved. For no [woman] shall be lawful unless taken in accordance with a valid marriage contract. The taking of a fifth woman, like the taking of a single one, is lawful in accordance with God's saying: "And [it is] lawful for you what is beyond that," provided she is taken in a lawful manner and in circumstances making the marriage lawful and not forbidden in principle.

But marriage between a man and a woman will not, under any circumstances, forbid other marriages to her paternal or maternal aunts—as God has forbidden his marriage to the wives' mothers—so her paternal and maternal aunts may be
S204-205 included in the category of who may lawfully be married, Just as it is lawful for a man to marry another woman if one of his four wives is separated from him [by death or divorce], so the maternal aunt becomes lawful, if the daughter of her brother is separated [from her husband].[62]

[*Forbidden Food*]

161. God said to His Prophet:

> Say: I do not find, in what is revealed to me, anything forbidden to one who eats of it, unless it be a dead animal, or blood outpoured, or

[61] Būlāq ed., p. 29.

[62] For further discussion on forbidden women, see Shāfiʿī, *Kitāb al-Umm*, Vol. V, pp. 2-5.

the flesh of swine, for it is an abomination, or an impious thing over which the name of a god other than God has been invoked [Q. VI, 145].

This communication may have two meanings: First, that nothing is forbidden at all except what God has [specifically] excluded. This is the clearest and the broadest meaning and any one presented with it will understand at once that nothing is forbidden except what God has specifically forbidden. If it S206
means otherwise, the scholars are under obligation to accept no other meaning save what the sunna of the Prophet specifies and they should say: "This is the meaning intended by God, Blessed and Most High."

Nothing in the Book of God nor in the sunna [of His Prophet] is regarded as a particular [communication] unless there is a specific [evidence] in either one or in both, and nothing is regarded as particular unless the divine communication is intended to mean particular. So what is not intended to be a [particular] communication, must never be so regarded.

So God's saying: "Say: I do not find, in what is revealed to me, anything forbidden to one who eats of it..." may mean S207
that the Apostle was asked [to specify] a certain thing to the exclusion of others. And it may [also] mean [nothing forbidden] in what you were eating. This [may be] the appropriate meaning in accordance with the evidence of the sunna. For Sufyān [b. ʿUyayna] told us from Ibn Shihāb from Abū Idrīs al-Khawlānī from Abū Thaʿlaba [al-Khushnī] that the Prophet prohibited "the eating of beasts having fangs."[63] And Mālik [b. Anas] told us from Ismāʿīl b. Abī Ḥakīm from ʿAbīda b. Sufyān al-Haḍramī from Abū Hurayra from the Prophet B29
who said: "The eating of any of the beasts which have fangs S208
is forbidden."[64]

[63] Muslim, Vol. XIII, pp. 81-83; Abū Dāwūd, Vol. III, p. 355; Shawkānī, *Nayl al-Awṭār,* Vol. VIII, p. 120; Shāfiʿī, *Kitāb al-Umm,* Vol. II, p. 219.

[64] Mālik, Vol. II, p. 496.

[*Women's Abstention during the* ʿIdda *of Their Husbands' Death*]

162. God said:

> Those of you who die, leaving wives, let them keep to themselves for four months and ten [days]; when they reach the end of their term, then it is no fault in you what they may do with themselves honorably. God is aware of what you do [Q. II, 234].

So God specified that [women] who [suffer] the death [of their husbands] are under obligation of the *ʿidda* [four months and ten days] and that upon the expiration of the term they shall be free to do honorably with themselves whatever they may wish, but He mentioned nothing else to be avoided during the *ʿidda*.[65]

The literal meaning of the divine communication is that [the widow] should abstain only from getting married during the *ʿidda* and that she should stay in her house.

[The communication] may [also] mean that [the widow] should [not only] abstain from marriage, but also from certain
S209 other things which were not forbidden to her before the *ʿidda*, such as [the use of] perfume and [the wearing of] ornaments.

Since the Prophet decreed that the widow must abstain from the use of perfume and the like, she is under obligation to do so [by virtue] of the duty imposed by the sunna, but her abstention from marriage and her stay in the house of her [deceased] husband are [imposed on her] by the Book and the sunna.

The sunna's role here as elsewhere is [merely] to specify on God's behalf what [the widow] should abstain from doing, just
B30 as it specifies [the duties of] prayer, alms, and pilgrimage. The
S210 sunna [also] provides [rules] laid down by the Apostle [for matters] on which there is no divine communication.

[65] Shāfiʿī, *Kitāb al-Umm,* Vol. V, pp. 205-208; Ṭabarī, *Tafsīr,* Vol. V, pp. 77-94.

Chapter VIII

[ON THE NATURE OF GOD'S ORDERS OF PROHIBITION AND THE PROPHET'S ORDERS OF PROHIBITION][1]

163. He [the interlocutor] asked: Will you explain to me the sum-total of God's orders of prohibition and the Prophet's orders of prohibition generally, leaving nothing [unexplained]?

164. Shāfiʿī replied: [God's] orders of prohibition fall in two [categories] of meanings:

First, the act prohibited must be in itself unlawful, never to be lawful except by a particular indication laid down by God in His Book or [specified] by His Prophet's tongue. Thus if the Apostle prohibits a certain act it shall be regarded as unlawful, and no particular act is permitted unless it falls [in the category of] a certain meaning [of permission] as I have already explained.

165. He said: Explain to me this kind of prohibition which you have just stated by an example which indicates the like meaning. S343

166. [Shāfiʿī] replied: all women are forbidden [to men] except in one of two ways: Either by *nikāḥ* (marriage), or *waṭī'*

[1] This chapter has been moved from the latter part of the *Risāla* (see paragraphs 926-960 of Shākir's edition), because it deals with a broad jurisprudential subject. The heading is borrowed from Shāfiʿī's *Kitāb al-Umm* (Vol. VII, pp. 265-67) where the same subject is briefly discussed; cf. *Jumāʿ al-ʿIlm*, ed. Shākir (Cairo, 1359/1940), pp. 125-34.

(intercourse with a slave-woman) by virtue of possession. These are the two ways made lawful by God [in His Book]. The Apostle laid down in the sunna the modes in which the *nikāḥ* makes previously forbidden women lawful, [such as] the need for a guardian, [the testimony of] witnesses and the consent of the *thayyib* woman.[2] The Prophet's stipulation concerning the woman's consent is an evidence that [prior] consent of the [two] spouses is a prerequisite without distinction between them. Thus if the marriage [contract] fulfils four conditions—consent of the *thayyib* woman and the man, [presence of the] guardian who arranges the marriage for the woman, and the witnesses—it would be lawful, except in certain cases which I shall cite later. But if it lacks any one of the four conditions, it becomes *fāsid* (invalid), because it would not
S344 be in accordance with the sunna laid down by the Apostle for a valid marriage. If a *ṣadāq* (bride-price) were added [as an additional condition] it would be commendable; but the marriage [contract] would not be *fāsid* without it, for God's stipulations concerning marriage do not include *mahr* (dowry)[3] (This subject has been treated elsewhere).[4] These conditions are as equally [applicable] to honorable as to dishonorable women, for each one is equal to the other in all matters that are lawful and unlawful, obligatory or unobligatory, punishable or unpunishable.

167. Shāfiʿī said:[5] The circumstances in which marriage is permissible—in accordance with what I have described—are those in which marriage is not prohibited, for if marriage is made in accordance with the prohibited circumstances, it would be regarded as void by the orders laid down by God in His Book and by the Prophet's tongue. For example: [Marriage is void] if a man marries his wife's sister, because God prohibited the taking of two sisters as wives; or if a man takes a fifth woman as wife,

[2] The *thayyib* woman may either be a widow or a divorcee, or not a virgin. See Lane, *Lexicon*, p. 363.

[3] See Q. II, 237.

[4] See Shāfiʿī, *Kitāb al-Umm*, Vol. V, p. 51.

[5] Būlāq ed., p. 48. The statement " Shāfiʿī said" in the previous paragraph of Shākir's edition is omitted.

because God permitted only four [at a time] and the Prophet made it clear that God prohibited the taking of any additional S346 one; or if one marries his wife's aunt, paternal or maternal, since this is prohibited by the Prophet; or if one marries a woman during her *ʿidda*. All these marriages are not lawful, for they are all prohibited, and no disagreement exists among scholars about them. B48

168. Shāfiʿī said: In like manner the Prophet prohibited [such marriages as] *al-shighār*,[6] and *mutʿa*.[7] He [also] prohibited the pilgrim, [whether man or woman] from marrying or getting married [during the performance of Pilgrimage]. We hold that all such marriage [contracts] in the circumstances in which he [the Prophet] prohibited them, must be dissolved, just as other marriages which we have already cited must be dissolved. S347 Some [scholars] may disagree with us on this matter, but we have discussed this elsewhere.[8] Similarly, the marriage in which the woman is married without her prior consent [must be dissolved]. She may give her consent later—which is not permissible—but the contract was void at the time it was concluded.

Similarly the Apostle prohibited the *gharar* sale,[9] the sale of dry dates for ripe dates except the sale of *al-ʿarāya*,[10] and others.

[6] *Shighār* is a mode of marriage which existed in Arabia before Islam by virtue of which a person may marry the sister or daughter of another person, and the latter reciprocating in like manner, so that neither one will need to collect the *mahr* (dowry) from the other. For Shāfiʿī further treatment of the subject, See *Kitāb al-Umm*, Vol. V, pp. 68-69.

[7] *Mutʿa* is a form of temporary marriage; its period is fixed, and the contract is dissolved automatically at the end of the period. This form of marriage, practiced in Arabia before Islam as well as in the early Islamic period (Q. IV, 24), was later declared abolished. The contradictory traditions reflect the controversy among early jurists as to its validity until it was rejected by the Sunni schools. It is still valid in Shīʿī law. For Shāfiʿī's further treatment of the subject, see *Kitāb al-Umm*, Vol. V, pp. 71 f.; and J. Schacht, *Origins of Muhammadan Jurisprudence*, pp. 266-67.

[8] See Shāfiʿī, *Kitāb al-Umm*, Vol. V, pp. 68-72; and *Ikhtilāf al-Ḥadīth (Kitāb al-Umm*, Vol. VII, pp. 238-41, 254-57).

[9] The *gharar* is a kind of sale in which uncertainty is involved, such as the sale of fish or birds before they are actually caught or produced by the vendor. See Shāfiʿī, *Kitāb al-Umm*, Vol. III, p. 75.

[10] The *ʿarāya* sale, a transaction on dates, although permitted by the Prophet,

For in principle one's own property is forbidden to another save in a lawful manner and by [the kinds of lawful] sale the Apostle did not prohibit, but no sale prohibited by the Apostle which is unlawful in principle renders one's property lawful to another. Disobedience of a prohibition of sale does not make lawful what was unlawful, for in principle the unlawful will not
S348 become lawful except in acts which constitute no disobedience. These [examples] fall in the category of [legal] knowledge for the public.

169. Someone may ask: What is the kind of [orders of] permission that is prohibited to men [only] in specific cases and is different from the kind of [orders of] prohibition which you have just stated?

170. [Shāfiʿī replied]: It is like the Apostle's order of prohibition against wearing a single robe by a person who folds it on one side leaving uncovered a certain private area
S349 of his body while a lad is eating before him. [The Prophet] prohibited eating from the top of the dish; he is reported to have prohibited—although this is not certain—eating two dates together, exposing the inside of the date [prior to eating], and halting on the road for rest.[11] Since the wearing of the robe, the eating of food (as much as one desires), and [walking
S350 on] the earth (which belongs to God, and all men are equally entitled to use it) are all lawful acts, the Prophet's order of prohibition refers to particular acts which are different from those he permitted. For the [Prophet's] order of prohibition [is limited] only to the wearing of the robe if it were folded in such a way that it leaves uncovered a certain part—the *ʿawra* (private parts)—but if the *ʿawra* were covered by the
S351 cloth, the prohibition against uncovering the *ʿawra* should not include the wearing of the robe, since one can wear it without uncovering the *ʿawra*. [Similarly] the Prophet's orders against the [lad's] eating of the food [before an uncovered *ʿawra*] and eating from the top of the dish, which are permissible,

may be said to fall in the same category as the *muzābana* sale. See paragraphs 346-347, below.

[11] See Bukhārī, Vol. III, p. 507; Muslim, Vol. XIII, pp. 228-29; Abū Dāwūd, Vol. III, p. 362; Vol. IV, p. 256.

are merely orders of etiquette, for it is more appropriate on behalf of the host to observe them while eating with his table-companion, instead of eating voraciously. [The Prophet] prohibited eating from the top of the dish because God's blessing descends on the top and it should continue descending on it. So once he has eaten the food on the sides, it would be permissible to eat the top. If one is permitted to walk along a road, he does so because it is permissible [in principle], since nobody owns it, to forbid others from passing; but S352
the Prophet prohibited halting for a certain specific reason, for he said: "It is the shelter of insects and a passage for snakes," not because halting is unlawful. He also prohibited halting if the road were narrow and crowded, for if one halts [for rest] others' right of passing would be encroached upon.

171. Someone may ask: What is the difference between this [kind of prohibition] and the other?

172. [Shāfiʿī] replied: He to whom the proof is established [concerning the validity of these orders] must know that the Prophet prohibited [the acts] which I have just explained, and he who acts contrary to them, despite his awareness of them, would be regarded as disobedient and should ask God's forgiveness and never repeat them again.

173. He may ask: Such [a man] is disobedient, and since you have already called [the man who violates] the marriage and S353
sale [contracts] disobedient in this [your] book, on what ground have distinguished between the two?

174. [Shāfiʿī] replied: I made no distinction between the two on the ground of disobedience, since I have regarded both as disobedients, although certain acts of disobedience may be greater than others.

175. He may ask: On what ground have you not regarded as disobedient the man who wears the robe, eats from the top of the dish and halts on the road, while you regarded as disobedient the man who violates the marriage and sale [contracts]?

176. [Shāfiʿī] replied: The first has been ordered to obey an order of permission and has done so, so I have regarded as

lawful what was permitted and unlawful what was prohibited. His disobedience to what was permitted would not render it unlawful in all circumstances; but it prohibited him from committing an act of disobedience.

177. He asked: For example?

178. [Shāfiʿī] replied: A man having a wife and a slave-woman is prohibited from intercourse with them whenever they are menstruating or fasting; if he did, the intercourse would be unlawful. However, neither is forbidden in other circumstances,
S354 for they are in principle lawful to him.

179. Shāfiʿī said:[12] One's own property is forbidden in principle to be taken by another, except in a lawful manner which permits another to do so. [Similarly], women are forbidden to men except by marriage or ownership. So if
B48 one makes a marriage contract with a forbidden [woman] or enters into a sale transaction concerning forbidden [goods], such contracts would be invalid, for what is forbidden cannot become lawful by an unlawful act. The act which is in principle forbidden remains so unless there is a specific text in the Book or a sunna or consensus or the like [which make it lawful].

180. Shāfiʿī said:[13] I have already given examples of [the kind of] prohibitions which were not intended to be [on the same footing as those] unlawful orders [specified] by indications
S355 which I do not want to repeat here. May God protect us against
B50 error and grant us success.

[12] Būlāq ed., p. 49.
[13] Būlāq ed., p. 50.

Chapter IX

[ON TRADITIONS]

Defects in the Traditions

181. Shāfiʿī said: Someone has asked me: We find that among the traditions from the Apostle some are in conformity with the Qur'ān; others are in conformity only with the S210 general meaning of the Qur'ān; and [still] others provide either specifications additional to those of the Quranic text or legislation on matters on which the Qur'ān is silent.

Further, there are certain traditions which agree with one another, and others which are contradictory to one another; the abrogating and the abrogated traditions are clearly distinguished [in some of them]; in others the traditions which are abrogating and abrogated are not indicated.

There are [certain traditions], consisting of orders of prohibition by the Apostle, the obligation of which you have regarded as binding, while there are others, consisting equally of orders of prohibition, the obligation of which you have regarded as optional.

We have noted that you have accepted certain contradictory traditions but not others; and that you have applied analogical S211 deduction on the strength of some of them only. Your [method of] analogy, however, was discriminatory, for you have applied it in some [cases] but not in others. On what ground have you been applying analogy to some while abandoning it in the case of others? Furthermore, you have been disagreeing with other scholars—some of you have abandoned certain traditions in favor of others of equal or even weaker status.

182. Shāfiʿī said: I have replied as follows:

The sunna which the Apostle has laid down on matters for which a text is to be found in the Book of God is always in full agreement with that text and clarifying on God's behalf a general text; the [Apostle's] specification is more explicit than the text. But as for the sunna which he laid down on matters for which a text is not found in the Book of God, the obligation to accept them rests upon us by virtue of the duty imposed by God to obey the [Prophet's] orders. As to the abrogating and abrogated sunnas—like the abrogating communications laid down by God to abrogate orders—they are in like manner laid down by the Apostle so that each sunna may be abrogated by another. And I have given
S212 him [the interlocutor] other examples which I have already discussed in this book, in explanation of what I have just described.

As to contradictory traditions where no indications exist to specify which is the abrogating and the abrogated, they are all in accord with one another and contradiction does not really exist among them. [For] the Apostle of God, being an Arab by tongue and by country, may have laid down a general rule intended to be general and another general rule intended to be particular, as I have already pointed out in my discussion on the Book of God and the sunna of His Apostle. Or a certain question may have been asked to which he gave a certain concise answer, leading some of the transmitters to relate the tradition in detail and others in brief, rendering the meaning of the tradition partly clear and partly vague. Or [it may happen] that the transmitter of a certain tradition related the answer he heard [from the Prophet] without knowing what the question had been, for [had he known] the question he would have understood the
S213 answer clearly from the reasoning on which the answer was based.

He [the Prophet] may have likewise laid down a sunna

covering a particular situation and another covering a different one, but some of those who [related what they] heard failed to distinguish between the two differing situations for which he had laid down the sunnas. And he may have laid down a sunna on a certain matter in conformity with the text [of the Qur'ān]—transmitted by one authority—and another in one form in agreement with the text and in another contradictory to it—owing to changes in the circumstances—transmitted by another authority. Hence the transmission by one authority appeared to many as contradictory to the other, while [in reality] no contradiction existed at all. He may have also provided a sunna consisting of an order of permission or prohibition the wording of which was general, and he may have provided a second specifying sunna which made evident that his order of prohibition was not intended to prohibit what he made lawful, nor that his order of permission made lawful what he had prohibited. For all possibilities of this kind parallel examples exist in the Book of God, which we have already described [in this book].

[Whenever] a certain sunna was abrogated by another [the Prophet] never failed to indicate in the abrogating sunna what he had intended to abrogate. If certain transmitters have **S214**
overlooked some information concerning the abrogating and **B30**
abrogated sunnas, [at least] one must have transmitted what the others did not, so that information concerning abrogations was never entirely lacking.

All such matters, as I have already explained, were accepted in accordance with what the sunna laid down and [men] knew how to distinguish between the sunna in the same way that [the Prophet] did, for obedience to his ruling distinguishing the sunnas one from the other was obligatory and no one had ever questioned that [the Prophet] did distinguish between one sunna and another. For if anyone says that the Prophet made no distinction between one [sunna] and another he would be ignorant [of what the Prophet said] or, what is worse, doubtful **S215**
of it. Surely, obedience to God [imposes the duty] of obedience to [the Prophet's orders].

The contradictory sunna is due either to incomplete transmission rendering it contradictory, as I have explained before, although what was lacking can be known from other [traditions], or it is the product of the transmitter's imagination. No contradictory tradition [from the Prophet] is known to us for which a possible explanation is lacking or the category to which it belongs is not known, as I have already pointed out.

We may find [the answer], on the other hand, by the indication as to which of the contradictory traditions is the most reliable; for if two contradictory traditions exist, they cannot possess equal validity and only the reliable or authentic tradition should be accepted. The evidence as to which tradition is authentic may be found either in the Book of God or in the Prophet's sunna, on the strength of which we accept the tradition for which the strongest evidence exist. However, we have known of no two contradictory traditions for which we could find neither explanation nor evidence as to which is
S216 the authentic one, [either on the ground of] its conformity with the Book or with other traditions or any other kind of evidence.[1]

Hence whatever the Apostle has prohibited is unlawful unless an evidence is found specifying that [his prohibition] was not intended to condemn the matter as unlawful.

Finally, [Shāfiʿī] said, analogy [on the basis] of the sunna falls into two categories, each subdivided into various forms.

183. He [the interlocutor] asked: What are they?

184. [Shāfiʿī] replied: God has imposed the obligation of obedience upon men through His Book and His Prophet's tongue, in accordance with the obligation of obedience set forth in His established judgment that men shall obey His will without challenge to His command.[2] The Apostle specified the meaning of what God made obligatory [in the tradition] or

[1] For a discussion on this subject, see Ibn Qutayba al-Dīnawarī, *Kitāb Ta'wīl Mukhtalaf al-Ḥadīth* (Cairo, 1326/1909).

[2] " *Lā muʿaqqib li ḥukmih,*" a Quranic expression (Q. XIII, 41) which Shāfiʿī borrows, has been differently translated by different writers, Cf. Richard Bell, *The Qur'ān,* Vol. I, p. 234; and A. J. Arberry, *The Koran Interpreted* (London, 1955) , Vol. I, p. 272.

in any narrative transmitted from him so that nothing is left unexplained and the scholars are under obligation to regard this narrative [as authentic] as other traditions if it expresses the identical meaning.[3] This [category of traditions] is subdivided S217 into many forms.

The second category of traditions consists of a general order of permission qualified by a particular order of prohibition. Men should regard [all acts under] the general order of permission as lawful and [the specific act under] the particular order of prohibition as unlawful. But in so doing they should not apply analogy to a particular order of prohibition, for the general rule is that an order of permission and analogy must be applied ordinarily on the general, not on the particular rule. The same [rule] must apply if the general order is one of prohibition and the particular order is one of permission, or if [God] imposes a [general] duty and the Apostle qualified it by a permission that is particular. Thus analogy is valid to us [only] S218 on the evidence of the Book, the sunna and precedents.

To have given an opinion contrary to an authentic tradition from the Apostle is something, I hope, for which I shall never be reproached. Nor has anyone the right to give such an opinion. However, a man ignorant of a certain tradition may give an opinion contrary to it by oversight or by a wrong interpretation, without having intended to do so.

185. [Shāfiʿī] said: Someone may ask me: Give me an example for each of the categories you have described, embodying in a concise statement[4] all that I have inquired about, beginning with the abrogating and abrogated sunnas of the Prophet, citing some of it together with the Qur'ān, even though you may be repeating some of what you have already S219 discussed.

186. [Shāfiʿī] replied: God ordered His Apostle to turn in prayer first toward Jerusalem. So Jerusalem became the *qibla* and as long as the Apostle faced that direction, to face any other was unlawful. But ever since God abrogated the *qibla* toward

[3] Būlāq ed., p. 34.
[4] Literally: "Avoiding a detailed treatment that I might forget."

Jerusalem and ordered the Apostle and men to turn toward the Kaᶜba, the latter became obligatory in accordance with the text [of the Book] and no other *qibla* should be faced, save in case of fear [of danger]. It became absolutely unlawful to turn toward Jerusalem. Each [*qibla*] was valid in its time: Jerusalem from the time when the Prophet turned toward it until he was ordered to change, and the Sacred House [Kaᶜba] from thence forward until the Day of Resurrection. All the other abrogated [communications], whether in the Book of God or the sunna, have in like manner been laid down.

187. [Shāfiᶜī] said: Such [a process of] abrogation is an evidence that whenever the Prophet laid down a sunna which
B31 God ordered him to revise, he laid down another sunna which men were ordered to obey in place of the earlier one so that they
S220 would no longer obey the abrogated sunna. Thus no one, except those unversed in the Arab tongue and in the [legal] knowledge concerning the place of the sunna in its relation to the Book (that it specified the meaning of the Book), should ever suppose [from the internal evidence of the sunna] that the Book abrogates the sunna.[5]

188. He asked: Would it be possible for the sunna to contradict the Book [of God]?

189. [Shāfiᶜī] replied: Impossible! For God, glorified be His praise, imposed on men the obligation [of obedience to the law] through two avenues—the origin of both is in the Book—His Book and the sunna: [The latter is binding by virtue of] the duty of obedience laid down in the Book that it should be followed. So it was not permissible for the Apostle to allow the sunna to be abrogated [by the Book], without [the Apostle himself] providing another sunna to abrogate it. The
S221 abrogating sunna is known because it is the later one, while most of the abrogating [communications] of the Book can be known only by [indications provided in] the Sunna of the Apostle.

So if the sunna [itself] indicates what the abrogating [communications] of the Book are and distinguishes between the

[5] See Chap. VI, above.

abrogating and the abrogated, it cannot be abrogated by the Qur'ān unless the Apostle himself provides another sunna—in conformity with the Qur'ān—which would abrogate an earlier sunna. Thus no doubt should ever remain in the minds of men that God has imposed the duty of obedience [to the Prophet].

190. He asked: Someone may say: If we find in the Qur'ān an explicit general meaning which a certain sunna may either make specific or to which it may give an implicit meaning that is contradictory, do you [not] agree that the sunna [in such a case] is abrogated by the Qur'ān?

191. [Shāfiʿī] replied: No scholar should ever hold such an opinion!

192. He asked: Why?

193. [Shāfiʿī] replied: Since God has imposed on His Prophet the duty to obey His communications to him, and He testified to his [right] guidance and imposed on men the duty to obey him, and since the Arab tongue—as I have already explained—may give a variety of meanings [for each word] so that some of the communications of the Book are general and intended to be particular and others particular and intended to be general, and some are general duties which the Apostle specified [in the S222
sunna]—a function which the sunna fulfils in its relation to the Book, the sunna cannot be contradictory to the Book of God, but will always follow the Book of God, in conformity with His divine communication, and clarify on God's behalf the meaning intended by God. Thus [the sunna] always follows the Book of God.

194. He asked: Will you give an evidence in support of your opinion from the Qur'ān?

195. [Shāfiʿī replied]: I quoted for him a part [of the argument] embodied in [my] book "*The* [*Conformity of the*] *Sunna to the Qur'ān*"[6] that God has imposed the duties of prayer, alms, and pilgrimage; but the Apostle specified the modes of performing the prayer, the number of prayers and the

[6] This is a reference to a book which has not come down to us, but none of Shāfiʿī's biographers have mentioned it either.

time for performing them each day and the rules [governing performance]; he specified the amount of the alms to be paid, the time of payment and the commodities exempted therefrom; and [he specified] the performance of pilgrimage and the rules as to what is permitted and what should be avoided. I have also cited to him God's saying:

> As for the thief, male and female, cut off their hands [Q. V, 38]

And:

> The fornicatress and the fornicator—scourge each one of them with a hundred stripes [Q. XXIV, 2].

And I pointed out that since the Apostle laid down in the sunna that cutting off the hand is the penalty for theft if the amount exceeds a quarter of a dīnār, and that the penalty of
S223 scourging [for fornication] on the part of unmarried free and adult persons—not free married or slave married persons—the sunna indicated that God implied [in the text of the Qur'ān] a particular [category of] adulterers and thieves despite the fact that the literal [meaning of the] communication is apparently general concerning the [penalty for] thieves and adulterers.

196. He said: I am in agreement with what you have just explained; but can you give an evidence against those who related a saying on the authority of the Prophet which runs as follows:

> Compare whatever is related on my authority with the Book of God;
> S224 if it agrees with it, I have said it, but if it does not agree, I have not said it.[7]

197. [Shāfiʿī] replied: This tradition was not related by one whose authority on any matter, significant or insignificant, has been recognized so as to constitute a proof for what he related.

[7] This tradition has been transmitted in a variety of forms and is regarded as weak. For a critical evaluation, see Ibn Ḥazm, *Kitāb al-Iḥkām Fī Uṣūl al-Aḥkām,* Vol. II, pp. 76-82. See also Shākir's edition of the *Risāla,* p. 224, n. 4; and J. Schacht, *Origins of Muhammadan Jurisprudence,* p. 28.

Besides, that is an interrupted transmission from an unknown person and is unacceptable to us.

198. He asked: Was anything related on the authority of the Prophet in support of your opinion?

199. [Shāfiʿī] replied: Yes. For Sufyān [b. ʿUyayna] told us from Sālim Abū al-Naḍr from ʿUbayd b. Abī Rāfiʿ from his father that the Prophet said: S225

> Let me find no one of you reclining on his couch, who, when confronted with an order of permission or prohibition from me, says: 'I do no know [whether this is obligatory or not]; we will follow only what we find in the Book of God.'[8]

So[9] the Apostle urged men never to reject his orders, on the grounds that God imposed the duty that they should obey his orders.

200. He asked: Will you give an example of general communications on which the scholars, or the majority at least, have agreed with you that the sunnas, together with the Book, give an indication that such a communication is intended to be particular, although its literal meaning is general?

201. [Shāfiʿī] replied: Yes; it is as I have already discussed in this book.

202. He asked: Repeat some portion of it.

203. [Shāfiʿī] replied: God said:

> Forbidden to you are your mothers and daughters, your sisters, your aunts, paternal and maternal, your brothers' daughters, your sister's daughters, your mothers who have given suck to you, your suckling sisters, your wives' mothers, your step-daughters, who are in your care being born of your wives you have been into—but if you have not yet been into them, it is no fault in you—and the spouses of your sons who are of your loins, and that you should take to you two sisters together, unless it be a thing of the past; God is All-Forgiving, All-Compassionate; and wedded women except what your right hands possess. So God prescribes for you. And lawful for you is what is beyond that [Q. IV, 23-24]. S226

[8] See paragraph 94, n. 15, above.

[9] "Shāfiʿī said" is omitted.

So[10] God stipulated what He prohibited and added: " Lawful
B32 for you is what is beyond that"; but the Apostle specified that no woman together with an aunt, paternal or maternal, shall be taken as a wife.[11] I know of no one who has disagreed with that
S227 specification.

There are two indications in that [tradition]: First, that the sunna of the Apostle can contradict the Book of God in no circumstance, but can only specify the general and particular communications of that Book. Second, that [the scholars] have accepted that [tradition] on the authority of a single transmitter. But I know of no transmitter other than Abū Hurayra who correctly related it on the authority of the Prophet.[12]

204. He asked: Would it be possible in your opinion to regard this tradition as contradictory to any literal meaning in the Book [of God]?

205. [Shāfiʿī] replied: Neither this [tradition] nor any other [can be contradictory to the Book of God].

206. He asked: What is, therefore, the meaning of God's saying: " Forbidden to you are your mothers," in which he
S228 stipulated the prohibition, and then added: " Lawful for you is what is beyond that" [Q. IV, 23]?

207. [Shāfiʿī] replied: God stipulated the instances [of women] forbidden in all circumstances, such as mothers, daughters, sisters, aunts—paternal and maternal—, the brother's daughters and the sister's daughters; those forbidden in all circumstances on the basis of kinship and suckling; and those forbidden to be taken with others, although if each were taken separately it would be lawful. So God's saying: " Lawful for you is what is beyond that," means that any woman is lawful in permissible circumstance; for the stipulation " lawful etc.," means marriage in a lawful manner, not taking a wife in an illegal marriage, or the taking of a fifth wife in addition to the other four,

[10] " *Qāla*" is omitted.

[11] See Mālik, Vol. II, p. 532; Bukhārī, Vol. III, pp. 422-23; Muslim, Vol. IX, pp. 190-93; Ibn Ḥanbal, Vol. V, p. 3530; Shawkānī, *Nayl al-Awṭār,* Vol. VI, pp. 156-59.

[12] For further discussion on this tradition, see Shāfiʿī, *Kitāb al-Umm,* Vol. V, pp. 4-5.

or the taking of two sisters or any other [woman] who is in a S229
forbidden category.

I have also given him the [example of the] duty of ablution laid down by God, and the Prophet's [precedent of] wiping the shoes, and the agreement of the majority of the learned on the acceptance of wiping.

208. He asked: Is [the Prophet's] wiping contradictory to any [textual communication] in the Qur'ān?

209. [Shāfiʿī] replied: In no circumstance can the sunna contradict the Qur'ān.

210. He asked: How would you explain it?

211. [Shāfiʿī] replied: Since [God] said:

> When you stand up for the prayer, wash your faces and your hands up to the elbows, and wipe your heads and your feet up to the ankles [Q. V, 6].

The sunna specified that whoever is in a state of purity, and who has not [subsequently become] polluted, is under no obligation to fulfil this duty [of washing the face, etc.] when he stands up in prayer; it also specified that the duty of washing the
feet is obligatory only on him who had not worn the two shoes S230
in complete purity.

I have also given him the [example of the] Prophet's prohibition of [eating the meat of] beasts possessing fangs. For God stipulated:

> Say: I do not find, in what is revealed to me, anything forbidden to one who eats of it, unless it be a dead animal or blood outpoured, or the flesh of the swine—for it is abomination—or an impious thing over which the name of a god other than God has been involved; but if one is compelled, not willingly or transgressing—then verily thy Lord is All-Forgiving, All-Compassionate [Q. VI, 145]; and specified what He prohibited.[13]

212. He asked: What is the meaning of this [communication]?

[13] See also Q. VI, 147-48.

213. [Shāfiʿī] replied: The meaning of "Say: I do not find... forbidden, etc..." is that nothing was forbidden of what men were accustomed to eat save a dead animal, etc... but what was regarded as forbidden should not be forbidden unless God or the sunna so stipulated in accordance with God's saying: "Making lawful for them the good things and unlawful the corrupt things" [Q. VII, 157]; so it is not just forbidden because
S231 the food was spoiled.

214. [Shāfiʿī] said: Further, I cited to him God's saying:

> God has permitted sale and forbidden usury [Q. II, 275].

And His saying:

> Do not consume your property among you in vanity, except there be trading by mutual consent on your part [Q. IV, 29].

The Apostle of God, however, has forbidden certain kinds of sales, such as the exchange of [gold] dīnārs for [silver] dirhams for a specified time as well as others, and the Muslims, following the Apostle of God, have forbidden them, too, although these [transactions] and others are not contradictory to the Book of God.

215. He asked: Define for me the meaning of what you have said in a more comprehensive and concise manner.

216. [Shāfiʿī] replied: Since it is evident in the Book of God that God placed His Apostle in the position of a mouth-piece [and an interpreter] on God's behalf and imposed on men the duty to obey his orders, therefore when He said: "God has permitted sale and forbidden usury," He meant that He permitted the [kind of] sale which was neither forbidden in His Book nor through the tongue of His Prophet. In like manner His saying: "And lawful for you is what is beyond that" [Q. IV, 23], means that God permitted the taking of women in lawful marriage as well as "what your right hand possesses" in
S232 accordance with His Book;[14] it is not an unqualified permission. This is clear Arabic speech.

[14] *Milk al-yamīn*, in the singular, is a citation from the Qur'ān concerning the taking of four lawful wives and what "your right hands possess" [Q. IV, 3].

217. Shāfiʿī said:[15] [In my reply] I have added the following: If it were permissible to abandon a tradition in place of the opinion of those who are ignorant of its place in relation to the Book, we would have abandoned the wiping of the shoes—which we have already explained—and we would have permitted everything that comes under sale, as well as taking as wives a woman together with her paternal and maternal aunts, and the eating of beasts possessing fangs and the like. It would also have been permissible to hold the opinion that the Prophet laid down the sunna concerning the cutting off of the thief's hand if the value of the stolen article exceeds a quarter of a dīnār before the divine communication: "The thief, male and female, cut off their hands" [Q. V, 38] was revealed. So everyone in this category would have his hands cut off.

In like manner it would be permissible to maintain that the Prophet decreed the stoning of the *thayyib* woman [as penalty for adultery] before he received the communication: "The fornicatress and the fornicator—scourge each one of them a hundred stripes" [Q. XXIV, 2], which meant that [the penalty] for the unmarried and *thayyib* women would have been S233
scourging, not stoning to death.

It would also have been permissible to maintain that all [the kinds of] sale forbidden by the Apostle had been forbidden before the divine communication "God has permitted sale and forbidden usury (*al-ribā*)" was revealed, and that thereafter they became lawful. Usury [may be found] when a man is indebted B33
to another, and the debt is due, and [the second] says [to the first]: Would you pay the debt or pay [in addition] the usury? Payment would be postponed, [in the latter event,] but the debt would grow larger.

Other examples parallel to it might be given. However, he who holds such an opinion would invalidate most of the sunnas of the Apostle; but such an opinion betrays ignorance indeed!

218. He said: That is correct.

219. [Shāfiʿī said]: The sunna of the Apostle is [obligatory] as I have already explained, and he who holds an opinion

[15] Būlāq ed., p. 33.

different from what I have stated, betrays a lack of knowledge about the sunna mixed with a false opinion on a subject in which he is ignorant.

220. He asked: Will you cite another example of a sunna
S234 abrogated by another?

221. [Shāfiʿī] replied: The abrogating and abrogated sunnas may be found in various places [of this book] and to repeat them here would take a long time.

222. He asked: Perhaps a few would be enough; will you cite them briefly and clearly?

223. [Shāfiʿī] replied: Mālik [b. Anas] told us from ʿAbd-Allāh b. Abī Bakr b. Muḥammad b. ʿAmr b. Ḥazm from ʿAbd-Allāh b. Wāqid from ʿAbd-Allāh b. ʿUmar who said:

> The Apostle of God prohibited the eating of the meat of sacrifice after three days [from the first Day of Sacrifice].[16]

ʿAbd-Allāh b. Abī Bakr said that he cited this [tradition] to ʿAmra, daughter of ʿAbd al-Raḥmān,[17] who said: That is true, I have heard ʿĀ'isha say:

> A few people from the desert came [to Makka] during the Day of Sacrifice in the time of the Prophet, who said: ' You may preserve [the meat of sacrifice] for three days and give the rest to the poor.' She said [a year] later the Prophet was asked: ' O Apostle of God! men were accustomed to make use of their sacrifices: They took its fat and used its [skins] to carry water.' So the Apostle inquired: ' Why
> S235 not?' You have prohibited preserving the meat of the sacrifice after three days,' they replied. ' I have prohibited that only for the sake of those who came [to the city] during the Day of Sacrifice. Surely you may eat of it; give to the poor and preserve the rest.'[18]

We are also told by [Sufyān] b. ʿUyayna from [Saʿd b. ʿUbayd] al-Zuhrī from Abī ʿUbayd, freed-slave of Ibn Azhar, who said:

[16] Sacrifices begin on the first day of the Great Feast. For the rules governing sacrifices, see Shāfiʿī, *Kitāb al-Umm,* Vol. I, pp. 187-91.

[17] Būlāq ed., p. 34.

[18] See Mālik, Vol. II, pp. 484-85; Muslim, Vol. XIII, pp. 130-31; Shawkānī, *Nayl al-Awṭār,* Vol. V, pp. 134-37. Cf. Bukhārī's version in *Ṣaḥīḥ* Vol. III, p. 64.

I have witnessed the Feast [of Sacrifice] with ʿAlī b. Abī Ṭālib whom I have heard saying: ' Nobody should eat from the meat of Sacrifice after three days.'[19]

And we are told by the trusted authority[20] from Maʿmar from al-Zuhrī from Abū ʿUbayd from ʿAlī who said: **S236**

The Apostle of God said: ' Nobody should eat from the meat of Sacrifice after three days.'[21]

Ibn ʿUyayna also told us from Ibrāhīm b. Maysara who said:

I have heard Anas b. Mālik say: We were accustomed to slaughter our sacrifices and preserve the remaining portion of it [for our journeys] to Baṣra.[22]

224. Shāfiʿī said: These traditions include many meanings [from which we may draw several conclusions]. [First,] the **S237** tradition transmitted by ʿAlī from the Prophet is in agreement with that of ʿAbd-Allāh b. Wāqid concerning the Prophet's prohibition against keeping the meat of sacrifice after three days. [Second,] there is an indication that ʿAlī heard the order of prohibition from the Prophet and that this order reached ʿAbd-Allāh b. Wāqid. [Third,] there is an indication that the Prophet's permission failed to reach both ʿAlī and ʿAbd-Allāh b. Wāqid, for had it reached them, they would have ceased to relate the order of prohibition, which was abrogated, and would have followed the order of permission which had become the abrogating [order]. [For if] the abrogated order of prohibition were known to them they would not have disregarded the abrogating order [of permission]. [Finally,] the opinion of Anas that they were accustomed to enter Baṣra with the meat of the

[19] This tradition is regarded as weak owing to interruption in the chain of authorities, but its content is in agreement with similar traditions. See Ibn Ḥanbal, Vol. II, p. 297, no. 1235.

[20] I. e., Yaḥya b. Ḥassān.

[21] Shāfiʿī fails to mention the name of his authority, but Ibn Ḥanbal gives the name of ʿAbd al-Razzāq. See Ibn Ḥanbal, Vol. II, p. 282. In another version of the tradition he gives the name of Muḥammad b. Jaʿfar. *Ibid.*, Vol. II, p. 280; al-Ḥāzimī, p. 120.

[22] al-Ḥāzimī, p. 121.

sacrifices may mean either that Anas had heard the order of permission but not the earlier order of prohibition—thus he acted on the order of permission without knowing the order of prohibition—or he may have heard both, but since the order of prohibition was abrogated, he failed to mention it. So each one of the two conflicting transmitters related what he had known. Thus it is obligatory on everyone who has heard anything from the Apostle of God, or related on his authority, to transmit what
S238 he had heard for the information of others.

225. Shāfiʿī said: Since ʿĀ'isha related from the Prophet first the order of prohibition concerning the keeping of the meat of sacrifice after three days and then the order of permission, and the Apostle's [reason] that he gave the order of prohibition for the sake of those who came from the desert—the complete tradition related by ʿĀ'isha from the Prophet is that which should include the first and the last parts, as well as the reason for the orders of prohibition and permission. It is obligatory on all who have known about it to follow it.

ʿĀ'isha's tradition is one of the clearest examples of the abrogating and abrogated sunnas. It also illustrates how a tradition may be split so that only a portion of it—not all—was related by one authority and another portion by others, each relating what he had remembered.

The order of permission concerning the keeping of the meat of sacrifice, eating it, and giving it to the poor may have only one of two meanings, each depending on one of two circumstances: Whenever the people of the desert enter [the city], the order
S239 of prohibition concerning the keeping of the meat after three days becomes obligatory; but if none should come, the order of permission is valid concerning eating, preserving, giving to the
B34 poor, and carrying it [on a journey]. It may also mean that the order of prohibition concerning the keeping of the meat after three days was abrogated—despite any [special] circumstance—
S240 so men can keep a portion of the meat after three days or give another to the poor.[23]

[23] Shāfiʿī seems to have adopted one interpretation at one time and another at another time. See his *Ikhtilāf al-Ḥadīth* (on the margin of the *Kitāb al-Umm,*

[*Categories of*] *Abrogating and Abrogated Traditions*

[A. First Category]

226. [Shāfiʿī said]: Muḥammad b. Ismāʿīl b. Abī Fudayk told us from Ibn Abī Dhi'b from al-Maqburī from ʿAbd al-Raḥmān b. Abī Saʿīd [al-Khudrī] from Abū Saʿīd al-Khudrī who said: S241-242

> We were withheld from performing prayer in [the battle of] the Trench for a long while, till [late at] night, but when we were relieved from fighting—as God said: ' God relieved the believers of fighting, God is All-strong, All-Mighty' [Q. XXXIII, 25]—the Apostle ordered Bilāl [to call the believers to prayer] and performed the noon-prayer as fully as if it were performed in its time, and performed the ʿ*aṣr*, the sunset, and the evening prayers in like manner. This [incident] took place before the communication concerning fear-prayer was revealed which runs as follows: ' If you fear [danger], pray either on foot or mounted.' [Q. II, 239].[24]

227. Shāfiʿī said: Since Abū Saʿīd related that the Apostle's prayer in the battle of the Trench was performed before the communication on fear-prayer (if you fear, etc.) was revealed, we concluded that the performance of fear-prayer took place after that time, for Abū Saʿīd was present [at the battle] and related the tradition concerning the deferment of prayers after their usual times[25] and stated that this [case] took place before the communication on fear-prayer was S243 revealed.

228. [Shāfiʿī] said: Thus in no circumstances shall fear-prayer be deferred from its usual time in the town, nor

Vol. VII, pp. 136-37, 247-48). Thus the matter was left undecided for further interpretations and the schools vary on this matter. See Shākir's ed., pp. 240-41, n. 3.

[24] See paragraph 148, n. 35, above.

[25] ʿ*Āmmatiha* means the times of all the prayers.

in performing [two] prayers at one time in travel, whether [men are] in fear [of danger] or not. Prayers must always be performed in the same manner as performed by the Apostle of God.

Our opinion concerning fear-prayer is based on what Mālik [b. Anas] told us from Yazīd b. Rūmān from Ṣāliḥ b. Khawwāt from men who performed the fear-prayer with the Apostle in the campaign of Dhāt al-Riqāʿ who said:

> A company [of believers] stood in rank [for prayer] with [the Prophet] while another watched the enemy. He performed one cycle with the company who stood with him and remained standing until the others completed [the prayer]. Having thus taken the position of those facing the enemy, the other company stood [with the Prophet], who performed the other cycle and remained sitting while the company completed their prayer until he uttered the salutation with them.[26]

229. [Shāfiʿī] said: We have been told by men who heard ʿAbd-Allāh b. ʿUmar b. Ḥafṣ relating on the authority of his brother ʿUbayd-Allāh b. ʿUmar from al-Qāsim b. Muḥammad from Ṣāliḥ b. Khawwāt b. Jubayr from his father from the
S244 Prophet a similar tradition. It[27] has also been related that the Prophet performed a fear-prayer differently from what Mālik had stated. We have, however, accepted [Mālik's] version, because it is more consistent with the Qur'ān and more deceptive to the enemy. This subject and the contradictory traditions related to it have been discussed in the *Kitāb al-Ṣalāh* [Book of Prayer].[28] We have dispensed with opposing views on this tradition since they are scattered in [the various chapters of] our books.

[26] See paragraph 148, n. 36, above.

[27] *Qāla* (he said) is omitted.

[28] See Shāfiʿī, *Kitāb al-Umm,* Vol. I, pp. 186-203. Cf. Shāfiʿī's *Kitāb Ikhtilāf al-Ḥadīth* (margin of *Kitāb al-Umm,* Vol. VII, pp. 221-26). Shāfiʿī's reference to his *Kitāb al-Ṣalāh* may well be to another book which is not in the *Kitāb al-Umm* (see Shākir's edition of the *Risāla,* p. 245, n. 4).

[B. Second] Category

230. [Shāfiʿī said]: God, Blessed and Most High, said:

> Those of your women who commit indecency, call four witnesses against them, and if they testify—then detain them in their houses until death takes them, or God appoints for them a way out. S245
>
> And when two of you commit indecency, punish them both; but if they repent and reform, then let them [Q. IV, 15-16].

The punishment for the two adulterers, according to this communication, was detainment and suffering; but since God has communicated to His Apostle that the penalty for fornication shall be: "The fornicatress and fornicator—scourge each one of them with a hundred stripes" [Q. XXIV, 2], and for the slave-woman shall be: " If then, having been taken under *iḥṣān*, they commit an indecency, they shall be liable to half the punishment of freewomen" [Q. IV, 25], detainment as a punishment for adulterers has been abrogated, but punishment [by suffering] was confirmed.

As to the communication concerning the punishment of slave-women that "they shall be liable to half the punishment of freewomen," God has obviously drawn a distinction between the punishment of slave- and free-women: He made it evident that half [of the punishment] cannot be other than scourging, for only scourging can be halved by the number of stripes while stoning to death cannot be halved, since death might be caused either by the casting of one or by a thousand stones. So what is incapable of being halved cannot be regarded as penalty, and death certainly cannot be halved by dividing the number of S246
stones cast at the person.[29]

God's communication: "The fornicatress and the fornicator—scourge each one of them with a hundred stripes" [Q. XXIV, 2] may either mean as a penalty to all free adulterers, or to some to the exclusion of the others; but the sunna of the Apostle specified who is liable for such a penalty. For B35
ʿAbd al-Wahhāb al-Thaqafī told us from Yūnus b. ʿUbayd from al-Ḥasan from ʿUbāda b. al-Ṣāmit that the Apostle of God said:

[29] See paragraph 123, above.

> Take it from me [repeated twice] God has decided on a way [for their punishment]: For the fornication of the unmarried couple [the penalty] is scourging with a hundred stripes and banishment for a year; for [the adultery of] the married couple, scourging with a hundred stripes and stoning [to death].[30]

231. [Shāfiʿī] said: The Apostle's saying that "God has decided on a way [for their punishment]" indicates that this was the first penalty imposed on adulterers in accordance with God's communication "until death takes them or God appoints
S247 for them a way out" [Q. IV, 15].[31]

Since the Apostle ordered the stoning of both Māʿiz and the wife of al-Aslamī rather than scourging them, the sunna made it evident that scourging [as a penalty] for fornication by the unmarried was abrogated.[32] For no such distinction in the penalty of freemen was ever made before except in the case of women under *iḥṣān* whether by marriage or otherwise. But the Prophet's saying that "God has decided on a way for their punishment, etc..." is an indication that the first [penalty] abrogated was banishment, and that any other kind of punishment must have been imposed later, since the penalty of banishment was imposed first. [For] Mālik [b. Anas] told us from Ibn Shihāb al-Zuhrī from ʿUbayd-Allāh b. ʿAbd-Allāh
S248 b. ʿUtba from Abū Hurayra and Zayd b. Khālid who said:

> Two men submitted a dispute to the Apostle of God. One of them said: 'O Apostle of God! Will you settle our dispute on the basis of the Book of God?' The other, who was more knowledgeable in the law, said: 'I concur, O Apostle, but I beg you to let me speak [first].' 'You may speak,' replied [the Prophet]. He said: 'When my son was in the employment of this [the plaintiff] he committed adultery with his wife. I was told that my son's penalty was stoning [to death]; but instead I paid a ransom of one hundred sheep and a slave-woman. Upon inquiry from those who are learned in the law, I have found that my son's penalty was a hundred stripes and banishment for a year, while the penalty for his [the plaintiff's] wife was stoning.' 'By Him in whose hand is my soul, I shall give my judgment on the basis

[30] See paragraph 122, above.
[31] Ṭabarī, *Tafsīr,* Vol. VII, pp. 72-81.
[32] See paragraph 123, above.

of the Book of God: your sheep and slave-woman should be given back to you,' ruled the Apostle of God, and ordered that the son should be scourged by a hundred stripes and banished for a year. He S249
also ordered Unays al-Aslamī to cross-examine the [plaintiff's] wife and to stone her if she admitted adultery. The woman confessed and was stoned [to death].[33]

Mālik [b. Anas] told us from Ibn ʿUmar that the Prophet ordered the stoning of two Jews for committing adultery.[34]

232. [Shāfiʿī] said: Thus the scourging of a hundred stripes and banishment were confirmed [as a penalty] for fornication on the part of the unmarried, and stoning for the married. But if punishment by scourging is imposed [on the two fornicators,] it should not be enforced together with stoning since the latter was abrogated; for if [the culprits] were regarded as married—therefore not liable for scourging—their penalty should be that S250
imposed on married adulterers.[35]

[The communication concerning] the penalty of stoning for the two married adulterers was revealed after that concerning scourging according to the Apostle, who made that [clear] on God's behalf. This is the meaning most consistent [with the Book of God] and most appropriate in our opinion. But God knows best!

[C. Third] Category

233. Mālik [b. Anas] told us from Ibn Shihāb al-Zuhrī from Anas b. Mālik, who said:

The Prophet, riding on horseback, was thrown and his right side was scratched. Thereupon he performed one of his daily prayers sitting and we performed ours behind him sitting, too. After prayer the

[33] Mālik, Vol. II. p. 822; Muslim, Vol. II, pp. 205-207; Cf. Abū Dāwūd, Vol. IV, pp. 145-46.

[34] Mālik, Vol. II, p. 819; Muslim, Vol. II, pp. 208-209; Abū Dāwūd, Vol. IV, p. 153; Shawkānī, *Nayl al-Awṭār,* Vol. VII, p. 97.

[35] See Shāfiʿī, *Kitāb al-Umm,* Vol. VI, pp. 119-21.

> Prophet said: ' The imām [prayer leader][36] is expected to be followed;
> if he performs the prayer standing, you should stand, too; if he bows
> you should bow; if he raises his hands, you should raise them; if
> he says: ' God listens to him who praises Him,' you should say:
> ' Praise be to you, Our Lord'; and if he performs his prayer sitting,
> S251 you should perform yours sitting, too.'[37]

Mālik [b. Anas] told us from Hishām b. ʿUrwa from his father from ʿĀ'isha, who said:

> When the Apostle was sick, he performed his prayer sitting in his house; but when the men behind him performed their prayer standing, he ordered them to sit. After prayer, [the Prophet] said: ' The imām is expected to be followed; if he bows, you should bow; if he raises his hand, you should raise yours, too; if he sits, you should sit all together.'[38]

This tradition, related by Anas [b. Mālik], is like the previous one, but the meaning of Anas' tradition is clearer.

Mālik [b. Anas] told us from Hishām b. ʿUrwa from his father, who said:

> The Apostle of God went out [from his house] while still sick [to
> perform his prayer in public]. While leading the prayer, Abū Bakr
> stepped aside [in favor of the Prophet], but the latter ordered him to
> S252 continue and sat beside him: Abū Bakr followed the Apostle [in his
> prayer], and men followed Abū Bakr.[39]

Shāfiʿī said that he was in favor of the opinion expressed in this tradition.[40]

[36] The imām, or prayer leader, is the Muslim sufficiently versed in the technique of prayer to perform the formalized recitals and postures. See Edwin E. Calverly, *Worship in Islam* (London, 1957), Chap. 4.

[37] Mālik, Vol. I, p. 135; Bukhārī, Vol. I, p. 180; Muslim, Vol. IV, pp. 130-31; Abū Dāwūd, Vol. I, p. 164; Shawkānī, *Nayl al-Awṭār,* Vol. III, pp. 148, 180-81.

[38] Mālik's version omits the statement " in his house" (see *al-Muwaṭṭa',* Vol. I, p. 135). See also Bukhārī, Vol. I, p. 180; Muslim, Vol. IV, p. 132.

[39] Mālik, Vol. I, p. 136; Bukhārī, Vol. I, p. 177; Muslim, Vol. IV, pp. 135-38; Shāfiʿī, *Ikhtilāf al-Ḥadīth* (*Kitāb al-Umm,* Vol. VII, pp. 99-100).

[40] This statement is an expression of Shāfiʿī's opinion, perhaps inserted by al-Rabīʿ as he heard it from Shāfiʿī; probably it was not part of the *Risāla.* See Shākir's edition, p. 253, n. 2.

234. [Shāfiʿī] said: A similar tradition has been related by Ibrāhīm al-Nakhaʿī from al-Aswad b. Yazīd from ʿĀ'isha from the Apostle and Abū Bakr to the effect that the Prophet performed his prayer sitting while Abū Bakr, [leading the prayer,] followed the Prophet and men followed Abū Bakr S253
standing.[41] B36

235. [Shāfiʿī] said: Since the Prophet performed his prayer during his death-sickness sitting while men performed it standing behind him, we concluded that his previous order permitting men to perform prayer sitting at the time of his fall from the horse was abrogated by his later order that they may perform prayer standing, because they [should] sit when the imām sits.[42]

Thus the evidence of the sunna and the consensus of the people [i. e, of the scholars] indicate that prayers should be S254
performed standing when men are able to stand, and sitting when they are unable to stand; but those who can perform it standing by themselves should never do so sitting.

Although the Prophet's sunna ordering men to perform their prayer behind him standing while he performed it sitting during his [death] sickness abrogated his previous sunna, it is in conformity with his sunna concerning the prayers of healthy and sick men, as well as the consensus of the people, that each man should fulfil his [prayer] duty in accordance with the rule stipulating that the sick man can perform his prayer sitting behind a healthy imām who performs the prayer standing.

So we maintain: [If sick,] the imām performs his prayer sitting, but the healthy men behind him should perform theirs standing. So each one fulfils his duty in his own way, although it is more appropriate if the imām deputizes another person [whenever he is sick].[43]

236. One scholar[44] held: "Nobody after the Prophet shall

[41] Cf. Shāfiʿī, *Kitāb al-Umm,* Vol. I, p. 156; and *Ikhtilāf al-Ḥadīth (Kitāb al-Umm,* Vol. VII, p. 100); and Shawkānī, *Nayl al-Awṭār,* Vol. III, p. 180.

[42] See Bukhārī, Vol. I, p. 180; and Shāfiʿī, *Kitāb al-Umm,* Vol. I, p. 151.

[43] For further discussion, see Shāfiʿī, *Kitāb al-Umm,* Vol. VII, p. 184.

[44] This implicit criticism is alleged to have been levelled against the followers of Muḥammad b. al-Ḥasan al-Shaybānī; but in reality it was against all the

S255 lead the prayer sitting"; but the tradition which he cited in support of his opinion was an interrupted one related by an unreliable authority, and therefore cannot be accepted as binding. [The text of this tradition runs as follows]: "Let no
S256 one after me [the Prophet] lead the prayer sitting."[45]

237. [Shāfiʿī] said: There are other parallel examples concerning the abrogating and abrogated sunnas which provide evidence in support of this viewpoint. There are likewise parallel
S257-258 examples in the Book of God; some have been described in this book and others scattered in their proper places in this book and in [the chapters on] the Qur'ān and the sunna.[46]

[*Contradictory Traditions*]

238. [Shāfiʿī] said: He asked: Give examples of contradictory traditions in which no indications are to be found concerning the abrogating and abrogated [sunnas] and the reason for accepting some and rejecting others?

239. [Shāfiʿī] replied: I have already cited a tradition to the effect that the Apostle performed the fear-prayer in the campaign of Dhāt al-Riqāʿ, in which he performed one cycle with one company while the other watched the enemy, etc. However,[47] Ibn ʿUmar related from the Prophet that he [the Prophet] performed the fear-prayer somewhat differently as follows:

> S259 He [the Prophet] performed one cycle with one company while another stood [for protection] between him and the enemy. The company that stood in rank [for prayer] replaced the one which had not prayed, taking a position between him [the Prophet] and the

Ḥanafī and Mālikī jurists. For differences between Shāfiʿī and Mālik, see Shāfiʿī, *Kitāb al-Umm,* Vol. VII, pp. 184-86.

[45] For further discussion, see Shāfiʿī, *Ikhtilāf al-Ḥadīth (Kitāb al-Umm,* Vol. VII, pp. 100-102).

[46] Cf. Būlāq ed., p. 37.

[47] "Shāfiʿī said" is omitted.

enemy. He performed the final cycle with this company, and uttered the salutation. Thus all performed the prayer together.[48]

Abū ʿAyyāsh al-Zuraqī related:

> The Prophet performed a [fear]-prayer in the campaign of ʿUsfān[49] while Khālid b. al-Walīd [and his army] stood between him and the *qibla* [watching the enemy]. He [the Prophet] stood in rank for prayer and performed one cycle [with his men]. When he bowed,
> one company bowed with him and the other watched the enemy. S260
> When he stood, the company that watched the enemy bowed. Thus all completed the prayer together.[50]

Jābir related [a tradition] the meaning of which is nearly identical to that one.[51] Other[52] contradictory traditions may be cited, but they are unreliable.

240. Someone has asked me: Why have you accepted [the
tradition concerning] the Prophet's prayer in the campaign of S261
Dhāt al-Riqāʿ to the exclusion of others?

241. [Shāfiʿī] replied: I would accept the tradition of Abū ʿAyyāsh and Jābir concerning fear-prayer if the reason given there for the Prophet's prayer were the same as that in the other [i. e., the tradition of Dhāt al-Riqāʿ].

242. He asked: What is it?

243. [Shāfiʿī] replied: The Apostle had under his command 1,400 men, while Khālid b. al-Walīd had only 200. Far away in the desert, [Khālid] was secure from attack owing both to the few under his command and the many under the Apostle's command. For if the enemy attacked [Khālid], they could be seen [by the Prophet] while performing the bowing as he was in such a position that they were always seen by him. However, if the enemy consisted of only a few and were at a

[48] Cf. paragraph 149, above.

[49] ʿUsfān, a place on the route between Makka and Madīna. The expedition to ʿUsfān, dispatched against the Banu Liḥyān, took place in 5/627. See Ibn Hishām, Vol. II, pp. 718-19; Guillaume's translation, pp. 485-86.

[50] See Shāfiʿī, *Kitāb al-Umm,* Vol. I, p. 191; and *Ikhtilaf al-Ḥadīth* (*Kitāb al-Umm,* Vol. VII, p. 225). See also Abū Dāwūd, Vol. II, pp. 11-12.

[51] See Shawkānī, *Nayl al-Awṭār,* Vol. III, pp. 338-39.

[52] *Qāla* (he said) is omitted.

distance, and no company stood between them [and those who performed the prayer], I am of the opinion that fear-prayer should be performed in such circumstances, as I explained before.

244. He asked: I realize that owing to changes in circumstances the tradition concerning the prayer of Dhāt al-Riqāʿ is in agreement [with your opinion]; why are you opposed to the tradition of Ibn ʿUmar?

245. [Shāfiʿī] replied: [The tradition of Dhāt al-Riqāʿ] was related by Khawwāt b. Jubayr. A not very different one was related by Sahl b. Abī Ḥathma. Moreover, ʿAlī b. Abī Ṭālib was reported to have performed the fear-prayer in the Night of al-Harīr,[53] in accordance with the tradition related by Khawwāt b. Jubayr from the Prophet. Finally, Khawwāt was an old and early companion of the Prophet.

246. He asked: Is there any evidence [for accepting Khawwāt's tradition] stronger than his [age and] early compan-
S263 ionship?

247. [Shāfiʿī] replied: Yes, it is its consistency with the
B37 meaning of the Book of God, as I have already explained.

248. He asked: What part of it is consistent with the Book of God?

249. [Shāfiʿī] replied: God said:

> When thou art with them and hast set up the prayer for them, let a party of them stand with thee, and let them take their weapons. When they bow, let them be behind you; and then let another party who has not prayed come and pray with thee, taking their guard and their weapons. The unbelievers wish that you should neglect your weapons and your baggage, then they would fall upon you all at once. There is no fault in you, if rain molests you, or you are sick, to lay down your weapons, but keep your guard [Q. IV, 102].

And He said:

[53] The Night of al-Harīr, known also as the Day of al-Harīr, was one of the days in the battle of Ṣiffīn (A. D. 657) between the Caliph ʿAlī and Muʿāwiya, then governor of Syria.

> When you feel secure again, observe the prayer. Verily, the prayer has become for the believer a thing prescribed for stated times [Q. IV, 103].

The meaning implied [in these texts] is that when men are secure, they should perform their [usual] prayer. But God knows best!

Since God has distinguished between fear and secure prayers in order to protect the followers of His religion from a sudden attack, we have found that by comparing the tradition of Khawwāt b. Jubayr with others contradictory to it, Khawwāt's
tradition seems to be more appropriate to follow for precau- S264
tionary [considerations]. It is recommended that the two parties should participate equally [in performing the prayer and in guarding against the enemy], for the party that performs the prayer first with the imām should be well guarded by the other which does not perform the prayer. The guarding party—relieved of the duty of prayer—should be fully occupied [in watching the enemy], whether standing or sitting, turning left or right, and prepared to defend should the enemy attack, giving warning whenever the enemy suddenly attacks and being ready to fight if necessary, never moving from their position between the enemy and the party performing the prayer. The imām should quickly perform the prayer if he fears a sudden attack by the enemy, upon a warning from the guarding party.

250. [Shāfiʿī] said: Both parties are equally right in fulfilling their duties, for in accordance with the tradition of Khawwāt, both are equally responsible. Each one, after it has performed its prayer, guards the other; thus each takes the place of the other fulfilling its duties. Such [a division of responsibility] is just.

251. [Shāfiʿī] said: The tradition contradictory to that of Khawwāt does not provide for such precaution, since one of the two parties protects the other only during one cycle while the other takes the place of the first in order to guard it before completing its prayer, so that when they were performing their prayer together they did not have any protection at
all. So the only one who fully performed his prayer was the S265
imām, who did not take part in guarding nor could he be

strong enough to guard [against the enemy]. This [kind of performance] is inconsistent with the order of precaution and preparedness against the enemy. Yet God has made it plain that He distinguished between the fear-prayer and other prayers so that the followers of His religion should not be exposed to a sudden attack by the enemy and that neither party should be held responsible more than the other. We note that God made
S266 no stipulation that either the imām or the two parties should perform substitution prayers. This indicates that the imām and the men following him have equally fulfilled their duty. This is [clearly shown] in Khawwāt's tradition, but not in the one contradictory to it.

252. He asked: Is there any other meaning in the tradition unacceptable to you which you have not described?

253. [Shāfiʿī] replied: Yes. [The tradition] may mean that if it is permissible to perform the fear-prayer in a manner different from other prayers, it should be permissible to perform it in whatever manner is possible, depending on the circumstances in which [the Muslims] or the enemy happen to be, provided the number [of cycles] is completed, even though [the mode of] performance may be different, but all [such performances] fulfil the duty.

Another Kind of Contradictory [*Traditions*]

S267 254. Shāfiʿī said: Someone has asked me: Traditions relating to the *tashahhud*[54] have been differently transmitted from the Prophet. Ibn Masʿūd related that he [the Prophet] instructed men how to recite the *tashahhud* just as he instructed them to recite a portion[55] of the Qur'ān, beginning with the three words: Salutations to God.[56] Which [tradition of] *tashahhud* have you accepted?

[54] The *tashahhud* is the recital of the salutations to the Prophet and the formula of the profession of the faith.

[55] Literally: " The sūra [chapter] of the Qur'ān."

[56] See Abū Dāwūd, Vol. I, p. 254; Shawkānī, *Nayl al-Awṭār*, Vol. II, pp. 280, 287.

255. Shāfiʿī replied: Mālik [b. Anas] told us from Ibn Shihāb from ʿUrwa [b. al-Zubayr] from ʿAbd al-Raḥmān b. ʿAbd al-Qārī who heard ʿUmar b. al-Khaṭṭāb on the pulpit instructing men how to recite the *tashahhud* say:

> Say: Salutations to God. Sanctities belong to God. Goodness and prayers to God. O Prophet, peace is upon you and God's blessings and mercies to you. Peace is upon us and upon all good servants of God. I profess that there is no god at all but God, and I witness that Muḥammad is His servant and Apostle.[57]

256. Shāfiʿī said: This is the tradition in which our learned predecessors have instructed us in our early age. We have known that tradition, including the names of authorities who related it, as well as others contradictory to it; but we know of no other transmission, whether it agrees or disagrees with it, which is more reliable than that one, although there are other reliable traditions also. For we are of the opinion that ʿUmar did not instruct men from the pulpit in the presence
of other companions of the Apostle save in what the Prophet S268
himself had instructed. So any other tradition related to us by other companions which confirms this tradition is acceptable to us.

257. He asked: What tradition?

258. [Shāfiʿī] replied: We are told by the trusted authority—Yaḥya b. Ḥassān—from al-Layth b. Saʿd from Abū Zubayr al-Makkī from Saʿīd b. Jubayr and Ṭāwūs from Ibn ʿAbbās, who said:

> The Apostle instructed us how to recite the *tashahhud* in the same
> manner as he taught us to recite the Qur'ān. He said: ' Blessed B38
> greetings and good prayers to God. O Prophet! Peace and God's
> mercies and blessings be upon you. Peace be upon us and upon all S269
> good servants of God. I profess that there is no god at all but God and that Muḥammad is the Apostle of God.[58]

[57] Mālik, Vol. I, pp. 90-91.

[58] For Shāfiʿī's remarks on this tradition as the dearest to him, see *Kitāb al-Umm*, Vol. I, p. 101; and *Ikhtilāf al-Ḥadīth* (*Kitāb al-Umm*, Vol. VII, p. 63). See also Abū Dāwūd, Vol. I, p. 256.

259. Shāfiʿī said: He asked: Why does the transmission [of these traditions] from the Prophet vary? For Ibn Masʿūd, Abū
S270 Mūsa and Jābir have related different versions, each varies from the other in certain words, and [the Caliph] ʿUmar has instructed men differently. Moreover, the *tashahhud* of ʿĀ'isha and Ibn ʿUmar vary in wording; one of them includes a few words additional to the other.

260. [Shāfiʿī] replied: The matter is quite clear.

261. He said: Explain it to me.

262. [Shāfiʿī] replied: The recitals glorifying God instructed by the Apostle were committed to memory by men in words varying from one person to another, from the time of [the Prophet's] instruction. The main concern [of the transmitters] was the change in meaning, not the words; but whenever the change in wording resulted in a change of meaning such a change was not permissible. For it is possible that the Prophet himself permitted each man to recite what he had learned provided that there was no change in the meaning of his recital. So the transmitters in turn regarded as permissible the variations in the wording of the recitals but not in their meaning.[59]

263. He asked: Is there any evidence making permissible what you have described?

S272 264. [Shāfiʿī] replied: Yes!

265. He asked: What is it?

266. [Shāfiʿī] replied: Mālik [b. Anas] told us from Ibn Shihāb from ʿUrwa [b. al-Zubayr] from ʿAbd al-Raḥmān b. al-Qārī, who said: I have heard ʿUmar b. al-Khaṭṭāb say:

> I have heard Hishām b. Ḥākīm b. Ḥizām reciting the sūra of the Furqān [Q. XXV] differently from my recitation—which the Prophet himself had instructed me how to recite—so I almost quarrelled with him, but I waited until he completed the recitation, whereupon I wrapped his mantle around his neck and dragged him to the Prophet, and I said: ' O Apostle of God! I have heard this man recite the

[59] For further discussion on such variations in the wording of the *tashahhud*, see Shāfiʿī, *Kitāb al-Umm*, Vol. I. pp. 103-105.

sūra of the Furqān differently from what you have instructed me.' ' Recite it,' said the Prophet to the man; and he recited it the way I had heard it from him. ' This is the way it was revealed [to me],' said the Apostle; and he asked me to recite, which I did in the way he had instructed me to recite it. ' This is the way it was revealed [to me]' said the Prophet and added: ' The Qur'ān has been revealed in accordance with seven modes[60] and you may recite what
is convenient of it.'[61] S273

267. [Shāfiʿī] said: Since God, owing to His sympathy toward man and His recognition of the weakness of his memory, has permitted various recitals of His book in accordance with seven modes—provided no change in the meaning is made—variation in the wording of other books should be all the more permissible as long as the meaning is not affected. So changes in the wording of any text, save that of a divine communication,
is permissible if the meaning is not changed. S274

268. A Successor said: I have heard some of the Companions [relating traditions from the Apostle] agreeing in meaning but disagreeing in wording. I have taken up this matter with one of them, who said: " It is permissible unless the meaning is changed."

269. He asked: Since there is nothing in the recital of the *tashahhud* but the glorification of God, changes in the wording should be permissible, since, as you pointed out, [no change is made in the meaning]. Similarly, as you said [an argument
might be advanced in favor of] fear-prayer, so that as long as S275
it was performed as fully as related from the Prophet, it should fulfil the duty, since God has distinguished between that kind of prayer and others. But on what ground have you made your choice of the tradition related by Ibn ʿAbbās on *tashahhud* to the exclusion of others?

[60] This is an ambiguous expression in the Qur'ān, the meaning of which scholars have not agreed upon. " Modes" seems to be the nearest word to *aḥruf*. See Ṭabarī, *Tafsīr,* Vol. I, pp. 58-72; and Suyūṭī, *al-Itqān Fī ʿUlūm al-Qur'ān,* Vol. I, pp. 46-48.

[61] Mālik, Vol. I, p. 201; Bukhārī, Vol. II, pp. 90-91; Muslim, Vol. VI, pp. 98-99.

270. [Shāfiʿī] replied: Since I have found that tradition comprehensive enough, comprising more words and meanings than others, and transmitted by reliable authorities from Ibn ʿAbbās, I have decided to accept it without any reflection on others who have accepted other reliable traditions.

Contradictory Transmission of Traditions Different From Other Kinds

271. [Shāfiʿī said]: Mālik [b. Anas] told us from Nāfiʿ from Abū Saʿīd al-Khudrī that the Apostle said:

> Let no one exchange gold for gold save in equal quantities, or increase one quantity against the other. Let no one exchange silver for silver save in equal quantities, or increase one quantity against
> S276 the other. Let no one exchange anything at hand for another not in evidence.[62]

B39 Mālik [b. Anas] told us from Mūsa b. Abī Tamīm from Saʿīd b. Yasār from Abū Hurayra from the Apostle, who said:

> The [gold] dīnār [shall be exchanged] for a [gold] dīnār and the [silver] dirham for a [silver] dirham; there shall be no increase in the one against the other.[63]

Mālik [b. Anas] told us from Ḥumayd b. Qays from Mujāhid from Ibn ʿUmar, who said:

> The dīnār [shall be exchanged] for a dīnār and the dirham for a dirham; there shall be no increase in the one against the other. This is the order of our Prophet to us and ours to you.[64]

272. Shāfiʿī said: ʿUthmān b. ʿAffān and ʿUbāda b. al-Ṣāmit related [other] traditions from the Apostle to the effect that
S277 he prohibited the increase of gold for gold as the transfer of

[62] Mālik, Vol. II, pp. 632-33; Bukhārī, Vol. II, p. 81; Muslim, Vol. XI, pp. 8-12. Cf. Abū Dāwūd, Vol. III, p. 249.

[63] Mālik, Vol. II, p. 632; Muslim, Vol. XI, p. 15.

[64] Mālik, Vol. II, p. 633.

ownership takes place immediately.[65]

We[66] accept these traditions, since there are others identical in meaning related by leading Companions and jurisconsults throughout the land.

Sufyān [b. ʿUyayna] told us that he heard ʿUbyad-Allāh b. Abī Yazīd say: I have heard Ibn ʿAbbās say: Usāma b. Zayd told me that the Prophet said:

> *Al-ribā* (usury) is to be found in *al-nasīʾa* (deferred payment).[67] S278

Ibn ʿAbbās[68] and some of his followers in Makka and elsewhere have accepted this [tradition].

273. Someone has asked me: Is not this tradition contradictory to earlier ones?

274. [Shāfiʿī] replied: It may be regarded as both contradictory and not contradictory.

275. He asked: In what respect is it in agreement?

276. [Shāfiʿī] replied: Usāma may have heard someone ask the Apostle about [the exchange of] two different kinds of S279 property such as gold for silver, dates for wheat, or any other different property the transfer of which was to take place immediately, and the Prophet said: "*Ribā* is in *nasīʾa*." Or he may have been absent when the question was asked, but heard only the answer. So he related the answer without the question. Or he may have guessed [what the question was], for there is nothing in Usāma's tradition which is not in agreement with other traditions.

277. He asked: Why do you maintain that [Usāma's tradition] may be regarded as contradictory to others?

[65] Literally: "As it passes from one hand to the other." See Mālik, Vol. II, p. 633; Muslim, Vol. XI, p. 11. Cf. Abū Dāwūd, Vol. III, p. 248, for a different wording.

[66] "Shāfiʿī said" is omitted.

[67] Muslim, Vol. XI, pp. 25-26; Abū Muḥammad al-Dārimī, *Sunan* (Damascus, 1349/1930), Vol. II, p. 259; Shāfiʿī, *Ikhtilāf al-Ḥadīth* (margin of *Kitāb al-Umm,* Vol. VII, p. 241).

[68] "Shāfiʿī said" is omitted.

278. [Shāfiʿī] replied: Because Ibn ʿAbbās, who related it differently, said:

> There is no *ribā* in a sale if the transfer of ownership takes place immediately; but *ribā* is in *nasīʾa*.[69]

279. He asked: On what ground have you abandoned this tradition, notwithstanding its contradiction of earlier ones?

280. [Shāfiʿī] replied: Although those who related traditions contradictory to Usāma's were not as well-known experts as he, they were in the meantime no less reliable than he. However, ʿUthmān b. ʿAffān and ʿUbāda b. al-Ṣāmit were earlier Companions and more intimately connected [with the Prophet] than Usāma. As to Abū Hurayra, he was regarded as
S280 one of the senior Companions and the most reliable transmitter of tradition in his time.

Since a tradition literally related by two authorities is likely to be more accurate and reliable than one related by one only, a tradition related by older and a greater number of authorities (e. g., five) should be the more acceptable than a tradition
S281 related by one only.

Traditions Regarded as Contradictory [by Others], But Not by Us

[A. First] Category

281. [Shāfiʿī said]: [Sufyān] b. ʿUyayna told us from Muḥammad b. al-ʿAjlān from ʿĀṣim b. ʿUmar b. Qatāda from Maḥmūd b. Labīd from Rāfiʿ b. Khadīj that the Apostle said:

> S282 Start your dawn-prayer at day-break,[70] for [its performance] at that time is the most rewarding to you.[71]

[69] See paragraph 147, n. 23, above; Shāfiʿī, *al-Musnad,* ed. Muḥammad ʿĀbid al-Sindī (Cairo, 1369/1950), Vol. II, p. 159; and *Ikhtilāf-Ḥadīth* (*Kitāb al-Umm,* Vol. VII, p. 241).

[70] Būlāq ed., p. 40.

[71] Tirmidhī, Vol. I, pp. 289-91; Dārimī, Vol. I, p. 277.

Sufyān b. ʿUyayna told us from al-Zuhrī from ʿUrwa from ʿĀ'isha, who said:

> They, the believing women, were in the habit of performing the dawn-prayer with the Prophet; then they went their way in the half-light, wrapped up in their robes and unrecognized by anyone.[72]

The Prophet's rising in the dawn was likewise related by Sahl b. Saʿd and Zayd b. Thābit and other Companions in traditions identical in meaning to ʿĀ'isha's.

282. Shāfiʿī said: Someone has said to me: We hold that we should perform the dawn-prayer at daybreak, in accordance S283
with the tradition of Rāfiʿ b. Khadīj—which we regard as meritorious—while you maintain that it is permissible to choose one of the two contradictory traditions [on this matter]. Your [discretion] in our opinion, is contradictory to ʿĀ'isha's tradition.

283. [Shāfiʿī] replied: If there is a tradition contradictory to ʿĀ'isha's, it would be obligatory on both of us to accept her tradition rather than another, for her tradition should be the standard according to which you and I make our choice. So whenever traditions are found to be contradictory, we should choose the one for which there is valid reason which makes us believe that it is more reliable than others.[73]

284. He asked: What would that reason be?

285. [Shāfiʿī] replied: It is that one of the two traditions should be more consistent with [the meaning of] the Book of God, for consistency with the Book of God is an evidence [of reliability].

286. He said: So we hold, too. B40

287. [Shāfiʿī] said: If there is no relevant text in the Book of God, we shall choose the more reliable of the two [traditions], the one related by an authority better known as an expert in transmission and who has a greater reputation for knowledge, or better memory; otherwise we choose S284

[72] Mālik, Vol. 1, p. 5; Bukhārī, Vol. I, p. 223; Muslim, Vol. V, pp. 143-44; Abū Dāwūd, Vol. I, p. 115; Tirmidhī, Vol. I, pp. 287-88.

[73] See Shāfiʿī's *Ikhtilāf al-Ḥadīth (Kitāb al-Umm,* Vol. VII, pp. 208, 219, 222, 234, etc.).

the tradition related by two or more authorities in preference to one related by one authority, or the one which is more consistent with the general meaning of the Book or with the other sunnas of the Apostle, or more acceptable to the scholars, or validated by analogy, and [finally] the one followed by the majority of the Apostle's Companions.

288. He said: So we hold, as do all other scholars.

289. [Shāfiʿī] said: ʿĀ'isha's tradition is more consistent with the Book of God [than others], for God says: "Be you watchful over the prayers, and the middle prayer is included" [Q. II, 238]. So he who performs the prayer at the early time is the one who
S285 performs it more in keeping [with the duty of prayer].

Furthermore, the authorities who related ʿĀ'isha's traditions are all reputed to possess reliability and better memory. For in addition to ʿĀ'isha there are three authorities who related a similar tradition; they are: Zayd b. Thābit and Ibn Saʿd.[74] It is likewise more consistent with the Prophet's sunnas than Rāfiʿ b. Khadīj's tradition.

290. He asked: What sunnas?

291. [Shāfiʿī] replied: The Apostle of God said: "To pray at the early time means that one receives God's satisfaction; to pray late [i. e., later than the proper time] means that one must ask
S286 His pardon."[75]

He [the Prophet] does not prefer anything to God's satisfaction. As to pardon, it may either imply pardon for negligence or for allowable [action]. Permission means that favor will be given for the fulfilment of its opposite [i. e., prayer at the early time], because there is no order to abandon the opposite [action] which is permissible in the former.[76]

[74] The third authority was perhaps left out by an error, for Shāfiʿī gives the name as Anas b. Mālik in his book, *Ikhtilāf al-Ḥadīth* (*Kitāb al-Umm*, Vol. VII, p. 207).

[75] See Shāfiʿī, *Ikhtilāf al-Ḥadīth* (*Kitāb al-Umm*, Vol. VII, p. 209). Doubt has been raised on the authenticity of this tradition. See Shākir's commentary on Tirmidhī, Vol. I, pp. 321-22.

[76] See Calverley, *Worship in Islam,* p. 6 f.

292. He asked: What do you mean by that? S287

293. Shāfiʿī] replied: Since we are not permitted to abandon the performance of prayer at the scheduled time, only to delay the time of its performance, it is therefore meritorious to fulfil the duty at the scheduled time, although delay would be regarded as negligence that can be exercised. For the Apostle has made that clear in an answer to a question which he was asked: "What is the most meritorious act?" "Prayer at the scheduled time," he replied.[77] He [the Prophet] certainly will not abandon meritorious acts, nor will he order men to do otherwise. No scholar is ignorant that the performance of prayer at the scheduled time is most meritorious, but men are apt to be busy, forgetful, and [may suffer from] illnesses. That is the meaning which is more consistent with the Book of God. S288

294. He asked: In what part of the Book?

295. [Shāfiʿī] replied: God said: "Be you watchful over the prayers, and the middle prayer is included" [Q. II, 238]. So he who performs the prayer at the scheduled time is more in keeping [with his duty] than are those who delay its performance. We have noted that men prefer to perform their obligatory and voluntary prayers as nearly on time as they can, for they are liable to be busy or forgetful or suffer from other illnesses [which may cause postponement]—these are matters which are understandable. [Furthermore], the tradition related by Abū Bakr, ʿUmar, ʿUthmān, ʿAlī b. Abī Ṭālib, Ibn Masʿūd, Abū Mūsa al-Ashʿarī, Anas b. Mālik and others concerning the prompt performance of the dawn-prayer at the scheduled time is a reliable tradition.

296. He asked: Was it by the prolongation of the recital that Abū Bakr, ʿUmar and ʿUthmān began their prayer in the half-light and completed it at day-break. S289

297. [Shāfiʿī] replied: They prolonged the recital [at one time] and shortened it [at another]; but the performance at the scheduled time is determined by when it begins, not by when it

[77] Bukhārī, Vol. I, p. 143; Muslim, Vol. V, pp. 147-50; Dārimī, Vol. I, p. 278. Cf. Shākir's commentary on Tirmidhī, Vol. I, pp. 325-26.

is completed. For they all began at half-light, and the Prophet completed [his prayer] at half-light [while the others completed theirs at day-break]. Thus you have disagreed with a reliable tradition from the Apostle which it was binding on you to accept; and you have disagreed with others by maintaining that one may begin the performance of his prayer at daybreak and complete it at daybreak, and that he can shorten the recital. So you have disagreed [with all the traditions] on the time of the beginning of the prayer and on the shortening of the recital as well as with the tradition that [the Prophet] completed his prayer at half-light.

298. He asked: Would you regard Rāfiʿ's tradition as contradictory to ʿĀ'isha's?

299. [Shāfiʿī] replied: No!

300. He asked: In what respect do they agree?

301. [Shāfiʿī] replied: Since the Apostle urged men to perform their prayer at the scheduled time and pointed out that [such performance] was meritorious, his [attitude] implied that he was in favor of performing the prayer at the end of day-
S290 break. So he said: " Pray at day break," by which he meant just at the time the dawn begins.

302. He asked: Is there any other possible meaning?

303. [Shāfiʿī] replied: Yes. It may mean either what you have held, or an intermediary position between your opinion and mine, or any other meaning that may be implied by [the term] daybreak.

304. He asked: What makes your opinion preferable to mine?

305. [Shāfiʿī] replied: That which I have already explained as well as the Prophet's saying:

> There are two dawns: The first is like the tail of the *sirḥān* [false dawn][78] in which [the performance of prayer] is neither prohibited nor permitted; [the other] is daybreak, at which the performance of prayer is permitted, but taking the meal is forbidden.

[78] Lane, *Lexicon,* p. 1345.

That is to say, [taking the meal] by him who intends to fast [for the coming day].[79] S291

[B. Second] Category

306. [Shāfiʿī said]: Sufyān [b. ʿUyayna] told us from al-Zuhrī from ʿAṭā' b. Yazīd from Abū Ayyūb al-Anṣārī that the Prophet said:

> Let him who eases nature or makes water not face the *qibla* or turn his back to it; but turn either eastward or westward.[80] B41

And Abū Ayyūb said:

> When we entered Syria we found water-closets already built facing the *qibla*;[81] we therefore turned to the other direction and asked God's forgiveness.[82]

Mālik [b. Anas] told us from Yaḥya b. Saʿīd from Muḥammad b. Yaḥya b. Ḥabbān from his uncle Wāsiʿ b. Ḥabbān from ʿAbd-Allāh b. ʿUmar, who said:

> Some people have said: Whenever you ease nature, you should face neither the *qibla* [toward Makka] nor Jerusalem. However, ʿAbd-Allāh [b. ʿUmar] said: When I was on the roof of our house I saw [at a distance] the Apostle easing nature, sitting on two clay bricks in the direction of Jerusalem.[83] S292

307. Shāfiʿī said: The Apostle of God, living among Arabs who, most if not all, possessed no water-closets even when they lived in houses, instructed them [on how to ease nature] in a manner which might have one of two meanings:

[79] This tradition is not cited in any of the six standard digests, but in Bayhaqī, *al-Sunan al-Kubra* (Hyderabad, 1344-55/1925-36), Vol. IV, p. 215; and Jalāl al-Dīn al-Suyūṭī, *al-Dur al-Manthūr* (Cairo, 1314/1897), Vol. I, p. 200.

[80] Bukhārī, Vol. I, p. 50; Muslim, Vol. III, p. 153; Abū Dāwūd, Vol. I, p. 3; Tirmidhī, Vol. I, pp. 13-14.

[81] Būlāq ed., p. 42. Cf. Mālik's wording in *al-Muwaṭṭa'*, Vol. I, p. 193.

[82] See note 82; and Shākir's commentary on Tirmidhī, *Sunan,* Vol. I, pp. 13-14.

[83] Mālik, Vol. I, pp. 193-94; Bukhārī, Vol. I, p. 50; Muslim, Vol. III, pp. 152-53; Shāfiʿī, *Ihhtilāf al-Ḥadīth* (*Kitāb al-Umm*, Vol. VII, pp. 269-70).

First, since [the Arabs] were in the habit of going out into the desert to ease nature, [the Prophet] ordered them neither to face the *qibla* nor to turn their backs to it, since it was easy to avoid facing the *qibla* and turning their backs to it in the
S293 open desert. Since it so often happened that those who went out to ease nature in the desert were seen uncovered by men performing prayer, they were ordered to respect the *qibla* of God by avoiding exposure of the uncovered portion of their bodies to men performing prayer. This is the meaning more consistent with [the Prophet's] instructions. But God knows best!

Second, it is possible that [the Prophet] prohibited men from going out to ease nature in the open desert in places which were likely to be in the direction of the *qibla* in order to protect it from filth which might hurt those who perform prayer on it.

308. [Shāfiʿī] said: It is possible that Abū Ayyūb heard the
S294 tradition related from the Prophet in a general manner, so he applied it both to the desert and the houses, making no distinction between facing the *qibla* in the open desert and in water-closets within houses in which those who ease nature would be hidden. He [Abū Ayyūb] seems to have related the tradition in a general manner as he had heard it. It is indeed the duty of all who may relate traditions in a general manner to do so as they heard them until they find [qualifying] evidence specifying them.

309. Shāfiʿī said: Because Ibn ʿUmar related that he had seen the Prophet easing nature while facing [the *qibla* of] Jerusalem, one of the two *qibla*s—facing the latter *qibla* means that he should turn his back to the Kaʿba—, he objected to
S295 those who held that one should neither face the *qibla* nor turn his back on it while easing nature. He asserted that nobody should prohibit an act which the Apostle himself had permitted.

He [Ibn ʿUmar] did not seem to have heard the Apostle's order concerning [easing nature in] the open desert in order to draw a distinction between that act in the desert and in houses, so that he would relate the order of prohibition applicable to the desert and the order of permission applicable to the houses. For [if he did] he would have cited the specification concerning the houses as he heard it and would have distinguished between the two in the way the Apostle did, owing to the differences in the conditions between houses and the open desert.[84]

This is an evidence that whoever heard an order from the Apostle should obey it, even though [in obeying the order] the difference between one specifying order and another was unknown to him until such [an order] from the Apostle became known to him. **S296**

There are several other parallel traditions, but we have cited sufficient examples from among others we did not cite.

[C. Third] Category

310. [Sufyān] b. ʿUyayna told us from al-Zuhrī from ʿUbayd-Allāh b. ʿAbd-Allāh b. ʿUtba from Ibn ʿAbbās, who said:

> Al-Ṣaʿb b. Jaththāma told me that he had heard the prophet asked about the sudden attack at night on unbelievers in an enemy territory [whether] their [women and children] are included? ' They are included,' the Apostle replied.

ʿAmr b. Dīnār, on the authority of al-Zuhrī, added: They [the children] fall in [the same category as] their parents.[85] **S297**

[Sufyān] b. ʿUyayna told us from al-Zuhrī from Ibn Kaʿb b. Mālik from his uncle, who said:

> When the Prophet dispatched men to [kill] Ibn Abī al-Ḥuqayq, he prohibited them from killing women and children.[86]

[84] Shāfiʿī's contention that Ibn ʿUmar was unacquainted with such a tradition seems to be contradicted by a tradition cited by Abū Dāwūd to the effect that Ibn ʿUmar was once seen urinating in the desert, sheltered by his camel, in the direction of the *qibla*. He was asked whether the Prophet had not prohibited this. Ibn ʿUmar said yes, but not if there was a barrier between him and the *qibla*. See Abū Dāwūd, Vol. I, pp. 3-4.

[85] Bukhārī, Vol. II, pp. 250-51; Muslim, Vol. XII, pp. 48-49; Abū Dāwūd, Vol. III, p. 54; Ibn Ḥanbal, Vol. VI, pp. 332, 334; Shawkānī, *Nayl al-Awṭār,* Vol. VII, p. 259.

[86] For an account of this incident, see Ibn Hishām, Vol. II, pp. 714-16; Guillaume's translation, pp. 482-83. See also Abū Dāwūd, Vol. III, p. 54 (the latter part of the tradition).

311. [Shāfiʿī] said: Sufyān held that the Prophet's saying: "They [women and children] are included," meant that their killing was permissible, but that [such a permission] was abrogated by his order relating to Ibn Abī al-Ḥuqayq; and [Sufyān] added that whenever al-Zuhrī related the tradition of al-Ṣaʿb b. Jaththāma, he added to it the tradi-
S298 tion of Ibn Kaʿb [prohibiting the killing of women and children].

312. Shāfiʿī said: The tradition of al-Ṣa'b b. Jaththāma dates from the time of the Prophet's *ʿumra* [or lesser pilgrimage].[87] So if it were related from the time of the first *ʿumra*, his order [of killing] Ibn Abī al-Ḥuqayq was either given before this *ʿumra*, according to one opinion, or in the same year, to another; but if the tradition were related at the second *ʿumra*, its date must
B42 be after the Prophet had given the order to [kill] Ibn Abī al-Ḥuqayq. But God knows best!

But we know of no order ever given [by the Prophet] permitting the killing of women and children which he later repealed. The reason for [the Prophet's] order prohibiting the killing of women and children, in our opinion, was to specify their exclusion from the order of killing whenever they could be distinguished from others [not because the killing of women and children was then permitted]. As to [the Prophet's] saying: "They [women and children] are included," the order means that [women and children] were subject to two rules: First, that they were immune neither by the
S299 faith [of Islam] which prohibits the shedding of blood of believers only, nor, [secondly,] by the rule governing only the territory [of Islam] which prohibits sudden attack on that territory.

Since the Prophet permitted sudden attack by night on enemy territory, on the strength of his order to attack the Banū al-Muṣṭaliq, [legal] knowledge prescribes that sudden attack by night, with the [consequential] killing of women and children,

[87] The Prophet twice performed the *ʿumra* (lesser pilgrimage): the first was in the year 7 of the hijra (A. D. 629), before the capture of Makka, and the second in the year 8 of the hijra (A. D. 630), shortly after the capture of Makka. See Ibn Hishām, Vol. II, pp. 788-89, 886-87; Guillaume's translation, pp. 530-31.

is lawful by an order of the Prophet, and that whoever kills them shall be subject neither to punishment nor to atonement [*kaffāra*], nor to blood-money [*diya*], nor to retaliation. Thus, if sudden attack by night is permitted the protection of Islam cannot save them. But whoever kills women and children should not do so intentionally, if they are recognizable and distinguishable.[88] He [the Prophet] prohibited the killing of children, because they do not comprehend disbelief sufficiently to be able to practice it, and the women, because they do not fight. They and the children might be taken as khawls (i. e., wives, slaves and servants) who will reinforce the followers of God's religion. S300

313. Someone said: Explain that by citing other examples?

314. [Shāfiʿī] replied: Enough has been given to the learned in distinction from others.

315. He asked: Will you give further evidence by citing a relevant text from the Book of God?

316. [Shāfiʿī] replied:[89] God said:

> It is not for a believer to kill a believer, unless it be by mistake. If anyone kills a believer by mistake, [the penalty is] the setting free of a believing slave, and blood-money is to be paid to his family, unless they forgo it as a free-will offering. If he [i. e. the victim] belongs to a people at enmity with you and is a believer, the compensation should be the setting free of a believing slave. If he belongs to a people between whom and you there is a compact, blood-money is to be paid to his family and the killer shall set free a believing slave. He who does not find the means to do that, shall fast two consecutive months—a repentance from God; verily God is All-Knowing, All-Wise [Q. IV. 92].[90]

So[91] God has imposed the penalty of paying the *diya* [blood-money] and the freeing of a slave for the killing of a believer

[88] For further discussion on this rule, see Shāfiʿī, *Kitāb al-Umm*, Vol. IV, pp. 156-57.

[89] In the text: " Shāfiʿī replied: Yes, God said."

[90] But " if anyone kills a believer intentionally, his recompense is hell, to abide therein. God will be angry with him and will curse him, and prepare for him a mighty punishment" [Q. IV, 93].

[91] " Shāfiʿī said" is omitted.

by mistake; and the payment of the *diya* and the freeing of a believing slave for the killing of a member [of a people] with whom Islam had made a compact. So in both cases killing is prohibited either by religion, or by compact, and by [residence in] the territory [of Islam]. If the believer kills
S301 another believer in a non-Muslim territory—wherein killing is not prohibited—faith prohibits him from so doing; he is therefore under [an obligation of] the *kaffāra* (atonement), but not the [payment of the] *diya*, for the shedding of the believer's blood is prohibited by the faith. Since the killing of non-Muslim children and women is neither prohibited by religion nor by residence in Muslim territory, compensation to the near of kin, retaliation, blood-money, and atonement are not obligatory.

[D. Fourth] Category[92]

317. He asked: Give some other kinds of traditions regarded by certain other scholars as contradictory.

318. [Shāfiʿī] replied: Mālik [b. Anas] told us from Ṣafwān b. Sulaym from ʿAṭa' b. Yasār from Saʿīd al-Khudrī, that the Apostle said:

> The Friday [complete] washing is obligatory on every adult [believer].[93]

S302 [Sufyān] b. ʿUyayna told us from al-Zuhrī from Sālim from his father, that the Prophet said:

> Let no one go to the Friday [prayer] before he performs the [complete] washing.[94]

[92] This heading is neither in the MS nor in the Būlāq edition. Shākir introduces it as the "Friday washing," but since it is another category of contradictory traditions no special title is deemed necessary.

[93] Mālik, Vol. I, p. 102; Bukhārī, Vol. I, p. 220; Muslim, Vol. VI, p. 132; Abū Dāwūd, Vol. I, p. 94; Shawkānī, *Nayl al-Awṭār,* Vol. I, p. 255; Shāfiʿī, *Ikhtilāf al-Ḥadīth* (*Kitāb al-Umm*, Vol. VII, p. 178).

[94] Mālik, Vol. I, pp. 102-103; Muslim, Vol. I, p. VI, 130; Abū Dāwūd, Vol. I, p. 94; Tirmidhī, Vol. II, pp. 366-67; Shawkānī, *Nayl al-Awṭār,* Vol. I, p. 252.

319. Shāfiʿī said: The Apostle's saying concerning "the Friday washing, etc.," and his order for its performance has two possible meanings: [First,] the literal, is that cleanliness for the Friday prayer cannot be fulfilled except by [complete] washing just as freedom from pollution cannot be attained without [complete] washing. [The second,] it is obligatory by discretion [i. e., commendable], for ethical or health reasons. [For] Mālik [b. Anas] told us from al-Zuhrī from Sālim [b. ʿAbd-Allāh b. ʿUmar], who said:

> A Companion of the Prophet entered the mosque on a Friday while the [Caliph] ʿUmar was reciting the sermon. ' What is the time?' ʿUmar asked. ' O Commander of the believers! I was at the market-place when I heard the call to prayer, so I performed the ablution at once [and hastened to this place,]' replied the Companion. ' [Have you performed] the ablution too? I understand that the Apostle S303
> ordered only [complete] washing,' said ʿUmar.[95]

I have been told, [says Shāfiʿī], by the trusted authority [Yaḥya b. Ḥassā] from Maʿmar [b. Rashīd] from al-Zuhrī from Sālim from his father a similar tradition, giving the name of the Companion who entered the mosque without washing as ʿUthmān b. ʿAffān.

320. [Shāfiʿī] said: Since ʿUmar knew well that the Apostle had ordered [complete] washing [on Fridays], and knew that ʿUthmān was well aware of the Apostle's order and reminded him of it, and ʿUthmān admitted that he knew it, therefore if anyone thought that ʿUthmān might have forgotten, he should remember that ʿUmar would have reminded him before he performed the prayer; and since ʿUthmān neither desisted from performing the prayer until he had washed nor was ordered
by ʿUmar to wash, this indicates that both must have been S304
certain that the Apostle's order for the [Friday] washing was optional—not obligatory—, since neither ʿUmar nor ʿUthmān would have neglected the order of washing unless, as I have already explained, it was regarded as optional.

[95] Mālik, Vol. I, pp. 101-102; Muslim, Vol. VI, p. 131; Shawkānī, *Nayl al-Awṭār,* Vol. I, p. 256.

321. [Shāfiʿī] said: [the scholar] of Baṣra has related that the Prophet said: He who fulfils the [duty of] ablution on
B43 Friday, [its fulfilment would be] satisfactory and virtuous; but he who performs the [complete] washing, washing would be
S305 preferable.[96]

Sufyān [b. ʿUyayna] told us from Yaḥya [b. Saʿīd] from ʿAmra [daughter of ʿAbd al-Raḥmān] from ʿĀ'isha, who said:

> S306 Men who were engaged in [daily] work and were in the habit of performing the [Friday] prayer [without washing] were told that it would be more appropriate if they first performed the [complete] washing.[97]

[A General] Order of Prohibition in One Tradition Made Particular in Another

322. Shāfiʿī said:[98] Mālik [b. Anas] told us from Abū al-Zinnād and Muḥammad b. Yaḥya b. Ḥabbān from al-Aʿraj from Abū Hurayra that the Apostle said:

> Let none of you seek a woman in marriage if his brother [in religion] already is seeking her.[99]

Mālik [b. Anas] told us from Nāfiʿ from Ibn ʿUmar from the Prophet, who said:

> Let none of you seek a woman in marriage if his brother already is seeking her.[100]

[96] Abū Dāwūd, Vol. I, p. 97; Shawkānī, *Nayl al-Awṭār,* Vol. I, p. 256.

[97] Bukhārī, Vol. I, p. 229; Tirmidhī, Vol. II, pp. 407-408; and Shawkānī, *Nayl al-Awṭār,* Vol. I, p. 257.

[98] Būlāq ed., p. 44.

[99] Mālik cites different authorities in *al-Muwaṭṭa',* Vol. II, p. 523.

[100] Mālik, Vol. II, p. 523; Bukhārī, Vol. III, p. 431; Cf. Muslim, Vol. IX, p. 197; Abū Dāwūd, Vol. II, p. 228; Dārimī, Vol. II, p. 135; Shawkānī, *Nayl al-Awṭār,* Vol. VI, p. 114.

323. Shāfiʿī said: Had there been no indication from the Apostle specifying the meaning of his order of prohibition that no one should propose marriage to a woman in competition with his brother, the literal meaning of the tradition would have been that it was unlawful for any one to propose marriage to a woman in competition with another from the time when the S307
suit was begun to the time of its withdrawal.

324. [Shāfiʿī] said: The Prophet's saying: "Let none of you propose, etc...," may have been an answer to a specific question, but the one who related the tradition did not know the reason for which the Apostle had given the answer. So either a certain portion, not all, of the tradition was related, or the portion which was subject to doubt was [consciously] not related. Thus it is possible that the Prophet was asked a question about a man who sought to marry a certain woman, and she agreed to marry him, but when another, whom she preferred to the first, sought to marry her, she rejected the first in favor of the second. So [the Prophet] prohibited the proposal to this woman. For if the woman rejected [the second man] after she had accepted him, the first to whom she wanted to S308
return might not agree to marry her. The consequences would be disadvantageous to both, [for it would be more difficult for them to find a partner to marry].

325. Someone may ask: Why do you maintain that the Prophet's order prohibiting one man to propose marriage in competition with another specified the meaning [in a certain situation], to the exclusion of others?

326. [Shāfiʿī replied]: Because there is a specific indication [in the tradition] to this effect.

327. He asked: Where is it?

328. [Shāfiʿī] replied: Mālik [b. Anas] told us from ʿAbd-Allāh b. Yazīd—freed-slave of al-Aswad b. Sufyān—from Abū Salma b. ʿAbd al-Raḥmān from Fāṭima, daughter of Qays, who said: Her husband had divorced her and the Apostle ordered her to fulfil the *ʿidda* [waiting period] in the house of Ibn Umm Maktūm before she could lawfully remarry, and told her to let him know when she had become lawful [for re-marriage]. S309
When the time had come, she told him that Muʿāwiya b. Abī

Sufyān and Abū Jahm had proposed to her. " Abū Jahm," said the Apostle, " is a man whose stick is never laid down from his shoulder, and Muʿāwiya is a begger who owns no property. Get married to Usāma b. Zayd." " But I do not like him," she answered. " Get married to Usāma," he repeated. " So I married him and God has blessed him abundantly and I am happy with him," said she.[101]

329. Shāfiʿī said: We are in favor of this opinion. For the evidence in the Apostle's proposition on behalf of Usāma to Fāṭima—after she had told him that Muʿāwiya and Abū Jahm had proposed to her—specified two points:

First, the Prophet knew well that the proposals of the two men [Abū Jahm and Muʿāwiya] had not been made [at the same time, but] one after the other. Since he did not tell her that one of them had no right to propose until the other had withdrawn, and since he [himself] proposed to her on behalf of Usāma—after she had been proposed to—we concluded that
S310 she must have rejected the earlier proposals, for [the Prophet] would have ordered her to marry the one she had accepted. So her intimation [to the Prophet] that two [men] had proposed to her was merely to inform him that she already had rejected them. She may have told him because she wanted his advice, for if she had accepted either one, she would not have sought his advice.

[Second], since the Prophet proposed to her on Usāma's behalf, we concluded that the circumstances in which he proposed to her were different from those which he regarded as unlawful. Nor does the circumstance [in which the Prophet proposed to her] distinguishing this proposal from the other-rendering the one lawful and the other unlawful—make the marriage valid unless she empowered her guardian [the Prophet] to arrange her marriage on her behalf. If the guardian [formally] arranges the marriage, [the contract] becomes [equally] binding on both, and she becomes lawful [only] to him. Otherwise,
S311 neither does the guardian have the right to arrange the marriage

[101] Mālik, Vol. II, pp. 580-81; Muslim, Vol. X, pp. 94-98; Dārimī, Vol. II, pp. 135-36; Shawkānīi, *Nayl al-Awṭār,* Vol. VI, p. 116.

without her permission, nor does her approval or disapproval [of the proposition] make any difference.

330. Someone may ask: [Do you not think that] the circumstances of her approval are different from those of her disapproval?

331. [Shāfiᶜī replied]: [Yes, they are] for if a man proposes to a woman and she rejects him with an affront, and she neither rejects him with an affront nor approves when he proposes again, her attitude is different and may be regarded as nearer to acceptance. Thus the circumstances in which she rejected him with an affront were different from those in which she did not reject him with an affront, for in the latter case her attitude was nearer to acceptance. Thus her attitude changed from non-commital to another nearer to approval than to non-approval.

No meaning other than the one which I have [just] described S312
is valid: [The Prophet] has prohibited a proposal of marriage
to a woman who had already been committed by her guardian, B44
with her approval, to another; and that unless the guardian's commitment had been made, her previous position had not changed. But God knows best.[102]

Orders of Prohibition [in Some Traditions] More Clearly Stated Than in Previous [Traditions]

332. [Shāfiᶜī said]: Mālik [b. Anas] told us from Nāfiᶜ from Ibn ᶜUmar that the Apostle said:

> The two parties to a sale [contract] have the right of option [to cancel
> the contract] so long as they have not separated, except the sale of S313

[102] Shāfiᶜī's controversy over this question was with Mālikī followers, since Mālik maintained that the Prophet's order of prohibition was confined only to the woman who had given prior approval to a person, specified the dowry and agreed to marry him. See Mālik, Vol. II, pp. 523-24. For a fuller discussion of Shāfiᶜī's reply, see *Ikhtilāf al-Ḥadīth (Kitāb al-Umm*, Vol. VII, pp. 296-301).

option (*bay*ᶜ *al-khiyār*) [i. e., that the right of option would be as stipulated in the contract].[103]

Sufyān [b. ᶜUyayna] told us from al-Zuhrī from Saᶜīd b. al-Musayyib from Abū Hurayra that the Apostle said:

Let no one sell to someone else what he already has agreed to sell to another.[104]

The meaning implied in this [communication] indicates that the Apostle decreed that "the two parties to a sale have the right of option so long as they have not parted," and his order of prohibition concerning sale by one person in contravention of his agreement to sell to another means that [such an order is applicable] only so long as the two [parties] have not departed from the place of the transaction. For the two cannot be regarded as two parties to the sale until they have made the contract. Once the contract is made, it becomes binding on the parties, and no disadvantage befalls the vendor if another man enters into another sale transaction with the purchaser whether relating to the same property or to different property after the property is sold. But so long as the two parties have the right of option and another vendor may offer, let us say, a suit of cloth for nine dīnārs while the other had asked ten, the purchaser
S314 is bound to cancel the sale transaction since he has the right of option before they separate. He may even cancel the first sale transaction and make no other one. So the other [vendor's] action could be disadvantageous to either the first vendor and the purchaser, or to either one of them. This is the explanation for the [Prophet's] order of prohibition that no man should enter into a sale transaction in contravention of his agreement to sell to another, and I know of no other. For do you not agree that if a man purchases a suit of cloth for ten dīnārs, and the sale contract is binding on the two parties before they separate, no damage accrues to the first vendor if a second vendor offers to sell the prospective purchaser one dīnār cheaper, because the

[103] Mālik, Vol. II, p. 671; Bukhārī, Vol. II, pp. 18-19; Muslim, Vol. X, p. 173. See also Shāfiᶜī, *Kitāb al-Umm,* Vol. III, p. 3.

[104] Cf. Shawkānī, *Nayl al-Awṭār,* Vol. V, pp. 195-96.

sale contract for ten dīnārs had become binding and could not be cancelled.

333. [Shāfiʿī] said: It has been related from the Prophet that he said:

> Let none of you bargain in competition with his brother [i. e., another Muslim].

If this tradition were reliable, although I do not consider it to be so, it would be parallel to the one which runs as follows:

> Let none of you propose marriage to a woman in competition with his brother.

"No one should bargain in competition with his brother" means that [no sale to another is permitted] if he [the vendor] has indicated an intent to sell before the sale takes place, so that if the contract is made it becomes binding. **S315**

334. If someone should ask: What is the evidence for that?

335. He would be told: The Apostle sold [a piece of property to a person] who paid a higher price. The sale of a property to one who paid a higher price is a bargain against another's bargain; but the vendor [in this case] did not accept the offer of the first person and demanded a higher price.[105]

[*Orders of*] *Prohibition Consistent with Previous Orders in Certain Matters and Inconsistent with Others*

[A. First Category]

336. [Shāfiʿī said]: Mālik [b. Anas] told us from Muḥammad b. Yaḥya b. Ḥabban from al-ʿAraj from Abū Hurayra, who said:

[105] Shāfiʿī disagreed with Mālik on the *khiyār al-majlis*, following more consistently the spirit of the Prophet's tradition, while Mālik, under the influence of local practice, rejected a tradition in favor of a sound legal rule. See Mālik, Vol. II, pp. 671-72; Shāfiʿī, *Kitāb al-Umm,* Vol. VII, pp. 204-205.

> The Apostle of God has prohibited the performance of prayer after the ʿaṣr till the sun has set, and after the break of dawn till it has risen.[106]

Mālik [b. Anas] told us from Nāfiʿ from Ibn ʿUmar that the
S316 Prophet said:

> Let no one intend to perform his prayer at the time of the sun-rising nor at the sun-setting.[107]

Mālik [b. Anas] told us from Zayd b. Aslam from ʿAṭā' b. Yasār from ʿAbd-Allāh al-Ṣunābiḥī that the Apostle of God said:

> S317 When the sun first rises, Satan's horns are associated with it; when it is up, they are separated; when it is at the meridian they join it; when it begins to descend, they are separated; when it approaches its setting, they join it again; and when it disappears, they are separated. The Apostle of God has forbidden the performances of prayer during these hours [when Satan's horns are associated with the sun].[108]

The Apostle's order of prohibition during these times may have two meanings:

The first, which is the more general, is that all kinds of prayers are incumbent on him who forgets or oversleeps, and those of that for any reason are incumbent on one are prohibited during these times, and no one is permitted to perform them. Should any one perform one of them, the duty would not be fulfilled, just as it would not be if he performed the prayer before its
S318-320 proper time.

The second, [the Prophet] may have intended to specify a certain [kind] of prayer, not others.

Prayers may be divided into two kinds: The one is obligatory which no Muslim is permitted to omit at its proper time, for if he

[106] Mālik, Vol. I, p. 221; Bukhārī, Vol. I, p. 154; Muslim, Vol. VI, p. 110; Shawkānī, *Nayl al-Awṭār*, Vol. III, p. 93.

[107] Mālik, Vol. I, p. 220; Bukhārī, Vol. I, pp. 154-55; Muslim, Vol. VI, pp. 110-12.

[108] Mālik, Vol. I, p. 219; Ibn Ḥanbal, Vol. VIII, p. 8; Shāfiʿī, *Musnad*, Vol. I, p. 55; cf. Tirmidhī, Vol. I, pp. 301-302.

ever does, he must make up for it. The other, the performance of which may draw [us] nearer to God, is supererogatory. He who omits a supererogatory prayer is under no obligation to make up for it.

We have found that obligatory [prayers] are to be distinguished from the optional if one is travelling as a rider. The B45
obligatory prayers can be performed on the ground, and no other way fulfils the duty, but the supererogatory ones may be performed while riding in whatever direction one desires. The two [kinds] may be distinguished [on the basis of] their performance whether in town or [in the country] while on travel: He
who can perform the obligatory prayers standing, should not S321
do so sitting, but he is permitted to perform the supererogatory ones sitting.

Since the two meanings [are permissible] it is obligatory on the learned not to become attached to any particular—in distinction from general—meaning unless there is a specifying indication in the sunna or an agreement among the scholars who do not agree on any matter contrary to the sunna.

337. [Shāfiʿī] said: Similarly, other traditions from the Apostle should be accepted as explicitly general unless an indication specifies otherwise, as I have explained, or unless there is an agreement of the Muslim [scholars] specifying that their meaning is implicit, not explicit [literal], and that it is particular, not general; and men should obey them in either case as such. [For] Mālik [b. Anas] told us from Zayd b. Aslam from ʿAṭā' b. Yasār from Buṣr b. Saʿīd and al-Aʿraj from Abū Hurayra
that the Apostle said: S322

> Whoever performed one cycle of the morning prayer before sunrise would be regarded as having performed the morning prayer, and whoever performed one cycle of the ʿ*aṣr* prayer before sunset, would be regarded as having performed the ʿ*aṣr* prayer.[109]

338. Shāfiʿī said: Thus [legal] knowledge indicates that he who performs one cycle of the morning prayer before sun-

[109] Mālik, Vol. I, p. 6; Bukhārī, Vol. I, p. 154; Muslim, Vol. V, p. 104; Abū Dāwūd, Vol. I, p. 112; Shawkānī, *Nayl al-Awṭār,* Vol. II, pp. 22-23; Shāfiʿī, *Musnad,* Vol. I, p. 63.

rise and he who performs one cycle of the ʿ*aṣr* prayer before sun-set, would be regarded as having performed his prayers at forbidden times, because both would be regarded as having been performed after the morning and ʿ*aṣr* prayers, coinciding with sun-rise and the sun-set, and these are times at which the performance of prayers is prohibited.

Since the Apostle considered those who perform their prayers at these times as having performed the morning and ʿ*aṣr* prayers, we concluded that his order of prohibition against performing prayer at these times governs supererogatory
S323 prayers [only], which are not obligatory, for he would not permit the performance of a prescribed prayer at a time forbidden for such prayers.

Mālik [b. Anas] told us from Ibn Shihāb from Ibn al-Musayyib that the Apostle said:

> Whoever forgot to perform a certain prayer should make up for it whenever he remembered it, for God said: ' And perform the prayer for my remembrance' [Q. XX, 14].[110]

Mālik [b. Anas] and ʿImrān b. al-Ḥusayn related a tradition from the Prophet similar to that of Ibn al-Musayyib, but one of them added: " [Whoever forgot. . .] or was asleep. . . "[111]

Shāfiʿī said: In his saying that ". . . she should make up for
S324 it whenever he remembered it," the Apostle, on God's behalf, appointed no specific time for it, but stated that it should be performed as soon as it was remembered.

[Sufyān] b. ʿUyayna told us from Abū al-Zubayr [al-Makkī][112] from ʿAbd-Allāh b. Bābāh from Jubayr b. Muṭʿim that the Prophet said:

> Men of ʿAbd-Manāf! Whoever of you may be in authority, shall never prevent anyone from performing the circumambulation of this

[110] Mālik, Vol. I, p. 14; Muslim, Vol. V, pp. 181-83; Abū Dāwūd, Vol. I, p. 119. See also Shāfiʿī, *Kitāb al-Umm,* Vol. I, pp. 130-31; *Ikhtilāf al-Ḥadīth* (*Kitāb al-Umm*, Vol. VII, p. 126); *Musnad,* Vol. I, p. 55.

[111] Muslim, Vol. V, p. 193; Shawkānī, *Nayl al-Awṭār,* Vol. II, p. 26; Shāfiʿī, *Ikhtilāf al-Ḥadīth* (*Kitāb al-Umm*, Vol. VII, p. 127).

[112] Būlāq ed., p. 46.

House [of the Kaʿba] or the prayer at any time, whether in daytime or at night.[113]

ʿAbd al-Majīd [b. ʿAbd al-ʿAzīz] told us from Ibn Jurayj from ʿAṭā' [b. Yasār] from the Prophet, a similar tradition, adding at S325
the beginning: " Men of ʿAbd al-Muṭṭalib, etc... "[114]

339. [Shāfiʿī] said: So Jubayr informed [us] that the Prophet gave an order permitting the performance of the circumambulation and prayer at any time that anyone wished to do so. This [order] clearly indicates that the [Prophet's] orders prohibiting the performance of prayers at certain times related only to optional prayers, not to obligatory prayers. For Muslims performed the funeral prayers, which were obligatory, generally after the morning and the *ʿaṣr* prayers [irrespective of the forbidden times].

Some of our followers argued that since ʿUmar b. al-Khaṭṭāb
performed the circumambulation after daybreak and, finding S326
the sun had not yet risen, went to Ṭuwa[115] and couched his camel and performed the prayer after sunrise, they prohibited the performance of the circumambulation prayer after both the *ʿaṣr* and the morning prayers just as they prohibited optional prayers.[116]

340. [Shāfiʿī] said: If ʿUmar delayed the circumambulation prayer, he delayed it because it was permissible for him to do so. For he may have been in need of a certain place at Ṭuwa to ease nature,[117] and it was permissible for him [to delay the prayer]. However, [ʿUmar] had heard only the general order of prohibition, and he punished al-Munkadir [b. ʿAbd-Allāh] by striking him for performing a prayer
after the *ʿaṣr* in Madīna, without realizing that the order S327
of prohibition was specified to the situation that I have just

[113] Abū Dāwūd, Vol. II, p. 108; Shawkānī, *Nayl al-Awṭār,* Vol. III, p. 101; Shāfiʿī, *Kitāb al-Umm,* Vol. I, p. 131; *Ikhtilāf al-Ḥadīth* (*Kitāb al-Umm,* Vol. VII, p. 127).

[114] See Shāfiʿī, *Kitāb al-Umm,* Vol. I, p. 131; and *Ikhtilāf al-Ḥadīth (Kitāb al-Umm,* Vol. VII, pp. 127-28).

[115] A place on the outskirts of Makka.

[116] For ʿUmar's prayer at Ṭuwa, see Mālik, Vol. I, p. 368.

[117] Būlāq ed., p. 46.

explained and so [he felt] himself under obligation [to punish al-Munkadir]. He who knows the reasons for the orders of prohibition and permission [should distinguish between the two], since the order of permission was different from that of prohibition, just as I have already explained in the [case of the tradition of] ʿAlī b. Abī Ṭālib concerning the Prophet's order of prohibition against keeping the meat of sacrifice beyond three days, because ʿAlī had heard the Prophet's [general] order but did not hear the reasons for that [particular] prohibition.

341. He said: Someone may ask: Did not Abū Saʿīd al-Khudrī do what ʿUmar had done?

S328 342. [Shāfiʿī] replied: The answer to this [question] is like the answer to other [questions].

343. He asked: Someone may ask: Is there any one who did contrary to what the two have done?

B46 344. [Shāfiʿī] replied: Yes! They were: Ibn ʿUmar, Ibn ʿAbbās, ʿĀ'isha, al-Ḥasan, al-Ḥusayn, and others. Ibn ʿUmar heard the order of prohibition directly from the Prophet. [For] [Sufyān] b. ʿUyayna told us from ʿAmr b. Dīnār, who said:

> ʿAṭa' b. Abī Rabāḥ and I saw Ibn ʿUmar perform the circumambulation after daybreak and a prayer of two *rakʿa*s before sun-rise.[118]

Sufyān [b. ʿUyayna] told us from ʿAmmār al-Duhnī from Abū Shuʿba that al-Ḥasan and al-Ḥusayn performed the
S329 circumambulation after the *ʿaṣr* and [then] prayed.

Muslim [b. Khālid al-Zanjī] and ʿAbd al-Majīd [b. ʿAbd al-ʿAzīz] told us from Ibn Jurayj from Ibn Abī Mulayka, who said:

> I have seen Ibn ʿAbbās perform both the circumambulation and the prayer after the *ʿaṣr*.[119]

345. [Shāfiʿī] said: The reason for stating the Companions' disagreement on this matter is to enable him who is aware of this disagreement to understand that the meaning could not

[118] Bayhaqī, *al-Sunan al-Kubra*, Vol. II, p. 462.
[119] *Ibid.*, p. 463.

be other than what we have just said, or that the sunna was unknown by him who acted differently from it, or that he who knew the sunna may have interpreted its meaning in a certain way or may have found justification for certain other interpretation.

So if a certain tradition from the Apostle is proved to be authentic, it is obligatory on all who are aware of it to accept it, and nothing else shall be accepted instead, for God has given no one else [authority] to give an order contrary to the [Prophet's] order. S330

[B. Second] Category:

346. Mālik [b. Anas] told us from Nāfiʿ from Ibn ʿUmar that the Apostle prohibited "*muzābana*." *Muzābana* is the exchange of the [fresh] fruit [of palm-trees] for dry dates in equal quantities, and of grapes for raisins in equal quantities.[120]

Mālik [b. Anas] told us from ʿAbd-Allāh b. Yazīd, freed-slave of al-Aswad b. Sufyān, that Zayd Abū ʿAyyāsh told him from
Saʿd b. Abī Waqqāṣ that he heard the Prophet asked about the S331
exchange of [dry] dates for fresh dates. "Do fresh dates lose weight after they dry?" inquired the Prophet. "Yes, they do," was the answer. Thereupon the Prophet ordered the prohibition
[of such a sale].[121] S332

Mālik [b. Anas] told us from Nāfiʿ from Ibn ʿUmar from Zayd b. Thābit, who related that the Apostle permitted [the owner of] an ʿ*arīya*, [to sell a branch which contains a quantity of dates roughly estimated].[122]

[Sufyān] b. ʿUyayna told us from al-Zuhrī from Sālim from his father from Zayd b. Thābit that the Prophet permitted the
sale of ʿ*arīya*s.[123] S333

[120] Mālik, Vol. II, p. 624; Bukhārī, Vol. II, p. 32; Muslim, Vol. X, p. 193; Abū Dāwūd, Vol. III, p. 251.

[121] Mālik, Vol. II, p. 624; Abū Dāwūd, Vol. III, p. 251.

[122] Mālik, Vol. II, pp. 619-20; Bukhārī, Vol. II, p. 32; Muslim, Vol. X, pp. 183-86. For meaning of ʿ*arīya*, see Abū Dāwūd, Vol. III, p. 252.

[123] *Ibid.*; and Shāfiʿī, *Ikhtilāf al-Ḥadīth* (*Kitāb al-Umm*, Vol. VII, p. 319).

347. Shāfiʿī said: The exchange of [fresh] dates for dry dates was prohibited on the strength of the Prophet's order of prohibition, and the Prophet made it clear that he prohibited [such an exchange] because fresh dates lose weight after they dry. He [the Prophet] prohibited the exchange of dates for dates except in equal quantities, because he noted the loss of weight when fresh dates become dry, so that the exchange cannot possibly be equal in quantities since the [amount] lost cannot be known. Thus the [Prophet's] order of prohibition includes two meanings: The differential in weight, and *al-muzābana*; the latter means the sale of a known for an unknown [i. e., shrinking] measure of the same kind.

Since the Apostle permitted the exchange of *ʿarīya*s for dry dates by measure, his special permission [of sale] should not be construed as permission for other kinds of sale, such as *al-muzābana* or the exchange of [dry] dates for fresh dates, for
S334 his order of prohibition is general excluding only [the sale of] *ʿarīya*s. This is an example of the general speech intended to mean the particular.[124]

[C. Third] Category

348. [Shāfiʿī said]: Saʿīd b. Sālim [al-Qaddāḥ] from Ibn Jurayj from ʿAṭā' [b. Abī Rabāḥ] from Ṣafwān b. Mawhab from ʿAbd-Allāh b. Muḥammad b. Ṣayfī from Ḥakīm b. Ḥizām, who
S335 said:

> The Apostle of God said to me: ' I have been told that you are engaged in selling foodstuffs.' ' Yes, O Apostle of God,' answered Ḥakīm. ' Let no one sell foodstuffs until it is purchased and its price is paid for,' said the Apostle.[125]

Saʿīd [b. Sālim] told us from Ibn Jurayj, who said: ʿAṭā' [b. Abī Rabāḥ] related to me a similar tradition from ʿAbd-Allāh b. ʿIṣma [al-Jushamī] from Ḥakīm b. Ḥizām, who heard it from the Prophet.

[124] Cf. J. Schacht, *Origins of Muhammadan Jurisprudence*, pp. 153-54.
[125] Cf. Abū Dāwūd, Vol. III, pp. 281-82.

The trustworthy authority [Yaḥya b. Ḥassān] told us from Ayyūb b. Abī Tamīma from Yūsuf b. Māhak from Ḥakīm b. Ḥizām, who said: S336

> The Apostle prohibited me from selling what I did not own.[126]

[" What I did not own,"] means what one has not received and became responsible for.

[Sufyān] b. ʿUyayna told us from Ibn Abī Najīḥ from ʿAbd-Allāh b. Kathīr from Abū al-Minhāl from Ibn ʿAbbās, who said:

> When the Apostle of God entered Madīna, he found men in the habit of paying for dates in advance for one or two years. Thereupon he S337 stipulated: ' Whoever pays in advance [for a commodity], he shall do so for a specified measure and a definite weight, to be delivered at a fixed time.'[127] S338

349. [Shāfiʿī] said: The Prophet's order of prohibition against the vendor's sale [of a commodity] not in his own possession means either that the vendor may sell the commodity B47 before it is seen by the buyer as it had been seen by the vendor at the time of sale, or that the vendor may sell a commodity he either did not have or had not taken possession of, so that the vendor was not responsible for it nor was it in his possession to be able to hand it over to the buyer. [Finally] the S339 Prophet's order may have another meaning, other than the two [mentioned].

Since the Apostle stipulated that " whoever pays in advance [for a commodity] should do so for a specified measure and a definite weight, to be delivered at a fixed time," such [kind of a commodity] falls in the category of sale in which the commodity is neither in the vendor's possession nor ready for delivery at the time of sale. But since the vendor is responsible [for such a commodity] at the time of delivery, the Prophet's order indicates that he prohibited only the kind of sale in which

[126] See Abū Dāwūd, Vol. III, p. 281.

[127] Cf. Būlāq ed., p. 47, where there is a repetition of the same stipulations. Paragraphs 917-918 in Shākir's edition are omitted for the same reason. See Bukhārī, Vol. II, p. 44; Muslim, Vol. XI, pp. 41-42; Abū Dāwūd, Vol. III, p. 275. Sale by paying in advance is called *salaf* or *salam* sale.

the commodity is not in the vendor's possession. But God knows best!

The [Prophet's] order of prohibition may have been intended
S340 against the sale of a commodity not in evidence, regardless of
whether it is in the vendor's possession or not, for it would
be liable to destruction or shrinkage before it were seen by the
buyer.

350. [Shāfiʿī] said: Thus every explicitly general statement
in the sunna of the Apostle should be accepted as such unless
another reliable tradition from the Apostle indicates that only
part of that explicitly general statement was intended to be
general, as I have already explained regarding this and other
similar points. It is obligatory on the scholars to accept the two
S341 kinds of traditions as complimentary—not as contradictory— in
so far as they can be regarded as complimentary, for if there is a
way for harmonizing them, without regarding either one more
binding than the other, [they should do so]. No two traditions
should ever be regarded as contradictory so long as there is a
possibility of harmonizing them; a contradictory tradition is one
B48 which is incapable of being harmonized except by abandoning
another, such as when two traditions relate to one [specific] act,
S342 the one permitting it and the other prohibiting it.

Chapter X

[ON SINGLE-INDIVIDUAL TRADITIONS][1]

351. Someone has asked me: Will you state what the minimum proof for a narrative related by a few [transmitters] should be in order to be binding upon scholars?

352. [Shāfiʿī] replied: [The minimum proof] is that the narrative must be related by one person from another [before him] back to the Prophet, or to one next to the Prophet.[2] The proof for such a tradition is not established unless certain S369
conditions are fulfilled:

He who relates a tradition must merit confidence in his religion, and be known as reliable in his transmitting, comprehending what he transmits, aware of any pronunciation that might change the meaning of the tradition, capable of transmitting the tradition word for word as he heard it, not merely transmitting [in his own words] its meaning; for if he transmitts only the meaning and is unaware of what might alter its S370
sense, he might unknowingly transmute the lawful into the unlawful and vice-versa.[3] So if he transmits word for word there remains no ground for fearing a change of the meaning. [Furthermore], he should have learned the tradition by heart, if he

[1] Būlāq ed., p. 51.
[2] Such a person might be one of the Prophet's companions.
[3] Būlāq ed., p. 51.

relates it from memory, and should have memorized the written text [of traditions] if he relates it in its written form; when he participates with others in relating a tradition from memory, that which they relate must agree. He must not be an interpolator,[4] attributing to someone whom he has not met that which he has not heard from him, or attributing to the Prophet something different from that which reliable authorities relate from him.

The same [qualifications] must be possessed by transmitters
S371 preceding him until the transmitter relates back to the Prophet or to him who carries it back closest to him, for each of them
B51 vouches for the tradition as he received it and verifies it for him to whom he passes it. So none of them should lack [the qualifications] I have just described.

353. He asked: Explain this to me by an example concerning which I am better informed, owing to my knowledge of it and my limited knowledge of what you have described in the traditions.

354. [Shāfiʿī] replied: Would you like me to cite an example for which this might be an analogy?

355. He said: Yes.

356. [Shāfiʿī] said: [Traditions] constitute a source in themselves and should not be regarded as analogous to anything else, for analogy is weaker than the original source.

357. He asked: I do not mean that you should consider it as an analogy. Will you give me an example of it from testimonies which are generally known?

S372 358. [Shāfiʿī] replied: Testimonies may disagree in certain matters and agree in others.

359. He asked: In what [matters] could they disagree?

[4] *Tadlīs* literally means "deceit," which consist either of interpolating the name of a trustworthy authority or eliminating the name or names of discreditable transmitters from the *isnād* or the chain of authorities. See Ibn Ḥajar, *Marātib al-Mudallisīn* (Cairo, 1322/1904), pp. 2-4; I. Goldziher, *Étude sur la tradition Islamique,* tr. Léon Bercher (Paris, 1952), p. 58; J. Schacht, *Origins of Muhammadan Jurisprudence,* p. 37.

360. [Shāfiʿī] replied: I accept a tradition from either one man or one woman,[5] but I will accept neither one alone in testimony. I accept the traditions [in the form]: "So-and-so related to me from so-and-so" if the transmitter is not an interpolater; but I do not accept it in testimony unless [the witness] says: "I heard [so-and-so]" or "I saw [so-and-so]" or "take me as a witness."

Traditions, however, vary; I accept some of them by *istidlāl* (inductive reasoning) on the basis of the Book [of God], the sunna, consensus, and analogy, but *istidlāl* is not applicable to testimony as well. There are many people whose testimony is acceptable, but I do not accept a tradition related by them owing to the possibility that it might contain many changes in meaning and might omit certain words affecting the meaning. But [traditions] may agree with testimony on matters other than S373
those I have already described.

361. He asked: I agree with what you have said concerning your refusal to accept a tradition from anyone except a trustworthy authority who had learned it by heart and is aware of what might change the meaning of the tradition. But why do you not accept such conditions in the case of testimony?

362. [Shāfiʿī] replied: Changes in the meaning of traditions are more difficult to detect than in the case of testimony. So I am much more careful in the case of a tradition than in the case of testimony.

363. He said: I agree with you; but if the person from whom someone quotes a tradition is reliable and he [in turn] transmits from a man whose reliability you do not know, then I do not accept your refusal to put confidence in his good reputation and S374
your insistence that he must narrate only from a reliable source even though you may not know who it is.

364. [Shāfiʿī] replied: If four persons of just character, well-versed in the law, testified confirming the testimony of two witnesses in favor of the claim of one man against another, would you take a decision if the four persons did not tell you that the two witnesses were of just character?

[5] Būlāq ed., p. 53.

365. He replied: No, I should by no means take any decision on the basis of their testimony until I knew their just character, either on the basis of the confirmation by the four persons of their just character, or of the confirmation of their just character by others, or on the basis of my own knowledge of their just character.

366. [Shāfiʿī] said: Why would you not accept their [testimony] for the same reason that you wanted me to accept the tradition, and say that they would not have testified in favor of anyone unless they considered him to be of just character?

367. He said: They might testify both in favor of someone whom they considered to be of just character, and in favor of someone whom they knew, although they did not know
S375 his just character. Since such a possibility might exist in their testimony, I could not accept the testimony of those who testified in his favor until [either] they declared him of just character or I was certain of his just character and the just character of those who testified before me concerning the just character of others. Nor do I accept the confirmation of the just character of a witness unless I know the just character of the person who confirms the just character of the witness.

368. [Shāfiʿī] said: The proof that you have adduced in this matter is against you, because you do not accept the narrative of a truthful [person] from someone whose truthfulness we do not know. People are more careful to testify only on behalf of the testimony of someone whose just character they know than they are in accepting a tradition only from someone whose transmission of traditions is known to be sound. This is because one man may meet another in whom he sees the mark of goodness and thinks well of him, so that he accepts the tradition from him and passes it on without knowing his character. Thus he may relate that a man called so-and-so transmitted to him such-and-such [a tradition] and hopes that he might find a trustworthy man who would know of the tradition so that he could accept it from him, or that he could relate it on the authority of a transmitter whether he approves of it or not; or he might be careless in transmitting the tradition from

him. For I do not know that I have ever met anyone who did
not relate [traditions] both from a trustworthy authority who S376
had learned them by heart and from other sources who were
quite different. In such cases I have done what was incumbent
upon me. Nor was my search for knowing the veracity of
him who related a tradition to me more of an obligation than
my quest for knowledge of the veracity of those from whom
he had received the tradition. For as far as all of them are
concerned I know all I need [to know] about those from whom
I receive a tradition, since all of them confirmed the narrative as
received from those before them and handed it on to those after S377
them.

369. He asked: What about [the possibility of] accepting a tradition from a person whom you have never known to be an interpolator, relating it from so-and-so, although it might be possible that he had never heard it?

370. [Shāfiʿī] replied: Muslims of just character are right
[when they testify] about themselves, but their status vis-à-vis
themselves is different from their status vis-à-vis others. Do you
not agree that if I knew them to be of just character [in matters]
concerning themselves, I should accept their testimony; but that
when they confirm the testimony of another witness I cannot
accept that testimony until I know the just character of the
other witness. For my knowledge of their just character does
not constitute knowledge of the just character of him whose
testimony they confirmed. We should accept the information
they relate about themselves and assume that their statements
are valid until their deeds indicate the opposite. We should
then be on our guard in the matter with regard to which
their deeds did not conform to what they ought to have B52
done.

Tadlīs has neither been practiced in our lands by our
predecessors in the past nor by our followers whom we have
known until recently, for some have taken it over from people
who practised it and who would have been better off if they had S378
left them alone [to indulge] in it.

It is the same to them whether a man says: "I heard so-and-so say 'I heard so-and-so,'" or whether he says: "So-

and-so related from so-and-so"; they only narrate what they have heard from others whom they have met from those whom we know who [operate in] this fashion. We accept the form: "So-and-so related to me from so-and-so," if he is not an interpolater.[6]

He whom we have known to interpolate on one occasion has exposed to us his fault in his transmission. This fault constitutes neither falsehood, which would cause us to reject his tradition, nor a real truth. Hence we accept from him that which we accept from those who speak the real truth. So [our position is] that we
S379 do not accept a tradition from an interpolater unless he says in it: "He related to me" or "I heard."

371. He said: I see that you accept the testimony [of a man] whose tradition you do not accept.

372. [Shāfiʿī] replied: This is because of the greater significance and position of traditions among the Muslims as well as for another obvious reason.

373. He asked: What is it?

374. [Shāfiʿī] replied: A word might be omitted from the tradition and thus alter its meaning; or a word might be pronounced differently from the way it was pronounced by the transmitter, thus altering the meaning of the tradition, even though he who pronounced it did not intend to do so. If he who transmits a tradition is ignorant of its meaning, he does not understand the tradition, and we do not accept it. [For] if he transmits what he does not understand, he is of those who do not transmit the tradition word for word; and he
S380 seeks to transmit the meaning of the tradition, but he does not understand the meaning at all.

375. He asked: Is it possible that the tradition of a man of just character might not be acceptable?

376. [Shāfiʿī] replied: Yes, for if he were [the type of person] I have just described, this would give rise to open suspicion that would cause his tradition to be rejected. A man might be just in testifying for other men, but suspect when he testifies

[6] Būlāq ed., p. 53.

for himself or for some of his relatives. For it is [perhaps] easier for a man to let himself fall from a height than to give a false testimony. However, whenever he becomes subject to suspicion his testimony is rejected for that reason. For distrust of those who do not transmit a tradition word for word and who do not understand its meaning is most clearly [indicated] in the case of those who testify in favor of someone whose testimony has been rejected because of dubious [elements] that it contains.

The testimony of witnesses should be [carefully] considered; if we detect a certain bias or an excessive interest in the person on whose behalf they are testifying, we do not accept their testimony. If they testify regarding a difficult matter beyond
their ability to comprehend, we do not accept their testimony, **S381**
for we do not believe that they understand the meaning of that to which they have testified. We do not accept the testimony of those whose transmission betrays many errors and which has no sound written source, just as we do not accept witnesses who make many errors in their testimony.

377. Shāfiʿī said:[7] Traditionists vary: Some are well known [for their knowledge] of tradition; they make every effort in their search for it, listening to their fathers, uncles, near of kin, and friends as well as spending long hours in the company of
scholars and disputants in the field. Such people stand in the **S382**
forefront of [the science of] tradition.[8] If [their transmission] is contradicted by someone who is less knowledgeable, it is better to accept the tradition of the former.

With regard to the traditionists, if they are jointly [engaged in considering] a tradition handed down by a certain man, they try to find out whether it agrees with what has been memorized by one of them and whether it is supported by those who have committed [the traditions] to memory, or whether it conflicts with what he and those who have memorized the traditions have learned by heart. If the transmitted [versions] differ, we seek guidance from [the versions that people] have memorized.

[7] Būlāq ed., p. 53.

[8] This is spurious, according to Būlāq ed., p. 54.

One can then tell from the errors and other indications therein what the truth is. We have explained about memorization and errors in another section [of this work]. I ask God to protect us against error and grant us success.[9]

378. He asked: On what ground do you accept a tradition related by a single individual even though you do not accept the [unsupported] testimony of one witness? What is your argument
S383 for holding that the single-individual tradition and testimony are ambiguous in most cases but different in others?

379. [Shāfiʿī] replied: You are repeating a question that I thought I had already answered: I do not compare [the single-individual tradition] with testimony. You asked me to give a parallel example more familiar to you than traditions. I gave you such an example, but I did not mean that analogical deduction is applicable to tradition. For the proof of a single-individual tradition is too strong to need the support of a parallel example; indeed it is an original source in itself.

380. He asked: How is it that traditions are like testimony in certain respects but not in others?

381. [Shāfiʿī] replied: [Traditions] are different from testimony in some respects, as I have already pointed out to you; but if I have said that they are similar to testimony in some respects
S384 and not others, I have done so for certain obvious reasons.

382. He asked: What are they, since the purpose of all testimony is the same?

383. [Shāfiʿī] replied: Do you mean in all cases or only in certain ones?

384. He said: In all cases.

385. [Shāfiʿī] asked: What is the minimum number [of witnesses] you would require in [a case of] adultery?

386. He replied: Four.

387. [Shāfiʿī] asked: If there are only three of them, would you order [the accusers] to be scourged?

388. He replied: Yes.

[9] Būlāq ed., p. 53.

389. [Shāfiʿī] asked: How many witnesses would you require in [the case of] murder, disbelief [i. e., apostasy], and highway robbery, all of which are punishable by death?

390. He replied: Two.

391. [Shāfiʿī] asked: How many witnesses would you require S385
in [cases of theft of] property?

392. He replied: One male and two female witnesses.

393. [Shāfiʿī] asked: How many witnesses would you require in [cases relating to] vices affecting women?

394. He replied: One woman.

395. [Shāfiʿī] asked: If there were lacking [either one] of the two witnesses or one of the male and two female witnesses, would you not order the [remaining] witnesses to be scourged as you did in [the case of] adultery?

396. He replied: No.[10] B53

397. [Shāfiʿī] asked: Do you consider that all these cases are similar?

398. He replied: Yes, I agree that the number [of witnesses] required is not the same and that only the witnesses in the case of adultery should be scourged.

399. [Shāfiʿī] asked: If I were to tell you that the same applies to the single-individual tradition, namely that I accept it as I do in testimony but that it is different with regard to the number [of witnesses], would that [not] constitute a strong argument S386
against you?

400. He replied: I have held my opinion concerning the variation in the [minimum] number of witnesses required in testimony on the strength of narrative and inductive reasoning.

401. [Shāfiʿī] said: Likewise, what I have held concerning the acceptance of the single-individual tradition is based on narrative and reasoning.

402. [Shāfiʿī] said: Do you maintain that if you did not accept the testimony of women in [a case concerning] childbirth that you would not accept it in [a case involving] property?

[10] "Yes" in the Arabic text (implying approval that the remaining witnesses should not be scourged).

403. He replied: [I should act] according to precedent [i. e., the practice followed by Muslims].

404. [Shāfiʿī] said: What would you do if someone told you
S387 that the Qur'ān does not stipulate [that there can be] less than one male and two female [witnesses]?

405. He replied: Nothing is stipulated against accepting less than that [number], so we have accepted what the Muslims have permitted, which is not contrary to the Qur'ān.

406. [Shāfiʿī] said: We have held the same opinion concerning the confirmation of the single-individual tradition, based on reasons all of which are stronger than that permitting the testimony of women.

407. He asked: Is there anything other than precedent that could justify a distinction between tradition and testimony?

408. [Shāfiʿī] replied: Yes, and I know of no scholar who
S388-390 does not accept it.

409. He asked: What is it?

410. [Shāfiʿī] replied: It is [the witness of] just character, whose testimony is acceptable in certain circumstances and unacceptable in others.

411. He asked: In what circumstances is his testimony unacceptable?

412. [Shāfiʿī] replied: [The circumstances are] when he testifies in cases in which his personal interests are principally involved, as when he defends himself against a certain debt, when he testifies in cases involving his son or his father or when
S391 he uses the testimony to defend them, and [finally] in any other circumstance liable to arouse suspicion.

Furthermore, in a matter of testimony, [if] a witness testifies that a certain person is liable for a debt or a punishment, or if he testifies that a debt should be paid to a man or a punishment be inflicted on his behalf, he [the witness] is not responsible for any debt which is not concerned with his [the accuser's] debt, nor for the dishonor which befalls him. However, the witness might become more partial if his son or father were involved. But his testimony would be accepted [in the cases stated above], because there is no obvious suspicion such as there would be in the case involving himself, his son, and his father or any other situations which might give ground for suspicion.

But the one who related traditions concerning what is lawful or unlawful is not obtaining any material advantage for himself or for others nor is he defending himself or anyone else, nor is he dealing with anything that involves punishment [meted out] against anybody or on behalf of anybody. Therefore, he and the Muslims from whom he related the tradition are on equal footing, whether [the tradition] concerns lawful or unlawful acts. He is like anyone else and his status is not different in this respect; on one occasion he might be suspected and his narrative rejected; on another occasion he might be free of suspicion and his narrative accepted, just as the status of any witness may differ whether he is an ordinary or notable **S392**
Muslim.

There are circumstances in which people relate information more accurately and there are [cases] in which they are more pious than others. When people are in fear during illness or travel, or are mindful [of death] under such conditions or similar ones making them alive to [the danger of] negligence, they strive to be more careful; they concentrate their thoughts more effectively and are less forgetful. In such conditions[11] the untruthful Muslim might become truthful and his information trustworthy. His narrative might be regarded as reliable and fully trustworthy, if not because he is pious at least because he is afraid that he might cause people to distrust a tradition that he is not trying to use to defend himself or exploit to his own advantage. Subsequently, however, he might revert to prevarication or cause people to have reservations about believing everything he has **S393**
said.

Since there are certain circumstances in which the public and the untruthful might be truthful to the satisfaction of transmitters of traditions, it is more appropriate that pious and truthful men should in all circumstances be more careful than others; for they are in a position of [public] trust and they are held up as examples for the faith and they are aware

[11] "Shāfiʿī said" is omitted.

of the obligation imposed on them by God to be truthful in all matters and that the traditions dealing with that which is lawful and unlawful are of the highest importance and hence above all should be beyond suspicion. Moreover, a tradition from the Apostle has given them a meaning that has never been given with regard to anyone else—namely, that the fate of him who attributes a falsehood to the Apostle shall be hell-fire.

413. Shāfiʿī said:[12] ʿAbd al-ʿAzīz [al-Darāwardī] has told us
S394 from Muḥammad b. ʿAjlān from ʿAbd al-Wahhāb b. Bukht from ʿAbd al-Wāḥid al-Naṣrī from Wāthila b. al-Asqaʿ from the Prophet, who said:

> The greatest of liars is he who ascribes to me that which I did not say, who claims to have dreamt what he did not dream, or claims
> S395 that he is the son of someone other than his own father.[13]

ʿAbd al-ʿAzīz [al-Darāwardī] related from Muḥammad b. ʿAmr [b. ʿAlqama] from Abī Salāma [b. ʿAbd al-Raḥmān] from Abū Hurayra, that the Apostle said:

> He who ascribes to me what I did not say shall surely occupy his place in the fire [of hell].[14]

Yaḥya b. Sulaym related to me from ʿUbayd-Allāh b. ʿUmar from Abū Bakr b. Sālim from Ibn ʿUmar, that the Prophet said:

> S396 He who tells a lie about me will have a house built for him in the fire [of hell].[15]

ʿAmr b. Abī Salāma told us from ʿAbd al-ʿAzīz b. Muḥammad from Asīd b. Abī Asīd from his mother, who said:

> B54 I asked Abū Qatāda: How is it that you do not relate [traditions] from the Apostle as other men do? ʻ I heard the Apostle say: He who

[12] Būlāq ed., p. 54.
[13] Bukhārī, Vol. II, p. 384; and Ibn Ḥanbal, Vol. VIII, pp. 85-86, and 243-44. Different authorities are cited.
[14] *Ibid.*
[15] Ibn Ḥanbal, Vol. VI, p. 333; Vol. VIII, p. 137; Vol. IX, pp. 137-38; Shāfiʿī, *Musnad,* Vol. I, p. 17.

> tells a lie about me is surely seeking for himself a resting place in the fire [of hell]. The Apostle began to say this while he was wiping the ground with his hand,' replied he.[16]

Sufyān [b. ʿUyayna] related from Muḥammad b. ʿAmr [b. ʿAlqama] from Abū Salāma [b. ʿAbd al-Raḥmān] from Abū Hurayra, that the Apostle said:

> You may relate from the children of Israel whatever you like, but S397
> whenever you relate from me you shall not relate an untruth.[17]

This is the most emphatic tradition ever related from the Apostle on this matter. We have relied on this as well as on other traditions in not accepting a tradition unless it is from a trustworthy transmitter and we know the trustworthiness of those who transmitted it from first to last.

414. Someone may ask: What evidence is there in this tradition for what you have stated?

415. [Shāfiʿī] replied: [Legal] knowledge teaches [us] that in no circumstance has the Prophet ordered anyone to attribute falsehood to the children of Israel or to anyone else. While he
permitted the relating of traditions from the children of Israel, S398
the ascription of falsehood to them was not permitted; he merely permitted the acceptance of traditions from one who related from them, without its being known whether he was truthful or untruthful.

Nor did he permit [the acceptance of traditions] from one whose untruthfulness was known, for it is related that [the Prophet] said:

> He who relates a tradition that he considers to be false is a liar.[18]

So whoever relates a tradition from a liar is not guiltless of falsehood because he has perceived the liar lying in his tradition, and except in a few special [cases] he relies on

[16] Muslim, Vol. I, pp. 66-72; Dārimī, Vol. I, pp. 76-77; Shāfiʿī, *Musnad*, Vol. I, p. 17.

[17] Ibn Ḥanbal, Vol.IX, pp. 250-51; Vol.XI, pp. 127, 207; Shāfiʿī, *Musnad*, Vol. I, p. 17.

[18] Muslim, Vol. I, p. 62.

the trustworthiness of the informant, or his lack thereof, for guidance as to the truth or the falsity of the tradition. In the latter case he can tell whether it is true or false if the transmitter relates what cannot possibly be the case, or what is contradicted by information that is better authenticated and
S399 is more indicative of the truth.[19]

Since the Apostle distinguished between traditions related on his authority and traditions from the children of Israel by saying: "You may relate on my authority, but do not, etc.," [legal] knowledge instructs us[20] that the untruthfulness which [the Prophet] prohibited was hidden untruthfulness, namely, [that which might occur in a tradition] related from a person whose truthfulness is unknown. For since untruthfulness is prohibited in all circumstances, there is no untruthfulness greater than that which is related on the authority of the
S400 Prophet, God's peace and blessings be upon him.[21]

Authentication of the Single-Individual Tradition

416. Someone might ask:[22] What is the proof for the authentication of the single-individual tradition, whether based on the text of a narrative, an indication in it, or on consensus?

417. [Shāfiʿī] replied: Sufyān [b. ʿUyayna] told us from ʿAbd al-Malik b. ʿUmayr from ʿAbd al-Raḥmān b. ʿAbd-Allāh b. Masʿūd from his father, that the Prophet said:

> God will grant prosperity to His servant who hears my words, remembers them, guards them, and hands them on. Many a transmitter of law is no lawyer himself, and many may transmit law to others who are more versed in the law than they. The heart of a Muslim shall never harbor vindictive feelings against three: sincerity in working for God; faithfulness to Muslims; and conformity to the

[19] See J. Schacht, *Origins of Muhammadan Jurisprudence*, pp. 37-38.
[20] Literally: "Knowledge makes it certain to us."
[21] Abū Dāwūd, Vol. IV, pp. 203-204.
[22] The opening statement "Shāfiʿī said" is omitted.

community of believers—their call shall protect [the believers] and
guard them from [the Devil's] delusion.[23] S401

Since the Apostle has urged men to listen to his words, guard
them, and hand them on, and since the man who hands them on
is only one person, this indicates that the Apostle ordered that
no one should transmit anything from him unless the proof were S402
established to him to whom it was transmitted, because what is transmitted is something lawful [to be observed] or unlawful to be avoided, a punishment to be inflicted, a property to be taken or paid, and advice in matters relating to religion and worldly [life].

It also indicates that one who is not an expert in law may transmit law; he may have learned it by heart even though he is not an expert in the law.[24] The Apostle's order that men should follow the Muslim community is a proof that the *ijmāʿ* of the Muslims is binding.

Sufyān [b. ʿUyayna] told us from Sālim Abū al-Naḍr [client of ʿUmar b. ʿUbayd-Allāh] from ʿUbayd-Allāh b. Abī Rāfiʿ from his father, who related that the Prophet said:

> Do not let me find anyone of you who, reclining on his couch, when
> confronted with an order of permission or prohibition from me, says: S403
> We do not know [whether this is authentic or not]; we follow only what we find in the book of God.[25]

Sufyān b. ʿUyayna said: Muḥammad b. al-Munkadir related to me a similar tradition from the Prophet without the names of the transmitters.

In this case the confirmation of the narrative was from the Apostle [himself] and they were informed that it was binding on them, even though they did not find any relevant text in the Book of God. This subject is discussed elsewhere in this book.[26]

Mālik [b. Anas] told us from Zayd b. Aslam from ʿAṭā' b. Yasār that a man kissed his wife while fasting and became

[23] Dārimī, Vol. I, pp. 74-76; Ibn Ḥanbal, Vol. VI, p. 96; Shāfiʿī, *Musnad,* Vol. I, p. 16. See also J. Schacht, *Origins of Muhammadan Jurisprudence,* p. 54.

[24] Faqīh.

[25] See paragraph 94, above.

[26] See Chap. V, above.

emotionally aroused. So he dispatched his wife [to the Prophet's wife] to ask her opinion about the matter. She found Umm Salāma, Mother of the believers [and wife of the Prophet], and
B55 told her about the matter. "The Apostle [himself] kisses when fasting," she replied. The wife returned and told her husband, who became increasingly worried and said: "We are not like
S404 the Apostle, for God may permit him [to do] what he desires!" Thereupon the wife returned to Umm Salāma and found the Apostle [with her], and he inquired: "What does this woman want?" So Umm Salāma told him about the matter. "Have you not told her that I do it myself?" he remarked. "I have told her, but her husband was not satisfied and said: 'We are not like the Apostle, for God permits him [to do] what he desires,'" she answered. The Apostle became angry and said: "By God, I am more fearful of God than you and better informed regarding punishments!"[27] I have heard someone who gave the names of
S405 all the transmitters of this tradition, but I do not remember the names.

418. Shāfiʿī said: In the Prophet's reply to Umm Salāma, in which He said: "Have you not told her, etc.," an indication that Umm Salāma's narrative from him [is of the category of traditions] which may be accepted, for the Prophet would not have ordered her to repeat what he had said, provided what she said contains a valid argument. The same would be true of the wife [of the man in question] if he considered her truthful.

Mālik [b. Anas] told us from ʿAbd-Allāh b. Dīnār from Ibn ʿUmar, who said:

> When men were performing the dawn prayer at [the mosque] of Qubā', a messenger arrived and said: A Quranic communication was revealed to the Apostle last night ordering him to face the *qibla* [of the Kaʿba]. So whereas they had been facing al-Sham [Syria], they [immediately] turned around toward the Kaʿba.[28]

[27] Mālik, Vol. I, pp. 291-92; cf. Bukhārī, Vol. I, p. 480; Muslim, Vol. VII, pp. 215-20. Mālik, however, did not approve of kissing while fasting *(al-Muwaṭṭa'*, Vol. I, p. 293).

[28] See paragraph 119, above.

419. Shāfiʿī said:[29] The men of Qubā' were among the first
Muslims of the Anṣār [the Prophet's supporters in Madīna] S406
and were versed in the law and they used to face the *qibla*
which God had ordered them to face. They would not have
abandoned God's [previous] command concerning the *qibla* if
the obligation to do so had not been established upon them, for
they had neither contacted the Apostle nor had they heard [from
him] what God had revealed concerning the change of the *qibla*;
so they faced the *qibla* in accordance with the [new text of the]
Book of God or the [new] sunna of the Prophet as they heard
it from the Apostle, and not according to a tradition related by
the public; they felt they were obligated to change the *qibla* on
the authority of one transmitter only since he was considered by
them a truthful person, and abandoned it because he told them
that the Prophet had changed the *qibla*. [Surely] they would not
have accepted this on the authority of one individual unless they
had known that the proof is established if the person who relates
the narrative is truthful. They would not have made such a great
innovation as this in the religion [of Islam] unless they had to do
so. Nor would they have failed to inform the Apostle of what S407
they had done.

If the information they had accepted from a single individual, related from the Apostle, concerning the shifting of the *qibla*—which was obligatory—were [not] permissible, the Apostle would have said to them: " You were facing a [certain] *qibla*, and it was not up to you to abandon it unless the proof for it were established through what you heard from me, from the public, or from more than one person [on my authority]."

Mālik [b. Anas] told us from Isḥāq b. ʿAbd-Allāh b. Abī Ṭalḥa S408
from Anas b. Mālik, who said:

When I was serving a drink made of grape-juice and dates to Abū Ṭalḥa, Abū ʿUbayda b. al-Jarrāḥ, and Ubayy b. Kaʿb, a messenger arrived saying: 'Wine has just been forbidden.' Thereupon Abū Ṭalḥa said: 'Come, Anas, break these jars!' So Anas took a mortar

[29] Būlāq ed., p. 56.

> that we had and struck the jars with the bottom of it until they broke.[30]

420. Shāfiʿī said:[31] These men were closely connected with the Prophet in knowledge and position, and the Prophet's companions occupied a position of prominence that is not denied by any learned man. The drink of which they were partaking was lawful to them, but when a single person came and informed them that wine had been declared unlawful, Ṭalḥa, the owner of the jars, ordered that they should be broken. Neither he nor the others said that they would consider
S409 the wine lawful until they should see the Apostle, who was
near by, or until they should learn about it through public channels. Otherwise they would not have wasted something lawful by pouring it out when they were not wasteful people. For they would have asked the Apostle what they should do, if they felt they were not bound to accept a single-individual tradition, and the Apostle himself would have prohibited its acceptance.

The Apostle ordered Unays to go to a certain man's wife who was said to have committed adultery and ordered him to stone her if she confessed. She confessed, whereupon Unays stoned her to death.[32] This tradition has been related by
S410 Mālik [b. Anas] and Sufyān b. ʿUyayna from al-Zuhrī from
ʿUbayd-Allāh b. ʿAbd-Allāh from Abū Hurayra and Zayd b. Khālid [al-Juhanī] from the Prophet. Sufyān added Shibl [b. Miʿbad] to the list of transmitters after Abū Hurayra and Zayd b. Khālid.

ʿAbd al-ʿAzīz [al-Darāwardī] told us from Yazīd b. al-Hādī
S411 from ʿAbd-Allāh b. Abī Salāma from ʿAmr b. Sulaym al-Zuraqī
from his mother, who said:

> When we were at Mina, ʿAlī b. Abī Ṭālib arrived on a camel and declared that the Apostle of God said: ' These are days [in which it is

[30] Mālik, Vol. II, pp. 846-47; Muslim, Vol. XIII, pp. 148-50.
[31] See Būlāq ed., p. 56.
[32] See paragraph 123, above.

permissible] to eat and drink, so no one shall fast.' ʿAlī went around on his camel crying out this message to the people.[33] B56

The Apostle would not have sent a single truthful person with his order of prohibition if that person's veracity and the words he reported from the Prophet were not acceptable without question to those who were the recipients of the Prophet's prohibition. Furthermore, there were pilgrims with the Apostle, and he would have been able either to go and speak to those [who were drinking the wine] himself or to send a number of men [on the mission], but he sent only one man whose veracity they knew. For he would not have sent any emissary to them unless the latter possessed [convincing] proof that bound them to accept his words as being those of the Apostle. S412

If such was the situation with the Prophet's, as I have said, having been in a position to send to them several men [instead of one], it would be most appropriate for those who came after him and who were not in a position to do what [the recipients of the Prophet's instruction] could have done or what the Prophet could have done with regard to them, to use the same procedure in establishing the truth of the narrative of a single veracious man.

Sufyān [b. ʿUyayna] told us from ʿAmr b. Dīnār from ʿAmr b. ʿAbd-Allāh b. Ṣafwan [al-Jumaḥī] from one of his uncles, Yazīd b. Shaybān, who said:

> When we were standing at a certain place at ʿArafa, while ʿAmr [b. ʿAbd-Allāh] was at a great distance from the Imām, Ibn Mirbaʿ al-Anṣārī arrived and said to us: ' I am the messenger of the Apostle of God to you; he orders you to stand [in reverence] at the places S413
> of devotion of yours, because they are part of the heritage of your father Abraham.'[34]

The Apostle sent Abū Bakr in command of the pilgrimage in the year 9 [A.D. 631]. Many pilgrims came from various

[33] This tradition is not cited in the standard digests. See Shawkānī, *Nayl al-Awṭār*, Vol. IV, p. 277, giving the names of different transmitters.

[34] Abū Dāwūd, Vol. II, p. 189.

countries and diverse peoples, and Abū Bakr led the religious rites and instructed them, on behalf of the Apostle, in their rights and duties.[35] In the meantime [the Prophet] sent ʿAlī b. Abī Ṭālib, who recited to the assembled pilgrims on the day of al-Naḥr some verses from the sūra of Barā'a,[36] enjoining some
S414 of them to equity while encouraging others and forbidding them to do certain things.[37]

Both Abū Bakr and ʿAlī were well-known to the people of Makka as virtuous, religious, and truthful men, and those pilgrims who did not know either one or both of them could have found someone to testify to their truthfulness and virtue. The Apostle would not have sent a lone messenger unless the latter's words bore convincing proof to him to whom the Prophet had sent the messenger.

The Prophet dispatched governors to various regions, and the names of the men and the places to which they were sent to are known to us. [For example], he sent Qays b. ʿĀṣim and al-
S415 Zibriqān b. Badr and [Mālik] b. Nuwayra to their own tribes, because they were known to them as truthful men.

A delegation from Baḥrayn came [to the Prophet] and became acquainted with the men around him. [The Prophet] sent [Abān b.] Saʿīd b. al-ʿĀṣ back with them [as governor of Baḥrayn].

[The Prophet] sent Muʿādh b. Jabal to al-Yaman with orders to lead those who followed him against those who resisted him.[38] Since Muʿādh and his status and veracity were known to them, the Prophet also ordered him to instruct them in their duties toward God and to collect the obligatory [tax] from them. So all those who were appointed [by the Prophet] as administrators [of various regions] were ordered by him to

[35] See Ibn Hishām, Vol. II, pp. 919 ff; Guillaume's translation, pp. 617 ff.

[36] Sūra (Chapter) 9.

[37] ʿAlī was commissioned to recite the sūra of Barā'a (Q. IX) terminating the general agreement between the Prophet and the unbelievers. That agreement provided that no one should be kept back from the Kaʿba and that no one need fear the other during the pilgrimage. The special agreement between the Prophet and Arab tribes for specified terms was terminated at the end of its term. See Ibn Hishām, pp. 919-20; Guillaume, pp. 617-18.

[38] The wording of the sentence is slightly re-arranged for clarity.

collect [the taxes] imposed by God on the people subject to their rule. None of those veracious men who were sent by [the Prophet] was ever told that he was only one individual and that he had no power to collect [the tax] until the Apostle [himself] had been heard to say it was obligatory, S416
I do not believe that the Prophet would have sent those who were well known for their veracity in the provinces to which they were sent if, as I have stated, men such as they did not carry binding proof to those to whom they were sent.

The same applies to those men who were commanders of [the Prophet's] expeditions. He [the Prophet] sent an expedition against Mu'ta and appointed Zayd b. Ḥāritha [his freed slave] as its commander; " If he is killed, Jaʿfar shall succeed him, and if [the latter] is killed, then Ibn Rawāḥa," he said. He also sent Ibn Unays on an expedition by himself.

All of the commanders of expeditions who were sent forth [by the Prophet] were competent judges of the matters on which they were sent, for they were responsible for appealing to those who had not yet received the call [of Islam] and for fighting those who had to be fought. The same was true of S417
every commander and expedition leader whom [the Prophet] sent forth, although he was in a position to send two, three, four or more [if he had wished].

421. Shāfiʿī said:[39] On one occasion [the Prophet] sent twelve messengers simultaneously to twelve rulers, inviting them to accept Islam. Those [messengers] were sent only [to people] who either had already received the summons to Islam and who had been confronted with its arguments, or who had received [from the Prophet] letters indicating to those to whom the messengers had been sent that the letters were from the Prophet. He [the Prophet] was careful to choose well-known men both as his messengers and as his commanders. For example, he sent Diḥya [b. Khalīfa al-Kalbī] to the region in which he was known. For if [the person] to whom the messenger was sent had not known him, he first would have had to ascertain

[39] Būlāq ed., p. 57.

that he had been sent by the Prophet so as to rid himself of any doubt as to whether it was the Apostle's message, thus obliging the messenger to wait until his identity had been certified.

The Prophet's orders of permission and prohibition were
S418 continuously sent to his governors, and none failed to carry them out because the Prophet sent only messengers who were known as truthful to those to whom they were sent, and whose veracity could be certified by those on the spot. In case the recipient suspected that the letter carried by the messenger had been altered, or found that there were circumstances
B57 giving rise to a suspicion that the messenger who brought the communication had been forgetful, it was his duty to seek enlightenment regarding that which he suspected so that he could carry out the orders of the Apostle after they had been confirmed to his satisfaction.

In the same category fall the letters of the [Prophet's] successors and their governors and the Muslim's agreement that the caliph, the judge, the commander, and the imām were respectively single individuals. So they chose Abū Bakr [as caliph], and Abū Bakr designated ʿUmar. ʿUmar appointed a council of electors to choose one man. They selected ʿAbd al-Raḥmān b. ʿAwf, who chose ʿUthmān b. ʿAffān.
S419 Thus those governors who were judges, as well as others, handed down decisions, had their decisions executed, and imposed penalties. Their decisions were carried out after them, and these decisions were narratives handed down from them.

From what I have said concerning the sunna of the Apostle and the consensus of the Muslims, there is indication of a distinction among testimony (*shahāda*), narrative (*khabar*), and a decree (*ḥukm*).

Do you not agree that the decision of a judge in favor of one man against another is [a similar kind of] narrative handed down by the judge on the basis of confirmed evidence or on the basis of a confession made to him by one of the parties upon whom it was executed? Since the judge is obliged to act on the basis of such a narrative according to [the best of] his knowledge, then in accordance with the interpretation of the person who transmitted the decision, he would have to declare [the matter in question] as lawful or unlawful on the basis of the testimony given with regard to it. S420

If a judge [other than the one in the present case] related a narrative from witnesses who testified to him against a person who was not on trial before him, or on the basis of confession of one of the parties to a dispute, [the judge in the case] is not obligated to take a decision on the basis of the evidence of the other judge, because the party was not referred to that judge, but to him [the judge in the case], or because the party was referred to another judge for trial. Then the judge [in the case] makes the decision on the basis of the testimony of one witness in addition to the other [judge], since the latter would be regarded as [only] one witness, and the testimony of one witness—whether he is a judge or any other person—is not acceptable unless his testimony is supported by that of a second witness, just as the testimony of [any] one witness is not acceptable unless supported by that of a second S421
witness.[40]

422. [Shāfiʿī said]: Sufyān [b. ʿUyayna] and ʿAbd al-Wahhāb [al-Thaqafī] told us from Yaḥya b. Saʿīd from Saʿīd b. al-Musayyib that ʿUmar b. al-Khaṭṭāb decreed that [the compensation] for the loss of a thumb was fifteen [camels],[41] ten for the next finger, ten for the middle finger, nine for the finger next to the little finger, and six for the little finger.

423. Shāfiʿī said: Since ʿUmar knew that the Prophet had fixed the compensation of the hand at fifty [camels], and since the hand consists of five fingers varying in attractiveness and usefulness, he gave each of them its proportional value based on the amount of the compensation for the hand. This was [a decision taken] on the strength of a narrative through analogical reasoning.

When, however, it was found in the letter of Āl ʿAmr b. Ḥazm that the Prophet said: " For every finger [the compensation] shall

[40] The wording of the sentence is slightly rearranged.
[41] Būlāq ed., p. 58.

be ten camels," they were inclined to follow it. But they did not
S422 accept the letter of al ʿAmr until it was confirmed to them that
it was from the Apostle.[42]

There are two indications in this tradition:

First, a narrative [from the Prophet] must be accepted.
Secondly, the narrative is to be accepted when it is confirmed,
even though none of the imāms may ever have done anything
similar to the narrative in question. This indicates also that if
S423 the action of one of the imāms subsequently were found to
be contrary to a narrative of the Prophet, the imām's action
must be abandoned in favor of the Apostle's narrative. It [also]
indicates that a tradition from the Apostle is self-confirming
and does not need to be confirmed by the action of anyone else
after him. For the Muslims never said: " ʿUmar acted differently
[from the Prophet] in matters concerning the Muhājirīn[43] and
the Anṣār."[44] Nor did you[45] or any other say anything about
other men's having acted differently; they accepted traditions
from the Apostle as they were bound to do and they desisted
from all acts contrary to them.

Had ʿUmar been aware of this tradition he would have
accepted it as he had accepted other things that emanated
from the Apostle, owing to his fear of God, his [readiness] to
carry out his obligation to obey the order of the Apostle, his
S424 knowledge that no one else's order is on a par with that of the

[42] Shāfiʿī's quotation from the Prophet's letter to ʿAmr is not in the text that was reproduced by Ibn Hishām, perhaps because the text was not reproduced in full. See Ibn Hishām's *Sīra,* Vol. II, pp. 961-62. Shāfiʿī attaches great significance to the Prophet's order in this letter and argues that if ʿUmar had known the Prophet's order that the compensation for the finger was ten camels, he would not have made a different decision (see *Ikhtilāf al-Ḥadīth* in *Kitāb al-Umm,* Vol. VII, pp. 17-19). ʿUmar's ignorance of the letter and the Prophet's order, however, may raise doubt as to the authenticity of the letter. The tradition cited by Shāfiʿī may be found in Abū Dāwūd, Vol. IV, p. 188; Shawkānī, *Nayl al-Awṭār,* Vol. VII, p. 61; Yaḥya b. Ādam, *Kitāb al-Kharāj* (Cairo, 1347/1929), p. 119.

[43] The Makkans who emigrated with the Prophet to Madīna in 1/622.

[44] The inhabitants of Madīna who supported the Prophet after his migration to that city.

[45] In this statement Shāfiʿī is addressing himself to the interlocutor, a follower of the Ḥanafī school of law.

Apostle, and that obedience to God is obedience to the Apostle's order.

424. Someone said: Give me an example indicating that ʿUmar changed his practice when a tradition from the Apostle became known to him.

425. [Shāfiʿī] replied: [What will be the advantage of] my giving you one?

426. He said: Such an example will establish two rules: First, that opinion may be accepted in case there is no sunna. Secondly, that if the sunna reveals that one must do a certain thing, one must abandon what he [previously] had been doing: For one must discard all practices contrary to the sunna. One must also abandon [the idea that] the sunna is confirmed only by a narrative that has preceded it, for he should know that it is not vitiated by anything that contradicts S425
it.[46]

427. [Shāfiʿī] said: Sufyān [b. ʿUyayna] told us from al-Zuhrī from Saʿīd b. al-Musayyib who said: ʿUmar b. al-Khaṭṭāb held that the *diya* should be paid by the *ʿāqila*, and that the wife cannot inherit from the *diya* of her husband; but al-Ḍaḥḥāk b. Sufyān told ʿUmar that the Apostle B58
had written to him ordering him to permit the wife of Ashyam al-Dibābī to inherit the *diya* [of her husband]. So ʿUmar changed his opinion. This tradition has been explained elsewhere.[47]

Sufyān [b. ʿUyayna] told us from ʿAmr b. Dīnār and Ibn Ṭāwūs from Ṭāwūs that ʿUmar said: Has God mentioned S426
anything that anyone has heard from the Prophet concerning [the *diya* for] foeticide? Ḥamal b. Mālik b. al-Nābigha replied that he had two concubines, one of whom struck the other [who was pregnant] with a rolling pin causing a miscarriage. The Prophet ordered the payment of a *ghurra* or a slave [as the *diya*].

[46] Shāfiʿī repudiates an ancient legal doctrine by virtue of which practice validates certain legal decisions even if they were contrary to traditions. See paragraph 423; and J. Schacht, *Origins of Muhammadan Jurisprudence*, pp. 59-60.

[47] For Shāfiʿī's discussion on this tradition see *Kitāb al-Umm*, Vol. VI, p. 77. For text of the tradition, see Mālik, Vol. II, p. 866; Abū Dāwūd, Vol. IV, p. 192.

"Had I not heard this, I would have decided it differently," said ʿUmar. Others related that [ʿUmar said]: "We almost decided this matter on [the basis of our] own opinion."[48]

S427 ʿUmar changed his decision on the strength of a tradition related by al-Ḍaḥḥāk that conflicted with his own decision. He declared that if he had not heard that tradition he would have arrived at a different decision and that he almost made a decision concerning foeticide on the basis of his own opinion.

428. Shāfiʿī said: [Since] the sunna specified that the *diya* for a life is a hundred camels, the *diya* for foeticide should be one hundred camels if the foetus is alive, and no *diya* if it is dead.

When the Apostle's order was related [to ʿUmar] he deferred to him and obeyed him despite his prior contradictory decision. His own decision had been taken without his having heard anything with reference to it from the Apostle, but when he learned that his action was not in accord with the Apostle's decree, he abandoned his practice in order to obey the Apostle's
S428 decree and did likewise in all other matters. It is equally incumbent upon men to act accordingly.[49] [For] Mālik [b. Anas] has told us from Ibn Shihāb from Sālim b. ʿAbd-Allāh that [the Caliph] ʿUmar returned before [visiting] men [in Syria] on the strength of a tradition related by ʿAbd al-Raḥmān b. ʿAwf. This was when he set out for Syria and then learned that a plague
S429 had broken out there.[50]

[48] Abū Dāwūd, Vol. IV, p. 191. Cf. Mālik, Vol. II, pp. 855-56; Shawkānī, *Nayl al-Awṭār,* Vol. VII, pp. 72-73; Bayhaqī, *al-Sunan al-Kubra,* Vol. VIII, pp. 115-16.

[49] For further discussion on this point, see Shāfiʿī's *Ikhtilāf al-Ḥadīth (Kitāb al-Umm,* Vol. VII, pp. 20-21).

[50] In A. D. 639 the Caliph ʿUmar visited the borders of Syria where he met Abū ʿUbayda, Governor of Syria, and other leading men. The Caliph was advised to return owing to the plague, when thousands of believers died, but, according to one version of the story, Abū ʿUbayda said: "What! You flee from the decree of God?" "Yes," replied ʿUmar, "if we flee, it is from the decree of God unto the decree of God." At this juncture ʿAbd al-Raḥmān b. ʿAwf arrived and said that he had heard the Prophet saying: "When you hear of it [the plague], you should not approach the land; if you were in the land where it was, you should not leave it." Thereupon ʿUmar, acting on the strength of this tradition, returned to Madīna. See Mālik, Vol. II, pp. 895-96; Muslim, Vol. XIV, pp. 205-206.

Mālik [b. Anas] told us from Jaʿfar b. Muḥammad [al-Ṣādiq] from his father [Muḥammad al-Bāqir] who said: Upon mentioning the Magians, ʿUmar said: " I do not know what we should do with regard to them." Thereupon ʿAbd al-Raḥmān b. ʿAwf said: " I bear witness that I heard the Apostle of God say: ' Follow the same usage with regard to them as you do with regard to the People of the Book.' "[51]

Sufyān [b. ʿUyayna] told us from ʿAmr b. Dīnār that he heard Bajāla say: ʿUmar did not collect the poll tax from the Magians S430
until ʿAbd al-Raḥmān b. ʿAwf told him that the Prophet had ordered it to be collected from the Magians of Hajar.[52]

429. Shāfiʿī said: all the traditions that I have cited [above] in an interrupted fashion were [originally] heard by me as uninterrupted, or are well-known traditions related by many people transmitting them from scholars who were acquainted with them through common knowledge; but I did not want to cite traditions that I had not fully memorized, nor did I have access to some of my books which I had lost [to verify them]; but I have verified the accuracy of what I memorized by checking it with the knowledge of scholars, and I have summarized it fearing that this book might become too long. I have, however, cited what might be sufficient without going into every aspect of it in an exhaustive fashion.

So ʿUmar accepted the tradition of ʿAbd al-Raḥmān b. ʿAwf concerning the Magians and collected [the *jizya*] on the basis of the Quranic communication:

> Of those who have been given the Book, until they pay the *jizya* out of hand and have been humbled [Q. IX, 29].

On the basis of the Qur'ān, which states that the unbelievers should be fought until they accept Islam, and since ʿUmar never heard anything from the Prophet [regarding the Magians] and thought that they were unbelievers and not people of the

[51] Mālik, Vol. I, p. 278.

[52] Hajar, on the coast of Arabia, was the principal town in Baḥrayn. The term Hajar also applied to the whole of Baḥrayn, which included al-Ḥasā' and Qaṭīf. See Yāqūt, passim.

Book, he accepted the tradition of ʿAbd al-Raḥmān b. ʿAwf and
S431 followed it.

The tradition related by Bajāla is uninterrupted; for he [Bajāla] had known ʿUmar b. al-Khaṭṭāb personally and had served as a scribe to some of his provincial governors.[53]

430. Someone might say: ʿUmar might have sought for another transmitter in addition to the one who related the narrative to him.

431. [Shāfiʿī said]: The answer would be: ʿUmar would not ask for another transmitter [to substantiate] a tradition related
S432 to him by a man, except for one of three possible reasons:

[First,] he may have wanted to be careful; for even though the proof is verified by the narrative of a single person, the narrative of two makes it even stronger. I have known [some men] who confirmed the narrative of a single person and sought a second narrative [to confirm it]. [If] a man possesses a sunna from five [different] sources and a sixth is related to him, he writes it down. For the more numerous the authorities of a tradition and the better known, the better it is authenticated and the more satisfactory to him who hears it. And I have known certain judges who, although two or three witnesses were confirmed to them as witnesses of just character, asked the person on whose behalf the testimony was given to produce more witnesses. By this they sought to satisfy themselves more fully. If the party on whose behalf the testimony was given did not produce more than two witnesses, the decision would have been given in his favor.

[Secondly,] it is possible that the transmitter might not have been known [to ʿUmar], so he would suspend judgment until
S433 another transmitter whom he knew confirmed it. Likewise, [a tradition] related from an unknown person, is not acceptable. A tradition is acceptable only from someone known to be qualified.

[53] Shāfiʿī cited this tradition in *Kitāb al-Umm,* Vol. VI, p. 96, on the authority of Sufyān b. ʿUyayna. See also Abū Dāwūd, Vol. III, pp. 168-69; Ibn Ḥanbal, Vol. III, p. 141, no. 1685; Abū ʿUbayd b. Sallām, *Kitāb al-Amwāl,* ed. Muh. Hamīd al-Fiqqī (Cairo, 1353/1935), pp. 31-32.

[Thirdly,] it is possible that the information related to ʿUmar by the transmitter was unacceptable to him; in this case he would reject the narrative until he could find someone else whose word was acceptable.

432. Someone might ask: In your opinion, which of these reasons motivated ʿUmar? B59

433. [Shāfiʿī] replied: According to the tradition related by Abū Mūsa, it was caution, for he regarded Abū Mūsa as a trusted authority.

434. If he says: What is your evidence?

We reply: Abū Mūsa's tradition was transmitted by Mālik b. Anas from Rabīʿa from more than one of their authorities. S434 ʿUmar, however, said to Abū Mūsa: "I did not suspect you; I was merely afraid that people might attribute something to the Apostle that he did not say."[54]

435. Should he ask: Is this [not] an interrupted [tradition]?

436. [Shāfiʿī replied]: This is a well-authenticated tradition.[55] For it is not permissible for an imām of the religion, whether ʿUmar or anyone else, to accept the tradition of a single individual on one occasion, when he is satisfied that it is well authenticated, and reject it on another. This is never permissible for an intelligent scholar, just as it is not permissible for a judge to take a decision on the basis of [the testimony of] two witnesses on one occasion and reject them on another, unless they have been proved wrong on grounds disqualifying them or because of his ignorance of their just character. For ʿUmar was an extremely knowing, intelligent, trustworthy, and meritorious man. In the Book of God is an evidence for what I have S435 discussed; God said:

> Verily, We sent Noah to his people [Q. LXXI, 1].

And He said:

[54] Mālik, Vol. II, p. 964; Bukhārī, Vol. II, p. 8; Muslim, Vol. XIV, pp. 130-33; Abū Dāwūd, Vol. IV, pp. 345-46.

[55] Shāfiʿī did not answer the interlocutor's question directly. He had already pointed out in paragraph 429 that although some of the traditions he cited were lacking the names of transmitters, he had either heard them with the full chain of transmitters or they were well-authenticated traditions.

> We did indeed send Noah to his people [Q. XI, 25; XXIII, 23; XXIX, 14].

And He said:

> We revealed to Abraham and Ishmael [Q. IV, 163].

And He said:

> And to ʿĀd [we sent] their brother Hūd [Q. VII, 65; XI, 50].

And He said:

> And to Thamūd [we sent] their brother Ṣāliḥ [Q. VII, 73; XI, 61].

And He said:

> And to Midian [we sent] their brother Shuʿayb [Q. VII, 85; XI, 84; XXIX, 36]

And He said:

> The people of Lot gave the lie to those who were sent to them. When their brother Lot said to them: ' Will you not fear God? I am for you a faithful apostle. So fear God and obey me' [Q. XXVI, 160-163].

And to His Apostle Muḥammad, God's blessings and peace be upon him, He said:

> Verily, we have revealed to thee as We have revealed to Noah and the prophets after him [Q. IV, 163].

And He said:

> S436 Muḥammad is only an apostle; apostles have passed away before him [Q. III, 144].

So [God] has given proof to His creatures through His prophets, who were distinguished by certain signs from others, and the proof was clear to those who witnessed the actions of the prophets and the indications which distinguished them from others as well as from those who came after them. One of them is as good as more than one, since the proof is established by one just as well as by more than one. For [God] said:

Coin a parable for them: the people of a town when the envoys came to it; when we sent to them two, and they called them liars; so we sent a third as reinforcement and they said: ' To you we are envoys.' They said: ' You are only human beings like ourselves, and the Merciful has not sent down anything; you are only speaking falsely' [Q. XXXVI, 13-15].

437. Shāfiʿī said: Thus God established the proof to them by sending two and later a third [prophet]; likewise He established it for various people by sending one, for the confirmation [of the proof by more than one] does not mean that it cannot be S437 established by one only, if God endows him with that which distinguishes him from those who are not prophets.

438. Shāfiʿī said:[56] Mālik [b. Anas] told us from Saʿd b. Isḥāq b. Kaʿb b. ʿUjra from his paternal aunt Zaynab, daughter of Kaʿb, who said that al-Furayʿa, daughter of Mālik b. Sinān, had told her that she [al-Furayʿa] went to the Prophet requesting him to let her return to her family among the Banū Khudra,[57] since her husband, who had gone forth looking for some slaves of his, had been killed by them when he met them near al-Qaddūm.[58] " I requested the Apostle to let me return to my family since my husband left no house of his own for me to live in," she said. " Yes [you may return]," replied the Apostle. So I left, but he called me back when I was either in [my] chamber or in the Mosque, and said: " What did you say?" S438 So I repeated the story of what had appeared to my husband. " Stay in your house until the end of the period stipulated in the Book," said the Prophet. " So I passed the period of the *ʿidda*, four months and ten days," she said. When ʿUthmān became caliph, he sent for me and inquired about this [tradition], and I related it to him. He followed it and took decisions on the strength of it.[59] Thus ʿUthmān, who was an imām and a man of

[56] Būlāq ed., p. 60.

[57] The tribe of Banū Khudra, belongs to the Anṣār (supporters of the Prophet), in Madīna.

[58] A place about six miles from Madīna.

[59] Mālik, Vol. II, p. 591; Abū Dāwūd, Vol. II, p. 291; Shāfiʿī, *Kitāb al-Umm*, Vol. V, pp. 208-209.

knowledge and virtue, settled disputes between the Anṣār and Muhājirīn on the strength of a tradition related by a woman.

S439 Muslim [b. Khālid] told us from Ibn Jurayj from al-Ḥasan b. Muslim [b. Yannāq] from Ṭāwūs, who said: I was with Ibn ʿAbbās when Zayd b. Thābit said to him: "Would you rule that a woman [who has begun to] menstruate should return from the pilgrimage before visiting the Sacred House?" "It is not for me to say so," replied Ibn ʿAbbās, "ask so-and-so, the woman
S440 from the Anṣār, whether the Prophet ordered her to do so." Zayd b. Thābit went away laughing and said: "I must say that what you said is right."[60]

439. Shāfiʿī said: Zayd had heard an order of prohibition [from the Prophet] against a pilgrim's returning from the pilgrimage before visiting the Sacred House, and thought that it included the menstruating woman. When Ibn ʿAbbās ruled that she could return if she had visited the House after the Day of Sacrifice (al-Naḥr), Zayd took exception to it, but when Ibn ʿAbbās related to him a tradition from a woman who was
S441 ordered to do so by the Apostle—and when the woman was asked, she confirmed the tradition—he believed the woman and saw that the right thing for him to do was to cease differing with Ibn ʿAbbās. But Ibn ʿAbbās had no other proof than the woman's narrative.[61]

440. [Shāfiʿī said]: Sufyān [b. ʿUyayna] told us from ʿAmr [b. Dīnār] from Saʿīd b. Jubayr, who said: I have told Ibn ʿAbbās that Nawf al-Bikālī claims that Mūsa, the companion of al-Khiḍr, is not the Mūsa of the children of Israel. "The enemy of God had told a lie," replied Ibn ʿAbbās, for Ubayy b. Kaʿb told me that the Apostle in speaking to him once mentioned the story of Mūsa and al-Khiḍr in such a way as to indicate that the Mūsa of the children of Israel was the Mūsa who was associated with al-Khiḍr.[62]

[60] Ibn Ḥanbal, Vol. III, p. 307, Vol. V, p. 89. Similar traditions are related on the authority of ʿĀ'isha. See Mālik, Vol. I, pp. 410-12; Bukhārī, Vol. I, pp. 393, 415-16.

[61] See Shāfiʿī, *Kitāb al-Umm,* Vol. II, pp. 154-55.

[62] Bukhārī, Vol. I, pp. 30-31; Vol. II, p. 354. Al-Khiḍr is a legendary figure identified with various early prophets and saints, including Enoch, Elijah, and

Thus Ibn ʿAbbās, pious and versed in the law as he was, S442
accepted the authenticity of a tradition related by Ubayy b. Kaʿb
from the Apostle as a proof against the opinion of a certain B60
Muslim. Ubayy b. Kaʿb had reported to him a tradition from the Prophet that Mūsa of the children of Israel was the same as the Companion of al-Khiḍr.

Muslim [b. Khālid al-Zanjī] and ʿAbd al-Majīd told us from Ibn Jurayj [from ʿĀmir b. Muṣʿab] that Ṭāwūs told him that he asked Ibn ʿAbbās about the two cycles (*rakʿatayn*) after the ʿ*aṣr* prayer, and Ibn ʿAbbās forbade him to perform them. "I replied: I was not going to abandon them," said Ṭāwūs. Thereupon Ibn ʿAbbās, [quoting the Qur'ān], said:

> It is not for any believer, man or woman, when God and his Apostle have decreed a matter, to have a choice in any matter affecting him. Whoever disobeys God and His Apostle has gone astray into
> manifest error [Q. XXXIII, 36].[63] S443

Ibn ʿAbbās was of the opinion that the proof against Ṭāwūs was established by his tradition from the Prophet and by his indicating through a citation from the Book of God that both sources deprived Ṭāwūs of any choice in a matter that had been decided by God and His Apostle. Although Ṭāwūs knew of the decision of the Apostle from a tradition related only by Ibn ʿAbbās, he did not reject it and tell [Ibn ʿAbbās]: "This is a tradition related by you alone. I do not consider that it is established as being from the Prophet, since it is possible that you have forgotten something with regard to it."

441. Someone might say: Would [Ṭāwūs] not hesitate to say such a thing to Ibn ʿAbbās?

442. [Shāfiʿī replied]: Ibn ʿAbbās was above being afraid to
tell anyone the truth as he saw it. For he forbade [Ṭāwūs] to S444
perform the two cycles after the ʿ*aṣr* prayer and told him not

St. George. See Ibn Ḥajar, *al-Iṣāba*, Vol. I, pp. 428-47, for a traditional account of al-Khiḍr's life as a prophet. For a more critical account, see Meijer de Hond, *Der Koranisirte Elḫidr* (Leyden, 1914).

[63] See Bayhaqī, *al-Sunan al-Kubra*, Vol. II, p. 453; and Suyūṭī, *al-Dur al-Manthūr*, Vol. V, p. 201.

to perform them before informing him that the Prophet had prohibited them.

443. [Shāfiʿī said]: Sufyān [b. ʿUyayna] told us from ʿAmr [b. Dīnār] from Ibn ʿUmar, who said: "We used to practice *mukhābara*[64] (share-cropping), seeing no harm in it until Rāfiʿ b. Khadīj claimed that the Apostle had prohibited it. So we gave it up because of what [Rāfiʿ] had said."[65]

Thus Ibn ʿUmar, who was profiting from *mukhābara* and regarded it as lawful, did not continue to practise it after a tradition was related to him by a trusted transmitter that the Apostle had prohibited it. Furthermore, he did not use his own
S445 judgment regarding what was related from the Apostle and say: "Nobody has so far reproached us for this, and we have been practising it till now." This clearly indicates that something that was practised after the Prophet's death and was not supported by a tradition from the Prophet does not vitiate a narrative from the Prophet.[66]

444. [Shāfiʿī said]: Mālik [b. Anas] told us from Zayd b. Aslam from ʿAṭā' b. Yasār that Muʿāwiya b. Abī Sufyān once sold [either] a gold or a silver drinking cup for more than [the value of] its weight. "I heard the Apostle prohibit that kind [of thing]," said Abū al-Dardā' to him. "I do not see any harm in it," said Muʿāwiya. "Who will support me against Muʿāwiya?" asked Abū al-Dardā'. "I relate to him [a
S446 tradition] from the Apostle, and he gives me his own opinion. I cannot live in the same land with you [Muʿāwiya]."[67] Thus Abū al-Dardā' was of the opinion that the proof against Muʿāwiya was established by a narrative related to him; but when Muʿāwiya did not agree with him, he departed from the land in which he had been to save his self-respect, since

[64] *Mukhābara* was the practice of renting the land by paying one fourth, or one third, or any specific portion of the produce after harvest. It is also called *al-muzāraʿa*. See Jurjānī, *Kitāb al-Taʿrīfāt*, p. 290.

[65] See Shawkānī, *Nayl al-Awṭār*, Vol. V, pp. 287-96. For a different transmission, see Mālik, Vol. II, p. 711; Abū Dāwūd, Vol. III, pp. 257-59.

[66] Būlāq ed., p. 61.

[67] Mālik says that Abū al-Dardā' informed ʿUmar about Muʿāwiya's action, and ʿUmar forbade Muʿāwiya to conclude the transaction. See Mālik, Vol. II, p. 634. Cf. J. Schacht, *Origins of Muhammadan Jurisprudence*, p. 55.

Muʿāwiya had rejected a narrative related by a reliable source from the Prophet.

445. [Shāfiʿī] said: We have been told that Abū Saʿīd al-Khudrī met a man to whom he related something from the Apostle; the man, however, related another narrative contradictory to it. " By God, may I never be [again] with you under the same roof," said Abū Saʿīd.

446. Shāfiʿī said: The transmitter [Abū Saʿīd] was chagrined because [the other man] did not accept the tradition he related from the Prophet, but quoted another contradictory to it. However, there were two aspects of the latter's tradition; one of them may have conflicted with Abū Saʿīd's tradition and the S447
other not.

447. Shāfiʿī said:[68] I was told by one whom I do not suspect [Ibrāhīm b. Abī Yaḥya][69] from Ibn Abī Dhi'b from Makhlad b. Khufāf, who said:

> I bought a slave whom I employed, but later I discovered a certain defect in him. So I took the case before [the Caliph] ʿUmar b. ʿAbd al-ʿAzīz, who made a decision in my favor that I could return the slave but decided against me that I should return the profit [I made on him]. When I called on ʿUrwa b. al-Zubayr and told him about the matter, he said: I shall go to [the Caliph] this evening and tell him that ʿĀ'isha related to me a tradition that the Apostle decreed that ' the profit belongs to him who bears the responsibility.' So I hastened to ʿUmar and I told him what ʿUrwa had related to me, on the authority of ʿĀ'isha, from the Prophet. ' What a hasty decision I have taken! God knows that I sought nothing but what was right. Now that you have informed me of a sunna of the Apostle concerning this matter,
> I shall revoke the decision of ʿUmar and carry out the sunna of the S448
> Apostle of God,' said ʿUmar. When ʿUrwa called on ʿUmar [to whom he related ʿĀ'isha's tradition], ʿUmar decided that I should take the
> profit from the man in whose favor the [earlier] decision was taken.[70] S449

I was told by an authority from Madīna [Ibrāhīm b. Abī

[68] Būlāq ed., p. 61.
[69] See Bayhaqī, *Manāqib al-Shāfiʿī,* folio 278.
[70] Abū Dāwūd, Vol. III, p. 284; Ibn Sallām, p. 73.

Yaḥya], whose truthfulness I do not suspect, from Ibn Abī Dhi'b, who said:

Saʿd b. Ibrāhīm took a decision against a certain man on the strength of an opinion of Rabīʿa b. Abī ʿAbd al-Raḥmān, whereupon I related to him [a tradition] from the Prophet that was contradictory to his decision. So Saʿd said to Rabīʿa: "Here is Ibn Abī Dhi'b, a trustworthy authority in my opinion, who related a tradition from the Prophet that is contradictory to what I have just decided." "You have exercised *ijtihād* (personal
B61 reasoning), and your decision has been given," replied Rabīʿa. "How strange! Shall I carry out the decision of Saʿd, son of Umm Saʿd[71] and reject the order of the Apostle of God?" said Saʿd. "No," he added, "I shall reject the decision of Saʿd, son of Umm Saʿd, and carry out the order of the Apostle of God." So he called for the written decision, tore it up, and made a decision in favor of the one against whom he had made the decision.

448. Shāfiʿī said: Abū Ḥanīfa b. Simāk b. al-Faḍl al-Shihābī told us from Ibn Abī Dhi'b from al-Maqburī from Abū Shurayḥ
S450 al-Kaʿbī that the Prophet, in the year of the conquest [of Makka], said:

> Whoever suffers the loss of a relative who is killed can make a choice between blood-money and retaliation.[72]

Abū Ḥanīfa asked Ibn Abī Dhi'b: "O Abū al-Ḥārith! Do you act according to this [tradition]?" Thereupon, [Ibn Abī Dhi'b] gave me a blow on the breast, shouted vociferously, abused me and said: "I relate to you a tradition from the Apostle and you ask whether I act according to it? Yes, I do, for this is an obligation imposed on me and on whoever hears it. God chose Muḥammad from all men and guided them through him and through his words. Men are bound to follow him willingly, for
S451-452 no Muslim can escape from that." He went on and on until I

[71] Her name was Umm Kulthūm; but it was customary to address any woman as the mother of so-and-so.

[72] Abū Dāwūd, Vol. IV, p. 172; Abū ʿĀṣim al-Ḍaḥḥāk, *Kitāb al-Diyāt* (Cairo, 1323/1906), p. 25.

implored him to stop.[73]

449. [Shāfiʿī] said: There are other traditions concerning the authentication of the single-individual traditions, but those cited here are sufficient. This is the source which our ancestors as well as succeeding generations have followed down to our time. Scholars in other countries tell us that they agree with us on this matter.

450. Shāfiʿī said: We have found that Saʿīd in Madīna says: Abū Saʿīd al-Khudrī related to me something that the Prophet said on the subject of exchange and it has been authenticated as a sunna.[74] He [Saʿīd] says: Abū Hurayra gave me information from the Prophet which has been accepted as an authentic sunna. Other [single transmitters] have also been quoted as the source of statements that have been accepted as authentic sunna. We have found that ʿUrwa says that ʿĀ'isha told him that the Apostle decreed that the " profit belongs to him who bears the responsibility," and it was accepted as an authentic sunna.[75] Many other traditions consisting of orders of permission and prohibition have been transmitted through her from the Prophet which were accepted as authentic sunnas.
We have also found him [ʿUrwa] relating on the authority of S453
Usāma b. Zayd and ʿAbd-Allāh b. ʿUmar and others from the Prophet. The tradition from each was accepted in each case as an authentic single-individual sunna. And we have found him relating on the authority of ʿAbd al-Raḥmān b. ʿAbd al-Qārī from ʿUmar, and on the authority of Yaḥya b. ʿAbd al-Raḥmān b. Ḥāṭib from his father and from ʿUmar; and each one of these is accepted as an authentic narrative from ʿUmar.

We have found al-Qāsim b. Muḥammad relating [at one time] on the authority of ʿĀ'isha from the Prophet, and at another on the authority of Ibn ʿUmar from the Prophet. In each case these narratives have been accepted as authentic sunnas. And he relates on the authority of ʿAbd al-Rahmān and Mujammaʿ,

[73] Shāfiʿī, *Musnad,* Vol. I, p. 21; J. Schacht, *Origins of Muhammadan Jurisprudence,* p. 55.

[74] See paragraph 271, above.

[75] See paragraph 447, above.

the two sons of Yazīd b. Jāriya, from Khansā', daughter S454 of Khidhām, from the Prophet. This narrative, [although] transmitted by one woman, was accepted as an authentic sunna.

We have found ʿAlī b. Ḥusayn relating on the authority of ʿAmr b. ʿUthmān b. ʿAffān from Usāma b. Zayd from the Prophet, say: " A Muslim cannot inherit from an unbeliever, nor an unbeliever from a Muslim." This was accepted as an authentic sunna by him and by men after him on the strength of the narrative. And we have found Muḥammad b. ʿAlī b. al-Ḥusayn relating on the authority of Jābir b. ʿAbd-Allāh from the Prophet, and from ʿUbayd-Allah b. Abī Rāfiʿ from Abū Hurayra from the Prophet, all of whose narratives have been accepted as authentic sunnas.

We have likewise found Muḥammad b. Jubayr b. Muṭʿim, Nāfiʿ b. Jubayr b. Muṭʿim, Yazīd b. Ṭalḥa b. Rukāna, Muḥammad b. Ṭalḥa b. Rukāna, Nāfiʿ b. ʿUjayr b. ʿAbd Yazīd, Abū Salāma b. ʿAbd al-Raḥmān [b. ʿAwf], Ḥumayd S455 b. ʿAbd al-Raḥmān [b. ʿAwf], Ṭalḥa b. ʿAbd-Allāh b. ʿAwf, Muṣʿab b. Saʿd b. Abī Waqqās, Ibrāhīm b. ʿAbd al-Rahmān b. ʿAwf, Khārija b. Zayd b. Thābit, ʿAbd al-Raḥmān b. Kaʿb b. Mālik, ʿAbd-Allāh b. Abī Qatāda, Sulaymān b. Yasār, ʿAṭā' b. Yasār and other transmitters from Madīna relating on the authority of one of the Prophet's companions or from their successors on the authority of one of the Prophet's companions, and all this has been accepted as authentic sunnas.

We have found that ʿAṭā', Ṭāwūs, Mujāhid, Ibn Abī Mulayka, ʿIkrima b. Khālid [b. al-ʿĀṣ], ʿUbayd-Allāh b. Abī Yazīd, ʿAbd-Allah b. Bābāh, [ʿAbd al-Raḥmān b. ʿAbd-Allāh] b. Abī ʿAmmar, and other Makkan transmitters; Wahb b. Munab- S456 bih in al-Yaman; Makḥūl in al-Shām (Syria); ʿAbd al-Raḥmān b. Ghanam, al-Ḥasan and [Muḥammad] Ibn Sīrīn in Baṣra; al-Aswad, ʿAlqama, al-Shaʿbī in Kūfa; and transmitters and B62 notables in other provinces have all accepted the authenticity of the single-individual traditions originating from the

Apostle and ending with him and agree that they may be used as the basis of fatwas. Each one of these [transmitters] has accepted the tradition from a preceding transmitter and from him it was accepted by a succeeding transmitter.

If it is permissible for anyone to hold the view of the specialists' knowledge that the Muslims, ancient and contemporary, are agreed in accepting the authenticity of the single- S457
individual tradition and its binding [force], since no Muslim jurist is known who did not do likewise, it would be permissible for me to say so also. But I can add that none of the Muslim jurists have told me that they differ over the authentication of the single-individual tradition, since they were all in agreement, as I have already pointed out.[76]

451. [Shāfiʿī] said: If it could be supposed that one person might say that a certain tradition was related from the Prophet in one way, while another person might say something contradicting that tradition, then in my opinion it would not be permissible for a scholar [to insist that] the tradition of a single person be confirmed by many and use it to declare things lawful and unlawful while he rejects others similar to it, unless he possesses a tradition that contradicts it. For he considers that which he has heard and those who heard it from [the single transmitter] as more trustworthy than those who told him something different from it. Or he who transmitted
might not have been a memorizer; or he might consider him S458
suspect; or he might suspect one of the previous transmitters; or the tradition might be ambiguous and he might accept one interpretation in preference to the other. But one should not imagine that an intelligent jurist could on one or more occasion accept the authenticity of a sunna on the strength of a single-individual narrative and then discard the same in favor of a narrative similar to or more reliable than the previous one, except for one of those causes that might cast doubt upon the interpretation of it (as in the case of the commentators on the Qur'ān) or because he either suspects

[76] Cf. Būlāq ed., p. 62.

the transmitter, or is aware of a narrative contradictory to it.

452. Someone might say: Few are the jurists anywhere who have not related many traditions acceptable to them while they have related [only] a few that were unacceptable.

S459 453. [Shāfiʿī replied]: It is not permissible [for a jurist] to reject a tradition save for one of the reasons I have discussed, or because he is relating from one of the successors or from someone from a succeeding generation a saying that he is not bound to accept. He relates it only as information and does not vouch for it; he may or may not accept it. If he does not follow any of these courses, he would commit a great error which would be inexcusable, although failure to follow some of them might be forgiven.

454. Someone might ask: Has your term "proof" different meanings?

455. [Shāfiʿī] replied: Yes, it has; God willing.

456. He asked: What are they?

457. [Shāfiʿī] replied: No one shall be excused for discarding something [that is supported by] a clear text of the Book or a generally accepted sunna, for there is no doubt concerning either one of them, and he who refuses to accept either one must ask
S460 forgiveness.

But if a sunna were derived from a narrative handed down by a few [persons] but there is disagreement concerning it because the narrative is open to different interpretations and came [originally] from a single source, then any argument regarding it would be that it should be binding on those who are informed about it. For they cannot reject it as long as there is a text to support it, just as they are bound to accept the testimony of witnesses of just character, since [such knowledge] is as certain as the text of the Book [of God] or a narrative well known to the public. So if someone were to cast doubt upon it, we should not tell him to repent. Instead, we should tell him that if he is a learned man he should not doubt, just as one should take a decision only on the strength of the testimony of witnesses of just character, even though they are liable to err, for one is bound to take decisions in this regard on the basis of the apparent truthfulness [of the witnesses], since only God knows those things about them that are hidden from a person.

458. He asked: Can an interrupted tradition be used as an argument by him who knows about it? Are such interrupted traditions different from others, or are they on the same level?

459. Shāfiʿī replied: Interrupted traditions vary. A tradition related by one of the successors who saw one of the Apostle's companions but did not carry the tradition back to the Prophet should be scrutinized from various angles: S461

[First,] one should examine the transmission of the tradition. If the transmitter is supported by trustworthy memorizers of traditions who have related from the Apostle traditions of similar meaning, this would be an indication of the soundness of those who passed on the tradition.

[Secondly,] if he were the only one to relate a tradition and no other was found to support him with a similar one, the tradition related by one individual should be accepted.

[Thirdly,] it should be considered whether he is supported by any other transmitter whose traditions were accepted by others but who did not belong to that group of men from whom he accepted his traditions. If such is found [to be the case], it would be an indication supporting the transmitter of the tradition, although [such an indication] would be weaker than the former one. In case such an indication is not found, the information related from the Apostle by some of his Companions should be examined. If they are found to be in agreement with [other] traditions from the Apostle, S462
its transmitter took [his information] only from a sound source.

Furthermore, if scholars in general are found to have given rulings consistent with a tradition said to have been related from the Prophet, and if the transmitter cites as his authorities persons who were neither unknown nor objectionable, it is indicative of the soundness of what was related from the transmitter, since such authorities constitute a proof of reliability.

If [a transmitter] seeks the opinion of a memorizer regarding a tradition that the latter has never contradicted, and if the memorizer contradicts it but his tradition is found to be defective, it is an indication of the soundness of the person
S463 who gave out the transmitter's tradition. If the opposite of what I have described happens, then the [transmitter's] tradition is adversely affected and no one can accept it. But[77] if certain
B63 indications [in favor] of the soundness of his tradition are found by the means I have described, we should prefer to accept his tradition.

We cannot, however, claim that the proof [for the interrupted tradition] would be as good as that of an uninterrupted [tradition]. The reason is that the interrupted tradition has something lacking, though it may have been related from a person who, if his name had been known, might prove to be acceptable. But some interrupted [traditions]—even if similar interrupted traditions agree with them—might have been related from the same source, which if known might prove to be unacceptable. If the narrator is stating his own opinion [regarding the soundness of the tradition], even if some of the companions of the Prophet agree with him, it is not a strong
S464 indication of the soundness of the source of the tradition; for it is possible that [the transmitter] might have mistakenly thought that some of the companions were agreeing with him just as he might have mistakenly thought that some of the jurists agreed with him.[78]

But as for those who came after the leading Successors who so often saw some of the Companions of the Apostle, I do not know a single one of them whose transmission would be acceptable for various reasons. The reasons for that are: First, they were not so particular as to those from whom they related traditions. Secondly, there are certain indications in that which they transmitted that betray weakness in the source of their transmission. Thirdly, there are many variations [in their traditions], and this raises the possibility of misunderstanding

[77] " Shāfiʿī said" is omitted,

[78] Cf. Ibn Ḥazm, Vol. II, pp. 2-6.

and lack of reliability on the part of him from whom it was received. S465

460. Shāfiʿī said:[79] My experience with certain scholars indicates that there are groups with [two] opposite tendencies: Some are satisfied with meager knowledge and want to derive knowledge from only one source, neglecting similar or more reliable ones. These are the ones who are lacking in knowledge. Others, who have criticized this approach and aspired to a broader and thorough knowledge [of tradition], have been driven by this [desire] to accept traditions from transmitters from whom it would have been better not to accept. I have noticed that most of them are inclined to be unreliable, because they accept [traditions] from the same transmitters whose similar and better traditions they have rejected. They accept traditions that are interpolated, as well as those from unreliable sources if they agree with their opinions, while they reject traditions from reliable transmitters if they happen to contradict their opinions.

Interpolations reach some of these people from various sources. He who scrutinizes the knowledge [of traditions] with
competence and care is shocked by the [number of] interrupted S466
traditions from those who are not well-known Successors, as shown from certain indications explicit in them.

461. He asked: Why do you distinguish between well-known early Successors who knew [many of the] Companions of the Apostle and those who knew only some of them?

462. [Shāfiʿī] replied: Because it was quite impossible for those who had never met most of the Companions to relate traditions from them.

463. He asked: Why do you not accept an interrupted tradition from them or from any of the jurists who came after them?

464. [Shāfiʿī] replied: For [the reasons] that I have already described.

465. He asked: Is there any interrupted tradition from the

[79] Būlāq ed., p. 64.

Apostle that was transmitted by a reliable person but not accepted by any of the jurists?

466. [Shāfiʿī] replied: Yes. For Sufyān [b. ʿUyayna] has told us from Muḥammad b. al-Munkadir, who said: A man asked the Prophet: "O Apostle of God! I have my own family and property, and my father has his own family and property; yet he
S467 wants to take my property and use it to feed his family." "You and your property belong to your father," replied the Apostle of God.[80]

467. He said: We do not accept this tradition; but some of your followers accept it.

468. [Shāfiʿī] said: No, [we do not accept this tradition] for he who accepts it will give [the right to] the rich father to take the property of his son.

469. He asked: That is right; nobody accepts it. But why do people dispute it?

470. [Shāfiʿī] replied: Because it is not established that it is from the Prophet. For when God decreed that a father can inherit from his son as others, he put him on the same basis as other heirs. He might also receive a smaller share than many other heirs—an indication that the son owns his property independently of the father.

471. He asked: Is Muḥammad b. al-Munkadir extremely reliable in your opinion?

472. [Shāfiʿī] replied: Yes, he is, for he is distinguished in matters of religion and piety; but we do not know from whom he accepted this tradition. [You will recall that] I have explained to you the case in which two witnesses of just character testify
S468 concerning two men,[81] and how their testimony could not be accepted until their just character had been confirmed either by the two men in question or by others.

473. He asked: Will you give a tradition [in support of this opinion]?

474. [Shāfiʿī] replied: Yes. The trusted authority [Yaḥya b. Ḥassān] told us from Ibn Abī Dhi'b from Ibn Shihāb,

[80] Cf. Ibn Ḥanbal, Vol. X, p. 206; Suyūṭī, *al-Jāmiʿ al-Ṣaghīr,* Vol. I, p. 365.
[81] Būlāq ed., p. 64.

who said: "The Apostle ordered a man who laughed during the performance of prayer to repeat both the ablution and the prayer." We did not accept this tradition because it is interrupted. Then the trusted authority [also] related the same tradition from Maʿmar from Ibn Shihāb from Sulaymān b. Arqam from al-Ḥasan from the Prophet. We consider Ibn Shihāb to be an authority on traditions and expert in the choice of reliable transmitters; he names some of the Companions of the Prophet and prominent Successors, and we know of no transmitter who can relate from men more reliable or better known than those from whom Ibn Shihāb relates.

475. He said: We think it strange that he related from Sulaymān b. Arqam. S469

476. [Shāfiʿī replied]: [Perhaps] he did so because he thought that [Arqam] was a man of virtue, knowledge, and reason. So he accepted traditions from him and had good opinion of him, but failed to mention his name, either because Arqam was younger than he, or for some other [reason]. But when Maʿmar asked [Ibn Shihāb] who related the tradition, he gave him as his authority. Thus though it is possible that Ibn Shihāb may have related a tradition from Sulaymān b. Arqam [the tradition should be accepted] in view of what I have said [in praise of] Ibn Shihāb; but other [transmitters] should not be trusted in similar cases.

477. He asked: Is there any sunna of the Apostle established by an interrupted chain of transmitters which everybody has B64 refused to accept.

478. [Shāfiʿī] replied: No; sometimes we do find people disagreeing about it among themselves, some accepting it and others not. However, we have never found people agreeing in opposition to a well-authenticated sunna as we have found them to do in the case of an interrupted tradition from the Apostle.[82]

479. Shāfiʿī said: I [also] pointed out [to the interlocutor]: You have asked for the proof on the basis of which an

[82] Būlāq ed., p. 65. For further discussion, see Shāfiʿī, *Kitāb Ikhtilāf al-Ḥadīth* (*Kitāb al-Umm*, Vol. VII, p. 338); and J. Schacht, *Origins of Muhammadan Jurisprudence*, p. 11.

interrupted tradition is rejected and you have rejected such
S470 a tradition; but you have gone too far in rejecting a well-authenticated tradition which, in our opinion, you are under an obligation to accept.

Chapter XI

[ON CONSENSUS (*IJMĀʿ*)][1]

480. Shāfiʿī said: Someone has asked me: I have understood your doctrine concerning God's commands and His Apostle's orders that he who obeys God obeys His Apostle, [for] God has imposed [on men] the duty of obeying His Apostle, and that the proof for what you held has been established that it would be unlawful for a Muslim who has known the Book [of God] and the sunna [of the Prophet] to give an opinion at variance with either one, for I know that this [i. e. acceptance of the Book and the sunna] is a duty imposed by God. But what is your proof for accepting the consensus of the public [on matters] concerning which no explicit command of God nor any [sunna] related on the authority of the Prophet is to be found? Do you assert, with others, that the consensus of the public should always be based on an established sunna even if it were not related [on the authority of the S471
Prophet]?

481. [Shāfiʿī] replied: That on which the public are agreed and which, as they assert, was related from the Apostle, that is so. As to that which the public do not relate [from the Prophet], which they may or may not relate as a tradition from the Prophet, we cannot consider it as related on the authority of the

[1] Although Shāfiʿī's treatment of *ijmāʿ* in this chapter is brief, he has discussed some aspects of it in other parts of the *Risāla*. See Chaps. VI, VII, IX, X, XIV, and XV.

Prophet—because one may relate only what lie has heard, for no one is permitted to relate [on the authority of the Prophet] information which may or may not be true. So we accept the decision of the public because we have to obey their authority, and we know that wherever there are sunnas of the Prophet, the public cannot be ignorant of them, although it is possible that some are, and we know that the public can neither agree on
S472 anything contrary to the sunna of the Prophet nor on an error.

482. Someone may ask: Is there any evidence in support of what you hold?

483. [Shāfiʿī] replied: Sufyān [b. ʿUyayna] told us from ʿAbd al-Malik b. ʿUmayr from ʿAbd al-Raḥmān b. ʿAbd-Allāh b. Masʿūd from his father, who said: The Apostle said:

> God will grant prosperity to His servant who hears my words, remembers them, guards them, and hands them on. Many a transmitter of law is no lawyer himself, and many may transmit law to others who are more versed in the law than they, etc.[2]

And Sufyān [also] told us from ʿAbd-Allāh b. Abī Labīd from
S473 ʿAbd-Allāh b. Sulaymān b. Yasār from his father, who said: ʿUmar b. al-Khaṭṭāb made a speech at al-Jābiya in which he said: The Apostle of God stood among us by an order from God, as I am now standing among you, and said:

> Believe my Companions, then those who succeed them [the Successors], and after that those who succeed the Successors; but after them untruthfulness will prevail when people will swear [in support of their saying] without having been asked to swear, and will testify without having been asked to testify. Only those who seek the pleasure of Paradise will follow the community, for the devil can pursue one person, but stands far away from two. Let no man be alone with a woman, for the devil will be the third among them. He who is happy with his right [behavior], or unhappy with his wrong
> S474 behavior, is a [true] believer.[3]

[2] Only the first three words of this tradition are cited, because Shāfiʿī considered it quite unnecessary to repeat a text which he has already given in full in paragraph 417 above. It is reproduced in full in the Būlāq edition, p. 65.

[3] In the year 638 the Caliph ʿUmar went to al-Jābiya, a village on the outskirts of Damascus, where he met several leading Companions. For the text of the

484. He asked: What is the meaning of the Prophet's order to follow the community?

485. [Shāfiʿī] replied: There is but one meaning for it.

486. He asked: How is it possible that there is only one meaning?

487. [Shāfiʿī] replied: When the community spread in the lands [of Islam], nobody was able to follow its members who had been dispersed and mixed with other believers and unbelievers, pious and impious. So it was meaningless to follow the community [as a whole],[4] because it was impossible [to do so], except for what the [entire] community regarded as lawful or unlawful [orders] and [the duty] to obey these [orders].

He who holds what the Muslim community holds shall be regarded as following the community, and he who holds differently shall be regarded as opposing the community he was ordered to follow. So the error comes from separation; but in the S475
community as a whole there is no error concerning the meaning of the Qur'ān, the sunna, and analogy.[5]

tradition, see Shāfiʿī, *Musnad,* Vol. II, p. 187; and Ibn Ḥanbal, Vol. I, pp. 112-13, 176-81.

[4] This sentence is twice repeated in the Arabic text, in the middle and toward the end of the paragraph.

[5] For a brief translation of the last two paragraphs, see J. Schacht, *Origins of Muhammadan Jurisprudence,* pp. 90-91.

Chapter XII

[ON ANALOGY (*QIYĀS*)][1]

488. He asked: On what ground do you hold that [on
B65 matters] concerning which no text is to be found in the Book, nor a sunna or consensus, recourse should be had to analogy? Is there any binding text for analogical deduction?

489. [Shāfiʿī] replied: If analogy were [stated] in the text of the Book or the sunna, such a text should be called either God's
S476 command or the Apostle's order rather than analogy.

490. He asked: What is analogy? Is it *ijtihād*, or are the two different?

491. [Shāfiʿī] replied: They are two terms with the same meaning.

492. He asked: What is their common [basis]?

493. [Shāfiʿī] replied: On all matters touching the [life of a] Muslim there is either a binding ruling or an indication as to the right answer. If there is a ruling, it should be followed; if there is no indication as to the right answer, it should be sought by *ijtihād*, and *ijtihād* is *qiyās* (analogy).[2]

494. He asked: If the scholars apply analogy correctly, will they arrive at the right answer in the eyes of God? And will it be permissible for them to disagree [in their answers] through analogy? Have they been ordered to seek one or different an-

[1] Būlāq ed., p. 66. Analogy is also discussed in the chapters on personal reasoning and juristic preference (Chaps. XIII–XIV).

[2] Cf. J. Schacht, *Origins of Muhammadan Jurisprudence*, p. 127.

swers for each question? What is the proof for the position that S477
they should apply analogy on the basis of the literal rather than the implicit meaning [of a ruling], and that it is permissible for them to disagree [in their answers]? Should [analogy] in matters concerning the scholars themselves be applied differently from the way it is applied in matters concerning others? Who is the person qualified to exercise *ijtihād* through analogy in matters concerning himself, not others, and who is the person who can apply it in matters concerning himself as well as others?

495. [Shāfiʿī] replied: [Legal] knowledge is of various kinds: The first consists of the right rulings in the literal and implied senses; the other, of the right answer in the literal sense only. The right decisions [in the literal and implied senses] are those based [either] on God's command or on a sunna of the Apostle related by the public from an [earlier] public. These [God's commands and the sunna] are the two sources by virtue of which the lawful is to be established as lawful and the unlawful as unlawful. This is [the kind of knowledge] of which nobody is allowed to be ignorant or doubtful [as to its certainty].

Secondly, [legal] knowledge of the specialists consists of
traditions related by a few and known only to scholars, but S478
others [the public] are under no obligation to be familiar with it. Such knowledge may either be found among all or a few [of the scholars], related by a reliable transmitter from the Prophet. This is the [kind of] knowledge which is binding on scholars to accept and it constitutes the right ruling in the literal sense such as we accept [the validity of] the testimony of two witnesses.[3] This is right [only] in the literal sense, because it is possible that [the evidence of] the two witnesses might be false.

[Thirdly], [legal] knowledge derived from *ijmāʿ* (consensus).[4]

[Finally], [legal] knowledge derived from *ijtihād* [personal reasoning] through *qiyās* [analogy], by virtue of which right

[3] Būlāq ed., p. 66. Shākir's edition reads: "just as we condemn to death the murderer on the strength of two witnesses," p. 479.

[4] This subject is dealt with in Chap. XI.

rulings are sought. Such rulings are right in the literal sense to the person who applies analogy, not to the majority of scholars, for nobody knows what is hidden except God.

496. [He asked]: If [legal] knowledge is derived through analogy—provided it is rightly applied—should [the scholars] who apply analogy agree on most [of the decisions], although we may find them disagreeing on some?

497. [Shāfiʿī replied]: Analogy is of two kinds: the first, if the case in question is similar to the original meaning [of the precedent], no disagreement on this kind [is permitted]. The second, if the case in question is similar to several precedents, analogy must be applied to the precedent nearest in resemblance
S479 and most appropriate. But those who apply analogy are likely to disagree [in their answers].

498. He asked: Will you give examples known to me explaining that [legal] knowledge is of two kinds, the one consisting of the right rulings in literal and implicit senses, and the other of the right rulings in the literal, not the implicit, sense?

499. [Shāfiʿī] replied: If we were in the Sacred Mosque and the Kaʿba is in sight, do you not agree that we should face it [in prayer] with certainty?

500. He said: That is right.

501. Shāfiʿī asked: [Since] the duties of prayer, [the payment of] the alms, performance of pilgrimage, and the like have been imposed on us, are we not under obligation to perform them in the right ways?

502. He replied: That is right.

503. [Shāfiʿī] asked: Since the duty imposed on us to punish
S480 the fornicator with a hundred stripes, to scourge him who casts an imputation [of adultery] with eighty, to put to death him who apostatizes, and to cut off [the hand of] him who steals, are we not under obligation to do so [only] to him whose offence is established with certainty on [the basis of] his admission?

504. He replied: That is right.

505. [Shāfiʿī] asked: Should not [the rulings] be the same whether we were obligated to take them against ourselves or

others, although we realize that we know about ourselves what others do not know, and we do not know about others by outward observation what we know about ourselves inwardly?

506. He replied: That is right.

507. [Shāfiʿī] asked: Are we not under obligation to face the Sacred House [in prayer] wherever we may be?

508. He replied: That is right.

509. [Shāfiʿī] asked: Do you hold that we [could always] face the Sacred House correctly?

510. He replied: No, not always as correctly as when you were able to see [the Sacred House]; however, the duty imposed on you was fulfilled.

511. [Shāfiʿī] asked: Is our obligation to seek the unknown object different from our obligation to seek the known object? **S481**

512. He replied: That is right.

513. [Shāfiʿī] asked: Are we not obligated to accept the just character of a man on the basis of his outward behavior, and establish marital and inheritance relationship with him on [the basis of] his outward acceptance of Islam?

514. He replied: That is right.

515. [Shāfiʿī] said: Yet he may not be just in character inwardly.

516. He replied: That is quite possible; but you are under no obligation to accept save what is explicit.

517. [Shāfiʿī] asked: So is it not lawful for us to establish marital and inheritance relationship with him, and to accept his testimony, and is it not unlawful for us to kill him on the basis of [our] explicit [knowledge] of him? But if others should discover him to be an unbeliever, would it not be lawful for them to kill him and to repudiate marital and inheritance relationship or whatever else he had been permitted to do?

518. He replied: That is right.

519. [Shāfiʿī] said: Thus the obligation imposed on us toward the same person differs in accordance with the degree of our understanding of it and others' understanding of it.

520. He replied: Yes, for each one fulfils his obligation on the basis of his own understanding.

521. [Shāfiʿī] said: Thus we hold concerning matters on which there is no binding explicit text that these should be sought by *ijtihād*—through *qiyās*—because we are under obligation to arrive at the right answers according to us.

522. He asked: Are you not seeking the answer to one question through different means?

523. [Shāfiʿī] replied: Yes, whenever the grounds are different.

524. He asked: Give me an example.

525. [Shāfiʿī] replied: If a man admits an obligation on his part to God or to another person, I should take a decision
B66 against him on the strength of his admission; if he does not admit, I should take the decision on the evidence established against him; if no evidence can be established against him, I should take the decision on the basis of an oath taken by him which might acquit him; if he refuses [to take the oath], I should ask the other party to take an oath and I should make the decision against him on the basis of the oath of the other party. It is understood that [one's own] admission against himself—owing to [one's natural] covetousness and greed—is more certain than the evidence of others, since they might make a mistake or tell a lie against another. The evidence of witnesses
S483 of just character against a person should be regarded as nearer to the truth than [the accused] refusal to take an oath, or [nearer to the truth] than the oath taken by the other party [against him], since the latter might not be just in character. Thus the decision is taken on several grounds, some of them stronger than others.

526. He said: That is all right, but if he refuses to take an oath, we [the Ḥanafī School] will take the decision [against him] on the ground of his refusal.

527. [Shāfiʿī] said: But you will have taken a decision on an evidence weaker than ours.

528. He said: Yes; however, I disagree with you on the source of evidence [on the strength of which you have taken the decision].

529. [Shāfiʿī] said: The strongest evidence for your decision was his admission, although one is liable to make an unfounded

or erroneous admission [on the strength of which] a decision might be taken against a person.

530. He said: That is correct; for you are under no other obligation than that. S484

531. [Shāfiʿī] asked: Do you not agree that we are under an obligation to take the right decision by one of two means: Either by certainty based on the literal and implicit meanings, or by certainty based on literal, not implicit meaning?

532. He replied: Yes, but is there any explicit text in the Book or the sunna in support [of your opinion]?

533. [Shāfiʿī] said: Yes, in such examples as I have [already] discussed concerning the determination of the *qibla* for myself and others. [For] God said:

> And they comprehend not anything of His knowledge save what He willeth [Q. II, 255].[5]

Thus God endowed knowledge to man in whatever amount or way He wanted; no one shall raise an objection to His decision; for He is quick at reckoning.[6]

And He said to His Prophet:

> They ask thee about the Hour: 'When is its arrival?' What hast thou to do with the mention of it? To thy Lord is its final coming [Q. LXXIX, 42-44].

Sufyān b. ʿUyayna told us[7] from al-Zuhrī from ʿUrwa, who said:

> The Prophet went on inquiring about the Hour until God communicated to him: 'What hast thou to do with the mention of it?' [Q. LXXIX, 43] so he stopped. S485

And God said:

> Say: No one in the heavens or on earth knows the unseen except God [Q. XXVII, 65].

[5] Cf. Ṭabarī, *Tafsīr,* Vol. V, pp. 396-97.
[6] Cf. Q. XXXIII.
[7] Būlāq ed., p. 67.

And God, the Blessed and Most High, said:

> With God is the knowledge of the Hour; He sends down the rain, He knows what is in the womb. No person knows what he will gain tomorrow, and no person knows in what land he will die. Verily God is All-Knowing, All-Aware [Q. XXXI, 34].

So men are under obligation to hold opinions and to act in accordance with what they have been ordered [to do], provided that they do not exceed the limits. However, they cannot reward
S486 themselves; only God can reward. So we ask God to reward us for fulfilling our duties to Him and to enlarge His reward [to us].

Chapter XIII

[ON PERSONAL REASONING (*IJTIHĀD*)][1]

534. He asked: On what ground do you hold that [the exercise of] *ijtihād* is permitted in addition to what you have already explained?

535. [Shāfiʿī] replied: It is on the basis of God's saying:

> From whatever place thou issuest, turn thy face in the direction of the Sacred Mosque; and wherever you may be, turn your faces in its S487
> direction [Q. II, 150].[2]

Regarding him who [wishes to] face the Sacred Mosque [in prayer] and whose residence is at a distance from it, [legal] knowledge instructs [us] that he can seek the right direction through *ijtihād* on the basis of certain indications [guiding] toward it. For he who is under an obligation to face the Sacred House and does not know whether he is facing the right or wrong direction may be able to face the right one through certain indications known to him [which help him] to face it as accurately as he can, just as another person may know other indications which help to orient him [in the right direction],

[1] Būlāq ed., p. 76.

[2] Paragraphs 1379 and 1380 (of Shākir's ed.) are omitted because Shāfiʿī's answer to the interlocutor's question on the meaning of " direction" is confined to citing a verse of poetry without actually giving directly the meaning of the term. Besides, this is a repetition of paragraph 109 (Shākir's ed.).

although the direction sought by each person may be different from that sought by the other.[3]

536. He asked: If I agree with you on this [matter], I should agree with you on the permissibility of disagreement in other matters.

537. [Shāfiʿī] replied: You may hold whatever opinion you like.

538. He asked: I hold that [that disagreement] is not permissible.

539. [Shāfiʿī] asked: Let us [assume that] you and I, who
S488 know [the direction of] this road, [hold different opinions]: I hold that the *qibla* is in this direction; but you may disagree with me. Who should follow the opinion of the other?

540. He replied: Neither one is under an obligation to follow the other.

541. [Shāfiʿī] asked: What should each one do?

542. He replied: If I hold that neither one should perform the prayer until he is certain [of the right direction], both might not know with certainty the unknown object. Thus either the prayer [duty] should be abandoned, or the obligation of the *qibla* waived so that each one can pray in whatever [direction] he wishes. But I am not in favor of either one of these two [opinions]—I am rather bound to hold that each one should pray in the direction he believes [is right] and he would be under no obligation to do otherwise. It is also possible to hold that while each one is ordered to seek the right [solution] on the strength of the literal and the implicit meaning [of the duty], neither shall be responsible for the error [which might be committed], in the implicit—not the literal—meaning [of the duty].

543. [Shāfiʿī] said: Whatever opinion you may hold is a proof against you, because you have distinguished between [the validity of] decisions taken in the literal and the implicit [senses], a distinction for which you have already criticized us by saying:

[3] The translation of this paragraph is based on the Būlāq edition (p. 67) owing to the difficulty, as Shākir rightly points out (p. 488, notes 2-3), of deciphering the Rabīʿ MS.

"If they disagree [on the *qibla*, etc.],"[4] one of them must be in error.

544. He replied: That is right [I did].

545. [Shāfiʿī asked: You have held that the prayer was permissible despite your awareness that one of them was in error; it is even possible that both may have been in error. I have added: Such [a distinction] would be binding on you in [the cases of] testimonies and analogical deduction. S489

546. He replied: I hold that [such an error] is inevitable, but it is not intentional.

547. [Shāfiʿī] said: God said:

> O believers, do not kill the game when you are in pilgrim sanctity; whosoever of you kill it intentionally, there shall be compensation equal to what he has killed, in flocks as shall be judged by two men of just character among you, an offering to be delivered at the Kaʿba [Q. V, 95].

Thus God ordered [men] to pay compensation [in kind], to be determined by two men of just character. Since the eating of game in general was prohibited, compensation for animals taken by hunting shall be by other [edible animals] equal to their size. Some Companions of the Prophet made decisions [to the effect] that the compensation for the hyena is a ram, for the S490
gazelle a goat, for the rabbit a she-goat, and for the jerboa a kid.[5] [Legal] knowledge instructs [us] that equal compensation means compensation in kind, not in prices, for if decisions were taken on the basis of prices they would vary, owing to the variation of the prices of game from one town and one time to another, even though legal decisions should be the same.

Knowledge instructs [us] that the jerboa is not quite equal in size to the kid, but since it is the nearest in size, it is regarded as equal [for this purpose]. This kind of analogy is closer to [the analogy of] the goat and the deer than to that of the kid and the jerboa.

[4] See Paragraph 536, above.

[5] A *jafra* is a small kid about four months of age. For the Companions' decision, see Shawkānī, *Nayl al-Awṭār,* Vol. V, pp. 18-19; Shāfiʿī, *Kitāb-al-Umm,* Vol. II, pp. 175-76.

548. Shāfiʿī said:[6] In the event equal compensation in kind is for four-footed game—not birds—[such compensation] is S491 permissible only in accordance with ʿUmar's opinion that game killed shall be compensated for in kind by another animal nearest in resemblance to it. If the game killed is larger, compensation shall be made by another animal nearest in size to it, as in the case of the hyena, the compensation for which is a ram; and the jerboa, though smaller than the little she-goat, a kid.

Since game birds do not resemble cattle, owing to differences in their physical make up, compensation for those which are not lawfully edible shall be made on the basis of precedent and analogy by paying their price to the owner. It is agreed[7] [among the scholars] that the decision as to the price should be on the basis of the price [of the game] in the place and the day [it was killed], for [prices] vary from one place and time to another, so that the price of a bird in one place may be one dirham and in S492 another only a fraction of a dirham.

549. Shāfiʿī said:[8] We are ordered to accept the testimony of [witnesses of] just character. Thus, if the acceptance of [the testimony of] "just character" is stipulated, the indication is that we should reject [the testimony] of those who are not [of just character]. [Since] there is no sign in the body or speech of the witness of just character which distinguishes him from the witness lacking it, such a sign should be sought in the truthfulness reflected in his behavior. Thus if his behavior were on the whole good—although certain things may be lacking, as nobody, as far as we know, is [completely] devoid of sin—[his testimony] must be accepted. If his sins and good deeds are mixed, only by *ijtihād* may the good be distinguished from the bad, but in such a case the *mujtahid*s are liable to disagree. If the just character [of a person] is apparent his testimony must be accepted by us; but if another person finds him deficient in just character, the testimony must be rejected. S493 Thus two judges may take a decision in which one of them

[6] Būlāq ed., p. 68.
[7] "Shāfiʿī said" is omitted.
[8] Būlāq ed., p. 68.

accepts [a testimony] while the other rejects it. This is [an example of] disagreement,[9] but each judge has fulfilled his duty.

550. He asked: Will you cite a tradition permitting [the exercise of] *ijtihād*?

551. [Shāfiʿī] replied: ʿAbd al-ʿAzīz b. Muḥammad [al-Darāwardī] told us from Yazīd b. ʿAbd-Allāh [b. Usāma] b. al-Hādī from Muḥammad b. Ibrāhīm [al-Taymī] from Buṣr b. Saʿīd from Abī Qays [the client of ʿAmr b. al-ʿĀṣ] from ʿAmr b. al-ʿĀṣ, who heard the Prophet say:

> If a judge makes the right decision through *ijtihād*, he shall be doubly compensated; if he errs, he shall be compensated once.[10] S494

ʿAbd al-ʿAzīz b. Muḥammad told us from Yazīd b. al-Hādī, who said: I have related that tradition to Abū Bakr b. Muḥammad b. ʿAmr b. Ḥazm, who said: The tradition was related to me by Abū Salāma b. ʿAbd al-Raḥmān from Abū Hurayra.

552. He said: This is a narrative transmitted by one individual which other [scholars] reject and [for which they] demand a proof [for its authenticity].

553. [Shāfiʿī] replied: You and I are capable of establishing its authenticity.

554. He said: Yes.

555. [Shāfiʿī] said: Those who reject it know what I have already stated concerning the authentication [of such a S495 tradition] as well as others.[11] Which[12] part [of the tradition] is in question?

556. He asked: Did not the Prophet specify in what you related from him[13] [what kind of] *ijtihād* is right and [what kind is] wrong?

557. [Shāfiʿī] replied: This is an argument against you.

558. He asked: How?

[9] Cf. Būlāq ed., p. 68.
[10] Muslim, Vol. XII, pp. 13-14; and Abū Dāwūd, Vol. III, p. 299.
[11] See Chap. X, above.
[12] " Shāfiʿī said" is omitted.
[13] Būlāq ed., p. 68.

559. [Shāfiʿī] replied: Because the Prophet stated that [the judge] shall be rewarded for the one [i. e., the right kind of *ijtihād*] more than for the other [the wrong]; but rewards are not granted for things forbidden nor for intentional errors. For if he [the judge] were ordered to exercise *ijtihād* on the basis of the literal meaning [of the text], and his *ijtihād* was indeed S496 on the basis of the literal meaning [of the text], his error would be forgiven, as I have pointed out. But the punishment for an error which is not permissible is not forgivable as far as I can see; however, God might forgive him. This is [another] example for what I have already discussed that one is ordered to exercise *ijtihād* on the strength of the explicit, not the implicit meaning [of the text].

560. He asked: This may well be, as you hold; but what is the meaning of "wrong" and "right"?

561. [Shāfiʿī] replied: Their meaning is the same as that [explained in the example] of the *qibla*. He who can see it with certainty would face it correctly; but if it is out of sight, whether he [the person facing it] is at a distance or close to it, he should search for it. So some may face it correctly and others wrongly. Thus the facing itself is liable to be right or wrong, just as if one intends to relate a certain narrative concerning right or wrong, S497 he says: So-and-so is right in seeking [the right solution] for he did not fall into error, but so-and-so fell into error although he B68 sought [the right solution].

562. He said: It is as you hold; but do you not agree that *ijtihād* might be right in a different sense?

563. [Shāfiʿī] replied: Yes; for one is under an obligation to exercise *ijtihād* only in the search for an unknown object. If one does so, he would be right by doing what he was obligated to do. This is right for him on the basis of the literal meaning [of the text]; only God knows the implicit meaning. For we know that those who disagree in their search for the *qibla* cannot be right if the *qibla* is in sight; but they would be right in seeking it by *ijtihād* even though they may disagree [on how to face it]. The same [reasoning] may be applied in such cases as [the testimony of] witnesses and others which I have described.

564. He asked: Will you give an example?

565. [Shāfiʿī] replied: I do not think it would be explained by a stronger example than this. S498

566. He asked: Will you give a different example?

567. [Shāfiʿī] replied: God has made it lawful to marry two or three or four women and what our right hand possesses; but he made it unlawful [to marry] mothers, daughters, and sisters.

568. He said: That is correct.

569. [Shāfiʿī] asked: If a man purchases a slave-woman, whom he found clear of pregnancy, is she lawful to him?

570. He replied: Yes.

571. [Shāfiʿī] asked: after he had gone into her and she had given children, he discovered that she was his sister. What is [your] opinion about such [a situation]?

572. He replied: His [intercourse with her] was lawful until he found out about her [that she was his sister]; but once he knew it she was no longer lawful to him.

573. [Shāfiʿī] asked: So one may hold that the same woman was both lawful and unlawful to one man, although neither he S499
nor she was responsible for the [wrong] act?

574. He replied: In the implicit sense she was his sister from the beginning to the last; but in the explicit sense she was lawful to him so long as he did not know she was his sister, and unlawful after he became aware of it. Other[14] scholars might hold that he committed an offence, but the punishment would be waived.

575. [Shāfiʿī] said: Whatever [the scholars] hold, they have distinguished between the explicit and the implicit [meanings of] decisions, waiving the penalty for him who exercises *ijtihād* on the strength of an explicit decision—despite the fact that he committed an error—but they do not waive it in the case of an intentional offence.

576. He replied: That is correct.

577. [Shāfiʿī] said: Similarly, a man might marry an unlawful woman unknowingly or take a fifth [wife] who turned out to be his [former] wife, after the death of one of the four, and so forth. S500

[14] " He [the interlocutor] said" is omitted.

578. He said: Yes, there are many other similar situations. But[15] it is clear to those of you who are certain of truthful information that *ijtihād* should never be resorted to except in seeking an unknown object by means of certain indications, although it is permissible to those who exercise *ijtihād* to disagree [in their decisions].

And he asked: How is *ijtihād* [to be exercised]?

579. [Shāfiʿī] replied: God, Glorified and Praised be He, has endowed men with reason by which they can distinguish between differing viewpoints, and He guides them to the truth either by [explicit] texts or by indications [on the strength of which they exercise *ijtihād*].

580. He asked: Will you give an example?

581. [Shāfiʿī] replied: God erected the Sacred House and ordered men to face it [in prayer], when it is in sight, and to seek its direction [by *ijtihād*] when they are at a distance from it. And He created for them the heaven and the earth and the sun and the moon and the stars and the seas and the mountains
S501 and the wind [as guiding indications by which they can exercise *ijtihād*]. For God said:

> It is He who has appointed for you the stars, that by them you might be guided in the darkness of land and sea [Q. VI, 97].

And He said:

> And landmarks and by the stars they might be guided [Q. XVI, 16].

Thus [God] instructed men to be guided by the stars and [other] indicators, and by His blessing and help they know the direction of the Sacred House. So those who can see it from their places [may perform the prayer] and those who cannot see it should either be informed by those who have seen it or seek guidance by means of certain indications such as a mountain, which might point to [the direction], or a star indicating the north and south, or the sun, whose rising and setting is known,

[15] " He said" is omitted.

pointing out the direction for him who performs the evening [prayer], or the seas [which might also be a guiding indication] and the like. S502

Thus men should seek, through the reasoning power which God has implanted in them, the direction in which He made it incumbent for them to face [during prayer]. If it is thus sought, through their reasoning power and their knowledge of the indications [pointing to it], men can fulfil their duty.

[God] has made it clear that the duty He imposed on them is [to pray in] the direction of the Sacred Mosque, not always to face the House [al-Kaʿba] itself. If the right direction is not known with the same certainty as is possessed by those who see it, it is not permissible to hold that one can face any direction one wishes without [a guiding] indication.

Chapter XIV

[ON JURISTIC PREFERENCE (*ISTIḤSĀN*)][1]

582. He said: I agree with you that *ijtihād* should not be exercised except for a specific object, and the object must be
S503 something definite that can be determined by means of evidence or resemblance to an established, object. Thus, it should be clear that it is unlawful for anyone to exercise *istiḥsān* whenever it is not called for by a narrative, whether the narrative is a text of the Qur'ān or a sunna, by virtue of which an [unknown] object is sought,[2] just as when the Sacred House is out of sight it should be sought by analogy. So nobody is allowed, to give an opinion save through *ijtihād*, and this, as you said, is seeking [to know] the right answer. Thus would you hold that it is permissible for anyone to exercise *istiḥsān* by means other than analogy?

583. [Shāfiʿī] replied: It is not permissible for everyone in my opinion, [to do so], for only the scholars—not others—may give an opinion, and the scholars hold that a narrative must be followed; if a narrative is not found, analogy might
B69 be applied on the strength of a narrative. For if analogy were abandoned, it would be permissible for any intelligent man,

[1] Būlāq ed., p. 69. This subject is also discussed in a separate treatise entitled *Kitāb Ibṭāl al-Istiḥsān* (see Shāfiʿī, *Kitāb al-Umm*, Vol. VII, pp. 267-70, 270-77.)

[2] Literally: "an object is sought by the *mujtahid*" (i. e, the person who exercises the *istiḥsān*).

other than the scholars, to exercise *istiḥsān* in the absence of a narrative. But to give an opinion based neither on a narrative nor on analogy, as I have already stated in the discussion on the Qur'ān and the sunna, is not permissible according to [the rules of] analogy. S504

584. He asked: The Qur'ān and the sunna give, indeed, evidence in support [of *ijtihād*]. For since the Prophet gave an order to exercise *ijtihād*, it should not be exercised save to seek an [unknown] object, and the object cannot be sought except through certain evidences [on the strength of] which analogical deduction may be made. Will you point out what are the analogy and the evidences which you have explained?

585. [Shāfiʿī] replied: Do you not agree that if a man injured the slave of another the scholars would not ask a [third] man to S505 fix the price of the slave, whether male or female, unless he were well informed about the market prices in order to estimate two prices [i. e. the market price and the estimated price] by which he would inform you of the price of a similar slave on that day? For such [pricing] cannot be done except on the basis of the [man's] knowledge of similar cases on the strength of which he applies analogy. So whoever deals with property should not be asked to estimate the price unless he is well informed [about the market price].

So it is not permissible to ask a jurist of just character who is not acquainted with the prices of slaves [the question]: "What S506 is the price of this male or female slave?," or "What is the wage of this worker?" for if he estimates such prices without regard to similar prices, he is making his estimate wrongly.

If that is the case in such matters as the pricing of property of little value, concerning which an error might easily be committed by one man against another, it is all the more necessary that God's orders as to what is right and wrong should not be applied by treating a case without due consideration or by dealing with it on the basis of *istiḥsān*. *Istiḥsān* is merely doing what is agreeable.

No one except a well-informed scholar fully acquainted with the [binding] narratives should exercise it [analogy]. And he who exercises it should do so only on the basis of

S507 [legal] knowledge, and legal knowledge consists of the binding narrative on the strength of which analogy may be applied by means of certain indications as to what is right. So the scholar should always follow a narrative or have recourse to analogical deduction on the strength of such a narrative, just as [in prayer] one should either lace the Sacred House when it is in sight or seek the direction in which it lies by the exercise of *ijtihād* through certain landmarks [when it is out of sight].

If he [the scholar] were to give an opinion based neither on a binding narrative nor on analogy he is more liable to commit a sin than is an ignorant person, if it were permissible for the latter to give an opinion. For God has not permitted any person since the Prophet's time to give an opinion except on the strength of established [legal] knowledge. [Legal] knowledge [after the Prophet's death] includes the Qur'ān, the sunna, consensus,
S508 narrative, and analogy based on these [texts], as I have already explained.

Nobody should apply analogy unless he is competent to
S509 do so through his knowledge of the commands of the Book of God: its prescribed duties and its ethical discipline, its abrogating and abrogated [communications], its general and particular [rules], and its [right] guidance. Its [ambiguous] communications should be interpreted by the sunna of the Prophet; if no sunna is found, then by the consensus of the Muslims; if no consensus is possible, then by analogical deduction.

No one is competent to apply analogy unless he is conversant with the established sunna, the opinions of [his] predecessors, the agreement (consensus) and disagreement of the people, and has [adequate] knowledge of the Arabic tongue. Nor is he regarded as competent in analogical [reasoning] unless he is sound in mind, able to distinguish between closely parallel precedents, and not hasty in expressing an opinion unless he is certain of its correctness. Nor shall he refrain from listening to the opinions of those who may disagree with him, for he might
S510 be warned against [possible] forgetfulness or be confirmed in his right [judgment]. In so doing he must exert his utmost power

not to be misled by personal [bias], so that he knows on what ground he has given one opinion and on what ground he has rejected another. Nor should he be more preoccupied with the opinion he has given than with the one with which he disagrees, so that he knows the merits of what he accepts as compared with that which he rejects.

He who possesses a mature mind but lacks the other qualifications we have described should not be permitted to express an opinion based on analogy, for he might not know the precedent on which he applies analogy just as a jurist of sound mind should not be permitted to estimate what a dirham will buy if he lacks the information on market [prices]. And he who possesses the [legal] knowledge I have described [solely] through memory, and is uncertain of its correctness, should not be permitted to express an opinion based on analogy, for he may not comprehend the meaning [of that knowledge].

Moreover, if he were good in memory but were lacking either in comprehension or in knowledge of the Arab tongue, he should not be permitted to apply analogy, for he would be lacking in the tool by means of which he applies analogy. However, we do not maintain that it is permissible only to follow [precedents] and not to use analogy.[3] But God knows best! S511

586. Someone asked: Will you give some examples of [binding] narratives on the strength of which analogy might be applied, and how would you apply it?

587. [Shāfiʿī] replied: Every order laid down by God or by the Apostle for which there is evidence, either in itself or in some other of the orders of God or His Apostle, was laid down for some reason. If a case should arise for which there is no [specific] textual order, it should be decided on the strength of the case identical to it in reason for which a [specific] order was laid down.

Analogy is of various kinds, and all are included under the term "analogy." They differ from one another in the S512
antecedence of the analogy of either one of them, or its source,

[3] See *Kitāb Ibṭāl al-Istiḥsān* (*Kitāb al-Umm*, Vol. VII, p. 274).

or the source of both, or the circumstance that one is more clear than the other. The strongest kind [is the deduction] from an order of prohibition by God or the Apostle involving a small quantity, which makes equally strong or stronger an order of prohibition involving a great quantity, owing to the [compelling] reason in the greater quantity. Similarly the
B70 commendation of a small act of piety implies the presumably stronger commendation of a greater act of piety; and similarly an order of permission involving a great quantity would render permissible something involving a smaller quantity.[4]

S513 588. Someone may say: Give an example of each one of these to explain their meaning.

589. [Shāfiʿī] said: The Apostle said:

> God has prohibited the shedding of the believer's blood and the taking away of his property, and [ordered] that only what is good should be thought of him.[5]

If [God] has made it unlawful for [the believer] to be thought of in any way contrary to the good which he manifests, then the thing greater than the thought implying in any way what
S514 is contrary to his good such as telling an untruth about him, should be all the more unlawful. The more this matter is indulged in, the stronger the order of prohibition becomes. [For] God said:

> Whoever has done a particle's weight of good, he shall see it; and whoever has done a particle's weight of evil, he shall see it [Q. XCIX, 7-8].

Thus what is greater than a particle's weight of good is a greater commendation [of an act of piety] and what is greater than a particle's weight of evil is a greater sin.[6]

He [God] has made lawful for us the life-blood and property of combatant unbelievers, excepting those who have made

[4] See *Kitāb Ibṭāl al-Istiḥsān* (*Kitāb al-Umm*, Vol. VII, p. 274).

[5] This is a *mursal* tradition for which no authority is given, although its substance might be found in other traditions.

[6] Bayḍāwī, p. 807.

a compact [with us], prohibiting nothing that I remember. So whatever we take of their bodies, except their life-blood, and of their property, except the whole of it, is all the more lawful.

Some scholars refuse to call these [rulings] analogical deduction, for they hold that they fall within the meaning of what God has made either lawful or unlawful, and has either com- S515
mended as an act of piety or repudiated; these things are included in the general order itself rather than an analogy based on another order. Similarly this is applicable to other matters: whatever is equivalent (*fī maʿna*) to something lawful is lawful and what is equivalent to something unlawful is unlawful. They refuse to call any thing an analogy unless there is a parallel precedent which can be determined in one of two ways, one of them being chosen as the answer to the exclusion of the other. Other scholars hold that any [ruling] other than the [explicit] text of the Book and the sunna is analogy, provided it is in harmony with their meaning. But God knows S516
best.[7]

590. Someone said: Give examples of analogy that illustrates its varieties of clarity and arguments and the proof for it, other than those already stated, which the public can understand.

591. [Shāfiʿī] replied: God said:

> Mothers shall suckle their children two full years, for anyone who wishes the period of suckling to be complete. It is for the father to provide for his [daughters] and clothe them honorably [Q. II, 233].

And He said:

> And if you desire to seek someone to suckle your children, it is no fault of yours when you hand over what you have given honorably (Ibid.).

And the Apostle ordered Hind, daughter of ʿAtba, to take from her husband's—Abū Sufyān's—property what was needed

[7] Cf. Schacht, *Origins of Muhammadan Jurisprudence*, pp. 124-25.

for her and her children without asking his permission, since they were his children.[8]

592. [Shāfiʿī] said: Thus the Book of God and the sunna of the Prophet indicate that it is [the duty] of the father to see to it S517 that his children are suckled and that they are supported as long as they are young.

Since the child is [an issue] of the father, he [the father] is under an obligation to provide for the child's support while [the child] is unable to do that for himself. So I hold by analogical deduction when the father becomes incapable of providing for himself by his earnings—or from what he owns—then it is an obligation on his children to support him by paying for his expenses and clothing. Since the child is from the father, he [the child] should not cause him from whom he comes to lose anything, just as the child should not lose anything belonging to his children,[9] because the child is from the father. So the forefathers, even if they are distant, and the children, even if they are remote descendants, fall into this category. Thus I hold that [by analogy] he who is retired,[10] and in need should be supported by him who is rich and [still] active.[11]

S518 The Prophet made a decision that a slave sold with a defect which became known only after he was employed could be returned, with the purchaser retaining the profit [derived from the slave's employment] on the ground that he was responsible for the slave [during the latter's employment].[12]

We conclude that if it were not stipulated in the sale transaction that the profit should be part of the price [the profit belongs to the purchaser], since the slave is a piece of property belonging to his owner, and if the slave should die, his price would be a loss to him who had purchased him. So the profit belongs to the purchaser because it was earned when the slave

[8] Bukhārī, Vol. III, p. 489; Shawkānī, *Nayl al-Awṭār,* Vol. VI, p. 342; Shāfiʿī, *Kitāb al-Umm,* Vol. V, pp. 77-78.

[9] Singular in the Arabic text.

[10] Literally: " Without an occupation."

[11] Cf. Ṭabarī, *Tafsīr,* Vol. V, pp. 30-44, 71-76.

[12] See paragraph 447, above.

was in his possession and under his responsibility. We hold [by analogy] the same opinion about the fruit of palm trees; the milk, wool, and young of cattle; the children of a slave-woman; and anything that may be produced while in the possession and responsibility of the purchaser, including the [right of] intercourse with a slave-woman who is a *thayyib*, and the use of her service.

593. [Shāfiʿī] said: Some of our fellow jurists as well as others have disagreed with us on this matter.

One of them held: The profit, the service,[13] and the property of male and female slaves, except the right of intercourse, belong to the purchaser, who has the right to return [the female slave] if he discovers any defect in her. He added: He has no right to return the female slave if he enters into sexual intercourse with her even if she were a *thayyib*. Nor is he entitled to the fruit of palm trees or the milk and wool of cattle, or the children of slave-women, for all of these—the cattle, the children of the slave-woman, the palm trees, and the profit—are not in the S519
category of the slave.

594. Shāfiʿī said:[14] I asked one of those who held this opinion: Do you not agree that the two [i. e., the slave and the profit, etc.] belong together in that both were produced while in the possession of the purchaser and there was no stipulation concerning them in the sale transaction?

595. He replied: Yes, but the two must be distinguished because the fruit which the purchaser has received from the palm, the children he has received from the female slave, and the young he has gained from the cattle have been produced by them, while the slave's profit does not accrue [directly] from him but results from his employment. S520

596. [Shāfiʿī] asked: If a critic raises an objection in line with your reasoning and says: Since the Prophet decided that the profit belongs to him who bears responsibility, and since the profit cannot be earned except by employment and this might B71
deprive the master of the slave's service, do you not agree that

[13] Būlāq ed., p. 72.
[14] *Ibid.*, p. 72.

the master is entitled to the slave's profit in lieu of the service rendered [to the employer] and the expenses for the [slave's] subsistence? But if a gift is given to him [the slave], which cannot divert him from his master's service, it should not be given to the second but to the first owner.

597. He replied: No, it should be to the second, in whose possession the slave was when the gift was given.

598. [Shāfiʿī] said: But [the gift] is not a profit, for it falls in a category other than that of profit.

599. He said: Although it is not, neither can it be considered [to have been produced] by the slave.

600. [Shāfiʿī] said: Its meaning must be distinguished from
S521 that of profit, for it belongs to a different category.

601. He said: Although it falls in a different category, it was given [to the slave] while he was in the possession of the purchaser.

602. [Shāfiʿī] said: The fruit and the other products were produced while their [sources] were in the possession of the purchaser. So if the fruit were picked from the palm tree it should no longer remain a part of the tree and might be sold without it just as the tree might be sold without the fruit. The same [reasoning] applies to the product of the cattle. However, the profit [from the slave] would more appropriately be returned with the slave, because sometimes it seems to acquire a quality which the fruit of the date palm has, if it were permissible that one of the two should be returned.

Some of our followers have agreed with us on [retention of] the profit and on the [permissibility of] sexual intercourse with the *thayyib* [slave-woman] and on keeping the fruit of the palm trees; but they have disagreed on [the right to retain] the children of the slave woman.

Since all of them have been produced while [the property
S522 was] in the possession of the purchaser, they fall in the same category and no other [opinion] is right; for the slave's master—the purchaser—can claim only the [slave's] profit and his service, but not what was given to him as a gift, nor what he may find, nor anything that he may obtain from a [hidden] treasure or the like—except in the form of profit or service rendered—

nor the fruit of palm trees, nor the milk of the cattle nor anything else, for all of them do not fall in [the category of] profit.

603. Shāfiʿī said:[15] The Apostle of God has prohibited [the exchange of] gold for gold, date for date, wheat for wheat, and barley for barley unless in equal quantities and delivered immediately.[16]

Since the Prophet excluded (with regard to these kinds of edibles, concerning which men were so greedy that they bartered S523
them by measure) two categories: one, that a thing should be sold for an equal quantity with one a cash sale and the other with deferred payment; and the second, that one of the things might be more than the other when delivered by hand, so whatever is in these categories is unlawful, by analogy. Such kinds are all edibles when sold by weight, for all have the common attribute that they are edible and potable, since the latter's meaning falls within the former's. To the public, these materials [foodstuffs] are either basic food or plentiful or both. I have found that when such foodstuffs (as honey, clarified butter, olive oil, sugar, and other [foodstuffs] which are edible and potable) become scarce, men sell them by weight, for weighing is more accurate than measuring and its meaning is included in measuring.

604. Someone may ask: Is it possible that the thing sold by weight is analogous to the thing sold by gold and silver in weight, so that things exchangeable by weight would be more S524
appropriate for analogy than things exchanged by measure?

605. [Shāfiʿī said]: To this it may be replied: That which prevented us from taking the position you have described, which confines the analogy of things that are weighed to other things that are weighed, is that valid analogy occurs when you make one thing analogous to another in decisions in which one case would be the same as the other. If you were to make honey and clarified butter analogous to dīnārs (gold coins) and dirhams (silver coins) and were only declaring the superiority of some

[15] *Ibid.*

[16] See paragraph 271, above, and Shāfiʿī, *Kitāb al-Umm,* Vol. III, p. 12.

things over others to be illegal when they are of one kind, on the analogy of gold and silver coins, then would it be proper for honey and clarified butter to be bought for cash with gold and silver coins on [the same basis as a transaction including] payment at an appointed time?

606. If he says: It [the sale] should be permitted in
S525 accordance with that which the Muslims permitted.

607. [Shāfiʿī said]: The reply to this may be: The permissibility of the Muslims indicated to me that they did not do so by analogy. If it were by analogy, the decision in one case would be the same as in the other. So it would not be legal unless [the thing] were sold for ready money, just as gold and silver coins may not be exchanged except for ready money.

608. Should he ask: If analogy were applied on the basis of measuring, would you apply the same rules?

609. [Shāfiʿī] replied: That is correct; I make no distinction under any circumstances.

610. He asked: Is it not permissible for you to purchase a *mudd* [a measure][17] of wheat, delivered on the spot, for three *raṭl*s [measures][18] of olive oil to be delivered at an appointed
S526 time?

611. [Shāfiʿī] replied: This is not permissible, for nothing edible or potable can be [exchanged lawfully] for other kinds of things to be delivered at an appointed time.[19] For the rule of [exchanging] foodstuffs by measure applies to [exchanging] foodstuffs by weight.

612. He asked: What is your opinion about the [exchange of gold] dīnārs for [silver] dirhams?

613. [Shāfiʿī] replied: That is unlawful in itself. Edible [things] are not analogous to it, for they are not in the same category. The [exchange of] measured edibles is not lawful in

[17] The *mudd* is a grain measure equivalent to 1⅓ of a *raṭl* in the Ḥijāz and 2 in ʿIrāq.

[18] The *raṭl* is a measure of weight approximately equivalent to a pound (in Egypt).

[19] This paragraph is written on the margin of al-Rabīʿ MS (Cf. Būlāq ed., p. 72).

itself; only the analogy of what is equivalent in measure or weight applies to it, because they fall in the same category.

614. He asked: What is the difference between the [exchange of] dīnārs for dirhams?

615. [Shāfiʿī] replied: I know of no scholar who disagrees on the permissibility of exchanging foodstuffs by measure or by weight for dīnārs and dirhams to be delivered at an appointed time, but [such an exchange] would be unlawful if it is made by [gold] dīnārs for [silver] dirhams. Nor do I know any scholar who denies that if I discover a mine and pay the right [tax] on my profit from it, I should each year pay its *zakāt* (legal alms) S527
if the silver or the gold from it remains a year [or more] with me. And if I were to harvest grain from my land, having paid its *kharāj* (land-tax), and it remained with me for a year, there would be no *zakāt* due from me for it. And if I were to destroy something belonging to a man, its value might be paid in gold or silver coins, because they are the [measure of] prices of all the property of a Muslim, except in cases of blood-money [which may be paid in camels].

616. He said: That is correct.

617. [Shāfiʿī] said: Thus things differ by [differentials] less B72
than what I have described to you.

618. [Shāfiʿī] said:[20] We have found that it was generally agreed among scholars that the Prophet decreed that [the *diya*] for unintentional homicide committed by a free Muslim against another shall be one hundred camels to be paid by the *ʿāqila*.[21] It is also generally agreed that the [*diya*] shall be [paid] within three years, one-third each year on the basis of specified years. Several meanings of analogical deduction are implied in this [decree]; some of them which I may remember are the following:

We have found that it was generally agreed among scholars that if a free Muslim commits an intentional offence against the life or limb of a person or destroys his property, the

[20] Būlāq ed., p. 73.

[21] The *ʿāqila* is a term applied to the killer's male relatives who are under obligation to pay the *diya* or blood-money.

compensation shall be paid out of his own property; but if the
S528 offence were unintentional, it shall be paid by his *ʿāqila*.

We have found them [the scholars] agreed that the *ʿāqila* pays one-third of the *diya* for an offence [in the category] of injuries and upwards. But they have disagreed on the payment of less than one-third [of the *diya*]. Some of our fellow jurists held: The *ʿāqila* should pay compensation for *al-muwaḍḍiḥa*[22] and upwards, [equal to] half of the one-tenth [of the *diya*] and upwards; but he should not pay for injuries less than that.[23]

I have said to some of those who stipulate the payment of half of the one-tenth but not anything less: Can analogy ever be
S529 sound on the basis of the sunna but in one of two forms?

619. He asked: What are they?

620. [Shāfiʿī] replied: First, since the Prophet decreed that the *diya* shall be paid by the *ʿāqila*, I should follow his ruling; anything less than the *diya* should be paid out of the offender's property. No other analogy can be applied on the basis of the *diya*, for in principle it should be more appropriate for the offender than for the others to pay the compensation for his offence, just as in the case of intentional injuries. Since God has decreed that whoever commits an unintentional killing shall pay the *diya* and set free one slave, I hold that the slave shall be paid out of the [offender's] property—since the offence is his—, but the *diya* would be excluded on the basis of the [Prophet's] ruling. On the basis of this ruling I hold that anything less than the *diya* should be paid out of the [offender's] property, since it is more appropriate for him to pay than for others, just as I hold that the wiping of the shoes is permitted on the strength of a tradition from the Prophet, without regarding it as a precedent for analogy. [Secondly], analogy may take another
S530 form.

621. He asked: What is it?

622. [Shāfiʿī] replied: Since the Prophet has excluded unintentional offence against life from offences other than those in-

[22] *Al-muwaḍḍiḥa* is a category of an offence involving a wound reaching to the bone.

[23] This is the doctrine of the Ḥanafī school of law.

volving life [i. e., the limb] and from intentional offence against life, requiring the *ʿāqila* to pay [the *diya*] for the unintentional offence because it is the greater amount, I hold that the *ʿāqila* shall be liable to pay for what is less [than the *diya*] in an unintentional offence, since it is more appropriate for him to pay it than the greater amount or what falls in that category.

623. He said: This is the more appropriate meaning as a basis for analogy, but it is not a case parallel to the wiping of the shoes.

624. [Shāfiʿī] said: That is in agreement with your opinion, for the scholars are agreed that the *ʿāqila* should pay one-third or more [of the *diya*]; and their agreement is an evidence that they applied the analogy of the payment of compensation of what is less than the *diya* on the [basis of the] payment of [full] *diya*. S531

625. He said: That is right.

626. [Shāfiʿī] said: Our master [Mālik b. Anas] said: "The best opinion that I have heard is that the *ʿāqila* should pay one-third of the *diya* upward," and he said that this is the opinion acceptable to him.[24] Do you not agree that a critic might advance two points [against such an opinion]?

627. He asked: What are they?

628. [Shāfiʿī] replied: You and I are agreed that the *ʿāqila* should pay one-third or more of the *diya*; but we are in disagreement on the payment of the smaller amount. So the proof is established by your agreement and mine on the payment of the one-third, but you are unable to produce a tradition in support of the payment of the smaller amount. What would be your answer?

629. He replied: I should say this: My agreement [with you] is based on a ground different from your agreement [with me], for my agreement is based on the analogy that since the *ʿāqila* pays the greater amount [of the *diya*] he should also be responsible for a smaller amount. For who has limited the amount to one-third? Do you not agree that someone might

[24] Mālik, Vol. II, p. 865.

argue: "The [ʿāqila] should pay nine-tenths [of the *diya*] rather than the smaller amount?"

630. [Shāfiʿī] said: If he holds that one-third [of the *diya*] is too much for whomever pays it, I hold [likewise] that it is too
S532 much and that it should be paid by some one jointly with him or on his behalf, but no one else should pay it if it were the smaller amount.

631. He said: Do you not agree that if some one possesses only two dirhams it would be too much for him to pay one-third [of the *diya*] and one dirham—since he would thus be deprived of his property—but that it would not be too much for one who possesses a fortune to pay one-third [of the *diya*]?

632. [Shāfiʿī] said: Do you not agree that he [Mālik] would not say, "This is our practice," unless the matter had been
S533 agreed upon among the scholars in Madīna?

633. He said: Is not an opinion agreed upon in Madīna stronger than a narrative related by one individual? For[25] why should he relate to us a weak narrative related by one individual and refrain from relating to us a stronger and binding matter agreed upon [among the scholars]?

634. [Shāfiʿī] asked: Supposing someone should tell you: It is because the narrative is rare and the agreement [about the matter] is too well known to be related; and should you yourself say: This is a matter agreed upon?

635. He replied: Neither I nor any of the scholars would say: "This is [a matter] agreed upon," unless it were [a matter] about which you would never find a scholar who would not repeat it to you and relate it from a predecessor, such as that the noon-prayer has four [cycles, *rakʿas*] and that wine
S534 is forbidden, and the like. I sometimes find one who says: "The matter is agreed upon," but I often find scholars in Madīna who say the opposite, and I find that the majority [of scholars] of other cities oppose what is said to be "agreed upon."[26]

[25] "He said" is omitted.

[26] On the controversy with Mālik and his followers, see Shāfiʿī, *Kitāb al-Umm*, Vol. VII, p. 188, and *Ikhtilāf al-Ḥadīth, ibid.*, pp. 147-48.

636. [Shāfiʿī] said: I pointed out to him that he [the critic] might object to your opinion: "No blood-money [should be paid] for less than *al-muwaḍḍiḥa*," just as he objected to the B73
payment of the one-third [of the *diya*].

637. He replied: The evidence for that is that the Apostle made no decision on cases relating to [offences] less than *al-muwaḍḍiḥa*.

638. [Shāfiʿī] asked: Do you not agree that a critic may raise an objection by saying: "I will make no decision relating to injuries less than *al-muwaḍḍiḥa*, because the Apostle made no decisions on such matters."

639. He replied: He has no right to say so, for if [the Apostle] made no decision on such matters, it does not follow that he waived the payment of compensation for such injuries. S535

640. [Shāfiʿī] said: He may also hold that if he [the Prophet] did not order the *ʿāqila* to pay blood-money for offences less than *al-muwaḍḍiḥa* he did not prohibit the *ʿāqila* from paying the blood-money for less than *al-muwaḍḍiḥa*; for if he had made a decision [relating to compensation paid by the *ʿāqila*] for *al-muwaḍḍiḥa*, but not for offences less than that, it does not follow that the *ʿāqila* should not pay compensation for offences less than *al-muwaḍḍiḥa* [on the ground] that if it pays the greater compensation it must pay the smaller one, just as you and I have already agreed on this matter when you raised an objection to us. If it is permissible for you to hold such an opinion, it would be permissible to hold it against you also.

If the Prophet made a decision that the *ʿāqila* should pay half of the one-tenth [of the compensation for *al-muwaḍḍiḥa*], would it be permissible to hold that [the *ʿāqila*] should pay either half of the one-tenth [of the *diya*] or the [full] *diya*, but not an amount between the two, for this should be paid by the offender! This is an opinion that it is not permissible for anyone to hold, nor should one hold that the *ʿāqila* should pay compensation for all unintentional offences, even if it were only one dirham.

641. [Shāfiʿī] said: Some of our fellow jurists held: If a free man commits an unintentional offence against a slave resulting

S536 either in the latter's death or in an injury less than death, the [compensation] shall be paid out of the offender's property—not by the ʿ*āqila*—for the ʿ*āqila* is under no obligation to pay the compensation for a slave.

We maintain that this is an offence committed by a freeman. For since the Apostle decreed that the compensation paid by the ʿ*āqila* covers an offence committed by a freeman unintentionally, [the freeman's] offence against a slave, if it were unintentional, must be included [in the Prophet's decree]. But God knows best!

You [the interlocutor] have already agreed with us [on this matter], and have held that he who holds that the ʿ*āqila* is not liable to pay compensation for a slave holds that no compensation shall be paid by the ʿ*āqila* for an offence committed by the slave, for the slave himself should be responsible for it, not his master. Thus you have held an opinion similar to ours and have regarded our argument, based on the sunna, as valid.

S537 642. He replied: That is right.

643. [Shāfiʿī] said: I have added: Your fellow jurist[s] as well as some of our fellow jurists held: Compensation for an offence committed against a slave is [equal to] the slave's price just as the compensation for an offence committed by a free-man is [equal to] his *diya*. Thus [the compensation] for the loss of an eye is half of the slave's price and for *al-muwaḍḍiḥa* half of the one-tenth of his price.[27] However, you have disagreed with us on this matter and have held that the [compensation] for the slave's offence is less than his price.

644. He replied: First, let me ask you to give the proof for the opinion that the [compensation] for the slave's offence is [analogous to] the *diya*. Is it based on a narrative or on an analogy?

645. [Shāfiʿī] replied: It is on a narrative from Saʿīd b. al-Musayyib.

646. He asked: Will you relate it?

[27] See Mālik, Vol. II, pp. 862-63.

647. [Shāfiʿī] replied: Sufyān [b. ʿUyayna] told us from Ibn Shihāb al-Zuhrī from Saʿīd b. al-Musayyib, who said: "The blood-money of the slave is [equal to] his price," and I have heard it repeated by him [al-Musayyib] several times. He may have added: "just as [the compensation] for an offence committed by a freeman is [equal to] the *diya*." Ibn Shihāb said: S538
Others have added: "[The price of the slave] shall be estimated in the same manner as that of a commodity."[28]

648. He asked: I have asked you to relate a [binding] narrative [i. e., a tradition] in support of your argument.

649. [Shāfiʿī] replied: I have already said that I know of no narrative from an authority earlier than Saʿīd b. al-Musayyib.

650. He said: His [Ibn al-Musayyib's] opinion is not a proof.

651. [Shāfiʿī] said:[29] I have not claimed that it is a proof to be rejected.

652. He asked: What is the proof?

653. [Shāfiʿī] replied: It is an analogy [based on the case] of the criminal offence committed by a freeman.

654. He said: [The compensation for the slave] differs from the *diya* of the freeman, because the latter is specified, while S539
the former is equal to his price, just as commodities—such as camels, beasts and the like—are priced.

655. [Shāfiʿī] replied: This argument, in support of those who hold that the *ʿāqila* should not pay compensation for the slave, is against you.

656. He asked: In what way?

657. [Shāfiʿī] replied: One may say to you: Why do you hold that the *ʿāqila* pays the slave's price [as compensation], if the offence is committed by a freeman who is in possession of the price, while if the offence is committed against a camel, the compensation should be paid out of the offender's property?

658. He said: Because it is unlawful to take the [slave's] life.

659. [Shāfiʿī] asked: Is not the camel's life unlawful to the slayer?

[28] Cf. Būlāq ed., p. 74; and Shāfiʿī, *Kitāb al-Umm,* Vol. VI, pp. 90-91.
[29] Būlāq ed., p. 74.

660. He replied: Not in the same [degree] as that of a believer.

661. [Shāfiʿī] asked: One may argue that the slave's life is not
S540 of the same [degree of] unlawfulness as that of the free-man. He
added: If it is, should the *ʿāqila* pay the blood-money?

662. He replied: Yes.

663. [Shāfiʿī] asked: [Is not] God's judgment concerning the unintentional killing of a believer that a *diya* should be paid and a slave freed?

664. He replied: That is right.

665. [Shāfiʿī] asked: Do you not hold that [the compensation] for a slave is the freeing of [another] slave equal in price—as in the case of a freeman—and that the price is like a *diya*?

666. He replied: That is right.

667. [Shāfiʿī] asked: Do you not hold that you would kill a freeman [in retaliation] for the killing of a slave?

S541 668. He replied: That is right.

669. [Shāfiʿī] said: Have we not both held that a slave shall be killed for the [killing of another] slave?

670. He said: I hold the opinion you hold.

671. [Shāfiʿī] said: It is your opinion and mine that [the slave] and the freeman are liable to the same penalty for whatever offense they may commit, and that the camel falls in the same category concerning the payment of compensation that is equal to its price? On what ground have you based your opinion that the [compensation for the slave's] offence should be equal to that for an offence against a camel, putting it in [the category of] the smaller amount rather than in the category of the *diya* of the freeman? [The slave] and the free man possess five things in common and differ in one. Would it not be more appropriate to apply analogy to the [situation in which the slave and the freeman possess] five points in common than to the situation in which they possess only one? In fact, the slave possesses further points in common with the freeman, [namely,] that whatever is unlawful for the one is unlawful for the other, and that both are liable to [the

same] penalties and that they are under the [same] obligations concerning the performance of prayer and the observance of fasting as well as other duties, while animals are under no such obligations.

672. He said: I hold that the [slave's] *diya* should be equal to S542
his price.

673. [Shāfiʿī] asked: [Since] you hold that a woman's *diya* is equal to half that of a man, why should [the compensation for] offences against her not be equal to her *diya*, just as [the compensation for] an offence against a man is equal to his *diya*? [Shāfiʿī] added: If the *diya* consists of camels [to be paid] in three years, do you maintain that the camels would be regarded as a debt? If so, why do you object to the sale of camels by deferred delivery? And [if you apply analogy], why do you do so on the basis of *diya* rather than on the basis of either the sale agreement [of the slave], or the dowry,[30] while you permit the camel to be regarded in all these cases as a debt? Thus you have [taken a position] contradictory to analogy as well as to the text of a tradition from the Prophet to the effect that he had borrowed a camel [the price of which] was paid later as a
debt? S543

674. He replied: Ibn Masʿūd has objected to this [kind of a transaction].

675. [Shāfiʿī] asked: Is there anyone whose authority is equal to that of the Prophet?

676. He replied: No, if [the tradition] from the Prophet is well authenticated.

677. [Shāfiʿī] said: It is well authenticated [by the Prophet's precedent] that he borrowed a camel which was later paid back—a case on *diya*s well known to you and to us. This [precedent] is a sunna.

678. He asked: What is the narrative for analogical deduction?

679. [Shāfiʿī] replied: Mālik [b. Anas] told us from Zayd b. Aslam from ʿAṭā' b. Yasār from Abū Rāfiʿ, who said:

[30] Shāfiʿī, *Kitāb al-Umm,* Vol. III, p. 106.

> The Prophet borrowed a camel from a certain man. Upon receiving several camels [later] he ordered me to pay back [the debt], but I told him: I find that every one of these camels is superior. ' Give it to him [the man from whom the camel was borrowed], for the best of men
> S544 shall have the best in payment [of the debt].'[31]

680. He asked: What is the narrative which cannot be regarded as a basis for analogy?

681. [Shāfiʿī] replied: Whenever God has established a textual order for which a qualifying sunna is provided by the Apostle specifying a certain modifying permission to the exclusion of another, such an order of permission should be obeyed provided it is not regarded as a precedent for other orders of permission. The same [reasoning] applies to certain specifying sunnas which the Apostle may have laid down to qualify general rules.

682. He asked: For example?

683. [Shāfiʿī] replied: God has imposed [the duty of] ablution on all who rise up from sleep to perform the prayer and said:

> When you stand up for the prayer wash your faces and your hands up to the elbows, and wipe your heads and your feet up to the ankles [Q. V, 6].

[God] meant that the washing of the feet is included [in
S545 the ablution], just as other limbs are included. But since the Apostle practised the wiping of the shoes, we should not wipe by analogy the turban, the veil, or the gloves. Thus the duty of washing the limbs is confirmed, while the wiping of the shoes is permitted only by the Prophet's order to the exclusion of wiping other things.[32]

684. He asked: Would you regard this [tradition] as contradictory to the Qur'ān?

[31] Abū Dāwūd, Vol. III, pp. 247-48; and Shāfiʿī, *Kitāb al-Umm,* Vol. III, pp. 103, 106-108.

[32] Some jurists maintain that there are traditions to the effect that the Prophet permitted the wiping of the turban. See Abū Dāwūd, Vol. I, p. 36; Tirmidhī, Vol. I, pp. 170-73; and Shawkānī, *Nayl al-Awṭār,* Vol. I, pp. 181-84.

685. [Shāfiʿī] replied: In no circumstance can the sunna contradict the Qur'ān.

686. He asked: What is the meaning [of this tradition] in your opinion?

687. [Shāfiʿī] replied: It means that one should [always] wash his feet if the shoes were not worn in cleanliness.

688. He asked: Is this [meaning] permissible in the [Arab] tongue?

689. [Shāfiʿī] replied: Yes, just as it is permissible for anyone who has [already] performed the ablution to stand up in prayer—for it is not the ablution that is desired—on the strength S546
of the Apostle's [precedent] that he performed two or more prayers with one ablution.[33]

Also, God said:

> The thief, male and female, cut off their hands as a recompense for what they have earned: [an exemplary] chastisement from God. God is All-Mighty, All-Wise [Q. V, 38].

Just as the sunna indicated that God did not mean by " cutting off" [a penalty] for all kinds of thieves, so the Apostle's sunna indicated that he meant by the prescription of the wiping of the shoes that he who wears them need not wash his feet if they were clean.

690. He asked: What are the like examples in the sunna?

691. [Shāfiʿī] replied: The Apostle prohibited the exchange of dates for dates except in equal quantities. Asked about the exchange of fresh dates for dry dates, he inquired: " Will the dates lose weight when dry?" " Yes," he was answered; and he ordered the prohibition of such an exchange. He also prohibited *muzābana*, an exchange of a known quantity for an unknown which may include *ribā*. These are examples which fall in one category. However, [the Prophet] permitted
the sale of *ʿarāya* for dry dates.[34] So we have permitted [the S547
sale of] *ʿarāya* on the strength of the [Prophet's] permission,

[33] Abū Dāwūd, Vol. I, p. 44; Tirmidhī, Vol. I, pp. 86-91; Shawkānī, *Nayl al-Awṭār,* Vol. I, pp. 230-31; Ṭabarī, *Tafsīr,* Vol. X, pp. 7-81.

[34] See paragraph 347, above.

although it is the exchange of fresh dates for dry dates, and it falls in the category of *muzābana* with its conjecturing. Thus we confirm all prohibited foodstuffs that are in the same category as *muzābana*, whether [sold] by measure or by estimate; but we have permitted [the sale of] *ʿarāya* as an exception on the basis of his permission, qualifying the general rule of prohibition. Thus neither one of the two traditions is invalidated by the other, nor are they invalid as a precedent for analogy.

692. He asked: What [possible] explanation would you give for that?

693. [Shāfiʿī] replied: There are two possible explanations. One, is that what [the Prophet] prohibited as a general rule did not include *ʿarāya*; the other is that he may have given his order of permission after he had given the general rule of prohibition. In either case we have to obey his orders, by accepting as lawful what he regarded as lawful, and as unlawful what he regarded
S548 as unlawful.

694. [Shāfiʿī] said:[35] The Apostle decreed that the *diya* for the unintentional killing of a believer is one hundred camels, to be paid by the *ʿāqila*. The compensation for intentional injuries must be distinguished from that for unintentional, and from wrongs, but the common factor is that a *diya* shall be paid.

Since the Prophet decreed that each person must pay
B75 compensation out of his own property, not from that of another, except in case the free Muslim is killed unintentionally, we hold that the *ʿāqila* should pay [the *diya*] for the unintentional killing of a freeman in accordance with the Prophet's decree, and that for the intentional killing of a freeman a *diya* must be paid by the offender out of his own property just as the penalty for any other offence committed intentionally should be paid out of his own property. However, the analogy of compensation for an
S549 unintentional offence should not be applied to compensation for intentional killing.[36]

[35] Būlāq ed., p. 75.

[36] See paragraphs 618 ff., above.

695. Someone may ask: What should be the compensation paid for offences committed intentionally?

696. [Shāfiʿī] replied: God said:

> And give the women their dowries as a gift [Q. IV, 4].

And He said:

> Observe the prayer and pay the *zakāt* [Q. II, 43].

And He said:

> But if you are prevented, then such offering as may be feasible [Q. II, 196].

And He said:

> For those who say, regarding their wives, ' Be as my mother's back,' and then retract what they have said, they shall set free a slave, before they touch each other [Q. LVIII, 3].

And He said:

> If any of you kill it intentionally, let there be compensation, equal to what he has killed, from his flocks, as two persons of just character among you shall decide—an offering to be delivered at the Kaʿba; or let there be an expiation, the feeding of poor people, or its equivalent in fasting, so that he may taste the mischief of his action. God has pardoned what is past, but if anyone repeats the offence God will take vengeance on him. God is mighty, taking vengeance [Q. V, 95]. S550

And He said:

> The expiation of it [the broken oath] is to feed ten poor persons with the food you ordinarily serve to your families, or to clothe them, or to set free a slave; but if anyone finds not the means let him fast for three days [Q. V, 89].

The Apostle decreed that the owners of property are responsible for its protection during the day [from damage by the flocks], but that the responsibility for any damage done [to the property] during the night rests with the flock's owners.[37]

The Book and the sunna—as well as the absence of disagreement among the Muslims—indicate that [compensation] must be paid by the person [responsible for the damage] in accordance with the due owing to God which God imposed on men in ways that bind them, and that no one is responsible for a damage done by another. Nor is it permissible for a person to commit an offence for which another would be held liable, except in the particular case for which the Prophet laid down a
S551 sunna, such as unintentional homicide and unintentional offences against other men.

The analogy of offence against an animal or damage to a property or the like, which I have already described, indicates that [compensation] should be paid by the offender, and it is commonly accepted that the greater [the amount of compensation] the greater the reason that it should be paid by the offender. So analogical deduction should not be applied to cases of the smaller [amount of compensation] while the greater and the [more] reasonable is abandoned. The compensation for an unintentional killing committed by a free-man against another, or any other unintentional killing or offence, should be paid by the ʿ*āqila* on the basis of both tradition and analogy.

697. Shāfiʿī said:[38] The Apostle decreed that the compensation for foeticide is a *ghurra* (a male or female slave). Scholars have estimated the price of the *ghurra* to be five camels.[39]

698. [Shāfiʿī] said: Since nothing has been related from the Apostle distinguishing between the compensation for male and female foeticide, it is taken for granted that he had put
S552 them on an equal footing; if the foetus dies after abortion the compensation for the male is one hundred camels, and for the female fifty.

But it is not permissible to apply the analogy of foeticide to other cases [the compensation for which is] specific and in which

[37] Mālik, Vol. II, pp. 747-48; Abū Dāwūd, Vol. III, p. 298; Shawkānī, *Nayl al-Awṭār*, Vol. V, pp. 342-44.

[38] Būlāq ed., p. 76.

[39] See paragraph 427, above.

a distinction is made between the female and male. Men do not disagree that if the foetus dies after abortion compensation must be full, namely, that it should be one hundred camels for the male and fifty for the female. The Muslims are agreed—as far as I know—that if a man causes the death of another none of them should be held liable to pay any *diya* or fine, and the [compensation for] foeticide should be paid [in like manner], whether dead or alive.

Since the Apostle made a distinction in his decision between the dead and the living, which was unknown before, other decisions should be taken on the strength of, and in obedience to, the Apostle's order.

699. He asked: Do you know of any possible explanation S553 for that?

700. [Shāfiʿī] replied: I know of one, but God knows best!

701. He asked: What is it?

702. [Shāfiʿī] replied: If [the child] were not known to be alive—thus it would be neither necessary to pray for it nor could one inherit from it—the offence would be regarded as being against its mother and the Apostle specified [a compensation] the price of which the Muslims fixed, just as he specified [the compensation] for *al-muwaḍḍiḥa*.

703. He said: That is one explanation.

704. [Shāfiʿī] said: Another one is that the tradition does not make it clear that the decision was made in favor [of the plaintiff]; therefore it would not be right to hold that such a decision was made [in favor of the plaintiff]. But if one holds that a decision was taken, it must be in favor of the wife not the husband (i. e., the mother, not the father) since if any offence was committed, it was against her. However, there is no decision to the effect that the child can be inherited from, for he who does not inherit cannot be inherited from.

705. He said: This is a sound opinion. S554

706. [Shāfiʿī] said: God knows best!

707. He asked: If this is not the [right] explanation what else should the decree mean?

708. [Shāfiʿī] replied: It is a sunna binding on men on the strength of which they should make decisions.

709. [He asked]: What should the other [i. e., analogy] be which the narrative indicates is a reason on the strength of which a decision may be made?

710. [Shāfiʿī] replied: It is the binding decision of a sunna the meaning of which is known and on the strength of which analogy may be applied in like situations.

711. He asked: Give an example other than what you stated,
S555 which you may remember, illustrating how analogy may or may not be applied.

712. [Shāfiʿī] replied: The Apostle decreed in [the case of] the *muṣarrāt*[40]—the she-camel and sheep and goats which the buyer has milked after the purchase—that he can either keep it or return it with one *ṣāʿ* (a measure) of dates.[41] He also decreed that "the profit (*al-kharāj*) belongs to him who bears responsibility."[42]

As to "the profit belongs to him who bears responsibility," in the event a slave is bought[43] and a profit is derived from his employment, it would be reasonable that when a defect is discovered [the buyer] has the right to return the slave without
B76 the profit for two reasons. First, since [the slave] was not in the possession of the seller, he [the latter] should not have a share in the profit. Second, [the slave] was in my possession and the
S556 responsibility was transferred from the seller to me, so that if the slave died the loss would be borne by me. Thus if I decide to keep the slave, the profit belongs to me.

On the strength of the tradition "the profit belongs to him who bears responsibility" I hold that anything accruing from the fruits of an estate that I have purchased, the young produced by the flock and the children of a slave-woman born after her purchase, should be regarded as a profit, because all of them

[40] *Al-muṣarrāt* is the animal which the vendor consciously does not milk for some time before the sale so that its yield of milk will be greater after the sale. The buyer soon discovers the trick of the vendor. See Muzanī, quoting Shāfiʿī on the meaning of *al-muṣarrāt*, in *Mukhtaṣar* (*Kitāb al-Umm,* Vol. II, pp. 184-85, margin).

[41] Bukhārī, Vol. II, pp. 26-27; Abū Dāwūd, Vol. III, p. 270; Shawkānī, *Nayl al-Awṭār,* Vol. V, pp. 226-27.

[42] See paragraph 447, above.

[43] Literally: "by me."

were produced or born after they have become the possession of the buyer, not the vendor.

Our opinion concerning the *muṣarrāt* is based on the Apostle's order, but this case should not be [a precedent] for analogy, because the sale transaction was made for a specific sheep carrying an unknown quantity of milk and at a specific price, and we know that [the prices of] the milk of the sheep and the she-camel vary. However, since the Apostle fixed [the price of] the unknown quantity of the milk to be one *ṣāʿ* of dates, we accept his decision [as an exceptional order]. S557

713. [Shāfiʿī] said: If a man buys a sheep which he, after milking her, decides to keep even though it turns out to be a *muṣarrāt*, but after a month he finds another hidden defect in addition to the *taṣriya* [for which he decides to return her], he has the right to do so, and the milk belongs to him, because it is in the category of profit (*kharāj*) and was not included in the sale transaction, but was produced when the animal was in the possession of the purchaser; but he must give one *ṣāʿ* of dates for the milk which was in the *muṣarrāt* [at the time of the sale], on the strength of the Prophet's decision. Thus our opinion on [the price of] the milk of the *muṣarrāt* is based on a tradition, but the ownership of the milk accruing after *taṣriya* is determined by an analogy based on [the Prophet's ruling]: "The profit belongs to him who bears responsibility." For the *taṣriya* milk must be distinguished from the milk that accrued later, since the former was included in the sale transaction, while the latter accrued after the buyer had taken possession [of the sheep]; it should not [therefore] be included in the sale transaction.[44]

714. Someone may ask: Is it possible that for one question two answers might be given?

715. [Shāfiʿī] replied: Yes, if it includes two or more different S558
reasons.

716. He asked: Will you give another example?

[44] Paragraphs 715-716 are summarized in J. Schacht, *Origins of Muhammadan Jurisprudence,* p. 123.

717. [Shāfiʿī] replied: A woman, upon hearing of the death of her husband waits for the period of the *ʿidda* and marries another man, but her [former] husband returns.[45] Separation [between the woman and her second husband] shall take place on the basis of the cancellation of the second marriage without resort to divorce and neither one shall be held liable for punishment. The woman has the right to keep the bride-price, but she has to wait for the period of the *ʿidda* [before she joins her former husband]. The child [if any] belongs to his father. Neither the woman nor the [second] husband can inherit from one another.

A decision in his [the second husband's] favor—since in the explicit sense [the marriage] is lawful—gives the woman the right to keep the bride-price, to wait for the *ʿidda*, the child [the right] to belong to his father, and waives the punishment. A decision against him [the second husband]—since in the implicit sense it is unlawful—invalidates the marriage [contract], forbids intercourse with her after [the two spouses] have known [about the first husband], prohibits inheritance between them, and separation takes place without divorce since she was not a lawful wife.

There are many other parallel situations, such as the marriage
S559 of the woman during the period of her *ʿidda*.

[45] Būlāq ed., p. 77. The structure of the passage is slightly changed for clarity.

Chapter XV

[ON DISAGREEMENT (*IKHTILĀF*)][1]

718. He asked: I have found the scholars, in former and present times, in disagreement on certain [legal] matters. Is it permissible for them to do so?

719. [Shāfiʿī] replied: Disagreement is of two kinds: one of them is prohibited, but I would not say the same regarding the other.

720. He asked: What is prohibited disagreement?

721. [Shāfiʿī] replied: On all matters concerning which God provided clear textual evidence in His Book or [a sunna] uttered by the Prophet's tongue, disagreement among those to whom these [texts] are known is unlawful. As to matters that are liable to different interpretations or derived from analogy, so that he who interprets or applies analogy arrives at a decision different from that arrived at by another, I do not hold that [disagreement] of this kind constitutes such strictness as that arising from textual [evidence]. S560

722. He asked: Is there any evidence which demonstrates your distinction between the two [kinds of] disagreement?

723. [Shāfiʿī] replied: Concerning [His] disapproval of disagreement,[2] God said:

> Those who have been given the Book did not become disunited until there had come to them the Evidence [Q. XCVIII, 4].

[1] Cf. Būlāq ed., p. 77.
[2] Būlāq ed., p. 77.

And He said:

> Be not like those who became disunited and went different ways after the Evidences had come to them [Q. III, 105].

Thus [God] disapproved of [people's] disagreeing on matters concerning which they have been provided with clear [textual] evidence. As to matters which shall be decided by *ijtihād*, I have already given you examples such as the *qibla*, testimony, and the like.

724. He said: Give me some examples of matters concerning which our predecessors have disagreed in their transmission and concerning which God has provided a textual command [in His Book] liable to different interpretations. Is there any indication
S561 [in that text] as to the correct interpretation?

725. [Shāfiʿī] replied: Few are the matters on which they have disagreed and concerning which we have found no evidence in the Book of God or the sunna of His Apostle, or an analogical deduction based on both or on one of them.

726. He said: Give some examples.

727. [Shāfiʿī] replied: God said:

> Divorced women shall keep to themselves for three [menstrual] periods (*qurū'*) [Q. II, 228].

ʿĀ'isha said: The [term] *aqrā'* or "periods" [means] purity; those who agreed with her in this meaning include Zayd b. Thābit, Ibn ʿUmar and others.[3] However, some of the Companions of the Prophet held that *aqrā'* [means] menstruation, so that the divorced woman cannot lawfully [remarry] until she performs the washing after the third menstruation.[4]

S562 728. He said: On what ground has each based his opinion?

729. [Shāfiʿī] replied: The common meaning of *aqrā'* [in
B77 the foregoing narratives] is periods, and the periods in this case are signs indicating to the divorced women that they

[3] See Shāfiʿī, *Kitāb al-Umm,* Vol. V, 191-92; Bayhaqī, *Sunan al-Kubra,* Vol. VII, pp. 414-16.

[4] Ṭabarī, *Tafsīr,* Vol. IV, pp. 499-515; Bayhaqī, *Sunan al-Kubra,* Vol. VII, pp. 416-18.

are not allowed to remarry until these periods have been completed. But, in our opinion, those who held that *aqrā'* means menstruation believe that [God] said that these periods constitute the minimum [time-limits], because such periods separate one [menstruation] from another, just as limits are the minimums that separate things from each other. Since [the period of] menstruation is shorter than that of purity, it is more appropriate to speak of it as a period, just as the new moon S563
marks the period of division between one month and another. He [who held this opinion] has perhaps based it on the Prophet's order that the women taken captives at Awṭās[5] should wait one menstrual period before indulging in intercourse.[6] So he concluded that the *ʿidda* constituted an *istibrā'*,[7] and that the *istibrā'* was one menstrual period. He also made a distinction between the *istibrā'* of slave and free women and held that the *istibrā'* of the free woman followed three full menstrual periods after which she attains the state of purity, while the *istibrā'* of the slave-woman was achieved after one full menstrual period after which she attained purity.

730. He said: This is one school of thought; but why have you accepted a different one, since you hold that the Quranic S564
communication is capable of two interpretations?

731. [Shāfiʿī] replied: The new moon, which marks [the beginning of] a period of time, is a sign provided by God to indicate the months; but the period marked by the new moon is different from the [time defined by the] day and the night, since it is the sum of either twenty-nine or thirty just as the numbers thirty or twenty are totals of other numbers and have no other meaning.[8] So if the [term] " period" (*qur'*) means time, it consists of a number of nights and days just as the *ʿidda* S565
consists of a number of nights and days of menstruation and

[5] Awṭās is a valley near the tribes of Hawāzin where the Prophet's men assembled before the battle of Ḥunayn. See Ibn Hishām, Vol. II, p. 840; Guillaume's translation, pp. 566-67.

[6] See Abū Dāwūd, Vol. II, p. 248.

[7] Clear of pregnancy.

[8] Būlāq ed., p. 78. Cf. Shākir's ed., where there is a certain ambiguity in the text, p. 565.

purity. Thus a period resembles limits, which may or may not be included within the thing bounded by the limits and not clearly distinguished. So [*qur'*] means period in a [special] sense.

732. He asked: What is that sense?

733. [Shāfiʿī] replied: Menstruation means the visible discharge of blood by the womb, while purity means that the
S566 womb retains the blood so that it is no longer apparent. [Both] purity and *qur'* refer to the retention—not the discharge—of blood; therefore, since purity might refer to a period of time, it is more appropriate to use it in the meaning of *qur'*; because it refers to the retention of the blood. Thus when ʿAbd-Allāh b. ʿUmar divorced his wife during her menstruation, the Apostle commanded ʿUmar b. al-Khaṭṭāb to order him to keep her until she achieved her state of purity, after which he could divorce her while she was in that state without entering into sexual intercourse with her. "This is the [period of the] *ʿidda*, during which God has decreed that woman can be divorced," said the Apostle.[9]

734. Shāfiʿī said:[10] This means that God said: "When you divorce women, divorce them during their *ʿidda*" [Q. LXV, 1].

The Apostle handed down God's word that the [term] *ʿidda*
S567 refers to [the state of] purity, not menstruation.[11] For God said: "[Women should wait for] three periods." So a divorced woman must wait for three periods; if the third period is prolonged, it is not lawful [for her to remarry] until she has menstruated again. If it is feared that she might not [menstruate] again, she must wait for [the prescribed] months of the *ʿidda*. Thus the washing [after the third menstruation] has no significance, since it is a fourth consideration apart from the other three. He who holds that it is obligatory for her would
S568 be holding that if a woman remained a year or more without washing it would not be lawful for her to remarry.

[9] Mālik, Vol. II, p. 576; Bukhārī, Vol. III, pp. 457-58; Muslim, Vol. X, pp. 59-61; Shawkānī, *Nayl al-Awṭār,* Vol. VI, p. 235. See Shāfiʿī, *Kitāb al-Umm,* Vol. V, p. 162.

[10] Būlāq ed., p. 78.

[11] See Bayḍāwī, p. 742; cf. Shākir's commentary, p. 567, n. 7.

Thus the opinion of him who holds that *aqrā'* means [periods of] purity, is closer to the meaning of the Book of God, and the language is clear as to the meanings of these words. But God S569
knows best!

735. Shāfiʿī said:[12] The Prophet's order that the *istibrā'* of the female captive should be one menstrual period means just what it says [i. e., in the literal sense]; for if a slave woman completed a full and genuine menstrual period following a state of purity, she obviously is not pregnant. Even though blood might appear, it would not [necessarily] constitute a true menstrual period, for the latter is valid [only] when it has been completed. Therefore any period of purity that has preceded the full and valid menstruation is to be regarded as free of pregnancy in the literal sense.

Women who are observing the *ʿidda* do so for two reasons:
To accomplish the *istibrā'* [in the sense of clearance from S570-571
pregnancy] and for a purpose other than this. When she accomplishes [in the sense of fulfilling the waiting period], she fulfils two menstrual periods and two [periods of] purity and [ends with] a third [period of] purity. If the purpose were [merely] *istibrā'* [in the sense of clearance from pregnancy] she would have repeated the performance of this *istibrā'* twice; but in addition to clearance from pregnancy there is also an obligatory [*istibrā'*, i. e., that provided in the Book of God].

736. He asked: Will you cite for me other similar [cases] in which scholars have disagreed?

737. [Shāfiʿī] replied: Yes, and perhaps we can give some clearer examples. We have already partially adumbrated this subject in our discussion of the sunnas concerning which transmitters disagree, which has a bearing on the questions you have asked as well as similar matters.[13]

738. Shāfiʿī said:[14] God said:

> Divorced women shall wait by themselves for three periods [Q. II, 228].

[12] Būlāq ed., p. 78.

[13] See Chap. IX, above; this subject is also dealt with in Shāfiʿī's *Kitāb Ikhtilāf al-Ḥadīth (Kitāb al-Umm,* Vol. VII, margin).

[14] Būlāq ed., p. 78.

And He said:

> As for your women who have despaired of [further] menstruation, if you are in doubt, their period shall be three months, and those who have not menstruated as yet. And those who are pregnant, their term
> S572 is when they are delivered of what they bear [Q. LXV, 4].

And He said:

> Those of you who die, leaving wives, they shall wait by themselves four months and ten [days] [Q. II, 234],

Some of the Companions of the Apostle said: Concerning divorced women, God prescribed that the [period of the] *ʿidda* of those who are pregnant should be [until] they are delivered; but those whose husbands have died should observe an *ʿidda* of four months and ten [days]. So the *ʿidda* of the widow who is pregnant must be four months and ten [days], even if she has been delivered, so that she fulfils two *ʿidda*s, since delivery itself does not mean the termination of the prescribed *ʿidda* save in the case of divorce.[15] They hold
B78 in effect that delivery is acquittance, while the [waiting for] four months and ten [days] is obligatory, and that the widow cannot [lawfully] remarry until the four months and ten days are completed.[16] They believe that she is under obligation in two senses, and that neither one can be waived. It is as if she were subject to the claims of two men, neither one of whom invalidated the other, or if she married [one of them] during the *ʿidda* and had intercourse with him, she would have to fulfil an *ʿidda* before she could marry the other one.

Other[17] Companions of the Apostle have held that if she [the widow] has been delivered, it is lawful for her to remarry even if her [dead] husband is not yet buried.[18]

[15] Mālik, Vol. II, pp. 589; Bukhārī, Vol. III, p. 478; Shawkānī, *Nayl al-Awṭār,* Vol. VI, p. 304. See also Shāfiʿī, *Kitāb al-Umm,* Vol. V, pp. 205-206.

[16] Būlāq ed., p. 79.

[17] " He said," is omitted.

[18] Mālik, Vol. II, p. 590.

739. Shāfiʿī said: Thus the Quranic communication can be interpreted in two ways at the same time, but the most reasonable literal one is that a state of pregnancy puts an end to the *ʿidda*.

740. [Shāfiʿī] said: The sunna of the Apostle indicates that delivery marks the end of the *ʿidda* in the event of the death [of the husband], just as in the case of divorce. [For] Sufyān [b. ʿUyayna] has told us from al-Zuhrī from ʿUbayd-Allāh b. ʿAbd-Allāh [b. ʿUtba] from his father, [who related] that a few nights after the death of Subayʿa al-Aslamiya's husband, she was delivered. When Abū al-Sanābil b. Baʿkak, who was passing by, saw her, he remarked: "You have already prepared yourself for remarriage! You still have four months and ten [days] to wait." So Subayʿa reported this to the Apostle, who said: "Abū al-Sanābil is not telling the truth" (or it
is not as Abū al-Sanābil said) "You are already lawful, so S575
remarry."[19]

741. He said: A person whose words are in conflict with the sunna has no proof. So give examples of disagreement concerning which no sunna is to be found, but concerning which there may be either textual or inferred evidence in the Qur'ān, or evidence based on analogical deduction.

742. [Shāfiʿī] replied: God said: S576

> For those who set aside their women, their women must wait four months; if they revert, God is All-Forgiving, All-Compassionate. But if they resolve on divorce, then verily God is All-Hearing, All-Knowing [Q. II, 226-227].

The majority of the Companions of the Prophet who related from him have said that they believed that when the [period of] four months has expired, he who has set aside his wife must make a decision either to go back to her or to divorce her.[20] Other Companions are reported to have said that the intent to divorce [the wife] is indicated by the expiration of the four

[19] Bukhārī, Vol. III, p. 478; Muslim, Vol. X, pp. 108-111; Abū Dāwūd, Vol. II, p. 293; Shawkānī, *Nayl al-Awṭār,* Vol. VI, p. 304.

[20] Mālik, Vol. II, p. 556; Bukhārī, Vol. III, p. 469.

S577 months.[21] However, we do not possess anything on this matter from the Apostle of God.

743. He asked: Which of the two opinions have you accepted?

744. [Shāfiʿī] replied: I hold that the divorce is not binding on him who has put his wife aside, and that if his wife claims her due [i. e., payment of the deferred bride-price] from him, I should not hold him liable for it until the four months had expired. When the four months had expired, I should tell him either to take her back or to divorce her. His taking her back is [indicated] by intercourse.

745. He asked: Why do you prefer this opinion over the opposite one?

746. [Shāfiʿī] replied: Because I consider it more consistent with the meaning of the Book of God and with what is reasonable.

747. He asked: Where is the evidence for it in the Book of
S578 God?

748. [Shāfiʿī] replied: In God's saying: "For those who set their women aside is a wait of four months" [Q. II, 226], the literal meaning is that he upon whom God for some reason has imposed [the obligation] to wait for four months is bound to wait until the four months expire.

749. He said: It is possible that God may have given him four months in which to take her back, just as you may say [to someone]: "I have given you four more months in which to finish building this house."

750. [Shāfiʿī] replied: No one to whom this statement had been made would imagine that it meant such a thing unless it had been stipulated during the course of the conversation, for if he [the owner of the house] says: "I have given you four months," it means that he has given him four additional months and that he has no claim against him unless the four months have elapsed and the house still is not finished. He [the builder] cannot be accused of failing to complete the house, or

[21] Tirmidhī, Vol. II, p. 222; and Ibn Rushd, *Bidāyat al-Mujtahid* (Istanbul, 1333/1915), Vol. II, p. 83. The Ḥanafī school supports this point of view. Cf. Ṭabarī, *Tafsīr*, Vol. IV, pp. 456-99.

of being late in completing it so long as any part of the four months remains unexpired. If the four months have completely expired [and the builder has not completed the house], he can S579
be charged with being in default, and there may well be an indication before the expiration of the four months that the house cannot be completed by the time the four months are over.

However, there is no indication in the [act of] taking a wife back that one cannot do so before the expiration of the four months, because the performance of intercourse may take only a twinkling of an eye. So if the person, as I have explained, keeps himself apart from his wife until the four months expire, and then continues to keep himself apart, then he is answerable to God, for he should either take her back or divorce her. If there had not been any indication in the latter part of the communication that its meaning never differed from what you held, we should have preferred the first interpretation for reasons we have described, since that is the literal meaning. The Qur'ān is to be taken at its literal meaning, unless there is an indication either in the Qur'ān itself, the sunna, or the *ijmāʿ*, that the true meaning is a hidden one, and not the literal meaning.

751. He asked: What is there in the tenor of the communication that supports what you have said? S580

752. [Shāfiʿī] replied: When God, Glorious and Mighty, said that those who put their wives aside will have four months, He added:

> If they take them back, God is All-Forgiving, All-Compassionate. But if they resolve on divorce, then verily God is All-Hearing, All-Knowing [Q. II, 226-227].

So [God] laid down two rulings conjointly and without separating them; they must both take effect after the expiration of the four months, for He gave the husband the choice of either taking her back or divorce; the choice is simultaneous, neither one precedes the other. He said that the choice must be made at one time, just as in the case of something pawned [the lender would say to the owner]: "Redeem it or else I shall sell it." The two are inseparable, for in all cases [where there is a choice] between good actions one has either to choose one or the other without separating [the two alternatives].

[As for the contention that] the two alternatives should have B79 been stated separately [on the ground that] the decision to take the wife back can be taken during the four months while the decision to divorce her [has to be made] at the end of the four months, [I should reply that] they are two judgments that have to be envisaged at the same time, and that one has plenty of time in which to take one of them but little time in which to decide S581 on the other.

753. He asked: If he takes her back before the expiration of the four months, do you hold that it is [a valid act]?

754. [Shāfiʿī] replied: Yes, it is, just as you would say that if you paid a debt before it was due, you would be quit of it, and you would be doing a good act in paying it of your own free will before you were required to.

755. [Shāfiʿī] asked: Do you hold that it would be wrong if every day he resolved to take her back but did not have intercourse with her until the four months had expired?

756. He replied: The determination to take her back is not consequential until he actually does so, and his taking her back is [accomplished only by the performance of] intercourse, if he is capable of it.

757. [Shāfiʿī] asked: If he performs intercourse without the intent to take her back, is he thereby freed from the obligation to divorce her, since that is the significance of intercourse?

S582 758. He said: Yes.

759. [Shāfiʿī] asked: Likewise, if he were determined not to take her back and swore daily that he would not take her back, but then had intercourse with her for a moment before the expiration of the four months, would he no longer be bound to divorce her, even though the intercourse did mean that he intended to take her back?

760. He replied: Yes.

761. [Shāfiʿī] asked: Is not his resolve not to take her back thereby invalidated? And if he has intercourse with her for pleasure and not because he intends to take her back, does this not, in our opinion and yours, prevent him from escaping from his obligation to divorce her?

762. He replied: It is as you said, for by having intercourse with her he gives up the right to divorce her, regardless of the reason for the performance of the intercourse. S583

763. [Shāfiʿī] asked: How could he resolve daily to take her back and then at the end of the fourth month be obliged to divorce her, even though he had not determined to do so and had not spoken of it? Do you consider that such an opinion would be regarded as reasonable by anyone?

764. He replied: What makes it lacking in reasonableness?

765. [Shāfiʿī] asked: If a man says to his wife " By God I shall never approach you," do you think that it is as if he says: " You are divorced for four months?"

766. He replied: Supposing I should say yes?

767. [Shāfiʿī] asked: What if he had intercourse with her before [the end of] the four months?

768. He replied: No, it would not be the same as saying: " You are divorced for four months."

769. [Shāfiʿī] said: Thus the pronouncement of the oath of putting aside is not a [pronouncement of] divorce, but merely an oath that is transformed into divorce after a certain period of time. Is it permissible for any person who comprehends what S584
he is talking about to say such a thing, unless it is based on a binding narrative?

770. He replied: Such an argument is against you.

771. [Shāfiʿī] asked: How?

772. He replied: You hold that if the period of four months expires, he [who has put his wife aside] has either to take her back or is compelled to divorce her.

773. [Shāfiʿī] said: The oath of putting her aside does not constitute divorce, but is an oath for which God specified a period during which He forbade the husband to harm her. He imposed on him the obligation either to take her back or to

divorce her, and the decision had to be made after the expiration of four months from the time he put her aside. But the period of the effectiveness of this injunction is temporary, for it compels the person concerned whichever of the two alternatives he wishes—to take her back or to divorce her. If he refuses to do
S585 either, he who has the power to do so is to take from what he can; i. e., he shall be divorced from her since it is not lawful for him to cohabit with her.

774. Shāfiʿī said:[22] They [the scholars] are disagreed on [the distribution] of inheritance. Zayd b. Thābit and his followers held that each heir should be given his designated share; if any surplus remains and the deceased has no agnate (*ʿaṣaba*)[23] relative or patron,[24] it goes to the Muslim community. Others have held that the residue should be given to the uterine relatives (*dhawī al-arḥām*). If a man is survived by [only] one sister, she
S586 inherits half of his estate and the other half is to be given to her.

775. Someone has asked: Why would you not give the residue of the estate [to the survivors]?

776. [Shāfiʿī] replied: Because of certain indications in the Book of God.

777. He asked: Where is the indication in the Book of God in support of your opinion?

778. [Shāfiʿī] replied: God said:

> If a man passes away and has no children, but he has a sister, she shall receive a half of what he leaves, and he is her heir if she has no children [Q. IV, 176].

And He said:

> If there be both brothers and sisters, the male shall receive the portion of two females [ibid.].

Thus [God] prescribed that if the sister is the only survivor, she is to receive half [of the estate of the deceased person]; if the

[22] Būlāq ed.. p. 80.

[23] An *ʿaṣaba* (pl. *ʿaṣabāt*) is a male relative of the father.

[24] Succession by contract (*walā'*) is an arrangement between one person and another that the one can inherit the other in case of death of one of them.

brother is the only survivor, he is to receive the entire estate. And He prescribed that if both brothers and sisters survive the deceased, the sister's portion shall be half the brother's. His [God's] decree concerning the sister's portion, whether she is the sole survivor or survivor with a brother, is the same, [namely] that she is not on an equal footing with the brother, but receives only half of what he is entitled to receive of the inheritance. Thus if you hold that [in the event] a man dies leaving a sister as [the sole] survivor and she receives half the
estate by inheritance and the other half as a residue, have you S587
not given her the entire estate as a sole survivor, while God prescribed for her only half of it whether she was alone or with others?

779. He replied: I should not give her the other half as an inheritance but as a residue [in the absence of other survivors].

780. [Shāfiʿī] said: What is the meaning of giving her [a residue]? Is this a matter on which you can exercise *istiḥsān* (discretion) and give it to whomever you wish so that you may give it to the [deceased's] neighbors or to one of his distant relatives? Is that for you to decide?

781. He replied: No, that is not for the discretion of the
judge, but I would give it to her [as a residue] on the grounds of B80
her uterine relationship.

782. [Shāfiʿī asked]: Would it be as an inheritance?

783. He replied: Supposing I should say yes?

784. [Shāfiʿī] said: You would then have let her inherit what S588
God did not.[25]

785. He said: I hold such an opinion on the strength of God's saying:

> Those who are uterine relatives are nearer to each other in the view of the Book of God [Q. VIII, 75].

786. [Shāfiʿī] said: [The Quranic communication]: "Those who are uterine relatives are nearer to one another" was revealed at a time when men were [first] entitled to inherit from one another on the basis of succession by contract, then

[25] See Shāfiʿī, *Kitāb al-Umm,* Vol. IV, pp. 6-7.

on the basis of the Islamic faith and the hijra [emigration] so that one emigrant was entitled to inherit from another while his heirs who did not emigrate [to Madīna], notwithstanding their closer blood relationship, could not inherit. So the communication: "Those who are related, etc." was revealed [to regulate inheritance] in accordance with what [God] prescribed for them.[26]

787. He asked: What is the evidence for that?

788. [Shāfiʿī] replied: [The communication]: "Those who
S589 are uterine relatives are nearer to one another" is the rule [of inheritance] in accordance with what [God] prescribed. Do you not agree that some of "those who are uterine relatives" inherit while others do not? The husband [who is not related in blood] receives a larger share than most of those who are uterine relatives. So if you permit people to inherit according to uterine relationship, the daughter would be on an equal footing with the brother, and all the uterine heirs would be entitled to inherit and would have a greater claim than the husband, who enjoys no uterine relationship. If the meaning of the communication were as you have described it, you would have objected to our position with respect to it, namely, that neither his sister, who is more closely related to him, nor his mawlas get all of the estate; half is given to his sister and half to his mawlas, even though they are not uterine relatives and the Book of God does not prescribe any share for
S590 them.[27]

789. Shāfiʿī said:[28] They [the scholars] have also disagreed on the grandfather's [share of inheritance]. Zayd b. Thābit, supported by ʿUmar [b. al-Khaṭṭāb], ʿUthmān [b. ʿAffān], ʿAlī [b. Abī Ṭālib] and Ibn Masʿūd, held that the [deceased's] brothers can inherit along with his grandfather. Abū Bakr and Ibn ʿAbbās, supported by ʿĀ'isha, Ibn al-Zubayr and ʿAbd-

[26] See Ṭabarī, *Tafsīr,* Vol. IV, pp. 90-91; Suyūṭī, *Libāb al-Nuqūl* (Cairo, 1373/1954), p. 114.

[27] Būlāq ed., p. 81; and *Kitāb al-Umm,* Vol. IV, pp. 10-11.

[28] Būlāq ed., p. 81.

Allāh b. ʿUtba, hold that the grandfather is on an equal footing with the father, and they eliminate the brothers.[29]

790. He asked: On what ground have you fixed the inheritance of the brothers on the same level with that of the grand-father? Is it on the strength of the Book of God or the sunna?

791. [Shāfiʿī] replied: I do not know of any explicit text in the Book of God or the sunna.

792. He said: The narratives are equally divided on the subject and the evidence of analogy supports those who held that [the grandfather] is on an equal footing with the father and that the brothers are debarred.[30]

793. [Shāfiʿī] asked: What is the evidence? S591

794. He replied: I consider it to lie in the binding title of "fatherhood," in your [the scholars'] agreement that because of it you debar the uterine brothers, and in your agreement that his [minimum share] is one-sixth; all of this is the ruling that applies to the father.

795. [Shāfiʿī] said: We do not believe that he should inherit only on the ground of his fatherhood.

796. He asked: Why?

797. [Shāfiʿī] replied: Because I might find that although the title of fatherhood applies [in his case] he could not inherit.

798. He asked: In what instance?

799. [Shāfiʿī] replied: If there were another father surviving—and the title of fatherhood applies to him [the grand-father] and so on back to Adam—the grandfather could not inherit. Moreover, if he were a slave, a disbeliever, or a murderer, he could not inherit. Thus, if it were only on the ground of fatherhood, he would inherit in all these instances. Our opinion that the grandfather debars the uterine brothers
is based on a narrative, not on the title of fatherhood. For S592
we hold that the son's female descendants in the male line, no matter how small the share to which they are entitled, debar the uterine brothers. As to [your argument that] the grandfa-

[29] Cf. Mālik, Vol. II, pp. 510-12.

[30] It is the Ḥanafī's opinion which the interlocutor supports.

ther's share cannot be less than one-sixth, we hold that this is applicable to the grandmother also.[31] In doing so we have followed a [logical] sequence, and we do not believe that if the rule applicable to the grandfather resembles that applicable to the father in certain respects, it does so in all respects. For if the latter were true, similar to those of the grandfather, the son's female descendants would enjoy rights and they would debar the uterine brothers. The rule applicable to the grandmother is similar to that governing the grandfather in that we should not
S593 make her share less than one-sixth.

800. He asked: What is your argument for rejecting our opinion that the grandfather debars the [deceased's] brothers from inheritance?

801. [Shāfiʿī] replied: Because it is far removed from analogical deduction.

802. He said: We thought that it was indeed [a valid] analogical deduction.

803. [Shāfiʿī] replied: Do you think that the grandfather and the brother each claims to be related to the deceased or is it to someone else?

804. He asked: What do you mean?

805. [Shāfiʿī] replied: Is the grandfather's [relationship] not based on his claim: "I am the father of the father of the deceased person" while the brother says: "I am the son of the deceased's father."

806. He said: That is right.

807. [Shāfiʿī] asked: Does not each claim his relationship to the father in accordance with his own position in that relationship?

S594 808. He replied: Yes.

809. [Shāfiʿī] asked: Supposing that the deceased person were the father, and his successors were his son and his father; what would each inherit from him?

810. He replied: The son's share would be five-sixths [of the estate] and the father's one-sixth.

[31] Shāfiʿī, *Kitāb al-Umm*, Vol. IV, p. 11.

811. [Shāfiʿī] replied: If, as you said, the son of the deceased is entitled to inherit a greater portion of the estate than is the father of the deceased and since the claim of the deceased's brother is based on his relationship through the deceased's father, [just as] the deceased's grandfather's claim is based on his relationship through the [deceased's] father, then why do you hold that the brother is debarred by the grandfather? If one of the two is to be debarred by the other, it is the grandfather who should be debarred by the brother, since the latter is entitled to a greater portion of the estate than is he [the grandfather] to whom the two [the father and the brother] both claim to be related? Otherwise, we should never allot the brother five-sixths [of the estate] and the grandfather one-sixth.

812. He asked: What prevents you from holding such an opinion?

813. [Shāfiʿī] replied: all those [scholars] who disagree [on S595
matters concerning inheritance] are in agreement that the grandfather [as a joint successor] with the brother is entitled to an equal or greater share than the brother. On this matter I am in full agreement with them without having recourse to analogy, since analogy is the common basis of all their rulings. I have taken the position that the brothers' right to inherit on a
par with the grandfather is the more appropriate ruling in view B81
of the evidence provided by analogy, which I have explained, as well as the opinion of the majority of jurists, ancient and modern. In addition, the brother's inheritance is firmly fixed by the [text of the] Book, while that of the grandfather is not. Furthermore, the sunna establishes the brother's inheritance more [clearly] than the grandfather's.

814. He asked: I have heard your views on consensus and analogy, in addition to your opinions concerning the decrees of the Book of God and the sunna of the Apostle. What is your position concerning the opinions of the Apostle's Companions, if they disagree?

815. [Shāfiʿī] replied: We accept those which agree with the S596
Book, the sunna, consensus, or which is soundest according to [the rules of] analogy.

816. He asked: What of the opinions of a single Companion, on which neither the agreement nor the disagreement of others is known: Would you seek evidence for accepting it in the Book, or a sunna, or a ruling that people in general have accepted so that such evidence constitutes what you call a narrative?

817. [Shāfiʿī] replied: We have not found anything concerning this matter in the Book or in any established sunna, but we have found that scholars accept the opinion of one of their number at one occasion and reject it on another. They also differ concerning some of the opinions which they accept from such a person.

S597 818. He asked: Which one would you accept?

819. [Shāfiʿī] replied: I would accept the opinion [of a Companion] if I did not find anything about it in the Book, or established sunna or consensus, or anything of similar meaning that would decisively support it, or any analogical deduction. But one seldom finds an opinion of one Companion that is not contradicted by another.[32]

820. He asked: You have [rightly] made decisions on the basis of the Book and the sunna; on what ground have you made decisions on the basis of consensus and analogy, placing them on an equal footing with a [text in the] Book and a sunna?

821. [Shāfiʿī] replied: Although I have made decisions [on the basis of consensus and analogy] just as I have made decisions on the basis of the Book and the sunna, [in the case of consensus and analogy] the principle on which I made my decision varies.

822. He asked: Can there be different bases for the same
S598 decision?

823. [Shāfiʿī] replied: Yes; we make decisions on the basis of the [text of the] Book and the generally accepted sunna, concerning which there is no disagreement, arid we maintain that therefore such decisions are right according to both the explicit and the implicit [meaning of these sources]. We also make decisions on the basis of a single-individual tradition on

[32] Cf. J. Schacht, *Origins of Muhammadan Jurisprudence*, p. 19.

which there is no general agreement, and we hold that we have made the decision correctly according to its explicit meaning, since it is possible that he who related the tradition may have made an error in it.

We also make decisions on the basis of consensus and analogy, although the latter is the weaker of the two instruments.[33] Analogy is used only in case of necessity, since it is not lawful if a tradition exists, just as performing the ritual ablution with sand[34] renders one pure when one is travelling and S599
there is no water; but it does not render one pure if water is available. It produces a state of purity only if water is not at hand. Similarly, a source other than the sunna can be used as the basis for a decision if there is no sunna. However, I have already discussed analogy and other sources [of the law].[35]

824. He asked: Will you give an example?

825. [Shāfiʿī] replied: I should make a decision against a person either on the basis of my knowledge that the accusation made against him was right, or on his [own] admission. If I neither had the knowledge or if he did not confess, I should decide against him on the basis of [the testimony of] two witnesses [of just character]. Since witnesses may make mistakes or be confused, my knowledge and the [defendant's] admission would be stronger [evidence] against him than the [testimony of] two witnesses. I should [also] decide against him on the strength of [the testimony of] one witness and the [plaintiff's] oath; but [such evidence] is weaker than the [testimony of] two witnesses. I should also decide against him if he refused to take an oath whereas the plaintiff did take an oath; but [such evidence] is weaker than the [testimony of] one witness and the oath, since the accused's refusal might have been the

[33] Shaykh Shākir maintains that the word "weak" qualifies both consensus and analogy—which is unlikely—and argues that since Shāfiʿī held that the consensus of the people is authoritative, his reference must be to the consensus of the scholars. Cf. Shākir's ed., p. 599, note 10.

[34] *Tayammum* is ablution by sand during travel instead of by water. Sand as a substitute for water is lawful for fulfilling the duty of ablution if water is scarce or unavailable during travel.

[35] See Chaps. XII and XIII, above.

result of his fear for his reputation or his feeling that the matter was too insignificant for an oath, whereas he who did swear
S600 an oath on his own behalf might be a covetous or debauched
B82 person.

The end.

TRANSMITTERS OF TRADITIONS

Abān b. Saʿīd b. al-ʿĀṣ
Companion; Madīna; d. 14 or 15/635 or 636

ʿAbd-Allāh b. ʿAbbās
Companion; authority of Makkans; d. 68/687

ʿAbd-Allāh b. Abī Bakr b. Muḥammad b. ʿAmr b. Ḥazm
Traditionist; Madīna; d. 130 or 135/747 or 752

ʿAbd-Allāh b. Abī Labīd
Traditionist; Madīna; d. circa 132/750

ʿAbd-Allāh b. Abī Najīḥ
Successor; Makka; d. 132/750

ʿAbd-Allāh. b. Bābāh
Successor; Makka; n. d.

ʿAbd-Allāh b. Dīnār
Traditionist; Madīna; d. 127/774

ʿAbd-Allāh b. ʿIṣma
Obscure (transmitted one tradition); Ḥijāz; n. d.

ʿAbd-Allāh b. Kathīr
Traditionist; Makka; d. 120 or 122/737 or 739

ʿAbd-Allāh b. Masʿūd
Companion; Madīna; d. 32/652

ʿAbd-Allāh b. Muḥammad b. Ṣayfī
Successor; Makka; n. d.

ʿAbd-Allāh b. Rawāḥa
Companion; Madīna; d. circa 8/629

ʿAbd-Allāh b. Sulaymān b. Yasār
Son of successor Abū Ayyūb Sulaymān; related traditions from his father; n. d.

ʿAbd-Allāh b. ʿUbayd-Allāh b. Abī Mulayka
Successor; Makka; d. 117/736

ʿAbd-Allāh b. ʿUmar
Companion; son of the Caliph ʿUmar; d. 73 or 74/692 or 693

ʿAbd-Allāh b. ʿUsayla al-Ṣunābiḥī
Companion; Madīna; n. d.

ʿAbd-Allāh b. Wāqid
Successor; Madīna; d. 119/737

ʿAbd al-ʿAzīz b. Muḥammad al-Darāwardī
Traditionist; Madīna; d. 187 or 189/802 or 804

ʿAbd al-Malik b. ʿAbd al-ʿAzīz b. Jurayj
Traditionist; Makka; d. 150/767

ʿAbd al-Malik b. ʿUmayr
Judge of Kūfa; d. 136/753.

ʿAbd al-Raḥmān b. ʿAbd-Allāh b. Abī ʿAmmār
Traditionist; Makka; d. circa 198/813

ʿAbd al-Raḥmān b. ʿAbd-Allāh b. Masʿūd (son of the Companion Ibn Masʿūd).
Successor; ʿIrāq; n. d.

ʿAbd al-Raḥmān b. ʿAbd al-Qārī
Successor; Madīna; d. 80 or 88/699 or 707

ʿAbd al-Raḥmān b. Abī Saʿīd al-Khudrī
Son of the Companion Abū Saʿīd; n. d.

ʿAbd al-Raḥmān b. ʿAwf
Companion; Madīna; d. 31 or 32/651 or 652

ʿAbd al-Raḥmān b. Ghanam
Companion; Syria; d. 78/698

ʿAbd al-Raḥmān b. Hurmuz al-Aʿraj
Successor; Madīna and Alexandria; d. 117/735

ʿAbd al-Raḥmān b. Kaʿb b. Mālik al-Anṣārī
Traditionist; Madīna; died during the caliphate of Sulaymān b. ʿAbd-al-Malik

ʿAbd al-Raḥmān b. al-Qāsim b. Muḥammad b. Abī Bakr
Successor; Madīna; d. 126/743

ʿAbd al-Raḥmān b. Yazīd b. Jāriya
Successor; Madīna; d. 93/711

ʿAbd al-Raḥmān b. al-Zabīr
Companion; Madīna; n. d.

ʿAbd al-Wahhāb b. ʿAbd al-Majīd al-Thaqafī
Traditionist; Madīna; d. 194/809

ʿAbd al-Wahhāb b. Bukht
Successor; Makka and Syria; d. 113/732

ʿAbd al-Wāḥid al-Naṣrī
Obscure; transmitted one tradition; n. d.

Abū ʿAyyāsh Zayd b. ʿAyyāsh al-Zuraqī
Companion; Madīna; died during the caliphate of Muʿāwiya

Abū Ayyūb Khālid b. Zayd b. Kulayb
Companion; Madīna; d. 52/672

Abū Ayyūb Sulaymān b. Yasār
Successor; Madīna; d. 107/725

Abū Bakr ʿAbd-Allāh b. Abī Quḥāfa
Companion; first Caliph; d. 12/634

Abū Bakr b. Sālim b. ʿAbd-Allāh b. ʿUmar
Successor; son of Ibn ʿUmar; d. 106/724

Abū al-Dardā' ʿUwaymir b. ʿĀmir (or Mālik) al-Khazrajī
Companion; Madīna; d. 32 or 37/652 or 657

Abū Ḥanīfa b. al-Faḍl al-Shiʿbī
Successor (obscure)

Abū al-Ḥārith al-Layth b. Saʿd
Traditionist; Egypt; d. 165/781

Abū Ḥumayd b. ʿAbd al-Raḥmān b. Ḥumayd b. ʿAbd al-Raḥmān b. ʿAwf
Traditionist; Kūfa; d. 192 or 196/807 or 811

Abū Hurayra ʿAbd al-Raḥmān b. Ṣakhr
Companion; Madīna; d. 57/676

Abū Idrīs ʿĀidh-Allāh b. ʿAbd-Allāh al-Khawlānī
Successor; Madīna and Syria; d. 80/699

Abū al-Juham b. Hudhayfa b. Ghānim
Companion; Makka and Syria; d. circa 60/680

Abū Khālid Ḥakīm b. Ḥizām
Companion; Makka and Madīna; d. 54/674

Abū al-Minhāl ʿAbd al-Raḥmān b. Muṭʿim
Successor; Makka; d. 106/720

Abū al-Muhallab (either ʿAmr or ʿAbd al-Raḥmān) b. Muʿāwiya (uncle of Abū Qilāba).
Successor; Baṣra; n. d.

Abū Muḥammad ʿAṭā' b. Yazīd
Successor; Madīna; d. 107/725

Abū Mūsa al-Ashʿarī
Companion; Madīna and ʿIrāq; d. 52/672

Abū al-Naḍr Sālim b. Abī Umayya
Successor; Madīna; d. 129/746

Abū Qatāda Ḥārith (or Nuʿmān)
Companion; Madīna; d. 54/665

Abū Qays (freed slave of ʿAmr b. al-ʿĀṣ)
Successor; Egypt; d. 54/673

Abū Qilāba ʿAbd-Allāh b. Zayd
Successor; Baṣra; d. 104 or 106/722 or 724

Abū Rāfiʿ Ibrāhīm or Aslam (freed slave of the Prophet)
Companion; Madīna; d. circa 35/656

Abū Saʿīd al-Ḍaḥḥāk b. Sufyān
Companion; Madīna; n. d.

Abū Saʿīd Saʿd b. Mālik al-Khudrī
Companion; Madīna; d. 74/694

Abū Saʿīd Yaḥya b. Saʿīd b. Qays
Traditionist; Madīna; d. 143/760

Abū Salāma ʿAbd-Allāh (or Ismāʿīl) b. ʿAbd al-Raḥmān b. ʿAwf
Successor; Madīna; d. 93 or 94/711 or 712

Abū al-Sanābil b. Baʿkak
Companion; Makka; n. d.

Abū Shuʿba (probably the freed slave of Suwayd Muqarrin)
Successor; Madīna; n. d.

Abū Shurayḥ al-Kaʿbī
Companion; Madīna; d. 68/687

Abū Sufyān b. Ṣakhr (father of the Caliph Muʿāwiya)
Companion; Makka; d. 32 or 34/653 or 655

Abū Suhayl b. Mālik (uncle of Mālik b. Anas)
Traditionist; Madīna; n. d.

Abū Thaʿlaba al-Khushanī
Companion; Madīna and Syria; d. 75/695

Abū ʿUbayd Saʿd b. ʿUbayd al-Zuhrī
Traditionist; Madīna; d, 98/716

Abū ʿUbayda ʿĀmir b. ʿAbd-Allāh b. al-Jarrāḥ.
Companion; Makka and Syria; d. 18/639

Abū ʿUthmān Rabīʿa b. Abī ʿAbd al-Raḥmān
Traditionist; Madīna; d. 130 or 136/747 or 753

Abū Zakarīya Yaḥya b. Ḥassān
Traditionist; Baṣra;'d. 208/823

Abū al-Zubayr Muḥammad b. Muslim b. Tadrus
Successor; Makka; d. 128/745

ʿĀ'isha (daughter of Abū Bakr)
Wife of the Prophet; d. 57/676

ʿAlī b. Abī Ṭālib
Companion; fourth Caliph; d. 40/661

Anas b. Mālik
Companion; Baṣra; d. 90/708

ʿĀmir b. Shurāḥīl al-Shaʿbī
Traditionist; Kūfa; d. 104/722

ʿAmr b. Abī ʿAmr (freed slave of Muṭṭalib b. ʿAbd-Allāh b. Ḥanṭab)
Traditionist; Madīna; n. d.

ʿAmr b. Shuʿayb b. Muḥammad b. ʿAmr b. al-ʿĀṣ
Traditionist; Madīna; d. 118/736

ʿAmr b. Sulaymān al-Zuraqī
Successor; Madīna; n. d.

ʿAmr b. ʿUthmān b. ʿAffān
Successor; Madīna; n. d.

ʿAmr b. Yaḥya
Traditionist; Madīna; n. d.

ʿAmra bint ʿAbd al-Raḥmān
Successor; Makka; d. 98 or 101/716 or 719

Asīd b. Abī Asīd
Son of the Companion Asīd; transmitted from his father; n. d.

ʿĀṣim b. ʿUmar b. Qatāda
Grandson of Companion Abū Qatāda; d. 117/735

al-Aswad b. Sufyān
Companion (?); Makka; n. d.

al-Aswad b. Yazīd
Successor; Madīna; d. 75/694

ʿAṭā' b. Abī Rabāḥ
Traditionist; Makka; d. 114/732

ʿAṭā' b. Yasār
Successor; Madīna; d. 97 or 103/715 or 721

Ayyūb b. Kaysān al-Sikhtiyānī
Successor; Baṣra; d. 131 or 135/748 or 752

Bajāla b. ʿAbd (or ʿAbada)
Successor; Baṣra; died in the Caliph ʿUmar's time

Bilāl b. Rabāḥ
The Prophet's mu'adhdhin; Makka and Madīna; d. 20 or 21/640 or 641

Buṣr b. Saʿīd
Traditionist; Madīna; d. 110/718

Diḥya b. Khalīfa al-Kalbī
Companion; Ḥijāz and Syria; died during Muʿāwiya's caliphate

Fāṭima bint Qays
Companion; Madīna; n. d.

al-Furayʿa bint Mālik b. Sinān
Companion; sister of the Companion Abū Saʿīd al-Khudrī; n. d.

Ḥakīm b. Ḥizām
Companion; Makka; d. 54/673

Ḥamal b. Mālik b. al-Nābigha
Companion; Madīna and Baṣra; n. d.

al-Ḥasan b. Abī al-Ḥasan
Traditionist; Baṣra; d. 110/728

al-Ḥasan b. ʿAlī b. Abī Ṭālib
The Caliph ʿAlī's first son; d. 48/669

al-Ḥasan b. Muslim b. Yannāq
Successor; Makka; transmitted from Ṭāwūs; n. d.

Hilāl b. Usāma
Successor; Madīna; n. d.

Ḥiṭṭān b. ʿAbd-Allāh al-Raqāshī
Successor; Baṣra; n. d.

al-Ḥusayn b. ʿAlī b. Abī Ṭālib
Caliph ʿAlī's second son; d. 61/680

Ibn ʿAbbās *(see* ʿAbd-Allāh b. ʿAbbās)

Ibn Jurayj *(see* ʿAbd al-Malik b. ʿAbd al-ʿAzīz)

Ibn Shihāb al-Zuhrī *(see* Muḥammad b. Muslim b. ʿUbayd-Allāh b. Shihāb etc.)

Ibrāhīm b. Abī Yaḥya
Traditionist; Madīna; d. 184/801

Ibrāhīm b. Maysara
Successor; Ṭā'if and Makka; d. 132/750

Ibrāhīm al-Nakhaʿī
Traditionist; Kūfa; d. 95 or 96/713 or 714

Isḥāq b. ʿAbd-Allāh b. Abī Ṭalḥa
Successor; Madīna; d. 134/751

Ismāʿīl b. Abī Ḥakīm
Traditionist; Madīna; d. 130/747

Jābir b. ʿAbd-Allāh al-Anṣārī
Companion; Madīna; d. 78/697

Jaʿfar b. Abī Ṭālib
Grandson of the Caliph ʿAlī; d. 148/765

Jarīr b. ʿAbd-Allāh
Companion; Kūfa; d. 51 or 54/671 or 673

Jubayr b. Muṭʿim
Companion; Madīna; d. 54 or 59/673 or 678

Khālid b. al-Walīd
Companion; Madīna and Syria; d. 21/641

al-Khansā' bint Khidhām
Daughter of the Companion Khidhām b. Khālid; Madīna; n. d.

Khārija b. Zayd b. Thābit
Son of the Companion Zayd; Madīna; d. 100/718

Khawwāt b. Jubayr
Companion; Madīna; d. 40 or 42/660 or 662

Maḥmūd b. Labīd
Companion; Madīna; d. 96/696

Māʿiz b. Mālik al-Aslamī
Companion; Madīna; n. d.

Makhlad b. Khufāf
Son of companion Khufāf; n. d.

Makḥūl b. Zayd
Successor; Damascus (Syria); d. 112 or 118/731 or 737

Mālik b. Anas
Founder of a school of law; Madīna; d. 179/795

Maʿmar b. Rashīd
Successor; Ṣanʿā'; d. 154/771

Muʿādh b. Jabal
Companion; al-Yaman; d. 18/639

Muʿāwiya b. Abī Sufyān
Companion; first Umayyad Caliph; d. 61/681

Muḥammad b. ʿAbd al-Raḥmān b. al-Mughīra b. Abī Dhi'b
Traditionist; Madīna; d. 158 or 159/774 or 775

Muḥammad b. al-ʿAjlān
Traditionist; Madīna; d. 148/765

Muḥammad b. ʿAmr b. ʿAlqama
Successor; Madīna; d. 144/761

Muḥammad b. Ibrāhīm al-Taymī
Successor; Madīna; d. 119 or 121/737 or 738

Muḥammad b. Ismāʿīl b. Abī Fudayk
Traditionist; Madīna; died circa 200/816

Muḥammad b. Jubayr b. Muṭʿim
Son of Companion Jubayr; Madīna; died during the caliphate of ʿUmar b. ʿAbd al-ʿAzīz

Muḥammad b. al-Munkadir
Traditionist; Madīna; d. 130 or 131/747 or 748

Muḥammad b. Muslim b. ʿUbayd-Allāh b. ʿAbd-Allāh b. al-Zuhrī
Traditionist; Madīna; d. 124 or 125/741 or 742

Muḥammad b. Sīrīn
Traditionist; Madīna and Baṣra; d. 110/728

Muḥammad b. Ṭalḥa b. Rukāna
Successor; transmitted from his father Rukāna; died circa 105/724

Muḥammad b. Yaḥya b. Ḥibbān
Traditionist; Madīna'; d. 121/738

Mujammiʿ b. Yazīd b. Jāriya
Companion; Madīna; n. d.

Mūsa b. Abī Tamīm
Traditionist; Madīna; n. d.

Muslim b. Khālid al-Zanjī
Traditionist; Muftī of Makka; d. 179 or 180/795 or 796

al-Muṭṭalib b. al-Ḥārith b. Ḥanṭab
Companion (?); Makka; n. d.

Nāfiʿ (freed slave of Ibn ʿUmar)
One of Mālik's chief authorities; transmitted from Ibn ʿUmar; d. 117 or 120/735 or 737

Nāfiʿ b. Jubayr
Son of the Companion Jubayr; Madīna; d. 99/717

Nāfiʿ b. ʿUjayr b. ʿAbd-Yazīd
Successor; Madīna; n. d.

Nawf b. Faḍāla al-Bikālī
Successor; Madīna; d. 90 or 100/708 or 718

al-Qays b. Muḥammad b. Abī Bakr
Successor; grandson of the first Caliph; d. 106/724

Rabīʿa b. Abī ʿAbd al-Raḥmān (called Rabīʿa al-Ra'y)
Traditionist; Makka; d. circa 136/753

Rāfiʿ b. Khadīj
Companion; Madīna; d. 74/693

al-Ṣaʿb b. Jaththāma
Companion; Madīna; d. 198/813

Saʿd b. Abī Waqqāṣ
Companion; Madīna; d. 55 or 58/674 or 677

Saʿd b. Ibrāhīm b. ʿAbd al-Raḥmān b. ʿAwf
Judge of Madīna; d. 127/744

Saʿd b. Isḥāq b. Kaʿb b. ʿUjra
Traditionist; Madīna; d. circa 146/757

Ṣafwān b. Mawhab
Successor; Makka; n. d.

Ṣafwān b. Sulaym
Traditionist; Madīna; d. 132/749

Sahl b. Abī Hathma
Companion; Madīna; n. d.

Sahl b. Saʿd b. Mālik b. Khālid al-Sāʿidī
Companion; Madīna; d. 88 or 91/706 or 709

Sahl b. Saʿd al-Sāʿidī
Last of the Companions; d. 88 or 91/707 or 710

Saʿīd b. Abī Saʿīd b. Kaysān al-Maqburī
Traditionist; Madīna; d. 123/740

Saʿīd b. Jubayr
Traditionist; Kūfa; d. 95/713

Saʿīd b. al-Musayyib
Companion; authority of Madīna; d. 93 or 94/711 or 712

Saʿīd b. Sālim al-Qaddāḥ
Successor; Makka; n. d.

Sufyān b. ʿUyayna
Traditionist; Madīna; d. 198/813

Sufyān al-Thawrī
Traditionist; Kūfa; d. 161/772

Suhayl b. Abī Ṣāliḥ b. Dhakwān al-Sammān
Traditionist; Madīna; n. d.

Sulaymān b. Abī Muslim al-Aḥwal (uncle of Ibn Abī Najīḥ)
Successor; Makka; n. d.

Sulaymān b. Arqam
Traditionist; Baṣra; n. d.

Sulaymān b. Yasār
(*See* Abū Ayyūb Sulaymān b. Yasār)

Suwayd b. Muqarrin
Traditionist; Madīna; n. d.

Ṭalḥa b. ʿAbd-Allāh b. ʿAwf
Successor; Madīna; d. 97/715

Ṭalḥa b. ʿUbayd-Allāh.
Companion; Madīna; d. 36/656

Tamīm b. Aws al-Dārī
Companion; Madīna; d. 40/660

Ṭāwūs b. Kaysān
Successor; Makka; d. 105 or 106/723 or 724

ʿUbāda b. al-Ṣāmit
Companion; Madīna; d. 34/654

ʿUbayd-Allāh b. ʿAbd-Allāh b. ʿUtba b. Masʿūd
Traditionist; Madīna; d. 94 or 95/712 or 713

ʿUbayd-Allāh b. Abī Rāfiʿ
Son of companion Abū Rāfiʿ; n. d.

ʿUbayd-Allāh b. Abī Yazīd
Traditionist; Makka; d. 126/743

ʿUbayd b. Kaʿb
Companion; Madīna; d. 22/642

ʿUmar b. al-Ḥakam al-Sulamī
Companion; not very well known; n. d.

ʿUmar b. al-Khaṭṭāb
Second Caliph; Companion; d. 23/643

ʿUmrān b. Ḥusayn
Companion; Baṣra; d. 52/672

Unays b. al-Ḍaḥḥāk al-Aslamī
Companion; Madīna; n. d.

ʿUrwa b. al-Zubayr
Successor; Madīna; d. 92/710

Usāma b. Zayd
Companion; Madīna; d. 54/673

ʿUthmān b. ʿAbd-Allāh b. Surāqa
Son of the Companion ʿAbd-Allāh b. Surāqa; transmitted from his father; n. d.

ʿUthmān b. ʿAffān
Third Caliph; Companion; Madīna; d. 35/656

ʿUwaymir al-ʿAjlānī
Companion; Madīna; n. d.

Wahb b. Munabbih
Traditionist; Ṣanʿā'; d. 110 or 114/729 or 730

Wāsiʿ b. Ḥabbān b. Munqidh
Traditionist; Madīna; n. d.

Wāthila b. al-Asqaʿ
Companion; Madīna; d. 83 or 85/702 or 704

Yaḥya b. Hassān
Traditionist; Baṣra; d. 208/823, in Egypt

Yaḥya b. Saʿīd al-Qaṭṭān
Traditionist; Baṣra; d. 198/813

Yazīd b. ʿAbd-Allāh b. Usāma b. al-Hādī
Traditionist; Madīna; d. 139/756

Yazīd b. Rūmān
Traditionist; Madīna; d. 130/747

Yazīd b. Shaybān
Companion; Makka; n. d.

Yazīd b. Ṭalḥa b. Rukāna
Companion (?); Madīna; n. d.

Yazīd b. al-Zinnād
Successor; Madīna; n. d.

Yūnus b. ʿUbayd
Successor; Baṣra; d. 139/756

Yūsuf b. Māhak
Traditionist; Makka; d. 110/728

Zayd b. Aslam
Traditionist; Madīna; d. 136/753

Zayd b. ʿIlāqa
Successor; Kūfa; d. 125/742

Zayd b. Khālid
Companion; Madīna; d. 72 or 78/692 or 698

Zayd b. Mirbaʿ (or Yazīd) al-Anṣārī
Companion (full name is unknown); n. d.

Zayd b. Thābit
Companion; Madīna; d. 45/665

Zaynab bint Kaʿb
Companion (or successor); wife of Abū Saʿīd al-Khudrī

al-Zubayr b. al-ʿAwwām
Companion; Madīna; d. 36/656

GLOSSARY

ʿAbd: slave

ʿAdl: justice; probity or the just character (of a witness)

Ahl al-Kitāb: People of the Book (people who possess a scripture)

ʿĀlim (pl. *ʿulamāʾ*): scholar

Allāh: God

ʿAmal: practice; precedent

ʿAqd (pl. *ʿuqūd*): contract

Al-ʿĀqila: the group of persons sharing liability with the person who committed homicide (or an injury), responsible for the payment of compensation (*diya*) in cash or in kind

ʿAql: intellect; reason

Al-Arkān al-Khamsa: the five pillars of Islam (profession of the faith, prayer, payment of alms, fasting, and pilgrimage)

ʿAṣaba (pl. *ʿaṣabāt*): clan; agnate

ʿAwra: private

Bāṭil: void

Bayʿ: sale transaction

Al-Bayān: declaration; clear speech

Bayt al-Māl: public treasury

Al-Bayyina: evidence; indication

Bidʿa: innovation

Dār al-Islām: territory of Islam

Ḍarar: damage

Daʿwa: claim

Dhawū al-Arḥām: uterine heirs

Dhawū al-Furūḍ: sharers

Dhikr: praise and glorification of God

Dīn: religion

Dīnār: the gold unit of coinage derived from the Greek *denarius*

Dirham: the silver unit of coinage derived from the Greek *drachma*

Diya: blood-money; compensation

Faqīh (pl. *fuqahāʾ*): jurist

Farʿ (pl. *furūʿ*): branch of the law

Farḍ (pl. *furūḍ*): duty, the performance of which is obligatory

Farḍ ʿAyn: individual duty, the performance of which is obligatory for every individual

Farḍ al-Kifāya: collective duty, the performance of which is obligatory for the community as a whole: if a sufficient number fulfil the duty, the rest are relieved of it; if the duty is not performed, all the community is liable for punishment

Fatwa: legal opinion

Fiqh: jurisprudence

Furqān: that which distinguishes or separates; a name for the Qur'ān

Ghanīma: spoil of war

Ghusl: complete washing; bathing

Ḥadd (pl. *ḥudūd*): penalty

Ḥadīth: tradition

Ḥajj: major pilgrimage to Makka (*see* ʿ*umra*)

Ḥalāl: lawful; permitted

Ḥaqq (pl. *ḥuqūq*): right; the truth

Ḥarām: prohibited; unlawful

Al-Hijra: migration of the Prophet Muḥammad from Madīna to Makka; the beginning of the Islamic era in A. D. 622

Al-Ḥikma: wisdom (divine wisdom embodied in the sunna)

Ḥukm (pl. *aḥkām*): decision; command; order; rule of law

ʿ*Īd*: feast

ʿ*Idda*: period of waiting after death of husband or cancellation of marriage contract before eligibility for remarriage

*I*ʿ*jāz*: miracle (of the Quranic revelation)

*Ijmā*ʿ: consensus; agreement

Ijtihād: personal reasoning

Ikhtilāf: disagreement or differences among jurists on matters of law

ʿ*Ilm*: legal knowledge

Imām: leader of a school of law; prayer-leader; caliph

Iqrār: confession; admission

Isnād: chain of authorities through whom a tradition has been handed down from the time of the Prophet

Istibrā': clearance of pregnancy; acquittance

Istidlāl: inductive reasoning

Istiḥsān: juristic preference

Istinjā': cleansing with stones after defecation

Jā'iz: permissible

Janāba (pl. *junub*): ritual impurity, the removal of which is obligatory before the performance of prayer

Jarḥ (pl. *jirāḥ*): offence; injury

Jihād: just war (popularly holy-war)
Jizya: poll tax
Kaʿba: central shrine in the city of Makka
Kaffāra: atonement; expiation
Kāfir: unbeliever
Kalām: theology
Khabar: narrative
Kharāj: land tax
Khiyār al-majlis: right of option of the parties to a transaction before they separate
Khuṭba: (Friday) sermon
Kitāb: book; scripture
Liʿān: accusation (of adultery)
Madhhab: school of law; doctrine
Mahr: bride-price; dowry
Majlis: sitting; assembly
Mansūkh: abrogated (legislation)
Masjid: place of worship; a mosque
Mīrāth: inheritance
Mu'adhdhin: the man who calls to prayer
Muftī: jurisconsult
Mujtahid: the man who exercises personal reasoning (see *ijtihād*)
Mukhābara: renting of an agricultural land by paying a portion of the produce after harvest
Mutʿa: temporary marriage
Muzāraʿa: *see mukhābara*
Nabī: prophet; messenger
Nafal: supererogatory (*see tanfīl*)
Nāsikh: abrogating (legislation); *see mansūkh*
Naskh: abrogation
Naṣṣ: text
Nikāḥ: marriage
Nīya: intention
Qadhf: accusation of unchastity and illegitimacy
Qāḍī: judge
Qarāba: blood relationship
Qibla: direction toward Makka in prayer
Qiyās: analogical reasoning

Rajm: stoning to death
Ramaḍān: month of fasting
Rasūl (pl. *rusul*): apostle
Ra'y: opinion
Ribā: usury
Sabī: women and children taken as spoil
Ṣadaqa: charitable alms
Ṣaḥīḥ: authentic (tradition)
Ṣalāt: ritual prayer
Sariqa: theft
Ṣawm: fasting
Shahāda: profession of the faith; testimony
Shāhid (pl. *Shuhūd*): witness
Sunna: custom; a precedent based on the Prophet's acts or sayings
Sūra: a portion or chapter of the Qur'ān
Tafsīr: exegesis; commentary
Ṭahāra: state of purity
Taḥkīm: arbitration
Takbīr: to glorify God by reciting the formula: " God is very great"
Tanfīl: supererogation (*see nafal*)
Tanzīl: revelation
Taqlīd: originally, conformity to the opinion of a leading jurist; later, conformity to one of the four schools of law
Tashahhud: recitation of the salutation to the Prophet and the formula of the profession of the faith
Tayammum: purification by fine sand instead of water
Tha'r: vendetta
Thayyib: a woman separated by death of the husband or by divorce, or a girl who is not a virgin
Umma: community (of the believers)
ʿUmra: minor pilgrimage (*see ḥajj*)
ʿUshr: tithe
Uṣūl: roots or sources (of the law)
Waṣīya (pl. *waṣāyā*): will; bequest
Wuḍū': ablution
Zakāt: legal alms
Zina: fornication; adultery

SELECT BIBLIOGRAPHY

It is the purpose of this bibliography neither to compile and set forth a complete list of works on Islamic jurisprudence nor to reproduce all those cited in the footnotes, but rather to provide the fundamental primary and modern works on the life and jurisprudence of Shāfiʿī and those that have a bearing on the substance of the *Risāla* in particular. Fairly exhaustive bibliographies of classical works can be found in Ḥajjī Khalīfa's *Kashf al-Ẓunūn,* ed. G. L. Flügel (Leipzig and London, 1835-58); Ibn al-Nadīm's *Kitāb al-Fihrist,* ed. G. L. Flügel (Leipzig, 1871); and C. Brockelmann's *Geschichte der arabischen Literatur* (Leiden, 2nd ed., 1944-49). For a modern critical study of the historical origins of Islamic jurisprudence, the reader may refer to J. Schacht's *Origins of Muhammadan Jurisprudence* (Oxford, 1950) and *Law in the Middle East,* eds. M. Khadduri and H. J. Liebesny (Washington, D. C., 1955). For an exposition of Islamic law in general, and the Shāfiʿī system in particular, there are available David Santillana's *Istituzioni di diritto musulmano malichita, con riguardo anche al sistema schiafi'ita* (2 vols.; Roma, 1938) and Theodor W. Juynboll's, *Handbuch des Islamischen Gesetzes nach der lehre der Schafi'itischen Schule* (Leiden, 1910). The reader may also refer to the relevant articles in the *Encyclopaedia of Islam* (old and new editions) and the *Shorter Encyclopaedia of Islam.*

Primary Sources

Abū Dāwūd, Sulaymān b. al-Ashʿath. *Sunan.* 4 vols. Cairo, 1935.

Abū Yūsuf, Yaʿqūb b. Ibrāhīm. *Kitāb al-Kharāj,* ed. Abū al-Wafā'. Cairo 1352/1934. French translation by E. Fagnan (Paris, 1921).

———. *Kitāb al-Āthār,* ed. Abū al-Wafā'. Cairo, 1355/1937.

Āmidī, Sayf al-Dīn Abū al-Ḥasan ʿAlī b. Abī ʿAlī Muḥammad, *al-Iḥkām Fī Uṣūl al-Aḥkām.* 3 vols. Cairo, 1347/1928.

Anas, Mālik b. *al-Muwaṭṭa',* ed. Muḥ. Fu'ād ʿAbd al-Bāqī. 2 vols. Cairo, 1951.

Bāqillānī, Abū Bakr Muḥammad b. al-Ṭayyib. *Iʿjāz al-Qur'ān,* ed. Aḥmad Ṣaqr. Cairo, 1954.

Bayḍāwī, Nāṣir al-Dīn. *Tafsīr.* Cairo, 1371/1951.

Bayhaqī, Abū Bakr Aḥmad b. al-Ḥusayn b. ʿAlī. *Kitāb Manāqib al-Imām al-Shāfiʿī* (MS, including a sequel, in 312 folios). Photographic copy at the Institute of Arabic Manuscripts of the Arab League, Cairo.

———. *al-Sunan al-Kubra.* 10 vols. Hyderabad, 1344-55/1925-36.

Bukhārī, Abū ʿAbd-Allāh Muḥammad b. Ismāʿīl. *Kitāb al-Jāmiʿ al-Ṣaḥīḥ,* ed. L. Krehl. 4 vols. Leiden, 1862-1908.

Dāraquṭnī, Abū al-Ḥasan ʿAlī b. ʿUmar. *Aḥadīth al-Muwaṭṭa',* ed. al-Kawtharī. Cairo, 1365/1946.

Dārimī, Abū Muḥammad ʿAbd-Allāh b. ʿAbd al-Raḥmān b. Faḍl b. Bahram. *Sunan.* 2 vols. Damascus, 1349/1930.

Fakhr al-Rāzī, Abū ʿAbd-Allāh Muḥammad b. ʿUmar. *Kitāb Manāqib al-Shāfiʿī.* Cairo, n. d.

Ghazzālī, Abū Ḥāmid Muḥammad b. Muḥammad b. Muḥammad. *al-Mustaṣfa Min ʿIlm al-Uṣūl.* 2 vols. Cairo, 1356/1937.

Ḥāzimī, Abū Bakr Muḥammad b. Mūsa. *al-Iʿtibār fī al-Nāsikh wa al-Mansūkh Min al-Āthār.* Cairo, 1346/1927.

Ibn ʿAbd al-Barr, Abū ʿUmar Yūsuf. *al-Intiqā' fī Faḍā'il al-Thalātha al-A'imma al-Fuqahā'.* Cairo, 1350/1932.

———. *Tajrīd al-Tamhīd Limā fī al-Muwaṭṭa' Min al-Maʿānī wa al-Asānīd.* Cairo, 1350/1932.

Ibn Abd-Allāh al-Khazrajī, Ṣafī al-Dīn Aḥmad. *Khulāṣat Tadhhīb al-Kamāl fī Asmā' al-Rijāl.* Cairo, 1322/1905.

Ibn Ādam, Yaḥya. *Kitāb al-Kharāj,* ed. Aḥmad Muḥammad Shākir. Cairo, 1329/1911, English translation, entitled *Taxation in Islam,* by A. Ben Shemesh. Leiden, 1958.

Ibn Ḥajar al-ʿAsqalānī, Shihāb al-Dīn b. ʿAlī. *Tawālī al-Ta'sīs bi-Maʿālī Ibn Idrīs.* Cairo, 1301/1883.

———. *Marātib al-Mudallisīn.* Cairo, 1322/1904.

———. *Tahdhīb al-Tahdhīb.* Vol. IX. Hyderabad, 1326/1909.

———. *al-Iṣāba fī Tamyīz al-Ṣaḥāba.* 4 vols. Cairo, 1358/1939.

———. *Bulūgh al-Marām Min Adillat al-Aḥkām,* ed. R. M. Riḍwān. Cairo, 1954.

Ibn Ḥanbal, Aḥmad. *al-Musnad,* ed. Aḥmad Muḥammad Shākir. 15 vols. (incomplete) Cairo, 1949- .

Ibn Ḥazm, Abū Muḥammad ʿAlī. *Kitāb al-Iḥkām fī Uṣūl al-Aḥkām.* 2 vols. Cairo, 1345/1927.

Ibn Hishām, Abū Muḥammad ʿAbd al-Malik. *Kitāb Sīrat Sayyidinā Muḥammad,* ed. Ferdinand Wüstenfeld. 2 vols. Göttingen, 1858-60.

Ibn Khaldūn, ʿAbd al-Raḥmān. *al-Muqaddima,* ed. E. M. Quatremère. 3 vols. Paris, 1858. English translation by F. Rosenthal (London, 1958).

Ibn Khallikān, Abū al-ʿAbbās Shams al-Dīn Aḥmad b. Muḥammad b. Abī Bakr. *Wafayāt al-Aʿyān,* ed. Muḥammad Muḥī al-Dīn ʿAbd al-Ḥamīd. 6 vols. Cairo, 1948.

Ibn Qutayba al-Dīnawarī, Abū Muḥammad ʿAbd-Allāh b. Muslim. *Kitāb Ta'wīl Mukhtalaf al-Ḥadīth.* Cairo, 1326/1909.

———. *Kitāb Ta'wīl Mushkil al-Qur'ān.* ed. Aḥmad Ṣaqr: Cairo, 1373/1954.

Ibn Saʿd, Muḥammad. *Kitāb al-Ṭabaqāt al-Kabīr*, ed. Eugen Mittwoch and Edward Sachau. 9 vols. Leiden, 1905-1940.

Ibn Sallām, Abū ʿUbayd al-Qāsim, *Kitāb al-Amwāl*, ed. Muḥ. Ḥamīd al-Fiqqī. Cairo, 1353/1935.

Iṣfahānī, Abū Nuʿaym Aḥmad b. ʿAbd-Allāh. *Kitāb Ḥilyat al-Awliyā' wa Ṭabaqāt al-Aṣfiyā'*. Vol. IX. Cairo, 1938.

Khaṭīb al-Baghdādī, Abū Bakr Aḥmad b. ʿAlī. *Ta'rīkh Baghdād*. 14 vols. Cairo, 1349/1931.

Khayḍarī, Quṭb al-Dīn b. Sulaymān. *Zahr al-Riyāḍ fī Radd mā Shannaʿahu al-Qāḍī ʿIyāḍ ʿala al-Imām al-Shāfiʿī* (MS, No. 181). Photographic copy at the Institute of Arabic Manuscripts of the Arab League. Cairo.

Muslim, Abū al-Ḥasan Muslim b. al-Ḥajjāj. *Ṣaḥīḥ* (including Nawawī's commentary). 18 vols. Cairo, 1347-49/1929-30.

Muzanī, Ismāʿīl b. Yaḥya. *al-Mukhtaṣar* (on the margin of Shāfiʿī's *Kitāb al-Umm*, Vols. I–V).

Naḥḥās, Abū Jaʿfar. *Kitāb al-Nāsikh wa al-Mansūkh*. Cairo, 1323/1906.

Nawawī, Abū Zakarīya Yaḥya. *Kitāb Tahdhīb al-Asmā'* (Biographical Dictionary), ed. Ferdinand Wüstenfeld. Göttingen, 1842-45.

Naysābūrī, Abū ʿAbd-Allāh Muḥammad b. ʿAbd-Allāh. *Kitāb Maʿrifat ʿUlūm al-Ḥadīth*, ed. Muʿazzam Ḥusayn. Cairo, 1937.

———. *al-Madkhal ila Maʿrifat al-Iklīl*, ed. J. Robson. London, 1953.

Naysābūrī, Abū al-Hasan ʿAlī b. Aḥmad al-Wahidī. *Asbāb al-Nuzūl*. Cairo, 1315/1897.

Pazdawī, Abū al-Ḥasan ʿAlī b. Muḥammad b. Ḥusayn. *Kashf al-Asrār*. 3 vols. Istanbul, 1307/1889.

Qur'ān. Despite the several renderings of the Qur'ān into the English language, there is yet no fully adequate translation. Not infrequently a modified rendering based on two or three of the following translations have been used for the purpose of this book:
A. J. Arberry, *The Koran Interpreted* (London, 1955), 2 vols.
Richard Bell, *The Qur'ān* (Edinburgh, 1937-1939), 2 vols.
E. H. Palmer, *Qur'ān* (World's Classics, 1928).
J. M. Rodwell, *The Koran* (Everyman's Library, 1909).

Rāzī, Abū Muḥammad ʿAbd al-Raḥmān b. Abī Ḥātim. *Kitāb Ādāb al-Shāfiʿī wa Manāqibuh*, ed. Muḥammad Zāhid b. al-Ḥasan al-Kawtharī. Cairo, 1372/1953.

Sarakhsī, Abū Bakr Muḥammad b. Aḥmad b. Abī Sahl. *Kitāb al-Uṣūl*, ed. Abū al-Wafā'. 2 vols. Cairo, 1372/1952.

Shāfiʿī, Muḥammad b. Idrīs. *Kitāb al-Umm*. 7 vols. Cairo, 1321-25/1904-08.

———. *Jumāʿ al-ʿIlm*, ed. Aḥmad Muḥammad Shākir. Cairo, 1359/1940.

———. *al-Musnad,* ed. Muḥammad ʿĀbīd al-Sindī. 2 vols. Cairo, 1369/1950.

———. *Kitāb Aḥkām al-Qur'ān,* ed. Muḥammad Zāhid al-Kawtharī. 2 vols. Cairo, 137-72/1951-52.

Shāṭibī, Abū Isḥāq. *al-Muwāfaqāt fī Uṣūl al-Sharīʿa,* ed. ʿAbd-Allāh Durāz. 4 vols. Cairo, n. d.

Shawkānī, Muḥammad b. ʿAlī b. Muḥammad. *Fatḥ al-Qaḍīr.* 5 vols. Cairo. 1349-1351/1931-1935.

———. *Nayl al-Awṭār.* 8 vols. Cairo, 1952.

Shaybānī, Muḥammad b. al-Ḥasan. *Kitāb al-Aṣl,* ed. Shafīq Shaḥāta (Chehata). Vol. I. Cairo, 1954.

Shīrāzī, Abū Isḥāq. *Ṭabaqāt al-Shāfiʿīya* (including al-Muṣannif's *Ṭabaqāt al-Shāfiʿīya).* Baghdād, 1356/1937.

Subkī, Tāj al-Dīn Abū al-Naṣr ʿAbd al-Wahhāb b. Taqī al-Dīn. *Ṭabaqāt al-Shāfiʿīya al-Kubra.* 6 vols. Cairo, 1324/1907.

Suyūṭī, Jalāl al-Dīn ʿAbd al-Raḥmān b. Abī Bakr. *al-Jāmiʿ al-Ṣaghīr.* 2 vols. Cairo, 1352/1933.

———. *al-Itqān Fī ʿUlūm al-Qur'ān.* 2 vols. Cairo, 1370/1951.

———. *Lubāb al-Nuqūl fī Asbāb al-Nuzūl.* Cairo, 1373/1954.

Ṭabarī, Abū al-ʿAbbās Aḥmad b. ʿAbd-Allāh b. Muḥammad b. Abī Bakr Muḥibb al-Dīn. *al-Qira Li-Qāṣid Umm al-Qura,* ed. Muṣṭafa al-Saqqā'. Cairo, 1367/1948.

Ṭabarī, Abū Jaʿfar Muḥammad b. Jarīr. *Ta'rikh al-Rusul wa al-Mulūk,* ed. M. J. de Goeje et al. 15 vols. Leiden, 1879-1901.

———. *Jāmiʿ al-Bayān ʿAn Ta'wīl Āy al-Qur'ān,* ed. Maḥmūd M. Shākir. New ed. Cairo, 1374/1954.

Tirmidhī, Abū ʿĪsa Muḥammad b. ʿĪsa b. Sawra. *Sunan,* ed. Aḥmad Muḥammad Shākir. 2 Vols. Cairo, 1356/1937.

Yāqūt (al-Rūmī). *Kitāb Irshād al-Arīb Ila Maʿrifat al-Adīb* (this work is also called *Muʿjam al-Udabā'),* ed. D. S. Margoliouth. Vol. VI. London, 1931.

Modern Works

ʿAbd al-Rāziq, ʿAlī. *al-Ijmāʿ fī al-Sharīʿa al-Islāmīya.* Cairo, 1947.

ʿAbd al-Rāziq, Muṣṭafa. *al-Imām al-Shāfiʿī.* Cairo, 1945.

Abū Zahra, Muḥammad. *al-Shāfiʿī.* Cairo, 1367/1948.

Anderson, J. N. D. "Law as a Social Force in Islamic Culture and History," *Bulletin of the School of Oriental and African Studies,* Vol. XX (1957), pp. 13-40.

Baghdādī, Dāwūd b. Sulaymān. *Manāqib al-Imām al-Shāfiʿī.* Makka, 1328/1910.

Bell, Richard, *Introduction to the Qur'ān.* Edinburgh, 1953.

Bercher, Léon. *I. Goldziher's Études sur la Tradition Islamique*. Paris, 1952.

Bishop, Eric E. F. "Al-Shāfiʿī, Founder of a Law School," *Moslem World*, Vol. XIX (1929), pp. 156-75.

Bousquet, G. H., and Schacht, J. *Selected Works of C. Snouck Hurgronje*. Leiden, 1957.

Fitzgerald, S. V. "The alleged Debt of Islamic to Roman Law." *Law Quarterly Review*, Vol. 67 (1951), pp. 81-102.

Gibb, H. A. R. *Mohammedanism*. London, 1949.

———. "Government Under Law in Muslim Society," in American Council of Learned Societies, *Government under Law and the Individual*, Washington, D. C., 1957.

Goldziher, Ignaz. "The Principles of Law in Islam," *The Historians' History of the World*, ed. H. S. Williams, Vol. VIII, pp. 294-304. New York, 1907.

———. *Die Zahiriten*. Leipzig, 1881.

Graf, L. I. *al-Shāfiʿī's Verhandeling over de Wortelen van den Fikh*. Leiden, 1934.

Guillaume, Alfred. *The Traditions of Islam*. Oxford, 1924.

———, and Arnold, Sir Thomas (eds.). *The Legacy of Islam*. Oxford, 1931.

Jeffery, Arthur. *Foreign vocabulary of the Qur'ān*. Baroda, 1938.

———. *The Qur'ān as Scripture*. New York, 1952.

Kawtharī, Muḥammad Zāhid. *Bulūg al-Amānī fī Sīrat al-Imām Muḥammad b. al-Ḥasan al-Shaybānī*. Cairo, 1355/1937.

Khadduri, Majid. *War and Peace in the Law of Islam*. Baltimore, 1955.

Khuḍarī, Muḥammad. *Uṣūl al-Fiqh*. 2nd ed. Cairo, 1352/1933.

MacDonald, Duncan B. *Development of Muslim Theology, Jurisprudence and Constitutional Theory*. New York, 1903.

Margoliouth, D. S. *The Early Development of Muhammadanism*. London, 1914.

Mez, A. *Die Renaissance des Islam*. Heidelberg, 1922.

Mubārak, Zakī. *Iṣlaḥ Ashnaʿ Khaṭa' fī Ta'rīkh al-Tashriʿ al-Islāmī: Kitāb al-Umm*, etc. Cairo, 1352/1934.

Muṣṭafa, Muḥammad. *Kitāb al-Jawhar al-Nafīs fī Ta'rīkh Ḥayāt al-Imām Ibn Idrīs*. Cairo, 1326/1908.

Nöldeke, Th. and F. Schwally. *Geschichte des Qorans*. Leipzig, 1919.

Roberts, Roberts. *Social Laws of the Qur'ān*. London, 1925.

Robson, James. "Tradition, the Second Foundation of Islam," *Muslim World*, Vol. XLI (1951), pp. 22-33.

———. "Tradition, Investigation and Classification," *Muslim World*, Vol. XLI (1951), pp. 98-112.

———. "The Material of Tradition," *Muslim World*, Vol. XLI (1951), pp. 257-270.

Rosenthal, F. *The Technique and Approach of Muslim Scholarship.* Rome, 1947.

Schacht, J. "Foreign Elements in Ancient Islamic Law," *Journal of Comparative Legislation and International Law,* 3rd. series, Vol. XXXII (November, 1950), pp. 9-17.

———. *Origins of Muhammadan Jurisprudence.* Oxford, 1950.

Tyan, Emile. "Méthodologie et source du droit en Islam," *Studia Islamica,* Vol. X (1959), pp. 79-109.

Wensinck, A. J. "The importance of Tradition for the Study of Islam," *Moslem World,* Vol. XI (1921), pp. 239-45.

———. *A Handbook of Early Muhammadan Tradition.* Leiden. 1927.

Index